"The book does an excellent job of documenting and explaining the role of agriculture in the development process. Economic concepts are introduced with real-world examples in a way that is accessible to students. Topics such as food, poverty, population growth, and trade are treated in a manner that gives a clear picture of the challenges and opportunities facing the world in the 21st century."

Jacob Ricker-Gilbert, Professor, Department of
Agricultural Economics, Purdue University, USA

"My students have consistently indicated that they like *Economics of Agricultural Development*. The discussion questions are especially useful in facilitating learning of theoretical concepts."

Corinne Valdivia, Professor, Agricultural Economics,
University of Missouri, USA

Economics of Agricultural Development

Economics of Agricultural Development examines the causes, severity, and effects of poverty, population growth, and malnutrition in developing countries. It discusses potential solutions to these problems, progress made in many countries in recent years, and the implications of globalization for agriculture, poverty, and the environment.

Topics covered in the book include:

- Means for utilizing agricultural surpluses to further overall economic development
- The sustainability of the natural resource environment
- Gender issues in relation to agriculture and resource use
- The contribution of improved technologies to agricultural development
- The importance of agricultural policies and institutions to development and trade
- Actions to encourage more rapid agricultural and economic development

This new edition reflects the following developments:

- Growth in environmental challenges due to climate change
- Continued progress in agricultural and economic development in many low-income countries while other countries and regions are being left behind
- Continued growth in demand for higher-valued farm products

This book is essential reading for undergraduate students seeking to understand the economics of agricultural development and the world food system, including environmental and human consequences, international trade, and capital flows. It contains a wealth of real-world case studies and is accompanied by a website.

George W. Norton is Professor Emeritus of Agricultural and Applied Economics at Virginia Tech, USA, and a Fellow of the Agricultural and Applied Economics Association. He is the author of 12 books and numerous scholarly articles.

Jeffrey Alwang is Professor of Agricultural and Applied Economics at Virginia Tech, USA, and has won several international research and outreach awards. He is the author of 14 books and more than 100 journal articles.

William A. Masters is Professor in the Friedman School of Nutrition and the Department of Economics at Tufts University, USA, and a Fellow of the Agricultural and Applied Economics Association. He is the author of numerous books and scholarly publications.

Routledge Textbooks in Environmental and Agricultural Economics

For more information about this series, please visit www.routledge.com/Routledge-Textbooks-in-Environmental-and-Agricultural-Economics/book-series/TEAE

Economics of Agricultural Development

World Food Systems and Resource Use

Fourth Edition

George W. Norton, Jeffrey Alwang, and William A. Masters

Routledge
Taylor & Francis Group

LONDON AND NEW YORK

Fourth edition published 2022
by Routledge
2 Park Square, Milton Park, Abingdon, Oxon OX14 4RN

and by Routledge
605 Third Avenue, New York, NY 10158

Routledge is an imprint of the Taylor & Francis Group, an informa business

First edition published by Routledge 2006
Third edition published by Routledge 2015

British Library Cataloguing-in-Publication Data
A catalogue record for this book is available from the British Library

Library of Congress Cataloging-in-Publication Data
Names: Norton, George W., author. | Alwang, Jeffery, author. | Masters, William A., author.
Title: Economics of agricultural development : world food systems and resource use / George W. Norton, Jeffery Alwang, and William A. Masters.
Description: 4th Edition. | New York : Routledge, 2021. | Series: Textbooks in environmental and agricultural economics | Revised edition of the authors' Economics of agricultural development, 2015. | Includes bibliographical references and index.
Identifiers: LCCN 2021005767 (print) | LCCN 2021005768 (ebook)
Subjects: LCSH: Agriculture—Economic aspects.
Classification: LCC HD1415 .N67 2021 (print) | LCC HD1415 (ebook) | DDC 338.1—dc23
LC record available at https://lccn.loc.gov/2021005767
LC ebook record available at https://lccn.loc.gov/2021005768

ISBN: 978-0-367-32147-5 (hbk)
ISBN: 978-0-367-32148-2 (pbk)
ISBN: 978-0-429-31699-9 (ebk)

Typeset in Sabon LT Std
by Apex CoVantage, LLC

Access the companion website: https://agecontextbook.wordpress.com/

Contents

Preface

Extreme poverty and undernutrition remain serious problems in many developing countries despite significant progress in reducing them globally over the last 30 years. *Economics of Agricultural Development* examines the causes, severity, and effects of these persistent problems. It identifies potential solutions and considers the implications of globalization and potential future reduction in globalization for agriculture, poverty, and the environment. It identifies linkages in the world food system and stresses how agricultural and economic situations in poor countries affect industrialized nations and vice versa. It focuses on the role that agriculture has played in improving economic and nutritional well-being and how that role can be enhanced. It explores causes and implications of agricultural commodity price volatility and potential effects of climate change on agriculture.

Much has been learned about the importance of technology, education, trade and capital flows, agricultural policies and institutions, and rural infrastructure in stimulating agricultural and economic development. In some cases, the same factors that contribute to economic growth can lead to price and income instability or environmental risk. These lessons and other issues are examined in the book using basic tools of economic analysis. The need is stressed for improved information flows to help guide institutional change in light of social, cultural, and political disruptions that occur in the development process.

The challenge in studying the economics of agricultural development is to build a broad view of the problem and to bring economic theory to bear on specific challenges faced by the rural sector and on means for utilizing agricultural surpluses to further overall economic development. The goal of this book is to help students and other interested practitioners gain an understanding of the agricultural development problem, including the environmental and human consequences of different development paths, the influence of international trade and capital flows, and the reasons for progress in reducing poverty and improving food security in some countries but not others. It is designed to help students develop skills that will enhance their capability to analyze world food and development problems.

This book interprets for undergraduates the economics of development and trade, including the importance of using economics to account for institutions, imperfect information, and the willingness of people to exploit others and to act collectively. This use of economics provides important insights for development policy and helps explain why some countries develop while others are left behind. The role of the government in promoting broad-based development is explored. The book also covers topics related to sustainability of the environment, gender roles in relation to agriculture and resource use, and the importance of macroeconomic policies as related to development and trade. This new edition of the book provides new insights into economic issues related to climate change and how they affect agriculture in developing countries.

INTENDED AUDIENCE

Economics of Agricultural Development is designed as a comprehensive text for the first course on the economics of world food issues and agricultural development. The book is aimed at undergraduate students, with the only prerequisite a course in introductory economics. Students in undergraduate courses that address world food and agricultural development represent a range of majors. Economic jargon is kept to a minimum and explained where necessary, and the book sequentially builds a base of economic concepts that are used in later chapters to analyze specific development problems. A second audience for the book is those who work for public and private international development organizations.

ORGANIZATION OF THE BOOK

Agricultural development is important for rural welfare and for overall economic development. Part 1 of the book considers the many dimensions of the world food–income–population problem in both a human and an economic context. Having established the severity and dimensions of the problem, Part 2 examines the economic transformation experienced by countries as they develop, sources of economic growth, and theories of economic development, including the role of agriculture in those theories. Part 3 provides students with an overview of traditional agriculture and agricultural systems and their determinants in developing countries, with particular attention to issues such as environmental sustainability and gender roles. Part 4 then identifies agricultural development theories and the technical and institutional elements required for improving the agricultural sector. It stresses the need to improve domestic institutions. Finally, Part 5 considers the importance of the international environment, including trade and trade policies, macroeconomic policies, capital flows, and foreign assistance, including food aid. The concluding chapter integrates various development components addressed in the book and discusses future prospects for agricultural development.

ACKNOWLEDGMENTS

This and previous editions of the book have benefited from the contributions of numerous individuals, including feedback from students in classes at Virginia Tech, Purdue, and Tufts. We thank Laura McCann and Laurian Unnevehr for reviewing an earlier draft. The encouragement and assistance of our colleagues at Virginia Tech, Purdue, and Tufts are gratefully acknowledged. We especially would like to thank Brad Mills, David Orden, Brady Deaton, Catherine Larochelle, Dan Taylor, Darrell Bosch, Anya McGuirk, Jerry Shively, Wally Tyner, and Sally Thompson. The book has benefited greatly from discussions and interactions on development issues over many years with Phil Pardey, Julian Alston, Stan Wood, Paul B. Siegel, Terry Roe, Bill Easter, John Mellor, Dan Sisler, Mesfin Bezuneh, Robert Thompson, Jacob Ricker-Gilbert, Scott Swinton, Randy Barker, Bob Herdt, Prabhu Pingali, Chris Barrett, Jock Anderson, Gershon Feder, and numerous graduate students.

We thank Cloe James, Natalie Tomlinson, Robert Langham, Lisa Thomsen, and other editors at Routledge Press for their assistance on various editions of the book. We thank William Jones and Hunter Sanderson for assistance with figures and illustrations.

George W. Norton
Jeffrey Alwang
William A. Masters

PART 1

Dimensions of world food and development problems

Rural family in Colombia

1 Introduction

OVERVIEW OF THE WORLD FOOD SITUATION

One of the most urgent needs in the world today is to solve the persistent problems of hunger and poverty in developing countries. Despite significant progress in reducing these problems over the past few decades, millions of people remain ill-fed, poorly housed, under-employed, and afflicted by a variety of poverty-related illnesses. These people regularly suffer the pain of watching loved ones die prematurely, often from preventable causes. In many countries, the natural resource base is also being degraded, with potentially serious implications for the livelihoods of future generations.

Why do these problems persist? How severe are they, and what are their causes? What role does agriculture play in economic development and how might it be enhanced? What does the globalization of goods, services, ideas, technologies, and capital mean for agriculture, poverty, and environment around the world? How do policies in developed countries affect developing countries? And, how does the situation in low-income countries affect wealthier nations? An understanding of the fundamental causes of the many problems in poorer countries and the progress that has been achieved is essential if solutions are to be recognized, encouraged, and implemented.

Much has been learned over the past several years about the roles of technology, education, international trade and capital flows, agricultural and macroeconomic policies, and rural infrastructure in stimulating agricultural and economic development. In some cases, these same factors can be a two-edged sword: they contribute to economic growth on the one hand, but lead to price and income instability or environmental risk on the other. These lessons and other potential solutions to development problems are examined herein from an economic perspective. The need is stressed for improved information flows to help guide institutional change in light of social, cultural, and political disruptions that occur in the development process.

World food and income situation

Are people hungry because the world does not produce enough food? No. In the aggregate, the world produces a surplus of food, and it has for a long time, even during the COVID-19 pandemic. If the world's food supply were evenly divided among the world's population, each person would receive substantially more than the minimum amount of nutrients

Many farm workers in Asia earn between one and two dollars per workday

required for survival. The world population has more than doubled over the past 50 years, but food production has grown even faster.

If total food supplies are plentiful, why do people perish every day from hunger-related causes? At its most basic level, hunger is a poverty problem. Only the poor go hungry. They are hungry because they cannot afford food or cannot produce enough of it themselves. The very poorest groups tend to include: families of the unemployed or under-employed landless laborers; the elderly, handicapped, and orphans; and people experiencing temporary misfortune due to abnormal weather, agricultural pests, health crises, or political upheaval. Thus, hunger is for some people a chronic problem and for others a periodic or temporary problem. Many of the poorest live in rural areas.

Hunger is an individual problem related to the distribution of food and income within countries and a national and international problem related to the geographic distribution of food, income, and population. About 9 percent of the world's population (roughly 700 million people) lives on less than $1.90 per day (the World Bank definition of extreme poverty), and about half the world lives on less than $5 per day. These people are found primarily in sub-Saharan Africa and South Asia, although poverty is also prevalent in East and Central Asia, Latin America and Caribbean, and Middle East and North Africa. Significant strides have been made in reducing global poverty, with the proportion of the world's population living in extreme poverty cut by more than half over the past three decades. However, much remains to be done to alleviate poverty-related problems.

While hunger and poverty are found throughout the world, over the past 40 years per capita food production has grown steadily in most regions, and in the last 20 years it has grown in every major region, including Africa (Table 1.1). The result has been substantial progress in reducing hunger and poverty, although per capita calorie availability remains below minimum nutritional standards in many sub-Saharan countries. Low agricultural productivity (farm output divided by farm inputs), wide variations in yields due to climatic, economic, and political causes, and rapid population growth have combined to create a precarious food situation in these countries.

Annual variation in food production is also a serious problem in several countries, particularly in Africa. This variation has meant periodic severe food shortages in some countries, especially when production problems have been compounded by political upheaval or wars that have hindered international relief efforts. Production variability causes wide price swings that reduce food security for millions who are on the margin of being able to purchase food.

Table 1.1 Food Production Index and Average Dietary Energy

Year	1997	2007	2017
Food Production Index (2004–06 = 100)			
World	82	106	131
Asia	77	109	140
Africa	74	104	135
Americas	83	106	126
Europe	99	98	111
Oceania	87	92	119
Ave. Dietary Energy Supply (KAL/Cap/Day)			
World	2716	2792	2908
Asia	2580	2650	2840
Africa	2432	2537	2561
Americas	3125	3210	3279
Europe	3237	3362	3380
Oceania	2889	2988	3023

Source: FAOSTAT, 2020, www.fao.org/faostat/en/#country

Food prices

From 1970 to 2000, the real price of food for most people trended down slightly, and from 2001 to 2020 it exhibited a slight upward trend. U.S. prices (in nominal or "current" dollars) of maize, rice, and wheat (the world's major food grains) are shown in Figure 1.1. Despite peaks in 1972, 1981, 1996, 2008, and 2011, the average prices of all three grains fluctuated around a relatively constant level. The prices of most other things rose more steadily over the entire period, so for most people the *relative* price of food fell slightly, except during the peak years noted above. This reduction in the price of food was both good and bad because prices affect economic growth and social welfare in a contradictory fashion. Lower food prices benefit consumers and stimulate industrial growth but can lower agricultural producer incomes and reduce employment of landless workers. To the extent that lower prices reflect lower production costs, impacts on producers may be mitigated.

The three grains shown in Figure 1.1 have exhibited sizable year-to-year price variations. Food price fluctuations directly affect the well-being of the poor, who spend a high proportion of their income on food. Food price instability can increase human suffering and threaten political stability. Food price swings have resulted from a combination of factors

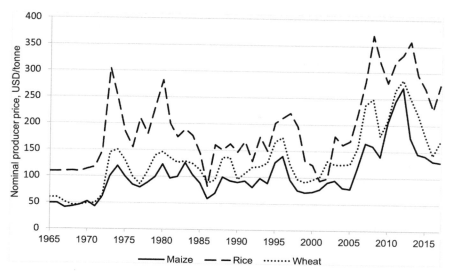

Figure 1.1 U.S. prices of major food grains in current dollars
Source: FAOSTAT, 2019

that shifted supply and demand. Supply factors included such items as adverse weather conditions and fuel and fertilizer costs. Demand factors included items such as demand for grains for bio-fuel use, population and income growth in many developing countries, changes in currency values, and policy changes in countries that affected their demand for imported food. Speculative investments in commodity markets have amplified commodity price swings for brief periods of time.

Malnutrition

Hunger is most visible to people in developed countries when a drought or other disaster results in images in the news of starving children. Disturbing as such images are, in a sense they mislead. The less conspicuous but more pernicious problem, in terms of people suffering and dying, is chronic malnutrition. While accurate figures of the number of malnourished in the world are not available, and even good estimates depend on the definition used, recent estimates indicate that almost 700 million people suffer from chronic undernutrition associated with food deprivation (Table 1.2), a number that has undoubtedly grown during the COVID-19 pandemic. Adverse health effects due to micronutrient deficiencies affect about two billion people. More than 5 million children die from preventable causes each year, about half due to malnutrition. Increasing per capita incomes have allowed more of the world's population to

Table 1.2 Estimated Number of Undernourished People in the World

Year	Number of Undernourished (millions)						
	2005	2010	2015	2016	2017	2018	2019
World	826	668	653	658	653	678	688
Africa	193	196	217	225	232	237	250
Asia	575	424	389	382	370	385	381
Latin America and the Caribbean	49	40	39	42	44	47	48

Source: FAO: The State of Food Security and Nutrition in the World, 2020, p. 340

eat better. But for those in lower income groups, the situation remains difficult.

Health

People born in developing countries live, on average, eight years less (in the least developed countries 14 years less) than those born in developed countries. Health problems, often associated with poverty, are responsible for most of the differences in life expectancies. Mortality rates for children under age 5 are particularly high, often ten times higher than in developed countries (Figure 1.2). Though countries with high rates of infant mortality are found in all regions, sub-Saharan African countries are particularly afflicted. The band of high infant mortality stretching from the Atlantic coast across Africa to Somalia on the Indian Ocean covers some of the poorest and most undernourished populations in the world.

Poverty affects health by limiting people's ability to purchase food, housing, medical services, and even soap and water. Inadequate public sanitation and high prevalence of communicable diseases are also closely linked with poverty. A major health problem, particularly among children, is diarrhea, usually caused by poor water quality. According to the World Health Organization, 1.4 million people die annually from causes related to diarrhea, including 500,000 children under the age of 5. Lower respiratory diseases account for an additional 3 million deaths and malaria another 400,000. Basic health services are lacking in many areas; on average, ten times as many people per doctor and per nurse are found in low-income countries as in developed countries.

A major health problem that continues to plague the developing world is acquired auto-immune deficiency syndrome (AIDS). The disease is difficult to contain in many developing countries because of lack

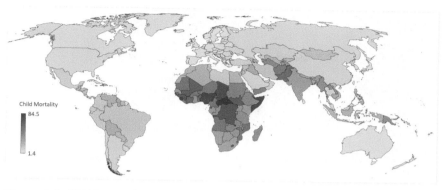

Figure 1.2 Child mortality rates per thousand live births, 2019
Source: World Bank, World Development Indicators 2019

of education about the disease, limited use of protective birth control devices, and in some cases, absence of government commitment to address the problem. Effects are felt in lost productivity and increased poverty in addition to its effects on direct human suffering. According to the World Health Organization, an estimated 37 million people worldwide were living with HIV/AIDS in 2018.

The COVID-19 pandemic in 2020 is estimated to have pushed an additional 50 million people into extreme poverty, according to World Bank data. The World Food Program estimates that 130 million people will be added to the list of those suffering from extreme hunger. Most health systems in developing countries were ill-equipped to address existing health problems, let alone a pandemic.

Population growth

Population growth is important to poverty and hunger problems for several reasons. First, population is growing less than 0.5 percent per year in developed economies, but about 1.7 percent per year in developing countries, excluding China, and 3 percent or more in some sub-Saharan African countries. High growth rates place pressure on available food supplies and on the environment in many low-income countries. Continual increases in food production are needed, because regardless of how successful efforts to control population growth are, world population will not stabilize for several years. Rapid urbanization is also occurring as populations continue to grow. Second, population growth has slowed significantly in some developing countries, allowing them to benefit over time from having a high proportion of their populations being of working age. However, in countries where population growth rates have been

Children in Honduras

slow for several years, such as in Germany, the United States, and more recently China, a key issue now is how to meet the medical and income needs of large and growing elderly populations.

Globalization

Food and economic systems in less-developed countries are affected by the international economic environment far more today than they were in years past. Trade and other economic policies abroad and at home, international capital flows, migration, disease transmission, and oil price shocks have combined to increase the instability of and opportunities for improving the food and economic security of developing and developed countries.

International trade in agricultural products (as with other products) has grown over the past half century, building on improvements in transportation and information systems. As exports and imports of farm products constitute a higher proportion of agricultural production and consumption, effects of agricultural policies aimed at farm sector and world prices become more important to farmers than they were previously. Possibilities for maintaining a nation's food security at the aggregate level are improved, although price volatility remains an issue. Production and policy changes abroad also tend to have an expanded effect on domestic agriculture as international trade grows. The need to be price competitive with other countries has grown, as has the need to participate in international negotiations to alter the policy environment. Growing demand in developed countries for non-traditional exports from developing countries, such as fresh fruits and vegetables, presents new opportunities for farmers. Quality and phytosanitary requirements in global markets create challenges for farmers wishing to exploit these opportunities.

International capital (money) markets, through which currencies flow from country to country in response to differences in interest rates and other factors, are as important as trade to the food and economic systems in less-developed countries. Capital flows affect the values of national currencies in foreign exchange markets. The foreign exchange rate, or the value of one country's currency in terms of another country's currency, is an important determinant of the price a nation receives for exports or pays for imports.

Many countries also have serious foreign debt problems. The decade following the 2008 global financial crisis was characterized by cheap credit for borrowers and increased private and public investments in developing countries. The need for foreign exchange to repay external debts has increased the importance of exports for these countries, forcing them to examine their trade and exchange rate policies. Fluctuations in global markets expose debtor nations to foreign exchange crises; when world commodity prices fall, heavy debt burdens can constrain domestic spending on social services and exacerbate political instability.

The lesson of two world wars, 9/11, the food price spike in 2008, and the recent COVID-19 pandemic is that we live in a globalized world that cannot be ignored, or if we do ignore it, it is at our own peril.

Environmental degradation

As populations grow, environmental problems become more severe. Deforestation, farming of marginal lands, overgrazing, and misuse of pesticides have contributed to soil erosion, desertification, poisoning of water supplies, and climate change. Global climate change has gradually warmed the climate and made weather more variable, contributing to stronger storms and harsher droughts. Water has become scarcer. Some environmental degradation is intentional, but most is the unintended result of people and governments seeking means of solving immediate food and economic problems, often at the cost of long-term damage to the environment. Some of this damage may compromise the ability of countries to raise incomes in the long run. When people are hungry, it is hard to tell them to save their resources for the future, and environmental conservation represents a form of savings. However, many potential solutions exist which are consistent with short-term increases in food production and long-term goals of simultaneously sustaining or improving environmental quality while raising incomes.

Risk and uncertainty

Most of the factors mentioned above are associated with increased exposure to risk and uncertainty. Fluctuating prices, exchange rate instability, agricultural pests, and rapidly changing weather patterns represent risk factors. Risks and risk management imply real costs that may compromise short- and long-run in well-being. For example, the COVID-19 pandemic spread rapidly throughout the world and exposed the limitations of public health systems in poor and wealthy countries alike. More than a million people perished as a result of the pandemic, and economic damage from it and efforts to contain it erased decades of progress in reducing global hunger and poverty.

Pandemics are devastating, but not all risks faced by individuals and countries are necessarily bad. Innovation and entrepreneurship are risky activities with high payoffs. It is how risks are managed that most influences economic growth. Risk management needs to be conducted efficiently; the proper balance must be found between managing risks and pursuing other goals.

The preceding overview provides brief highlights of some of the dimensions of the food–income–population–environment problem.

Slum close to river bank in Katmandu, Nepal

These problems are discussed in more depth in subsequent chapters, and solutions are suggested.

Meaning of development

The term *development* means a change over time, typically involving growth or expansion. *Economic* development involves changes in people's standard of living. For most of human history there was little such change, but over the past 300 years there has been a rapid and (so far) sustained increase in almost every kind of human activity. Growth occurred first and has been sustained the longest in Northwest Europe and North America, but similar kinds of expansion have occurred all around the world. Economic growth reduced the poverty headcount in China from 66 percent of the population in 1990 to about 1 percent in 2015, based on the World Bank poverty definition of earning less than $1.90 of income per person per day.

Development is a process with many economic and social dimensions. For most observers, *successful* economic development requires, as a minimum, rising per capita incomes, eradication of absolute poverty, and reduction in inequality over the long term. The process is a dynamic one, including not only changes in the structure and level of economic activity, but also increased opportunities for individual choice and for improved self-esteem.

Development is often a painful process. Adjusting to new circumstances is always difficult: as Mark Twain famously wrote, "I'm all for progress – it's change I can't stand". There is often dramatic social upheaval with traditional ways of life being displaced, existing social norms being challenged, and increasing pressures for institutional and political reform. The physical and cultural landscape of a country can change radically during economic development. And at the individual level, the standard of living for the poorest people in a society can decline, at least for a while, even as average real incomes increase. Usually, the fruits of improvement are unequally distributed. By any measure, poverty and deprivation remain widespread, despite the astonishing improvements in living standards experienced by many across the globe.

As economic activity continues to expand, there is continuous concern with the constraints imposed by natural resources and environmental factors. The World Commission on Environment and Development has defined sustainable development as "development that meets the needs of the present without compromising the ability of future generations to meet their own needs".[1] Thus, the term "development" encompasses not only an economic growth component, but also distributional components, both for the current population and for future generations.

Sustainable Development Goals

In 2015, United Nations countries adopted a set of 17 Sustainable Development Goals for the world to meet by 2030 (Figure 1.3). The first three goals are: no poverty, zero hunger, and good health and well-being. These goals appear ambitious, but having targets helps to focus attention on serious global problems and encourages measurement of progress in each country toward achieving improved and sustainable well-being for its citizens. In 2000, a set of similar goals were established for 2015, such as cutting extreme poverty and hunger in half. Some of these goals were achieved. The prominence among the goals of reduced poverty and hunger and of improved health reinforces their over-riding importance for the well-being of people around the world.

Measures of development

Achieving development is difficult to measure, illustrated in part by the sheer number of Sustainable Development Goals in Figure 1.3. However,

Figure 1.3 United Nations Sustainable Development Goal poster
Source: UNDP: Sustainable Development Goals, 2020, www.undp.org/content/undp/en/home/sustainable-development-goals.html

measurement is often necessary in order to assess the impacts of specific, particular programs, including foreign assistance, and for evaluating progress in meeting goals. Because of its several dimensions, single indicators of development can be misleading. Measures are needed that are consistent with the objective of raising the standard of living broadly and sustainably across the population. Average per capita income is frequently used as a measure of development (Figure 1.4). Is it a good measure?

Average per capita income is not a perfect measure of living standards for several reasons, but finding an alternative indicator that can incorporate each dimension of sustainable development is impossible. Because development is multidimensional, collapsing it into a single index measure requires placing weights on different dimensions. Average per capita income is an inadequate measure even of the economic dimensions because it misses the important distributional elements of development and is a crude measure of people's well-being. The World Bank converts local currencies into U.S. dollars to allow income comparisons to be made across countries. It does this conversion using either official foreign exchange rates (Atlas method) or by a method called purchasing power parity (PPP method) that considers cost differences across countries. Because the cost of living is generally lower in developing countries than the United States, the PPP method usually gives a higher estimated per capita income for developing countries than does the Atlas method.

Alternative multidimensional development indicators have been suggested. One of the oldest is a level of living index proposed by M.K. Bennett that weights 19 indicators.[2] Examples of indicators include caloric intake

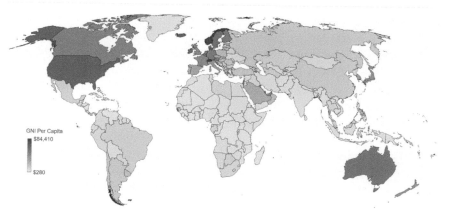

Figure 1.4 GNI per capita (Atlas method)
Source: World Bank, World Development Indicators Online Database, 2019

per capita, infant mortality rates, number of physicians per 1000 of total population, and years of schooling. Another index is the Human Development Index[3] (HDI), which weights life expectancy, education, and income. Weighting schemes are subjective, however, and average per capita income is highly correlated with many of the indicators. Consequently, average per capita income, measured as gross national income (GNI) or gross domestic product (GDP) per capita, is often employed as a first approximation; then measures such as income distribution, poverty rates, literacy rates, life expectancy, gender empowerment, and child mortality, among others, are examined separately or as part of an index. Even these supplementary indicators can be misleading due to regional disparities within countries.

Incomes and development

Poverty and low incomes are most frequently associated with underdevelopment, while growing per capita incomes should indicate increasing levels of development. As discussed earlier, increasing average incomes may not necessarily mean more development, because the distribution of this income often determines whether poverty and inequality are diminished as the mean grows. Some of the relationships between poverty and inequality are discussed in Box 1.1.

Numerous measures of inequality and the extent of poverty exist. For example, the Human Poverty Index (HPI) measures the extent of deprivation with respect to life expectancy, education, and income.[4] An Inequality-adjusted Human Development Index (IHDI) is also available.[5] If, as is argued earlier, the meaning of development contains some element of poverty reduction or increased equality of income distribution, then clearly the incomes of the poor and destitute should be raised during the development process.

Policies undertaken to promote development have diverse effects on the incomes of the poor. Some people benefit, but often some do not, and, at times, incomes fall for certain population groups. It is important to consider the winners and losers in the development process. Income distributions and changes in them are indicators of the impact of development policies on different groups in society.

Value judgments or premises about what is desired or not are inextricably related to development economics. Concerns for economic and social equality, poverty eradication, and the need to improve health and education derive from subjective beliefs about what is good and what is not. Solutions to specific development problems often involve tradeoffs, and decisions about public resource allocations always involve tradeoffs. Governments make such tradeoffs every day, as most public actions are costly to some people even as they benefit others. Economics can be a

BOX 1.1 POVERTY AND INEQUALITY

Poverty is generally defined as the failure to achieve a minimum standard of living. It refers not just to *averages*, but to *distributions*. Poverty is not, however, synonymous with inequality; countries with perfect equality could contain all rich or all poor people. Measurement of poverty requires three steps: determining an appropriate measure or indicator, deciding on its minimum level, and counting the number or percentage of people falling below it. Alternatively, a measure of degree or intensity of poverty would indicate the amount by which people fall below the poverty line.

Poverty refers to a level or position with respect to a measure such as income, while inequality refers to the distribution of that measure among a population. For example, evidence from 21 developing countries indicates that, on average, 6 percent of household income is received by the poorest 20 percent of the households, whereas 48 percent of household income is received by the richest 20 percent. In some countries, the extremes are even more dramatic. It is possible for poverty to decrease in a country during the development process, but for inequality to increase, at least for a period of time.

powerful tool for evaluating these tradeoffs, providing insights into the costs and benefits of different actions, winners and losers, and longer-run consequences of policy, investment, and consumption decisions. Economics is, however, less well-suited for making value decisions.

ROLE OF AGRICULTURE

Many alternative development paths or strategies exist. The strategy followed by an individual country at a point in time is, or at least should be, influenced in part by its resource endowments and stage of development. Some countries with vast oil and mineral resources have generated capital for development by exporting those resources. Others have emphasized cash-crop exports such as coffee, cocoa, and tea. Some have focused on industrial exports, while others have stressed increases in basic food production. The optimal development path will vary by country, but the choice of an inappropriate path, given the existing resource endowments and stage of development, can result in long-term stagnation of the economy.

Agriculture is not very productive in most low-income countries. Early in the development process, much of the population is employed in agriculture, and a high percentage of the national income is derived from that sector[6] (see Table 1.3). As development proceeds, population grows and per capita income increases. As incomes grow, more and different types of food are demanded; either agricultural production or imports

Table 1.3 Relationship among Per Capita National Income, the Proportion of National Income in Agriculture, and the Proportion of the Labor Force in Agriculture, Selected Countries, 2018

Country	Per capita income (in PPP dollars)[1]	Agriculture GDP as a percentage of total GDP	Percentage of active labor force in agriculture	
			Female	Male
Uganda	1,753	24	76	65
Mali	1,982	39	63	66
Bangladesh	4,057	13	59	31
Moldova	6,770	10	28	36
Philippines	9,540	9	15	31
Ecuador	10,128	9	24	29
Indonesia	11,256	13	28	32
Colombia	12,859	6	8	22
Brazil	14,068	4	4	13
Thailand	16,129	8	28	33
Argentina	17,623	6	0	0
Mexico	17,672	3	4	18
Italy	36,218	2	2	5
Korea, Rep.	36,757	2	4	5
Japan[2]	40,344	1	3	4
France	40,459	2	2	4
Canada[3]	43,632	2	1	2
Australia	44,041	2	2	3
United States[4]	56,651	1	1	2

Source: World Bank, World Development Indicators Online Database, 2019

1 PPP stands for purchasing power parity and means that the incomes are converted to dollars that consider cost of living differences across countries.

2 Per capita income and agriculture GDP share for Japan are for 2017.

3 Agriculture GDP share for Canada is for 2015.

4 U.S. agriculture GDP share is for 2017.

must increase. Because agriculture commands so many of the resources in most low-income countries, few funds are available for importing food or anything else unless agricultural output grows.

The capacity of the agricultural sector to employ an expanding labor force is limited. As incomes continue to rise, the demand for non-food commodities grows as well. Therefore, economic development requires a structural transformation of the economy involving relative expansion of nonagricultural sectors. The agricultural sector must contribute food, labor, and capital to that expansion. It also provides a market for nonagricultural goods.

This economic transformation is illustrated in Table 1.3. Agriculture accounts for a large percentage of total income, and an even larger percentage of total employment for the lower income countries. The contribution of agriculture to national incomes declines from 30 to 50 percent for the lower-income countries, to 15 to 20 percent for the middle-income range, and below 3 percent for the highest income countries.

The initial size and low productivity of agriculture in most developing countries suggests an opportunity for raising national income through agricultural development. Because of the initial size of and low per-capita income in the agricultural sector, there is real scope for improving the distribution of income and enhancing the welfare of a major segment of the population through agricultural development.

One key to agricultural development is to improve information flows. In primitive societies, economic activities are local and information is basically available to all. Inappropriate activities are constrained by social and cultural norms. As development begins to proceed and economies become more complex, information needs increase, but traditional forms of information transmission are incapable of meeting these needs. Modern information systems are slow to develop, creating inequalities in access to new and accurate information. Those with greater access than others can take advantage of this situation to further their own welfare, often at the expense of overall agricultural and economic development.

Some changes required to foster broad-based and sustainable development require institutional changes and capital investments. Institutional changes typically require government involvement. Capital investments necessitate savings. Such savings are channeled into private and public investment, the latter to build the infrastructure needed for development. Saving requires striking a balance between present and future levels of living because it requires abstention from current consumption. Means must be sought to reduce this potential short-run versus long-run conflict during the development process. However, certain types of investments necessary for development, such as education, provide both short- and long-run benefits, as do investments in technologies and employment-intensive industries.

Improving agriculture

How can agriculture be improved to facilitate its role in providing food and contributing to overall development? There are still a few areas of the world, particularly in parts of Latin America and Africa, where land suited for agricultural production is not being farmed. Most increases in agricultural production will have to come, however, from more intensive use of land currently being farmed. Such intensive use will require improved technologies generated through research as well as improved irrigation systems, roads, market infrastructure, and other investments. It will require education and incentives created through changes in institutions such as land tenure systems, input and credit policies, and pricing policies (Box 1.2).

BOX 1.2 HISTORICAL PERSPECTIVE ON AGRICULTURAL DEVELOPMENT

The historical progression of agricultural development can be broadly broken into four distinct periods, marked by three "revolutions" in production technology and social institutions.

First, from the time that we first appeared on earth, human beings hunted and gathered their food. Hunter–gatherer societies typically lived in small groups and experienced little population growth.

Second, more than 10,000 years ago, a combination of climate changes and other factors created conditions for the development of settled agriculture. In the Middle East and elsewhere, people began to collect and cultivate the seeds of plants that eventually became modern barley, wheat, and rye. This development is known as the *first agricultural revolution*, and it permitted a slow but significant increase in human population density.

Third, a few hundred years ago, rising population density and opportunities for trade led to a *second agricultural revolution*. In Northwestern Europe and elsewhere, farmers developed crop rotations and livestock management systems that permitted rapid growth in output per person, fueling the *industrial revolution* and the eventual mechanization of many important tasks.

Finally, in the late nineteenth and early twentieth centuries, scientific breeding, chemical fertilizer, and other innovations allowed rapid increases in output per unit of area. The spread of these biological technologies to developing countries, known as the *green revolution*, was a powerful engine of economic growth and poverty alleviation, allowing low-income people to produce more food at lower cost than ever before.

These historical trends played out at different speeds and in different ways across the globe. Very few people, and only in the poorest countries, still devote substantial energy to hunter–gatherer activities, although millions of farmers still cultivate the same seeds in the same ways as their ancestors. Because of population growth, these techniques and institutional arrangements yield less output over time. The development and spread of higher-productivity systems to suit people's needs is among the major humanitarian challenges of our time.

Some of the basic dimensions of the world food–poverty–population–environment problem were examined. The aggregate world food situation was reviewed, and questions such as who the hungry are, and why they are hungry even though the world produces a surplus of food, were addressed. The significance of population growth and a series of forces in the global economy that influence developing countries were stressed.

SUMMARY

The meaning and measures of development were discussed and Sustainable Development Goals were identified. While alternative development strategies can be followed, agriculture has an important role to play in overall development in most developing countries. Development will require a complex set of improved technologies, education, and institutions.

IMPORTANT TERMS AND CONCEPTS

Agricultural productivity
Development
Enhanced information flows
Environmental degradation
Food price instability
Foreign exchange rates
Globalization
Health problems
Institutional change

International capital markets
International trade
Measures of development
Population growth
Poverty
Purchasing power parity
Structural transformation of the economy
Sustainable Development Goals
Technology

LOOKING AHEAD

In order to visualize more clearly the relationships among food supplies, food demand, population growth, and nutrition, it is important to examine facts, scientific opinion, and economic theory. We make this examination in the remaining chapters of Part 1 in this book. We turn first in Chapter 2 to the causes and potential solutions to hunger and malnutrition problems.

QUESTIONS FOR DISCUSSION

1 Are people hungry because the world does not produce enough food?
2 Has food production in developing countries kept pace with population growth there?
3 Is malnutrition more widespread today than in the past?
4 Why did food prices rise sharply beginning in 2008?
5 What are some factors that will influence the price of food over the next 10 to 20 years?
6 Is there much hope of bringing more land into production to help increase food production?
7 Why is agricultural development particularly important in less-developed countries?
8 Approximately what proportion of the world's population lives on per capita incomes of less than $2 per day?
9 What is development? To what extent are values important when discussing development issues?
10 Is average per capita income a good measure of level of living?
11 Why is most of the labor force engaged in agriculture in many less-developed countries?
12 Does economic development require expansion of the nonagricultural sector in low-income countries?
13 What is the conflict between increasing near- versus long-term levels of living in developing countries?
14 What are some of the major health problems in developing countries and what are their primary causes?
15 How fast is population growing in developing countries?
16 Why has international agricultural trade become more important over the past 40 years?
17 Why have international capital markets become more important to developing countries over the past 40 years?
18 Why might low food prices be both good and bad?

19 Why has environmental degradation become an increasing problem in developing countries?

NOTES

1 World Commission on Environment and Development, *Our Common Future* (New York: Oxford University Press, 1987), p. 43.
2 See M.K. Bennett, "International Disposition in Consumption Levels", *American Economic Review*, vol. 41 (September 1951), pp. 632–649.
3 United Nations Development Program, *Human Development Report 2011* (New York: Palgrave Macmillan, 2011), with the HDI, http://hdr.undp.org/en/statistics/hdi/.
4 United Nations Development Program, *Human Development Report 2007* (New York: Palgrave Macmillan Press, 2007), p. 357.
5 United Nations Development Program, *Inequality Human Development Report 2011* (New York: Palgrave Macmillan, 2011), with the IHDI, http://hdr.undp.org/en/statistics/ihdi/.
6 A warning about measurement is appropriate: in most countries it is difficult to measure the number of people employed in agriculture. Multiple job holdings, seasonal labor use in agriculture, and unpaid household labor all complicate the measurement problem. Often, data on the number employed in agriculture are obtained by (generally high-quality) census estimates of the rural population. Even in rural areas, many people are employed outside of agriculture.

RECOMMENDED READINGS

Food and Agriculture Organization of the United Nations, *State of Food Security and Nutrition in the World 2020* (Rome: FAO, 2020).

Norton, George W., *Hunger and Hope: Escaping Poverty and Achieving Food Security in Developing Countries* (Long Grove, IL: Waveland Press, 2014), Chapter 1.

Runge, C. Ford, Benjamin Senauer, Philip G. Pardey, and Mark W. Rosegrant, *Ending Hunger in Our Lifetime: Food Security and Globalization* (Baltimore: Johns Hopkins University Press, 2003).

Todaro, Michael P., *Economic Development* (New York: Prentice Hall, 2011), especially Chapters 1–3.

United Nations Development Program, *Human Development Report 2013* (New York: Palgrave Macmillan, 2013).

World Bank, *World Development Report 2008, Agriculture for Development* (New York: Oxford University Press); see earlier and later volumes as well.

2 Poverty, hunger, and health

THIS CHAPTER

1 Describes the world food situation
2 Examines different forms of poverty, hunger, and malnutrition: their magnitudes, consequences, and how they are measured
3 Identifies principal causes of and potential solutions to problems with poverty, hunger, and malnutrition in developing countries

THE WORLD FOOD SITUATION

World food demand and supply

On a global level, sufficient food is produced to feed everyone on earth. And the overall food situation has improved significantly over the last 50 years. Cereals are the most important sources of food, and since the mid-1960s, world cereal production has risen by roughly 1 billion tons per year. It is likely that an additional billion tons of production per year will be needed by 2040 to meet food needs of a world population expanding in numbers and in income. It is also likely that cereal imports by many developing countries will continue to grow.

Until recently, overall numbers and projections had suggested gradual improvement in reducing undernutrition in the world. However, several countries, mostly in sub-Saharan Africa, have seen per capita food production and consumption stagnate for decades, or not increase enough to significantly reduce the number of malnourished. According to data from the Food and Agriculture Organization of the United Nations (FAO), the index of per capita food production in Africa has grown only about 10 percent since 1970, with most of the increase coming in the period between 2000 and 2014. In some countries, per capita food production and consumption has declined since 1970. For example, the Democratic Republic of the Congo has experienced a 50 percent decline in per capita food production since 1970, due in part to conflict-related disruptions.

Even in countries with growing average food consumption, some groups may not see their consumption levels increase: household food consumption is closely related to household incomes, and the most disadvantaged are afflicted by low and uncertain incomes. In addition, the rate of growth in agricultural output for the world as a whole has slowed since the 1980s, and the use of cereals and sugar to produce bio-fuel products has created competition for use of these products as food. For people in many countries, the struggle for food will continue. Therefore, we turn now to how poverty and access to food manifest themselves in terms of hunger, malnutrition, and, in some cases, famine.

POVERTY

Poverty has many faces and is one of the major challenges facing the development community. Poverty is widely understood to be an inability to meet basic needs, and the poor tend to be hungry, lack adequate shelter, and have limited access to health care. The poor lack opportunity, and their powerlessness often leads to hopelessness and despair. To most people reading this book, poverty is an invisible and abstract problem, somewhere out there. We seldom think about it, and when we do, we often don't know what to do about it. Global poverty has been cut roughly in half since 1990, but stark challenges remain. In 2019, almost 700 million people – about 9 percent or a sixth of the world's population – lived in extreme poverty, as defined by making less than $1.90 per day. About 1.3 billion people in developing countries are "multidimensionally poor", according to a survey by the UN Development Program. However, for the first time since 1998, the number of extremely poor rose rapidly in 2020 due to jobs lost during the COVID-19 pandemic, likely by more than 100 million people and perhaps by hundreds of millions.

Measuring poverty

Since poverty is multidimensional, efforts to measure it can be complicated by attention to its different dimensions. Two broad types of measurement schemes exist: monetary and non-monetary. Monetary measures consolidate the different dimensions of poverty into a single unit of measure – money. Their strengths include the ability to make comparisons in a common unit, a non-arbitrary measurement scheme, and ability to quantify the extent, depth, and severity of poverty (see Box 2.1). However, monetary approaches often fail to capture dimensions of poverty that may be especially important and intractable, such as social exclusion and political powerlessness.

BOX 2.1 MONETARY MEASUREMENT OF POVERTY[1]

Three primary challenges in measuring poverty are: (1) deciding what to measure, (2) identifying a value, below which a household is deemed to be poor, and (3) adding it up for the population. Poverty involves an inability to control sufficient resources to meet a minimum level of well-being, and analysts use household income or consumption expenditure to measure it. Consumption is generally preferred because income, particularly in rural areas, is seasonal and variable, while consumption is smoother and often easier to measure. The poverty line is the value of income or expenditures on a daily, monthly, or annual basis below which a person is deemed to be poor. This poverty line can be determined many ways. In the United States, the poverty line was created in 1963 using the minimum cost of achieving an adequate diet based on U.S. Department of Agriculture food plans. Non-food expenditures were accounted for by observing that poor households generally spend about a third of their total budget on food: the food poverty line was multiplied by 3 to obtain the total poverty line. This line has been updated over time by adjusting for changes in the cost of living. A commonly used international poverty line is the World Bank's use of $1.90 person per day (in 2011 prices) to reflect extreme poverty and $3.20 per day (2011 prices) to reflect moderate poverty.

With a household survey, incomes or expenditures can be compared to the poverty line: households with values below the line are poor. Policymakers are not only interested in which households are poor, but also in where the poor are located, what they do, and how poverty has changed over time. Monetary indices of poverty are used to address these concerns, and the most commonly used poverty index, called the Foster, Greer, Thorbecke (FGT) Index,[2] is one that reflects the prevalence (proportion of the total population that is poor), depth (the degree of shortfall below the poverty line), and severity of poverty (the degree of inequality among the poor). This index gives policymakers a nuanced view of the total poverty picture: for example, a policy may increase the depth of poverty among some while reducing the total proportion of the population that is poor. For example, 40 percent of the population in South Asia was poor in 2005 compared to 51 percent in sub-Saharan Africa. In contrast, the poverty severity measures were 3 percent for South Asia compared to over 10 percent for sub-Saharan Africa, indicating a far more serious problem in poverty severity in sub-Saharan Africa than in South Asia at the time.

---

[1] For more information, see: www.worldbank.org/en/topic/poverty.
[2] J. Foster, J. Greer, and E. Thorbecke, A Class of Decomposable Poverty Measures, *Econometrica*, Vol. 52, 1984, pp. 761–766.

Non-monetary measures include qualitative assessments and indices that combine different dimensions, such as the Human Development Index (HDI) and Human Poverty Index (HPI) described in Chapter 1. These indices often face the criticism that the weights used are arbitrary, and measures vary significantly when the weights are changed. They also fail to capture dimensions such as social exclusion and powerlessness.

The different approaches complement each other, and their combination has allowed a deeper understanding of poverty. For example, qualitative participatory poverty assessments that engage in discussions with groups of poor people about their conditions and the unique challenges they face often accompany monetary assessments, and the combination can help in understanding how policies can be formulated to reduce poverty.

Vulnerability: transitory and chronic poverty

Poverty is not a constant state for many developing-country households. Weather, pests, diseases, and policies cause fluctuations in income that translate into movement in and out of poverty – households are vulnerable to becoming poor. This in-and-out of poverty situation is important because different policies may be needed to address transitory compared to chronic poverty. Evidence shows that transitory poverty – movement in and out of poverty over time – accounts for a substantial portion of overall poverty. As a result, means of protecting people from transitory income shortfalls may substantially improve the global poverty picture. Formal and informal insurance schemes, social safety nets, and other means of reducing or managing risks can help achieve this aim. Rural public work programs, such as dam-building, irrigation and water supply schemes, road construction, and maintenance programs are examples of social safety nets that may reduce vulnerability to poverty and build infrastructure for agricultural development. Pension programs, cash transfers, and feeding programs are examples of social protection schemes that affect food demand.

Chronic poverty is often caused by very different factors: households do not have access to enough human, physical, natural, and other assets to earn sufficient incomes for minimum levels of well-being. Poverty traps caused by insufficient assets, severely degraded natural resources, and other factors are difficult to escape and often require long-term investments in asset building, access to new factors of production, and improved institutions.

Agricultural development and the poor

A common misconception about poverty is that it is largely an urban problem. Pictures of teeming slums with inadequate sanitation and rotting infrastructure help bolster this perception. In contrast, rural residents are thought to live in relatively spacious conditions and to be able to rely on their own production of foods in times of dire need. In fact, on a global level, the rural poor make up about 70 percent of the total poor, and rural poverty is twice as prevalent as urban poverty. Rural poverty is a major problem and, as we will see throughout this book, agricultural development can play a significant role in its reduction, but agricultural development can also alleviate urban poverty.

Agricultural technology has direct impacts on the rural poor by increasing incomes of farmers, many of whom may be poor. Care must be taken during development and subsequent release of new technologies to ensure that they are accessible to poor producers. Indirect benefits to the poor from growth in agriculture come from two primary sources: increased demand for labor on farms and increased supply of food, causing food prices to drop. In many countries, especially in South Asia, landless laborers comprise a large proportion of the rural poor, and increased demand for agricultural labor benefits this group. The latter benefit can be substantial and is an important reason why global poverty fell from the early 1980s until recently. Food price declines have led to higher levels of living even for people who do not depend directly on agriculture. When global food markets tighten, as they have for brief periods, poverty rises due to the indirect effect of higher food prices.

HUNGER, MALNUTRITION, AND FAMINE

Hunger is a silent crisis in the world. In times of famine, it can tear at the heartstrings as media attention focuses on its dramatic effects. The most extreme type of hunger is severe calorie and protein undernutrition during a famine. However, more pervasive is chronic undernutrition and malnutrition associated with poverty, illness, ignorance, maldistribution of food within the family, and seasonal fluctuations in access to food. Low-quality diets can cause many forms of malnutrition, contributing to cardiovascular and metabolic disease through obesity, diabetes, and other conditions, but in this chapter, we focus on hunger and undernutrition. We begin our discussion with the contrast between famine and chronic malnutrition.

Famine

Famine is marked by an acute decline in access to food that occurs in a definable area and has a finite duration. Access to food usually falls due to crop failures, often in successive years, due to drought, flood, insect infestation, or war. During a famine, food may actually be present in the affected area, but its price is so high that only the wealthy can afford it. Food distribution systems may break down so that food cannot reach those who need it.

Famines have occurred throughout history. In recent years, their prevalence has been highest in sub-Saharan Africa, such as the ones in Yemen in 2019–20, South Sudan in 2017, and Somalia in 2011. All of these were caused to some degree by political problems and conflict. Famines also occurred in North Korea in the mid-1990s, Cambodia in 1979, Bangladesh in 1974, India in 1966 to 1967, and China in 1959 to 1961. The latter was the worst famine of the 20th century and resulted in the deaths of more than 16 million people.

Famine is the extreme on the hunger scale because it causes loss of life and concurrent social and economic chaos over a relatively short period of time. As access to food falls, people begin by borrowing money and then selling their assets to acquire money to purchase foods. Subsistence farmers sell their seed stocks, livestock, plows, and even land. Landless laborers and other poor groups lose their jobs, or face steeply higher prices for food at constant wages. As the famine intensifies, whole families and villages migrate in search of relief. The telltale signs of acute malnutrition and, eventually, sickness and death appear.

Fortunately, progress is being made against famine. Although large variations occur in annual food production in individual countries and world population continues to grow, the frequency and intensity of famines has decreased due to improved information and transportation networks, increased food production and reserves, and dedicated relief organizations. Much of the starvation we see during famines now occurs in areas where transportation systems are deficient and where conflict thwarts relief efforts, such as in Yemen. The relatively recent famines in Yemen, South Sudan, and Somalia were all due to a combination of natural disasters, conflict, and lack of political will to alleviate the problem.

Chronic hunger and malnutrition

As devastating as famines are, they account for only a small fraction of hunger-related deaths. Famines can be attacked in a relatively short period of time if political conflict in the affected country does not hamper relief efforts. Chronic hunger and malnutrition affect a much greater number of people and are more difficult to combat (Table 2.1).

Table 2.1 Estimated Number of People Affected by Preventable Malnutrition Worldwide

Deficiency	Morbidity	Estimated Prevalence	Population Group Most Affected
Protein + energy[1]	Wasting (underweight)	49,500,000	Children under 5
Protein + energy[1]	Stunted growth	149,000,000	Children
Iron[2]	Anemia	613,200,000	Women 15 to 49
Vitamin A[3]	Blindness/ Measles/Diarrhea	105,700 (deaths)	Children under 5
Iodine[4]	Brain damage	18,000,000	Infants

Sources:
1 UNICEF-WHO-World Bank, Joint Child Malnutrition Estimates, regional and global joint estimates, 2019
2 2018 Global Nutrition Report – Chapter 2
3 *Lancet Global Health*, Vol. 3, Issue 9, 528–536
4 WHO, Investing in the future: A united call to action on vitamin and mineral deficiencies, Table 3: Human toll of vitamin and mineral deficiencies. Global Report 2009

According to FAO, nearly 690 million people were undernourished in 2019, or about 8.9 percent of the world population. An estimated 2 billion people did not have regular access to safe and nutritious food that included sufficient intake of macronutrients and micronutrients. Preschool children and pregnant and nursing women are particularly vulnerable to the dangers of malnutrition.

Serious macronutrient malnutrition in developing countries reflects primarily undernourishment – a shortage of food in the diet – not an imbalance between total calories and protein. The availability of calories per capita by country is illustrated in Figure 2.1. Many of the countries with very low per capita calorie availability are found in sub-Saharan Africa. A close, but not perfect, correspondence exists between low calorie availability and the low-income countries identified in the previous chapter. When commonly consumed cereal-based diets meet energy (calorie) requirements, it is likely that most protein needs will also be satisfied for people older than about 2 years of age. Thus, for everyone except infants, the greatest concerns are the total quantity of food available to eat and micronutrient consumption. In settings where overall energy intake meets minimum needs, remaining protein or micronutrient deficiencies can often be improved with rather small investments to improve the quality of the diet. However, for millions of people, especially women and children, these investments are not being made (Table 2.1).

Iodine deficiency is common in regions far from the sea, for example parts of the Andes in South America. Iron deficiency is a particularly serious problem among women of childbearing age all over the world, and vitamin A deficiency is a widespread concern, especially among children.

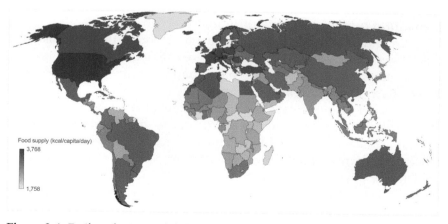

Figure 2.1 Daily calorie availability per capita, 2017
Source: FAOSTAT data

Consequences of hunger and malnutrition

Stunted growth, reduced physical and mental activity, muscle wasting, increased vulnerability to infections and other diseases, and, in severe cases, death are the most common consequences of calorie deficiencies. Death most frequently results from dehydration caused by diarrhea, whose severity is closely linked to malnutrition. Chronic protein malnutrition results in stunted growth, skin rash, edema, and change of hair color. A diet relatively high in calories but low in protein can result in an illness known as kwashiorkor, while a diet low in both calories and protein can result in an illness known as marasmus. People can live about a month with kwashiorkor, three months with marasmus; 7–10 million people die each year from the two diseases.

Iron deficiency anemia affects muscle function and worker productivity. Vitamin A deficiency is a leading cause of childhood blindness and often results in death due to reduced disease resistance. Iodine deficiencies cause goiter and brain damage.

There is little doubt that hunger and malnutrition result in severe physical and mental distress, even for those who survive the infections and diseases. Malnourished children are more likely to not attend school, and when they do, they learn less than their well-nourished counterparts. Malnutrition can affect the ability of a person to work and earn a decent livelihood, as mental development, educational achievement, and physical productivity are reduced. People with smaller bodies because of inadequate childhood nutrition are paid less in agricultural jobs in many countries. Lower earnings perpetuate the problem across generations, leading to a vicious cycle of malnutrition and poverty.

Measuring hunger and malnutrition

Measuring the extent of hunger and malnutrition in the world is difficult. Disagreement surrounds definitions of adequate caloric and protein requirements, while data on morbidity and mortality reflect the combined effects of sickness and malnutrition.

Nutritional assessments are usually attempted through food balance sheets, dietary surveys, anthropometric (body measurement) surveys, clinical examinations, and administrative records. Food balance sheets place agricultural output, stocks, and imports on the supply side and seed for next year's crops, exports, animal feed, and wastage on the demand side. Demand is subtracted from supply to derive an estimate of the balance of food left for human consumption. That amount left can be balanced against the Food and Agricultural Organization of the United Nations' (FAO) tables of nutritional requirements to estimate the adequacy of the diet. This method provides rough estimates at best, due to difficulties in estimating agricultural production and wastage in developing countries.

Food balance sheets provide only a picture of average food availability. Malnutrition, like poverty, is better measured if the distribution of food intake or of other indicators is also considered. Average national food availability can be adequate, while malnutrition is common in certain areas, or among particular population groups. Even within families, some members may be malnourished while others are not. To measure malnutrition accurately, information on households or individuals is required.

Household and individual information can be obtained from dietary or expenditure surveys and from clinical or field measurements of height, weight, body fat, and blood tests. These methods are expensive and seldom administered on a consistent and widespread basis for an

Women and child in Ethiopia
Source: **Photo by Mesfin Bezuneh**

entire country. They can be effective, however, in estimating malnutrition among population sub-groups. Since preschool children are most vulnerable to nutritional deficiencies, random surveys to measure either their food intakes or anthropometry can provide a good picture of the extent of malnutrition. Another means of estimating the extent of malnutrition is to utilize existing data in hospital, health service, and school records. Unfortunately, these statistics can be biased because the records for rural areas are scarce, the poor are the least likely to have sought medical attention, and the quality of the information in the records is uneven. For example, many countries record the heights, weights, and ages of first-year elementary school children. Unfortunately, some members of the poorest population groups do not attend school. Because of these biases, estimates of malnutrition among school-aged children generally understate the true problem. One reason why malnutrition is misunderstood is that its measurement is so difficult.

CAUSES OF POVERTY, HUNGER, AND MALNUTRITION

A variety of factors contribute to poverty, hunger, and malnutrition, but inadequate income is certainly the most important underlying cause. If people, for whatever reason, produce too few goods and services and lack income to buy food, they go hungry. Even in times of famine, decreased purchasing power rather than absolute food shortage is often the major problem, as food may be available in nearby regions. Incomes in the affected area have declined so that people cannot afford to buy food from unaffected areas.

Figure 2.2 contains a schematic diagram of the determinants of household well-being and individual nutritional status. Access to productive assets such as land, labor, natural resources, and the policy regime (prices and other factors) determine household income and well-being. Income, including the value of own production and in-kind transfers determine how much food can be purchased or consumed by the family. Total food purchases and consumption do not, however, tell the entire story. Health status and family food preparation, along with how food is distributed among members of the family, help determine how food available to a family is related to individual nutritional status.

Health and malnutrition

Poverty's interaction with malnutrition is often compounded by infectious diseases and parasites that reduce appetites, cause malabsorption

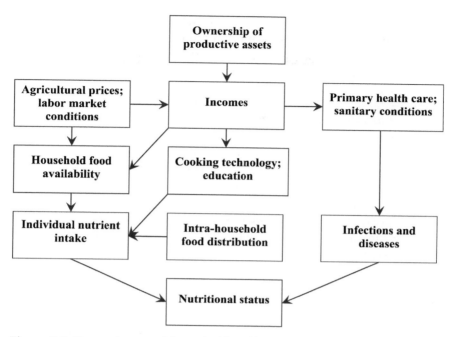

Figure 2.2 Determinants of household well-being and individual nutritional status

of food, or result in nutrient wastage due to fever and other metabolic processes. Health problems and malnutrition exhibit a synergistic relationship: infections and parasites lead to malnutrition while malnutrition can impair the immune system, increasing the risk of infection and the severity of illness. Measles, parasites, intestinal infections, and numerous other health problems are prevalent in developing countries. Many health and sanitation problems lead to diarrhea, which in turn can cause dehydration and death. Health is determined by, among other things, household sanitary conditions, which are influenced by household assets and income, and by government programs. There is room for optimism related to many childhood diseases. The World Health Organization reports that because of sustained efforts to vaccinate children, the majority of the world's children under 1 year old are now vaccinated against six common childhood diseases. However, the last 30 years has seen HIV/AIDS become a persistent problem, especially in Africa and Asia. Thirty-eight million people were HIV positive in 2018 and about 770,000 people died from AIDS-related illnesses. Malaria also remains a serious problem in many countries, with more than 200 million cases per year and 435,000 deaths. Seventeen countries, mostly in Africa, account for 80 percent of those deaths.[1] Fortunately, programs to combat malaria are broadly successful. The distribution of bed nets and efforts to reduce the malaria-transmitting insect – the female Anopheles mosquito – have reduced rates of infection in many countries.

Poor nutritional practices

Insufficient knowledge of good nutritional practices, maldistribution of food within the family, and excessive demands on women's time can all contribute to malnutrition and perpetuate poverty. The results of studies that have examined each of these factors provide conflicting evidence as to their importance. Each factor is undoubtedly significant in some areas of the world but not in others. In parts of South Asia, evidence indicates that adult males often receive a disproportionate share of food in the family compared to young females, but this is not universally the case.

Evidence shows that whether the male or female controls income within a family helps determine how food is distributed. When women earn incomes, the extra resources are more likely to be spent on food for the family.[2] There also is strong evidence that increased educational opportunities for women are linked to improved nutritional practices and more equitable distribution within the family.

Seasonal and cyclical hunger

As with poverty, many people in developing countries move in and out of a state of malnutrition. There are hungry seasons, hungry years, and hungry parts of the life cycle. Given individuals may or may not survive these periods and can experience lasting physical, mental, and emotional impacts even if they do survive.

Hungry seasons occur because of agricultural cycles. In the weeks preceding a harvest, food can be in short supply. This normal seasonality can be exacerbated if crops in a particular year are short or households are unable to effectively store food. In certain seasons, particularly the rainy seasons, disease and infection are more common. Likewise, droughts, floods, and insect infestations happen in some years but not in others. Young children are vulnerable, in part due to dangers associated with diarrhea. Pregnant and lactating women experience extra nutritional demands on their bodies, while the elderly suffer disproportionately as well, particularly if they lack the support of their children.

Ugandan children with seasonal hunger

SOLUTIONS TO POVERTY, HUNGER, AND MALNUTRITION PROBLEMS

Solutions to hunger and malnutrition problems depend on the types and causes of problems, but poverty alleviation is needed for a long-term solution. Famine relief strategies differ from solutions to chronic hunger and malnutrition, but even in famines, the poor are most vulnerable to starvation. Unfortunately, there is no single solution to reducing poverty. Fortunately, certain interventions can help reduce hunger and malnutrition even in the presence of poverty, and a concerted effort across many fronts is required.

Raising incomes
Lifting vulnerable people out of poverty is central to any long-term strategy to alleviate malnutrition in the world. For small-scale farmers, this implies raising productivity, increasing access to land, or creating off-farm employment opportunities. For the population in general, it

implies a need for increased employment opportunities combined with higher productivity per person. The latter requires growth in jobs and in the amount of capital per job in the non-farm sector. Enhanced education, an investment in human capital, will also increase productivity and incomes. Equal access to jobs and expanded economic opportunities in impoverished regions can also help reduce poverty. Economic growth without increased employment for the poorest segments of the population will do little to reduce hunger. Programs to increase employment and earnings opportunities for women are particularly important, partly because these opportunities help accelerate the transition to lower birth rates (for reasons discussed in Chapter 4) and contribute to women's empowerment.

Agricultural productivity
Agricultural productivity is important for the incomes and nutritional status of the poor because in developing countries many low-income people have no choice but to farm and to feed themselves and their families using their own labor and available land. Increased productivity for farmers raises incomes and purchasing power, and resulting production may lower the price of food for those who must buy it to feed their families. Increased investments in agricultural research and education, improved access to purchased inputs, marketing, and credit, improved agricultural policies, and investment in infrastructure such as roads, storage, and irrigation systems can each help generate agricultural production and productivity growth.

Safety nets
As noted above, much poverty is transitory and caused by fluctuations in income. These fluctuations, in turn, can have dramatic impacts on nutrition, and they can lead to longer-term poverty because households often invoke harmful coping mechanisms to deal with them. For example, in the face of income downturns, some families remove their children from school to reduce outlays on school-related items and provide additional workers to generate income. Safety net programs, such as cash and in-kind transfers, public works programs, and fee waivers for health and education, can assist people in need and provide insurance against risks. By protecting vulnerable farmers against the adverse consequences of risk, safety nets allow them to make better investment decisions and to adopt new technologies and production practices (such as new seeds and

fertilizers) that increase incomes. Safety nets need to be properly targeted and efficiently administered to avoid waste, but much has been learned in recent years about their design and implementation. Many countries have successfully implemented a variety of safety net programs, including cash transfers, unemployment insurance, and old age pensions.[3]

Food intervention programs

Food price subsidies, supplementary feeding programs, and food fortification can each help reduce nutritional deficiencies. Few developing countries have come close to eliminating malnutrition without some combination of these practices. However, these programs alone cannot solve problems of chronic malnutrition.

Several countries have instituted supplementary feeding programs for vulnerable groups such as children and pregnant and nursing mothers. In some cases, these programs provide food to be consumed in a specific location, such as in schools or health centers, while in others food may be consumed at home. In either case, while total family food consumption rises, that of the food recipient usually grows by less than the total donation. Some food is shared with family members. The evidence on supplementary feeding programs indicates that they often are associated with measurable improvements in nutritional status, but they tend to be expensive for the benefits received. Some of these programs have been supported with food aid from other countries.

Another food intervention program involves fortification by adding specific nutrients during processing. The most successful fortification example is iodine fortification of salt to prevent goiter. Vitamin A also has proven relatively inexpensive to add to foods such as tea, sugar, margarine, monosodium glutamate, and cereal products. Attempts have been made to fortify food with iron to prevent anemia, but reducing iron deficiency anemia has proven to be a complex problem. In general, the effectiveness of adding nutrients to food is reduced by the fact that the poor buy few processed foods, there is often cultural resistance to the fortified product, and the cost of fortification is prohibitive. In many cases, the "fortified" food has been shown to have no more nutrients than unfortified foods; quality control can be prohibitively expensive in developing countries. Recent success in incorporating vitamins and minerals such as vitamin A, vitamin B, iron, and zinc into food crops such as rice, sweet potatoes, and cassava through biofortification provides an alternative avenue for reducing these micronutrient problems.

Health improvements

Efforts to improve sanitation, reduce parasite infections, and prevent dehydration caused by diarrhea can reduce malnutrition and mortality substantially. For example, oral rehydration therapy, involving the use of water, salt, and sugar in specified proportions to replace fluid lost during diarrhea, can significantly reduce diarrhea-related deaths. Investments in sanitation services, such as potable water and latrines, when combined with effective education programs, can improve nutritional status by reducing diarrhea. The percentage of the world with access to clean water has grown dramatically since 1990, but even some countries with good indicators of potable water availability face stresses related to water shortages. Better health services like immunization and deworming programs can reduce the incidence and intensity of diseases and parasites that contribute to malnutrition.

Political, social, and educational changes

Political stability can help alleviate both famine conditions and chronic hunger. Famines in Ethiopia in 1983–84, Somalia in 2011, South Sudan in 2017, and Yemen in 2019–20 were exacerbated by political upheaval that hampered relief efforts. Hunger in North Korea also has political roots. Because programs to curb chronic hunger and malnutrition require long-term commitments, they are necessarily rendered less effective by political instability. Responsible political action can improve income distribution in a country, thereby reducing poverty and malnutrition.

Social, cultural, and educational factors also come into play. For example, low rates of breastfeeding in some countries have contributed to malnutrition as substitutes can be less nutritionally complete, are often watered down, and in some cases are even unsanitary. In other cases, breastfeeding may continue too long without the addition of needed solid foods. While social and cultural factors change slowly, and economic factors influence decisions, education can help. In fact, few consumption practices are totally unaffected by education. Nutrition education programs, especially when combined with income-generating projects or efforts to increase a family's access to nutrients, such as home gardening, have been shown to lead to improved nutritional status.

International actions

International actions can help alleviate poverty, famine, and chronic malnutrition. Because increased incomes are so important to improved nutrition, opening of markets in more-developed countries and debt

Rural health center in Colombia

relief are actions that can help, especially in the long run. Foreign assistance can provide short-run relief and, when properly designed, facilitate long-run development.

Reduced barriers by developed countries to imports from developing countries will enable low-income nations to gain greater access to world markets. The foreign exchange earned can be used for development efforts and food imports when needed.

Foreign assistance includes food aid as well as technical and financial assistance. Gifts and loans of food at low interest rates can help solve part of the hunger problem if the food assistance is properly administered. Food aid can save lives during short-term famines and be used over longer periods in supplementary feeding programs and in food-for-work programs to help generate wealth in developing countries. Financial and technical assistance can help developing countries expand their capital bases and improve methods for producing food and other products, allowing them to import or develop the new technologies they need to break out of poverty.

SUMMARY

In this chapter, the types and consequences of poverty, hunger, and malnutrition were examined. We now have much better information on the distribution and extent of poverty than we did a few years ago. Even though it is difficult to measure accurately the extent of hunger and malnutrition in the world, it is known that chronic malnutrition affects more people than do famines. Malnutrition results in reduced physical and mental activity, stunted growth, blindness, anemia, goiter, brain damage, mental anguish, and death.

The causes of hunger are many, but virtually all causes are related to poverty. Infections, diseases and parasites, poor nutritional practices, and variability in food supplies all contribute to the severity of malnutrition. Solutions to hunger and malnutrition include raising incomes, increasing agricultural productivity in developing countries, food intervention programs, improving health systems; political, social, and educational changes; international programs such as food aid and other foreign assistance; opening of foreign markets; and price stabilization.

IMPORTANT TERMS AND CONCEPTS

Anthropometry
Chronic malnutrition
Debt relief
Dietary surveys
Famine
Food aid
Food balance sheets
Food fortification
Food price subsidies
Foreign assistance
Kwashiorkor, marasmus,
  goiter, anemia
Maldistribution of food

Micronutrients
Oral rehydration therapy
Political upheaval
Poverty
Price stabilization
Protein and calorie deficiency
Safety nets
Seasonal and cyclical hunger
Supplementary feeding programs
Transitory poverty
Vitamin and mineral deficiency
Vulnerability

LOOKING AHEAD

Hunger and malnutrition imply a need for food but not necessarily a demand for food unless that need is backed by purchasing power. Food demand is influenced by income, prices, population, and tastes and preferences. In the next chapter, we will examine tools that can help measure or project the extent to which various demand factors affect food consumption. We will explore how demand interacts with supply to determine prices. The tools discussed are the first of a set of theories and methods presented in this book that can improve your ability to analyze and not just observe food and development problems and policies.

QUESTIONS FOR DISCUSSION

1 What are the causes of transitory poverty? What can be done to alleviate the problem?
2 Why is it important to have information on the depth and severity of poverty in addition to the poverty prevalence?
3 Has poverty gone down globally over time?
4 Is famine more common today than in the past?
5 If people in the United States moved to a diet in which they consumed more grain and less meat, would there be more food for people in poor countries of the world? Why or why not?
6 What are the principal causes and consequences of hunger?
7 How do we measure the adequacy of food availability in a country?
8 What are some solutions to hunger and malnutrition problems?
9 How might safety net programs contribute to long-term development?
10 Why and how does political upheaval contribute to famine?
11 What are the major interactions between health and nutritional problems?

NOTES

1 World Health Organization, 2020, www.who.int/gho/malaria/en/.
2 See Abhijit Banerjee and Esther Duflo, *Poor Economics: A Radical Re-thinking of the Way to Fight Global Poverty* (New York: Public Affairs, 2011).
3 See Margaret Grosh, Carlo del Ninno, Emil Tesliuc, and Azedine Ouerghi, *For Protection and Promotion: The Design and Implementation of Effective Safety Nets* (Washington, DC: The World Bank, 2008).

RECOMMENDED READINGS

Banerjee, Abhijit, and Esther Duflo, *Poor Economics: A Radical Re-Thinking of the Way to Fight Global Poverty* (New York: Public Affairs, 2011).
Food and Agriculture Organization of the United Nations, *The State of Food Security and Nutrition in the World* (Rome: FAO, 2020), p. 286.

Foster, Phillips, and Howard D. Leathers, *The World Food Problem* (Boulder, CO: Lynne Reinner Publishers, 2017).

Grosh, Margaret, Carlo del Ninno, Emil Tesliuc, and Azedine Ouerghi, *For Protection and Promotion: The Design and Implementation of Effective Safety Nets* (Washington, DC: The World Bank, 2008).

Holloway, Kris, *Monique and the Mango Rains* (Long Grove, IL: Waveland Press, 2007).

United Nations Development Program, *2019 Human Development Report* (New York: UNDP, 2019), p. 252.

Walraven, Gijs, *Health and Poverty: Global Health Problems and Solutions* (London: Earthscan, 2011), p. 192.

3 Economics of food demand

THIS CHAPTER

1 Discusses the importance of income, population, preferences, and prices in determining the demand for food as development occurs
2 Explains the importance of income and price elasticities of demand for projecting consumption patterns and for understanding how development is related to food consumption
3 Describes how supply interacts with demand over time to determine price levels and trends

EFFECTIVE DEMAND FOR FOOD

The need for food and the effective demand for food are related but distinct concepts. Food needs correspond to the nutrient consumption required to maintain normal physical and mental growth in children and to sustain healthy bodies and normal levels of activity in adults. The effective demand (often just called demand) for food is the amount of food people are willing to buy at different prices and income levels, given their needs and preferences.

In this chapter, we consider the means of analyzing food demand changes resulting from income and price changes. The goal is to help you understand the likely impacts of a change in these factors on consumption. We will see how food demand pressures interact with feed and bio-fuel demand and with supply conditions to determine changes in economic well-being.

Determinants of food demand

The quantity demanded of food, or of any commodity, is influenced by two major factors: its price, relative to all other goods, and consumers' incomes, relative to all prices. In order to isolate each effect, economists use a thought-experiment in which we imagine a change in only one variable at a time, and trace out the resulting change in another.

When considering the effect of a change in price on quantity consumed, we expect a higher price to cause a lower quantity consumed and vice versa. This inverse relationship between price and quantity consumed is often called the *law of demand*, and is illustrated on a graph using a market *demand curve* (Figure 3.1). The slope and location of the market demand curve are determined primarily by income per person, the number of people in the market, and the distribution of income among those people, prices of other goods, and other factors such as consumer preferences. Changes in any of these factors cause the demand curve to shift, as shown by the shift from the lower income demand curve to the higher income demand curve in Figure 3.1. Such a shift might be caused by a rise in per capita income, which increases the quantity demanded at a given price. Alternatively, the shift might be caused by population

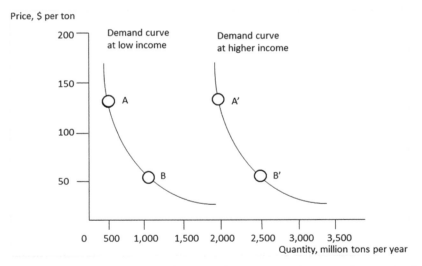

Figure 3.1 Hypothetical demand curves for a commodity. A reduction in the price of the commodity, all other things being equal, will cause a movement along a demand curve, say from point A to point B, and an increase in quantity demanded. Changes in the determinants of demand – population, income, prices of other goods, and preferences – can cause a shift in demand, say from point A on the lower income demand curve to point A' on the higher income demand curve.

growth at a constant per-capita income. This income effect on demand varies by commodity. Because the influence of income on food demand is not constant across countries, within countries, or by commodity, it is important to have a measure of the sensitivity of demand for food and for particular goods to changes in income. The measure used is called the *income elasticity of demand*.

Income elasticities of demand

The *income elasticity of demand* is defined as the percentage by which the quantity demanded of a commodity will change for a one percent change in income, other things remaining constant.[1] For example, when per capita income increases by 1 percent, if quantity demanded of a commodity increases by 0.3 percent, its income elasticity of demand is 0.3. Typically, for a very low-income country, the income elasticity of demand for food as a whole is around 0.8, while for a very high-income country it is around 0.1. This difference in income elasticities means that changes to income have a much larger relative impact on food demand in low-income countries than in high-income countries.

By necessity, poor people have no choice but to spend the bulk of their income on food – at times as much as 80 percent – and when their incomes rise, they spend a high proportion of that increase on more food. Eventually, however, further increases in income tend to be spent on other things. This change in the proportion of the family's budget spent on food, or *Engel's law*, says that as income increases, people spend a smaller proportion of their total income on food. This process is reflected in Figure 3.2, which shows the percentage of total income spent on food for a number of countries with different levels of per capita income. The distinct downward slope associated with Engel's law would be similar if the graph were constructed for individuals within a country, where richer people spend a smaller fraction of their income on food compared to poorer people.

Engel's law reflects, in part, the limited capacity of the human stomach, but note that total expenditures on food generally continue to rise with income, even as the proportion of the budget spent on food declines. Rising incomes lead people to consume more total calories, and also to consume more expensive foods. These foods are often more highly processed (for example, as people switch to bread instead of porridge) and include more animal products (meat, dairy, eggs, and fish) as well as more fruits and vegetables. The transition in consumption from a few inexpensive starchy staples such as cassava, rice, or corn to this greater variety of more expensive foods is known as *Bennett's law*. But note

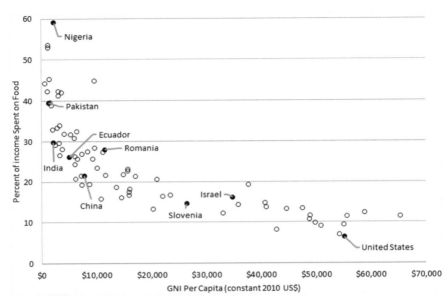

Figure 3.2 Relationship between per capita income and percentage of income spent on food, most countries
Source: **World Bank, World Development Indicators, 2019**

that when consumers switch from starchy staples to animal products, demand for animal feed can rise very fast: consumers may reduce their direct consumption of cereal grains as food, while increasing their total usage of cereal grains as animal feed.

Diversification and improvement of the diet with rising incomes implies that income elasticities vary by commodity and by income level. To show patterns of demand among some of the poorest people in the world, Table 3.1 provides examples of estimated income elasticities in various regions of sub-Saharan Africa for a range of commodities. Estimated income elasticities of demand for other countries and commodities are presented in Table 3.2. Note that income elasticities for animal products are higher than for food grains and root crops. Wheat and rice income elasticities tend to be higher than those of coarse grains, while roots and tubers have consistently small elasticities. As income grows, consumers switch away from roots and tubers toward rice and wheat. The substantial variation in income elasticities across countries reflects differences in income and in preferences for foods. For example, the income elasticity of demand for beef is low in Latin America compared to Africa, partly because initial levels of beef consumption are high in Latin America.

Table 3.1 Selected Income Elasticities of Demand for Agricultural Commodities in sub-Saharan Africa

Region	Wheat	Rice	Maize	Millet	Roots and tubers	Pulses
The Sahel	0.92	0.93	0.46	0.15	−0.04	−0.14
West	0.87	0.65	0.15	0.09	0.12	0.42
Central	0.55	0.93	0.66	0.28	−0.21	0.14
Eastern	0.51	0.58	0.28	0.01	0.29	0.02
Southern	1.46	0.56	0.35	0.17	−0.15	−0.002

Source: Cheryl Christensen et al., *Food Problems and Prospects in sub-Saharan Africa: The Decade of the 1980's* (Washington, DC: U.S. Department of Agriculture, Economic Research Service, Foreign Agricultural Research Report No. 186, August 1981)

Table 3.2 Selected Income Elasticities of Demand for Cereals and Livestock Products, Various Counties

Country	Cereals	Beef	Pork	Poultry	Cow's milk	Eggs
Brazil	0.15	0.58	0.29	0.64	0.45	0.55
Egypt	0.04	0.80	0.70	1.30	1.00	0.70
Indonesia	0.29	1.50	0.80	1.50	0.20	1.20
Kenya	0.35	1.00	0.70	1,20	0.59	1.30
South Korea	0.09	0.80	0.73	1.00	0.49	0.80
Malaysia	0.14	0.49	0.41	0.87	0.57	0.73
Nigeria	0.17	1.20	1.00	1.00	1.20	1.20
Philippines	0.22	1.20	0.93	1.00	1.50	1.00
Thailand	0.06	0.56	0.47	0.50	0.80	0.50
Turkey	−0.05	0.80	0.50	1.20	0.80	0.80

Source: J.S. Sarma, *Cereal Feed Use in the Third World: Past Trends and Protections to 2000* (Washington, DC: International Food Policy Research Institute, Research Report No. 57, December 1986), p. 64

Most of the estimated income elasticities in Tables 3.1 and 3.2 range between 0 and 1. These goods are called *normal* goods. Goods with income elasticities greater than 1 are called *superior* and represent foods that can be thought of as luxuries in the diet in a particular country. If the income elasticity is less than 0, the goods are called *inferior* as consumption of them actually declines as income increases.

The fact that income elasticities vary by commodity means that increases in income will result in an asymmetrical expansion in demand for different commodities. Demand for some commodities will expand by a greater percentage than that for others. Depending on the nature of supply, asymmetric expansion of demand can cause different pressures on commodity prices. These changes in commodity prices can influence which crops producers grow and can help determine the direction of development.

Price elasticities of demand

So far, we've focused on per-capita income as the major determinant of food consumption per person, but quantity demanded also responds to price changes. That price response was represented by movements along the demand curve in Figure 3.1, such as movement from point A at a high price to point B with a relatively low price and a higher quantity demanded. The degree of response in demand from a change in price is measured by the (own) *price elasticity of demand*, defined as the percentage change in quantity demanded of a commodity given a 1 percent change in its price, other things remaining unchanged.[2] For example, an own-price elasticity of –0.5 means that with a 1 percent change in price, the quantity demanded will change in the opposite direction by 0.5 percent. Own-price elasticities are typically negative, reflecting the

Potatoes in Ecuador

negative slope of the demand curve. If the own-price elasticity of demand is greater (in absolute value) than one, the demand is said to be *elastic*. If it is equal to one, it is said to be *unit-elastic*. If it is less than one, it is said to be *inelastic*. In a demand curve such as shown in Figure 3.1, an elastic demand has a relatively flat slope, as small price changes lead to large quantity changes.

Price elasticities of demand are useful for projecting demand changes that might result from policies that manipulate prices or from supply shifts. *Cross-price elasticities*, which represent the percentage change in quantity consumed of one commodity for a 1 percent change in the price of another commodity, holding all else equal, also are important.[3] If the cross-price elasticity of demand is greater than zero, the two commodities are said to be *substitutes*. If the cross-price elasticity is zero, the commodities are unrelated and if it is less than zero they are called *complements*.

When the price of a commodity changes, the change in relative prices causes most consumers to adjust the composition of the commodity bundle they purchase so that they buy less of the good that increased in price. This substitution is known as the *substitution effect*. Also, if the price of a commodity increases, the real purchasing power of a given amount of income is reduced, causing demand to change because of an *income effect*. In most cases, this income effect is a second factor that reduces demand for the commodity experiencing the price increase.[4] For inferior goods, however – commodities such as potatoes and cassava in some countries – the income effect may work in the opposite direction and partially offset the reduced consumption induced by the relative price increase.

A price increase for a good will increase consumption of substitutes and decrease consumption of complements. Part of these consumption changes are caused by changes in relative prices and part of them are due to income effects. Because the income elasticity of demand for food is large for low-income consumers, and because they spend a high proportion of their income on food, low-income consumers often make larger adjustments in their commodity purchases than do high-income consumers when prices change.

Small-scale producers generally both produce and consume staple crops, and their response to price changes is complicated by this dualism. When prices rise, they gain as producers (their products are worth more), yet they lose as consumers. The net effect of price changes depends on the net sales position of the farmer. If total sales exceed total consumption, then the household will benefit from price increases, but if consumption exceeds sales, price increases will hurt (Box 3.1).

BOX 3.1 IMPACTS OF RICE PRICE POLICY ON THE POOR IN THAILAND

Household-level data from Thailand were used to examine how policies affecting the price of rice would affect households in rural and urban areas and at different levels of income. Because rural households are both producers and consumers of rice, increased prices may or may not benefit them. They will gain as producers, but lose as consumers (all urban rice consumers will lose as a result of higher rice prices). The key to the analysis is to determine the "net benefit ratio" or the difference between the value of production and the value of consumption divided by total household expenditures. This ratio varies by total household income, and the analysis shows that middle income producers will benefit most from rice price increases. High-income rural households benefit very little from high prices (they earn their incomes outside agriculture or do not produce much rice). Very low-income rural households benefit by relatively small amounts, because their marketed surplus is low. Compared to plantation-type products (such as sugar and bananas), where price increases benefit larger-scale producers, rice price policy has its strongest impact on the middle of the income distribution in rural areas of Thailand. The study shows that the impacts of price policy depend on the commodity in question and the socioeconomic conditions of producer and consumer groups.

Source: Angus Deaton, *The Analysis of Household Surveys* (Baltimore: Johns Hopkins University Press, 1997), pp. 187–190

Obtaining elasticity estimates

The effects of changes in consumer behavior discussed earlier have important implications for food policies and nutrition in less-developed countries, so food-policy analysts often need updated local estimates of the sizes of the income elasticities, own-price elasticities, and cross-price elasticities of demand for various commodities. For example, if a policymaker wants to project domestic food demand and the increased production or imports needed to meet that demand, the income elasticity of demand for food is one of the pieces of information needed. If an estimate of the effect on the calorie and protein intakes of the poor resulting from a decrease in the price of rice is needed, it is important to have the own-price elasticity of demand for rice and the cross-price elasticities of demand between rice and other major foods in the country, disaggregated by income group.

How are elasticity estimates obtained? There are several approaches, and the appropriate procedure depends on the data available and the questions being asked. One type of estimate uses national aggregate data on consumption, production, trade, and prices. Often these data are published by international sources for several countries. If data are available on the same factors for several countries or for several regions in one country for one period of time, they are called *cross-sectional data*. If data are available for the same factors for one country for several years, they are called *time-series data*. These aggregate data are not very useful for studying short-term consumption behavior for commodities within countries because tastes and preferences vary by country. However, the data may be helpful in making long-term projections.

Sometimes, household-level, cross-sectional data are obtained by sampling many households to obtain information on income, expenditures on different commodities, prices paid, and educational levels and other demographic characteristics. Occasionally the data are collected over time as well, although not often because of the cost involved. If one is interested in microeconomic issues associated with consumer behavior for different income groups, household-level data are preferred.

Data (aggregate or household-level) are usually analyzed graphically and then in a statistical or *econometric* (statistical model which incorporates economic theory) model containing a set of demand equations.[5] These equations include variables representing the factors mentioned above. Elasticities are calculated from the estimated coefficients. Sometimes when data do not exist in one country or at a period in time, studies from other countries or at a different period of time are used. Elasticity estimates from other studies may not be ideal, but they are frequently used.

Some countries have serious deficiencies in aggregate and household-level data. Often these data are unreliable or even nonexistent. Policy analysts who have little time or money to collect new data and estimate a model sometimes rely on relationships from economic theory to obtain rough approximations of missing elasticities. For example, there is a useful working assumption (called the homogeneity condition) that the sum of the own-price elasticity, the income elasticity, and the cross-price elasticities of demand for a commodity is equal to zero.[6] Typically, the sum of the cross-price elasticities for a commodity greater than zero (and usually small) and the own-price elasticity is negative. Therefore, the absolute value of the own-price elasticity is usually a little larger than the income elasticity of demand. One may have an estimate of the income elasticity of demand but not the own-price elasticity. The homogeneity condition can be used to obtain a rough estimate of the size of the price elasticity of demand given the income elasticity and assumptions about cross-price elasticities. The homogeneity condition is just one example of the use of demand theory. The main points are that data availability and quality limit the potential for economic analysis, but a variety of techniques can often be exploited to interpret the available data in useful ways.

USING CONSUMPTION PARAMETERS FOR POLICY AND PLANNING

The purpose of obtaining income and price elasticities for foods is to assist with food policy analyses and planning. A variety of questions can be answered with the help of these elasticities. For example, what will happen to the consumption of rice, wheat, sugar, or meat when income rises? What will happen to the aggregate demand for food? How will the demand change for different commodities as absolute and relative prices change? What will be the effects of food price and income policies on the poor? The answers to these questions help policymakers anticipate future demand changes and production needs, and provide information for designing price and income policies (Box 3.1).

Income-induced changes in the mix of commodities demanded

For commodities with high income elasticities, demand can grow very rapidly when income rises. Anticipating income growth, policymakers may want to support research or use other policies to encourage increased production of those commodities. Otherwise, prices will rise or imports increase in response to demand growth.

Many highly income-elastic commodities such as milk and vegetables have high nutritional value. However, some goods with relatively high nutritional value have low income elasticities.[7] If a government wants to increase consumption of a good with a low income elasticity, it may have to resort to promotion, educational, or subsidy programs. Educational programs help change people's perceptions about physical (nutrient) needs and the amount of these needs the food provides. These programs essentially lower the costs associated with acquiring information about nutrient needs and food nutrient content.

Cattle in Ethiopia

Differences in income elasticities by commodity imply that as global per capita income grows over time, a relative shift will occur in demand toward agricultural commodities with high income elasticities. Many of these are high protein foods such as livestock products. One can also expect the grains fed to livestock, such as corn, to increase in demand relative to food grains such as rice. These types of changes have already been occurring.

Another impact of these patterns of income elasticities is that the average income elasticity of demand for food grains will decrease as development occurs. Low income elasticities are associated with small price elasticities of demand. With lower price elasticities, increased production of food grains would put sharp downward pressure on prices. Lower prices should help poor consumers who continue to spend large shares of their budget on grains, but may force many of the farmers producing these grains to switch to other commodities or to leave agriculture.

Changes in aggregate food demand as development proceeds
The demand for food is influenced by population, per capita income, prices, and preferences. As development proceeds, the two primary

factors that shift the demand for food outward are increases in population and in per capita income. These two major forces are captured by the simple relation $D = p + ng$, where D = rate of growth in the demand for food, p = rate of population growth, n = income elasticity of demand for food, and g = rate of increase in per capita income.

In this equation, population influences food demand in two ways. First, as presented by the term "p", it causes a proportional increase in demand. However, per capita income equals total income divided by population. Therefore, the net effect of population growth will not be a proportional increase in demand because population growth may slow the rate of per capita income growth.

At the extreme, if income does not expand at all with increased population, the drop in per capita income will almost completely off-set the direct effect of population growth. For example, developing countries often experience a population growth rate of about 3 percent per year during the early stages of development. The income elasticity of demand for food may be as high as 0.8. If total income remains constant, then per capita income will decline by 3 percent per year and the rate of growth of demand will be $D = 3 + 0.8(-3) = 0.6$.[8]

On the other hand, if per capita income grows at 4 percent per year while population is growing at 2.5 percent (rates that are not uncommon in middle-income developing countries), even if the income elasticity of demand for food drops to 0.6, the rate of growth in demand for food would be 4.9 percent per year. Relatively few countries have been able to maintain such a rate of growth in agricultural production over time. Thus, food imports may be needed to meet growing demands.

These examples ignore the fact that income growth in most less-developed countries is heavily dependent on agricultural output. If agricultural output fails to grow, per capita income will rise very slowly. As development proceeds, the proportion of employment and of total national income derived from agriculture shrinks. Even so, total per capita income still may be affected by the rate of growth of agricultural production because agriculture provides food, capital, and a market for nonagricultural products. These issues will be more fully discussed in subsequent chapters.

The determinants of food demand are interrelated; but as development proceeds, certain patterns tend to hold for some of these factors. As incomes increase, population growth rates generally increase slightly at first as death rates decline, but for reasons discussed in the next chapter, population growth rates eventually fall as income continues to grow. The rate of per capita income growth is usually highest in the middle-income countries, and the income elasticity of demand for food declines continually as income grows. The result is that the rate of growth in food demand is highest for middle-income countries. These are the countries that are most likely to need food imports. Middle-income countries frequently exhibit the largest increase in per capita income and food imports even though they also experience the largest increases in agricultural production. Eventually, as incomes continue to grow to the point that the countries are considered "developed", population growth rates and income growth rates are low and income elasticities of demand for food are small. The result is that growth rates in the demand for food and for food imports are low for these countries.

DEMAND FOR FARM PRODUCTS FOR NON-FOOD OR FEED USES

Many agricultural products are used for not only food and feed, but also industrial purposes such as starch, fiber, and energy. In recent years, food crops such as maize, soybeans, and sugarcane have been diverted to production of bio-fuels such as ethanol and biodiesel. As the demand for these energy products grows, it competes directly with the demand for food and feed, driving up the overall demand (and prices) for farm products if growth in supply does not keep pace with growth in overall demand.

Demand for bio-fuels has grown because the demand for energy has risen due to population and income growth around the world, while energy – primarily oil and gas – supplies have not always grown as rapidly, thus driving up the price of energy products. Technology to produce ethanol and biodiesel has improved over time, which has made the net energy balance (energy used to produce as compared to energy obtained from a gallon of bio-fuel) more favorable, reducing the cost of supplying bio-fuels. Governments, led by the United States and Brazil, also subsidized research on and production of bio-fuels. The last decade has seen energy prices moderate as high energy prices of a few years back stimulated energy production, especially of natural gas, and encouraged development of energy saving technologies. Energy supply from solar and wind has also grown.

At any given time, speculators are in the market, driving prices up or down as they make bets on the future supply and demand situations for energy products. Due to speculation and uncertainty, prices may rise above or drop below the level that fundamental supply and demand factors would dictate they should be. However, prices eventually adjust (and remove over-adjustment) as new information becomes available.

A good example is the price patterns for maize, rice, soybeans, and other basic cereals in 2007–2008. Grain prices rose sharply in those years after being relatively constant for several years.

SUPPLY AND ITS INTERACTIONS WITH DEMAND

If markets operate freely with numerous buyers and sellers, supply inter-acts with demand to determine the quantity supplied and demanded as well as the price. Market supply is defined as the amounts of a product offered for sale in a market at each specified price during a specified period of time in a specified location (see Figure 3.3).

A given supply curve assumes that the following factors are held con-stant: (1) technology of production (the way the good is produced), (2) prices of inputs used in production, (3) prices of products that may be substituted in production, and (4) number of sellers in the market. Changes in these factors can cause the supply curve to shift inward or outward. For food as a whole, changes in technology are a major factor causing shifts in supply over time. A new technology that lowers the per-unit cost of production will shift the supply curve downward to the right

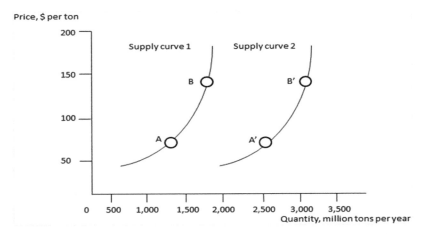

Figure 3.3 Hypothetical supply curve for a commodity. An increase in the price of the commodity, all other things being equal, will cause a movement along a supply curve, say from point A to point B, and an increase in quantity supplied. Changes in the determinants of supply – technology, input prices, other output prices, number of sellers – can cause a shift in the supply curve, say from A along supply curve 1 to A' along supply curve 2, or vice versa if there is a worsening of productivity.

(such as from supply curve 1 to supply curve 2 in Figure 3.3). Weather events such as droughts, floods, or abnormally hot or cold periods can also shift the supply curve, but usually weather-induced shifts are short-term, while shifts due to technical change last longer. Climate change can cause both short- and long-run shifts in supply.

Price implications

The rate of growth or decline in agricultural prices over time depends in large part on the net effects of supply and demand shifts (see Figure 3.4). Because of outward shifts of the demand curve caused by population and income growth, it is unlikely that agricultural prices will experience major declines resulting from supply growth in a country during the early stages of development.[9] If the supply curve for food shifts out very little, population- and income-driven demand growth could lead to price increases in places that do not have access to trade with the rest of the world, or the government has chosen to isolate its markets from trade with others. On average, these increases are likely to be small because of the close relationship between agricultural production growth and income growth during early stages of development. As noted earlier, it is

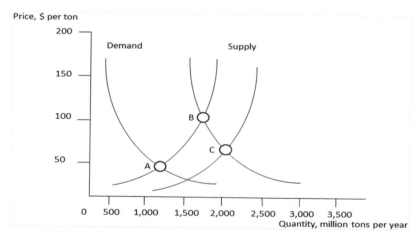

Figure 3.4 Hypothetical supply and demand curves for a commodity in region without access to trade. Changes in determinants of demand – for example, income and population – can cause a shift in demand while changes in the determinants of supply – for example, technology – can cause a shift in supply. When both are shifting, whether the net effect is a price increase or decrease (whether A is higher or lower than C) depends on the relative size of shifts of supply and demand and the slopes of the curves.

difficult to get large increases in income, and therefore effective demand, without corresponding increases in agricultural production.

Other important determinants of the effect of supply and demand shifts on agricultural prices are the elasticities of supply and demand. The more elastic the supply curve (roughly the flatter it is in Figure 3.4), the less prices will change as demands grow. Open economies (those where imports and exports are common) tend to be characterized by more elastic commodity supplies. One means of minimizing demand-induced price increases is to permit food imports. Another is to increase the responsiveness of the food production sector. However, open economies are also susceptible to sizable price swings if changes in supply and demand occur elsewhere in the world. These implications are examined in greater detail in Chapters 16 and 17.

Price policies

Early in the development process, there is a need to place emphasis on policies to shift out the agricultural supply curve and to raise incomes rather than on pricing policies. Many pricing policies distort incentives and create economic inefficiency (see Chapter 15). Price policies are also difficult to remove once they are in place. For example, many countries in the Middle East and North Africa have long subsidized consumer prices of wheat as bread is widely consumed in the region. As populations and incomes have grown, domestic production of wheat has not kept pace with demand growth and the countries have become highly dependent on wheat imports. This dependence creates vulnerability to world market price fluctuations; during the global commodity price spike of 2008, it was difficult or impossible to source wheat, and shortages led to food riots in countries such as Egypt. The subsidies also lead to distorted prices in the domestic market, creating incentives to produce wheat on some of the world's most fertile land in the Nile River Delta. The focus of public investment needs to be where the return is highest, whether it is inside or outside of agriculture. Because it is difficult to increase incomes of the poor without increasing employment, the country may need to focus investments on labor-intensive commodities and industries.

As development proceeds, incomes grow, and demand shifts outward, the possibilities for rapid increases in food prices arise even in countries experiencing rapid growth in agricultural production. The reasons for this were discussed earlier. Therefore, middle-income countries experiencing rapid rates of income growth are likely to need increased agricultural imports. Price policies that hinder such trade are likely to constrain economic development.

BOX 3.2 MARKETS AND REGIONAL PRICE VARIATION

Developing countries or the least developed regions within them are often characterized by poor transportation systems, sparsely populated areas, or isolated pockets of high population densities. Because of these factors, regional food markets within these countries may be isolated and relatively independent. Prices may vary widely from region to region, with limited relationship to average national prices and quantities, or to the prices prevailing in markets in large cities. In addition, local prices may be more variable than national prices if, with few market participants, changes in behavior by small numbers of participants induce large swings in supply and demand and thus affect prices.

The consequences of these market problems can be high regional food prices and less ability to meet consumption needs for given incomes. High price variability causes uncertainty to producers and consumers of the products. These factors worsen national welfare and can contribute to isolated pockets of poverty. Increases in national supply will do little to improve such situations.

Regional supply differences caused by high marketing costs can be lowered by improvements in infrastructure and market information. Poor information causes these differences when costs associated with gathering price and demand information impair the effectiveness of the marketing system. Measures to enhance information flows include collection and dissemination of market-related information and telecommunications systems to transmit the information.

Eventually, when high income levels are reached, income elasticities of demand for food and population growth rates become smaller. These small income elasticities relieve the upward pressure on food prices but create the potential for food surpluses and low farm prices. Policies at this stage tend to be concerned with easing the cost of moving large portions of the labor force out of agriculture, directing producers into those commodities for which the country has a relative advantage in world markets, and stabilizing domestic farm prices, which tend to be more heavily influenced by swings in international prices now than they were in the past.

The existence of structural changes in the market for agricultural goods over time suggests a strong need to tailor agricultural development policies to each country's stage of development. It also suggests a need for each country to consider the stages of development of other countries in the world and changes in energy markets when making projections about future demands for agricultural products.

Food systems and value chains

Food production, consumption, and prices are driven fundamentally by factors that affect supply and demand, but food systems are diverse, complex, and dynamic; all the more so as economic development occurs. A value chain is a network of stakeholders involved in growing, transforming, and shipping food and processed food products to the consumer. Policies influence actors at every node in the food value chain. For example, energy policy affects the cost of producing, processing, and transporting foods so that policy changes have economy-wide effects. The value chain becomes longer as agricultural development proceeds since income growth creates demand for processed and convenience foods, healthy food, and higher-quality food. This lengthening implies that more value is added off the farm as development proceeds and also that stakeholders far from the farm feel effects of food policy.

Environmental, economic, cultural, social, demographic, marketing, information, and political systems all influence the food system and hence nutritional and health outcomes. Each country has a unique history in its interactions with other nations, with implications for commodity mixes, agricultural policies, and international markets for farm products. Many of the economic, nutritional, health, and environmental outcomes of the food system feedback on farmers and their incentives to alter their production practices. The diversity of food and agricultural systems and the changes that tend to occur to them with development are discussed in Chapter 8. Agricultural markets, value chains, and price policies that affect those systems are discussed in Chapter 15. International trade policies that influence food systems and value chains are presented in Chapter 16.

SUMMARY

The effective demand for food is determined by the physical and psychological need for food combined with the ability to pay for it. Demand is influenced by prices, population, income, and preferences. The level of per capita income is a major determinant of food demand in low-income countries. The income elasticity of demand for food varies systematically by income level, by commodity, and by places and socioeconomic groups within a country. The income elasticity of demand for food declines as development proceeds, and shifts in consumption occur away from starchy staples toward higher-protein foods. Own- and cross-price elasticities of demand are useful for projecting demand changes. Several procedures are available for obtaining income and price elasticities. Middle-income developing countries generally experience the most rapid rates of growth in demand for food. Changes in energy markets have added an additional factor to consider when projecting food price changes.

IMPORTANT TERMS AND CONCEPTS

Aggregate versus household data
Bennett's law and why it holds
Bio-fuels
Cross-price elasticity of demand
Cross-sectional versus
  time-series data
Econometric model
Effective demand
Elastic versus inelastic
  demands
Engel's law and why it holds
Factors that shift the demand curve
Factors that shift the supply curve
Food policies
Food systems and value chains

Homogeneity condition and its use
Income effect
Income elasticity of demand
Law of demand
Major determinants of long-run
  price trends
Normal, superior, and inferior
  goods
Own-price elasticity of demand
Role of agricultural prices
Stage of development
Substitutes and complements
Substitution effect
Supply
Value chain

LOOKING AHEAD

Rapid population growth over the past few years has dramatically increased the world's population and made the task of raising per capita income and reducing hunger in some countries more difficult. Population growth is influenced by many factors, and several policies have been tried or suggested for controlling it. In the next chapter, you will learn about population growth, including implications for food consumption and natural resource use. You will examine population projections and policies for the future.

QUESTIONS FOR DISCUSSION

1 As incomes increase, do people spend greater, smaller, or the same proportion of their income on food?
2 Distinguish between an income elasticity of demand and a cross-price elasticity of demand.
3 What tends to happen to the income elasticity of demand for food as the per capita income of a nation increases? Why?
4 To estimate the effect on the calorie and protein intake of a population resulting from a decrease in the price of rice, why is it important to know something about the cross-price elasticities of demand between rice and other major foods in the country?
5 Assume the price elasticity of demand for eggs in India is –0.75. By what percentage would the price of eggs have to change to increase egg consumption by 15 percent?
6 Do you expect the price of food in the world to be higher or lower ten years from now? To answer this question, draw a graph with supply and demand curves and show how you expect the curves to change over time and why.
7 If population is growing at 2.6 percent per year, the income elasticity of demand for food is 0.6, and per capita income is growing at 4 percent per year, what would be the growth in demand for food per year, assuming prices remain constant?
8 What tends to happen to the mix of foods consumed as per capita income in a country increases? Why?
9 If agricultural development is successful at increasing the level of per capita food production in several less-developed countries over the next ten years, why might these same countries become less self-sufficient in food (have to import more food than before) during that period of time?
10 Assume you have the following cross-price elasticities for a particular country:

Commodity	Cross-price elasticity
Rice and beans	–0.35
Rice and wheat	0.40
Rice and chicken	–0.10
Rice and milk	–0.05
Rice and other goods	0.0

   a You are a planner for the country represented above and you want to raise the consumption of rice by 6 percent to improve calorie intake of the population. The income elasticity of demand for rice is 0.4. Use the information above and the homogeneity condition to determine the necessary percentage change in the price of rice.

   b If rice consumption increases by 6 percent, what else besides the calories obtained from rice would you need to consider when assessing the impact on calorie consumption?

11 What distinguishes the need for food from the effective demand for food?

12 Which of the following factors shift primarily the demand curve and which factors shift primarily the supply curve: per capita income changes; new technologies; population growth; tastes and preferences; prices of inputs used in production; prices of other goods consumed; prices of substitute goods in production?

13 Why is there a close relationship between agricultural production growth and a nation's income growth during the early stages of development?

14 Even if agricultural production increases rapidly, why is it unlikely that countries in early stages of development will experience major food price decreases as a result?

15 Why do middle-income countries experiencing rapid rates of growth in food production often need food imports while very poor countries that are experiencing slower rates of food production growth do not?

16 What is a food system and a food value chain?

NOTES

1 If we define n to be the income elasticity of demand for a good, ΔQ to be the change in quantity demanded for that good, and ΔI to be a change in income, then:

$$n = \frac{\%\Delta Q}{\%\Delta I} = \left(\frac{\Delta Q/Q}{\Delta I/I}\right) = \left(\frac{\Delta Q}{\Delta I}\right)\left(\frac{I}{Q}\right).$$

2 If E is the price elasticity of demand for a good, ΔQ to be the change in quantity consumed, and ΔP is the change in its price, then:

$$E = \frac{\%\Delta Q}{\%\Delta P} = \left(\frac{\Delta Q/Q}{\Delta P/P}\right) = \left(\frac{\Delta Q}{\Delta P}\right)\left(\frac{P}{Q}\right).$$

3 If we let E_{12} = the cross-price elasticity for commodity 1 as the price of commodity 2 changes, ΔQ_1 = the change in the quantity demanded of commodity 1, and ΔP_2 = the change in price of commodity 2, then:

$$E_{12} = \frac{\%\Delta Q_1}{\%\Delta P_2} = \left(\frac{\Delta Q_1}{\Delta P_2}\right)\left(\frac{P_2}{Q_1}\right).$$

4 If the consumer is also a producer of the good, which is often the case in rural areas of developing countries, this income effect can be positive. Commodity price increases can actually raise disposable income by increasing farm profits. This profit effect can be important when examining price responses of agricultural households that both consume and produce goods.

5 See Angus Deaton, *The Analysis of Household Surveys* (Baltimore: Johns Hopkins University Press, 1997), especially Chapter 1, for an advanced treatment of types of data and their uses for policy analysis.

6 That is, for the ith commodity out of T commodities, $E_i + \eta_i + \sum_{\substack{j=1 \\ i \neq j}}^{T} E_{ij} = 0$.

7 Elasticities reflect people's preferences for different attributes of the good, including taste, convenience, and nutritional value. A low value for an elasticity in not necessarily "bad"; it reflects consumer choices given income, preferences, prices, and information about the good.

8 The negative consequences of such a scenario should be obvious: total demand will increase by 0.3 percent but per capita demand will decline.

9 However, there may be substantial local or regional variation (see Box 3.2), and agricultural prices in a country may go up or down as well due to changes in supply and demand in international markets.

RECOMMENDED READINGS

Foster, Phillips, and Howard Leathers, *The World Food Problem* (Boulder, CO: Lynne Rienner, 2017), Chapter 8.

Runge, C. Ford, C., Benjamin Senauer, Philip G. Pardey, and Mark W. Rosegrant, *Ending Hunger in Our Lifetime* (Baltimore: Johns Hopkins University Press, 2003), pp. 39–56.

4 Population and migration

THIS CHAPTER

1 Presents basic facts about the distribution of the world's population, the rate of population growth, and the consequences of rapid and slow population growth rates
2 Explains the determinants of population growth and policies that can affect that growth
3 Examines causes and implications of migration from rural to urban areas

BASIC FACTS ABOUT POPULATION GROWTH

The human race dates back about 3 million years. During more than 99 percent of this time, there was virtually zero population growth. Average life expectancy was 20 to 25 years, and world population probably never exceeded 10 million people. After agriculture replaced hunting and gathering of food, around 6000 to 8000 B.C., population began to grow because larger numbers of people could be supported by food production. By the year 1 A.D., there were about 300 million people and by 1650, 500 million.

Population began to grow more rapidly during the industrial revolution in the eighteenth century, and growth accelerated after World War II when populations in developing countries began to increase dramatically. World population reached 1 billion around 1800, 2 billion in 1930, and 3 billion in 1960. It grew to 4 billion in 1975, 5 billion in 1986, 6 billion in 1999, and 7 billion in 2011 (see Figure 4.1). It is projected to reach 8 billion in 2023 and 9 billion in 2037.

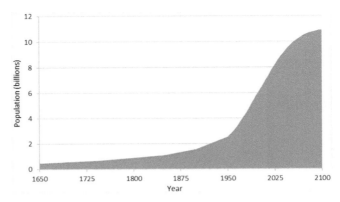

Figure 4.1 Past and projected world population, 1750 to 2050, medium estimate.
Source: Population Division of the Department of Economic and Social Affairs of the United Nations Secretariat, *World Population Prospects: The 2019 Revision*, and J.C. Caldwell and T. Schindlmayr, "Historical population estimates: Unraveling the consensus", *Population and Development Review*, vol. 28(2) (2002), pp. 183–204

The rate of population growth in the world peaked at 2.0 percent per year in 1965 and has declined since then to its current (2020) rate of 1.05 percent. However, population itself will continue to grow for many years since the future number of parents will be much larger than the current number because of rapid growth in the recent past.

Distribution of the world population

The world's population is distributed unevenly across the globe, reflecting the degree to which each location attracted migrants and was able to sustain growth in its local population over time. The earliest human ancestors lived in sub-Saharan Africa and migrated from there to other regions. By far the greatest accumulation of population has occurred in Asia, which holds over 60 percent of the world's people and has the highest population densities. Large populations are also found across Europe, along the coasts of North and South America, and within Africa.

The current size and density of the ten most populous countries are shown in Table 4.1. The list is dominated by China and India, but several other Asian countries have large populations and also have very high density, with over 100 people per square kilometer. These countries account for the bulk of historical population growth. Today, population growth in Asia and elsewhere has slowed substantially, and the fastest-growing countries are all in sub-Saharan Africa (Table 4.2 and Figure 4.2). The fastest growing countries all have annual rates of

Table 4.1 The World's Most Populous Nations

Nation	Mid-2019 population (millions)	Population density (people/square kilometer)
China	1,398	146
India	1,391	423
United States	329	33
Indonesia	268	141
Pakistan	217	246
Brazil	209	25
Nigeria	201	218
Bangladesh	164	1,111
Russia	147	9
Mexico	127	64
Total (10 nations)	4,451	
Total (world)	7,691	52

Source: Population Reference Bureau, Inc., 2019 World Population Datasheet

Table 4.2 Rate of Natural Increase in Population in the World's Fastest and Slowest Growing Nations (with 3 Million or More People)

Fastest growing nations	Annual growth rate (percentage, 2019)	Mid-2019 population (millions)
Niger	3.8	23.3
Mali	3.6	19.7
Angola	3.5	31.4
Benin	3.3	11.8
Chad	3.3	16.4
Uganda	3.2	44.3
Congo, Dem. Rep.	3.2	86.8
Burundi	3.1	11.5
Somali	3.1	15.4
Burkina Faso	3.0	20.3
Zambia	3.0	17.9
Tanzania	3.0	58.0
Madagascar	3.0	27.0

(Continued)

Table 4.2 (Continued)

Slowest growing nations	Annual growth rate (percentage, 2019)	Mid-2019 population (millions)
Bulgaria	−0.7	7.0
Ukraine	−0.6	42.0
Serbia	−0.5	6.9
Hungary	−0.4	9.8
Romania	−0.3	19.4
Belarus	−0.3	9.5
Japan	−0.3	126.2
Greece	−0.3	10.7
Portugal	−0.3	10.3
Italy	−0.3	60.3

Source: Population Reference Bureau, Inc., 2019 World Population Datasheet

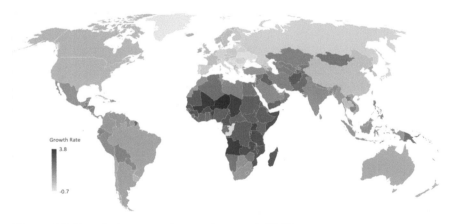

Figure 4.2 Population growth rates (percent), 2019
Source: **Population Reference Bureau, 2019 World Population Data Sheet**

population increase at or above 3.0 percent per year. Population growth of more than 3.0 percent was almost unprecedented in human history until the last 70 years. It is occurring today in the world's poorest places, where purchasing power per capita is below $2.00 a day, and where rapid population growth is a recent phenomenon. The slowest-growing countries are also presented in Table 4.2, and all of these are losing population. Countries with negative population growth rates are mainly the former socialist countries of Eastern Europe, but also include high-income countries such as Japan, Italy, Greece, and Portugal.

Consequences of rapid population growth

Rapid population growth can be a problem for developing countries because it changes the age composition of the country. It increases the proportion of young dependents, imposes a strain on the natural resource base, can make it difficult to find employment, reduces food production gains per capita, contributes to pollution, and strains the capacity of schools and other social services. It would be an oversimplification to say that rapid population growth is the root cause of natural resource problems, unemployment, and so forth, but it certainly intensifies these problems.

Differences in age structure associated with different rates of population growth are illustrated in Figure 4.3. Countries with rapid growth have many very young children relative to working-aged people. This high dependency causes increased current consumption and reduced

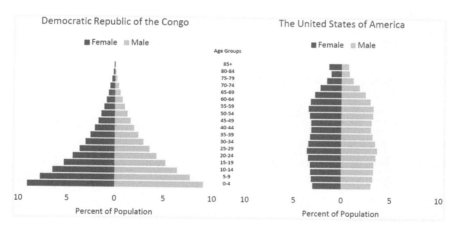

Figure 4.3 Population profiles, growth, and momentum

The age distribution of the people in a country has a major impact on the future rate of growth of its population. The population pyramid is a tool that demographers use to describe this distribution. Shown here are two population pyramids, reflecting differing rates of current and future population growth. The broad base on the Democratic Republic of the Congo pyramid means that the population growth "momentum" will cause population to grow, even if fertility, or the number of children that each family has, slows immediately to replacement levels. As the large number of people in the younger age groups in the Congo reach childbearing age, the number of births will rise dramatically, even if the number of births per couple falls. The United States has a relatively even age distribution and is unlikely to experience a large increase in population.
Source: U.S. Census Bureau, 2010

savings and investment. The impacts of rapid population growth on schooling can be particularly significant. Since about 25 percent of the people in developing countries are of school age, compared to 15 percent in typical developed countries, equal amounts of budget outlay for education translate either to low expenditures per pupil or low enrollment rates. Inadequate investments in either physical or human capital will hurt the long-run possibilities for development.

Hunger and poverty were serious problems long before population began its rapid rise. However, the population explosion has made it difficult for some countries to invest and has magnified problems of social justice in others. Continued rapid population growth puts strain on resources, especially in a period of increased vulnerability created by climate change.

Consequences of slow population growth

Population growth rates in many developing countries, such as China, Brazil, and Chile, have declined substantially in recent years. These countries have benefited from the new age-structure of their populations. When fertility rates are reduced, families have fewer young dependents than before, and a higher proportion of their resources can be devoted to savings and investment. This investment helps the economy to grow and per capita incomes increase. Part of the economic growth in countries such as China over the past 40 years was fueled by this *demographic dividend*, which was created when the working age population grew faster than other age groups.

The population dividend typically lasts 30–40 years. However, as countries such as China eventually age and have fewer workers, the burden on these workers to support their elders eventually increases. Savings during the demographic dividend stage are necessary for future support of the elderly. Expanded pension plans are essential as countries become richer. Several countries, including highly populous ones such as India and Bangladesh, are currently experiencing the population dividend, while others, such as China, have recently passed through that stage, and others such Niger, Tanzania, and Uganda have not yet entered it. The good news is that a substantial number of countries in Asia, Latin America, and even sub-Saharan Africa have recently experienced drops in fertility rates and are entering the population dividend stage. Their working age population is growing faster than other age groups, which bodes well for investment and economic growth.

CAUSES OF FERTILITY CHANGE AND POPULATION GROWTH

Population growth occurs for the world as a whole when births exceed deaths.[1] Years ago, births and deaths were both high, on the order of 40 to 50 every year per 1000 people in the population. About half of the deaths occurred before age 10, and death rates fluctuated from year to year with contagious diseases and with variations in food supplies. During this time, population fluctuated but did not grow rapidly for any sustained period of time.

Sustained population growth began in Europe and other now-industrialized regions during the eighteenth century, with a slow but steady decline in the death rate. Technological and economic progress resulted in improved nutrition and health, which reduced infant deaths and extended life expectancy well before scientists or medical doctors understood what caused disease or knew how to cure people once they fell ill. Population growth accelerated as death rates fell with no change in the birth rate for about one hundred years, until the late nineteenth century, when birth rates began to fall as women delayed marriage and had fewer children (Figure 4.4). Birth and death rates declined in tandem until the 1950s, when death rates stabilized and the total population growth rate slowed. It took roughly 200 years for the now-industrialized countries to transition from high birth and death rates in the early eighteenth century to low birth and death rates in the late twentieth century. During

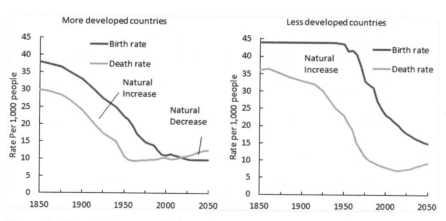

Figure 4.4 Population growth through natural increase, 1950–2100
Source: United Nations, Department of Economic and Social Affairs, Population Division (2019). World Population Prospects: The 2019 Revision, custom data acquired via website

this period, births exceeded deaths by about 10 per 1,000 people, for a population growth rate of 1 percent per year.

In contrast, today's developing countries experienced no significant decline in mortality until the twentieth century, when their death rates declined more rapidly than they ever had in the now-developed countries. This precipitous drop in the death rate was not due to slow improvements in nutrition and health, but rather to the sudden introduction of technological improvements developed through scientific research. Once scientists and doctors understood the causes of disease and the principles of nutrition, especially after World War Il, countries rapidly deployed the new antibiotics, immunizations, and insecticides to control disease-bearing insects. They invested heavily in sanitation and maternal and child health programs. After the decline in death rates, it took several decades for birth rates to begin falling – but by then the gap between deaths and births was on the order of 20 per 1,000 people, or 2 percent per year, and in many countries the rate was over 3 percent per year.

In summary, population growth has been much faster in today's low-income countries than it ever was in today's high-income countries for one reason: the low-income countries' death rates fell faster, due to the sudden introduction of life-saving technologies. It is hard to imagine any serious observer wishing that those techniques had *not* been introduced, since they saved millions of lives and made possible much of the population we have today – but the speed of introduction made it relatively difficult for those countries to raise per-capita incomes, until the transition to lower birth rates could be completed.

The historical *demographic transition* shown in Figure 4.4 has repeated itself in country after country. Each has a different timing and speed of transition, but all began with high birth and death rates and a relatively stable population size, then a decline in the death rate that initiated population growth. For those countries that have completed the demographic transition, a decline in the birth rate has followed, closing the gap between birth and death rates and stabilizing the population size at a new, higher level.

The fact that this demographic transition has been observed in many countries in the past does not, of course, guarantee that it will be observed in the future. If population growth outstrips a society's resources, death rates can rise again, and it has in some countries in Africa due to the ravages of HIV/AIDS and continued high levels of child malnutrition, poor sanitation, and disease. To understand how the demographic transition can be completed without rising death rates, we need to examine the causes of fertility (birth) rate changes and consider policies that might influence those changes.

Causes of fertility changes

Family size is largely determined by parental motivation, and this motivation reflects rational and, in many cases, economic decisions. Tastes, religion, culture, and social norms all play a role; yet, evidence suggests that differences in economic factors as well as family planning education and access to birth control play the major roles. Female education is particularly important in reducing family size.

People receive pleasure and emotional satisfaction from children. Thus, there is a consumption benefit from having children, and in poor societies there may be little competition from other consumption goods. It costs time and money to raise children, but these costs (both out of pocket and in terms of earnings foregone while caring for children) may be relatively low, especially in rural areas.

Children are also an investment. This investment value increases the benefits associated with having children. They frequently work during childhood. In rural areas, they gather firewood, collect water, work in the field, care for livestock, and do other chores. In urban areas, a child's ability to contribute work to the family is more limited; however, income opportunities exist for very young children in urban areas of most developing countries. An important source of employment of urban children is the "informal sector", often in petty trading and services. For some families, incomes provided by children working in the informal sector can be critical to survival. When older children leave home, especially if they go to the city, they may send cash back home. Children also provide security during old age, needed because many developing countries have a minimal or no social security system. These benefits from additional children raise the number of desired children in developing countries, especially among poor families. In many countries, child mortality is high, so that extra births may be necessary to ensure that the desired number children survive. All these factors increase birth rates.

As people obtain more education and earn more money, they delay marriage and have fewer children. Parents have more options and come to prefer keeping their children in school rather than earning income from children's work. An increase in per capita income is inherently a rise in the value of time. A rise in the value of time, particularly if women have expanded employment opportunities outside the home, creates strong incentives to have fewer children and to invest more in the health and education of each child.

Thus, poverty and high fertility are mutually reinforcing. Social and economic factors such as income, literacy, and life expectancy account for as much as 60 percent of the variation in fertility changes among

Child weeding onions in the Philippines

developing countries. The strength of family planning programs also accounts for a significant share.

Birth rates do not decline immediately when incomes begin to increase. Expectations about desired family size may take years to evolve, and they change at different rates for different social groups. Within each country, people with fewer opportunities – especially fewer opportunities for women – will often continue to have higher birth rates than other groups, further slowing the transition. And the speed of reduction in birth rates depends on the availability of effective family planning techniques. To reduce fertility, households must both want to reduce their total family size and be able to control the number and timing of births through effective contraception.

Policies that influence population growth

Most people favor public and private actions to reduce death rates in countries where they are high, but measures to reduce birth rates are more controversial. Controversy can arise if some people question the cost-effectiveness of family planning programs and if others find efforts to control fertility in conflict with their strongly held values and beliefs.

Those who favor public actions to help curb birth rates argue that public costs (schools, hospitals, pollution, etc.) associated with large families exceed social benefits. Therefore, society has a right to at least inform its citizens of ways to control births. Evidence from countries with strong family planning programs shows that these programs can be effective. Any measures to improve income growth and distribution, develop social insurance and pension programs, and expand education and employment opportunities for women can help to reduce birth rates. These efforts take time, however, which is why the policy debate often centers on family planning issues.

Many countries in Latin America took advantage of favorable macroeconomic conditions associated with the commodity price boom in the 2000s to reform their old-age pension systems. Due to belt-tightening in the 1980s, many Latin American countries privatized their pension systems and moved from a defined benefit to a defined contribution model. Privatization caused problems when many of the elderly could not prove they had contributed, exchange rate devaluations punished those who had saved, and some systems were impoverished by outright fraud. In the 2000s, governments introduced modest noncontributory pension schemes, some of which were merged with private systems, some of which are means targeted. China and India have also recently introduced noncontributory pension schemes with rural coverage. While these systems pay only modest benefits, they should reduce pressures on adult children and lower fertility rates over time.

China combined educational programs, social pressure, and economic incentives to reduce birth rates for many years. These actions were effective, but some people considered China's family planning program to be too strong, especially its emphasis on using abortion to control family size when other measures failed. Critics also have argued that China's one child policy lasted too long and will result in labor shortages and insufficient support for its rapidly aging population.

Future population projections
The United Nations has projected that by the year 2050, world population will have grown to around 9.7 billion people, and by 2100 to 10.9 billion.[2] Most of the growth will be concentrated in the developing countries, more than half of it in sub-Saharan Africa. Future population projections are somewhat uncertain because they depend on income increases, educational improvements, family planning programs, and the future progression of disease pandemics that are hard to predict. If present trends in growth rates continue, however, the population will have grown by about 28 percent by 2050 compared to the population in 2020. Almost half of the projected increase will be concentrated in

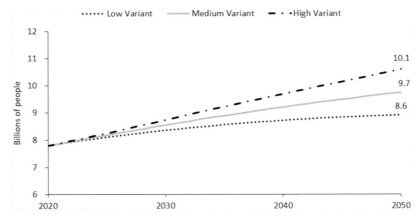

Figure 4.5 Future population projections
Source: United Nations, World Population Prospects, the 2019 Revision

just eight countries: Democratic Republic of the Congo, Egypt, Ethiopia, India, Indonesia, Nigeria, Pakistan, and Tanzania.

More than 50 countries are expected to experience at least a 1 percent loss in population by 2050 because of low fertility rates, and some, such as Bulgaria and Ukraine, at least a 20 percent loss. Since 2018, the number of people in the world over age 65 has outnumbered children under 5. Not only are fertility rates dropping but life expectancy is also growing. It reached 72 years in 2019, up eight years since 1990. Life expectancy, however, is seven years lower on average in the least developed countries.

URBANIZATION

The world population is now over 50 percent urban. Regardless of the total increase in population, it is clear that urbanization will continue at a rapid pace, and the world is projected to be two-thirds urban by 2050. While total population in developing countries grew almost 2 percent annually from 1990 to 2020, urban population grew at an annual rate of almost 3 percent. Natural population increases in urban areas account for about 60 percent of this growth rate, and another 8 to 15 percent is attributable to re-classification of rural areas to urban areas. At least 25 percent of the rapid growth in urban areas is caused by migration from rural to urban areas. Because a large proportion of the migrants are of childbearing age, a sizable part of the "natural increase" in urban populations also can be attributed to births by recent migrants. The percentage of urban population growth due to migration is highest in those countries in the early stages of development.

Causes of rural-to-urban migration

Rural-to-urban migration is, in a broad sense, a natural reflection of the economic transformation from agriculture to industry and services which economies undergo during the development process. As we discuss in Chapter 5, the process of industrialization increases the demand for labor in the manufacturing and service sectors. In the early stages of development, much of this labor must come from the rural areas. Some of the structural transformation out of agriculture occurs within rural areas as farm households increase their involvement in nearby non-farm activities, but rural-to-urban migration is an important part of the story.

By and large, people move to urban areas because they expect increased opportunities in terms of both earnings and access to goods or services. Economic opportunities are limited in rural areas due to high transport and other costs that constrain economic transactions among people. Landlessness and rural poverty, natural calamities, lack of educational opportunities, unequal public services provision, and other factors come into play as well. Pervasive risk of crop failure induces families to send people to urban areas as a sort of insurance policy. Climate change increases risks in some areas, making them less able to support agricultural livelihoods. Although living costs are higher in urban areas, migrants are searching for a better level of living; they are pushed out of rural areas by poverty and desperation, and pulled to the cities by hope and opportunity.

Most people who migrate to cities perceive that the benefits of the move exceed its costs (these costs include foregone rural income and the cost of the move), or they would not make the move. Migrants tend to be young, disproportionately single, and better educated than the average of those left behind. The first two of these characteristics tend to lower the costs of the move, while the third raises the benefits. Better-educated people can expect higher returns from their education (wages) in urban areas. Most migrants to large cities in developing countries have relatives or friends already living there, a fact that tends to lower the cost of the move.

Rural-to-urban migration has been persistent despite high unemployment rates in urban areas. The likely reasons for this persistence are that workers consider both rural–urban wage differentials and the probability of obtaining a job (which is often much less than 100 percent) and

Some rural-to-urban migrants in Dhaka Bangladesh work as bicycle rickshaw drivers

still perceive that they will be made better off by moving. Many of these migrants realize it is unlikely that they will obtain a high-paying or "formal" job immediately, but they are willing to work in low-paying jobs such as selling goods on street corners, "watching over" parked cars, or doing other jobs in the informal sector. In that sense, they are not completely unemployed. For some of these migrants, high-paying jobs may come only to their children, and then only if the children receive a better education than their parents.

The importance of educational opportunities and other public services cannot be overlooked as reasons for rural-to-urban migration. In many countries, an urban political bias has created a large disparity between the levels of services, including quality of public education, provided in rural compared to urban areas. Furthermore, and perhaps more importantly, the political bias extends to economic policies such as pricing policies. Food prices may be kept artificially low (through policies discussed later in this book). This policy helps urban consumers but discourages investment in food production and lowers incomes in rural areas. These distortions help explain some of the attractions of cities.

Consequences of rural-to-urban migration

Urbanization per se is not a problem. According to the United Nations, at least 56 percent of the world now lives in urban areas. There are economies of scale resulting from the concentration of suppliers and consumers for industry and public services. Innovative and knowledge-intensive industries are more likely to form and prosper in high population-density areas, so that urbanization is necessary for long-term economic growth. The problem arises when cities become "too large, too quickly", often because rural-to-urban migration increases the urban population at a rate faster than industry, schools, sewage systems, and so forth can expand. The result is substandard housing, poor sanitation, and lack of other services for recent migrants (Box 4.1). While migrants have been shown to be assets to the cities, the shanty towns that surround most large cities in less-developed countries attest to the growing disparities that occur if urbanization occurs too rapidly. Many people live in squalor, often without sewage systems and sometimes in garbage dumps. Social distancing during a virus pandemic is impossible. The World Bank estimates that about a billion people worldwide live in such

BOX 4.1 PROBLEM WITH URBAN SLUMS

India's economy has boomed in recent years, but many of its urban poor live in some of the most depressed conditions on earth. People are packed into overcrowded, dilapidated shacks with little ventilation, few sanitation facilities, and unclean drinking water. The Lalbagh slum near Azadpur is one of Delhi's largest, with more than 300,000 people squeezed into one square kilometer. Its stagnant water, clogged drains, garbage heaps, and human waste provide a perfect breeding ground for flies and mosquitoes that can carry disease. In the rainy season, standing water is everywhere. Children play near garbage dumps, seemingly oblivious that they might become infected with disease. Many toilets and bathing enclosures lack doors and running water. Toilets are full of filth and human excreta as the water supply is not functioning. The local school lacks water and electricity. The playground is littered with rubbish. Many houses contain six to eight people per room. Streets are narrow and sewage stagnates in open surface drainage ditches. About one-third of the global slum population lives in India.

Source: Summarized from Vishal Sethi, "Life in a Slum: Ugly Face of India", *The Times of India*, August 17, 2016.

slums.[3] The fact that people are willing to live in these areas highlights the poverty and lack of opportunity in rural areas.

Evidence suggests that farm output has not been affected greatly by the loss of migrants and their labor to urban markets. In fact, without sufficient rural-to-urban migration, returns to labor in rural areas can become too low compared to returns in urban areas. In many low-income countries, the number of farmers keeps rising despite rural–urban migration, because total population is growing faster than cities can expand. And migrants help sustain their relatives on the farm when they remit money back to rural areas. Some rural areas have suffered because the brightest and most educated workers have migrated, although in many countries farm wages are rising as labor markets tighten, which can help farm workers. Part of this tightening is due to migration, and rising wages will speed the agricultural transition described in the next chapter.

Governments have employed various approaches to the task of slowing down rural-to-urban migration. Some countries have restricted migration, implemented resettlement schemes, and provided services to smaller towns and cities. It appears, however, that unless the urban bias in economic policies is removed and economic development proceeds to the point that living conditions improve substantially in rural areas, rural-to-urban migration will continue in many countries at a rapid rate.

Once rural-to-urban migration slows in a country, a problem can develop of persistent place-based poverty for people that remain in rural communities left behind. Governments need to implement policies to improve the quality of life and encourage business investment by local entrepreneurs in those communities.

INTERNATIONAL MIGRATION

In 2019, 272 million people, representing 3.5 percent of the world's population, lived in a country in which they were not born. A majority of these people had moved to countries within the same region of their birth. During the decade 2010–2019, a total of 30 million more people immigrated to Europe, North America, Australia/New Zealand, and North Africa/Western Asia than emigrated from these regions to the rest of the world. The reverse was true for the regions of Central and South Asia, East and Southeast Asia, Saharan Africa, and Latin America/Caribbean. The United States received the largest number of immigrants and had a total of 51 million residents in 2019 who had immigrated at some point from their native country. These people represent 15 percent of the U.S. population. Roughly 1 million people have immigrated to the United States annually over the past 20 years, although the number declined to 600,000 net migrants (arrivals minus those who leave) in 2019. Three-fourths of recent immigrants are of working age.[4]

Many international immigrants leave their birth country and move permanently to another country to work for wages and salaries or to start a business. Others move as refugees fleeing war or other types of violence and remain temporarily or permanently in a new nation after applying for asylum. Others migrate due to climate stress and crop failures related to drought, flooding, and other natural calamities (Box 4.2). Others, usually without dependents, arrive as temporary workers, typically in low-paying jobs, and return home after working several months. Temporary workers in the United States are a key source of agricultural

---

BOX 4.2 CLIMATE CHANGE AND INTERNATIONAL MIGRATION

Climate-related migration is a growing phenomenon worldwide; it is estimated that approximately 16 million people were dislocated by climate stress in 2018. Floods (5.4 million people), extreme storms (9.3 million people), droughts (764,000 people), and wildfires (424,000 people) were the main sources of climate-related movement. As climate change becomes more acute, migration will increasingly disrupt lives in sending and receiving areas. People in rural areas are more susceptible to many climate hazards, such as drought, temperature increase, and more violent weather events. These hazards are projected to increase in areas with many poor people, such as South Asia, sub-Saharan Africa, and North Africa and the Middle East. The poor have larger family sizes and greater population growth, so increased climate stress will interact with political and economic stress to increase out-migration from vulnerable areas. Smallholder agriculture is more sensitive to such hazards because poor farmers are dependent on rainfall, farm in vulnerable areas, and have limited capacity to adapt to drought and temperature increases.

Source: Robert McLeman, "International Migration and Climate Adaptation in an Era of Hardening Borders", Nature Climate Change, vol. 9 (2019), pp. 911–918.

labor. Most immigrants arrive legally, but some cross borders without permission or arrive legally on tourist or other temporary visas and then overstay the visa. In the United States, about 20 percent of existing immigrants are in the country illegally, some for decades.

Three questions are often asked with respect to international immigration: (1) What are the economic impacts of immigration on countries that receive immigrants and those that supply them? (2) Given the sizable wage differences across countries, why do even more people not migrate to developed countries than currently do? (3) Why does immigration generate such strong views and emotions?

Economic impacts of international immigration

Economic impacts of immigration on countries receiving immigrants include effects on workers, producers, consumers, public expenditures, tax receipts, and economic productivity, among others. Economic effects on countries that the immigrants have left include loss of workers with varying levels of education and economic gains from money sent back to relatives. Low wage immigrants compete with natives for jobs in their new country, but less so than some people believe for several reasons. First, many take jobs that even unemployed workers will not. Most hired farm workers in the United States today are immigrants, without whom food in the country would be more expensive. Second, immigrants demand additional goods and services, which increases the overall demand for labor as well. Third, the influx of immigrants slows down mechanization that would otherwise replace labor. Fourth, the new workers are more productive than they would have been in their original country, provide extra products and services for consumers, and pay taxes in their new country. Many highly skilled immigrants do take jobs from natives, some of them create businesses that employ large numbers of workers. More than 40 percent of Fortune 500 businesses today were created by immigrants or their children. Immigrants often have ambition, patience, and a drive to succeed that helps them to succeed economically in their new country. Most economists agree that the net effects of migration are positive from an economic standpoint, often substantially so.[5]

Why relatively few people migrate internationally

Low-skilled migrants to developed countries earn substantially more than if they had stayed behind. Given the sizable wage gaps across borders, why don't even more people migrate internationally? For one thing, rich countries will not allow it. Yes, many people immigrate illegally, but the number is small compared to the number of people that could migrate. Developed countries have strong immigration restrictions in place that make it difficult to move. More importantly, the vast majority of people do not want to leave their homeland. Most prefer to stay where they are unless violence drives them out, at which point they may become refugees, usually moving to countries in close proximity. Those that do move for economic reasons often have connections to relatives or friends in their new country because those without connections find it hard to get a job. Moving is costly and having friends lowers the cost. Most people do not want to leave their culture and their extended family at home. They prefer not to take risks and they fear failure if they move.

Why international immigration generates strong views

Average annual international immigration is a small fraction of one percent of the global population, but its political impact has been sizable throughout history. People worry that immigrants will lower wages and employment prospects for natives, will be a net cost to taxpayers, will commit crimes, will not assimilate well, or may affect the political balance. With the exception of highly skilled immigrants, data do not support a negative view on wages and native employment. Studies have found that immigrants pay more in taxes than they cost in government payments. Most migrants are workers and the restrictions in place in most countries, including the United States, reduce their draw on public funds. Immigration is not charity. Statistics, at least in the United States, show that the number of crimes committed per thousand people is substantially less for immigrants than for the native population. Some people may not be aware of these statistics, and politicians often distort them by pointing to a few exceptions, but the primary reason the public opposes immigration is likely to be the fear that immigrants are different and will not assimilate well. People fear that immigrants will change the local culture and perhaps the balance of political power. First-generation immigrants often do assimilate slowly and tend to be socially conservative and fiscally liberal, although these differences tend to disappear by the second generation.[6] Economic growth globally and in most countries receiving migrants would be higher with additional international migration from developing to developed countries, but this fact seems counterintuitive to many people, and the fear of change is difficult to overcome.

SUMMARY

The current world population of more than 7.8 billion is growing at an annual rate of 1.05 percent, a high rate by historical standards. The developing world, especially in sub-Saharan Africa, is experiencing rapid population growth caused in part by a decline in death rates due to improved health and nutrition. Birth rates have also decreased in many regions due to higher incomes, family planning, education, and other factors, but world population is likely to continue to grow for the next century. Effective measures to manage population growth and its effects should consider the economics of fertility, how various economic and social policies affect childbearing decisions, and policies to prepare countries for their eventual aging. Rural-to-urban migration is proceeding at a rapid rate in many developing countries as migrants seek to achieve higher standards of living. Rapid urbanization has caused a strain on public services and created other problems but is expected with economic development. International migration receives a lot of attention but is relatively small compared to rural-to-urban migration.

IMPORTANT TERMS AND CONCEPTS

Birth rates and death rates
Causes of fertility changes
Causes of rural-to-urban migration
Characteristics of migrants
Consequences of rapid and
slow population growth
Demographic transition

Family planning
International Migration
Population density
Population dividend
Population growth
Rural-to-urban migration
Why death rates decline

LOOKING AHEAD

This chapter concludes our overview of several dimensions of the world food income–population problem. Hunger and poverty problems are severe and complex. We move now to a set of two chapters examining economic theories that attempt to identify the heart of the development process. We begin in the next chapter with a discussion of economic transformation and sources of growth. The subsequent chapter incorporates these factors into development theories.

QUESTIONS FOR DISCUSSION

1 Has population increased at a fairly constant rate since prehistoric times?

2 What is the current world population and how fast is it growing? When will it stop growing?

3 At present growth rates, how long will it take to add 1 billion people to the world population?

4 Why is population increasing more rapidly today in developing countries than it did during early stages of development in Europe and the United States?

5 What are the major determinants of birth rates in developing countries?

6 What are the impacts of rapid population growth?

7 What policies can be used to help reduce population growth?

8 Are population growth rates more likely to increase or decrease over the next 15 years?

9 Which are the fastest and slowest growing countries in the world (in terms of population)?

10 What proportion of the world's population lives in Asia?

11 Why are we seeing rapid rural-to-urban migration in many developing countries?

12 What are the consequences of rapid rural-to-urban migration?

13 Describe the characteristics of the most common type of migrant.

14 How can high fertility be viewed as a consequence of poverty as well as a cause of it?

15 Describe the demographic transition that tends to occur as development takes place and why it occurs.

16 What are the economic impacts of international migration?

17 What percent of the world migrates internationally each year?

18 Why does international migration generate such strong views?

NOTES

1 Population in individual countries also depends on immigration and emigration.

2 United Nations, *World Population Prospects: The 2019 Revision* (New York: United Nations, 2019).

3 World Development Report, *2009: Reshaping Economic Geography* (Washington, DC: The World Bank, 2009).

4 See UN Department of Economic and Social Affairs, International Migration 2019, U.S. Census Bureau, 2010, https://www.census.gov/prod/cen2010/cph-2-1.pdf;

International Organization for Migration, *World Migration Report* (Geneva: IOM, 2020).

5   Bryan Caplan and Zach Weinersmith, *Open Borders: The Science and Ethics of Migration* (New York: First Second Press, 2019); Abhijit Banerjee and Ether Duflo, *Good Economics for Hard Times* (New York: Public Affairs, 2019), Chapter 2.

6   Banerjee and Duflo, *Good Economics for Hard Times*, Chapter 2.

RECOMMENDED READINGS

Banerjee, Abhijit, and Esther Duflo, *Good Economics for Hard Times* (New York: Public Affairs, 2019), Chapter 2.

Boo, Katherine, *Behind the Beautiful Forevers* (New York: Random House, 2012).

Caplan, Bryan, and Zach Weinersmith, *Open Borders: The Science and Ethics of Migration* (New York: First Second Press, 2019).

De Brauw, Alan, Valerie Mueller, and Hak Lim Lee, "The Role of Rural-Urban Migration in the Structural Transformation of sub-Saharan Africa", *World Development*, vol. 62 (November 2014), pp. 33–42.

PART 2

Development theories and the role of agriculture

Rice in Peru

5 Economic transformation and growth

THIS CHAPTER

1 Describes the economic transformation that occurs with economic development, involving a decline in the size of agriculture relative to the nonagricultural activities
2 Identifies potential sources of economic growth

THE ECONOMIC TRANSFORMATION

Economic growth is almost always accompanied by an *economic transformation* from agriculture into other activities. As the economy expands, the agricultural sector grows more slowly than manufacturing and services, and agriculture accounts for a declining share of employment, output, and consumer expenditures. The transformation from farm to non-farm activities as incomes rise applies to regions, countries, and the world as a whole. It is among the most dependable relationships in the world economy and has major effects on peoples' lives. This chapter explores its causes and its consequences, both within agriculture and for society as a whole.

The tendency for richer countries to derive a smaller share of their income from agriculture is illustrated in Figure 5.1, and their tendency to have a smaller share of total employment in agriculture is illustrated in Figure 5.2. These two figures show remarkable similarity and an interesting difference. The similarity is the clear downward trend. All poor countries derive a significant share of their income from agriculture, while all rich countries derive only a small fraction from it. Note that agriculture never disappears entirely in the rich countries, and there

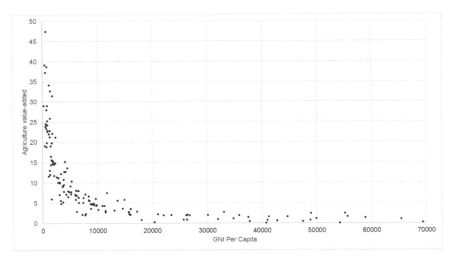

Figure 5.1 Agriculture's share of total output and gross national income per capita, 2019
Source: World Bank, World Development Indicators Online Database, 2019

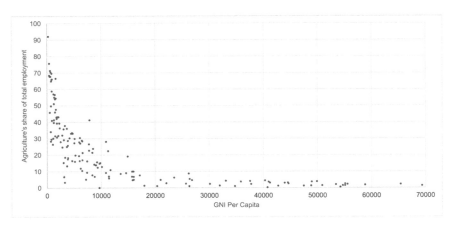

Figure 5.2 Agriculture's share of total employment and gross national income per capita, 2019
Source: World Bank, World Development Indicators Online Database, 2019

is wide variation in its share among the poorest countries. A key difference between the two figures is that, in poor countries, agriculture accounts for a larger fraction of employment than of output. Roughly speaking, countries below $5,000 per year in per-capita income have 30–70 percent of the workforce engaged in agriculture, and these people earn 10–50 percent of their country's total income. In other words, within poor countries, on average each farmer earns roughly half of what non-farmers earn.

The economic transformation from agriculture into other activities is vividly illustrated by economic changes that have occurred over time in the two most populous countries, China and India. From 1991 to 2017, the share of agriculture in overall gross domestic product shrank from 40 percent to 7 percent in China and from 40 percent to 25 percent in India. This transformation was accompanied by a period of dramatic poverty reduction in China and sizeable poverty reduction in India. Using the World Bank poverty definition of $1.90 per person per day, from 1991 to 2017 extreme poverty shrank from 65 percent of the population to 1 percent in China and from 45 percent of the population to 21 percent in India.

Causes of the economic transformation

In low-income countries, labor productivity is low and people, out of necessity, spend much of their income on food. Labor and small amounts of land and livestock are their primary assets, and many have no choice but to devote at least some of their labor to farming, to feed themselves and their family. Many low-income farmers are net food buyers, using small amounts of non-farm income or the sale of high-valued crops and livestock to supplement the basic foods they grow on the farm. To emerge from poverty, these semi-subsistence farmers must improve their productivity either on the farm or in non-farm activities.

As the productivity of labor and other factors increases, four major factors drive the transformation from farm to non-farm activities. The first factor is that incomes rise due to the productivity increase, causing a gradual shift in demand from food to non-food items. This consumption shift occurs primarily because the income elasticity of demand for food is less than one and tends to fall as income grows. Declining income elasticities mean that for each percentage increase in income, progressively lower proportions are spent on food (see Engel's law in Chapter 3). These changes in demands for agricultural and nonagricultural products imply that, as development proceeds, relatively more labor inputs and other resources are devoted to nonagricultural activities.

The second factor driving the transformation is that at any given income level, the quantity of food demanded changes relatively little when its price changes. In other words, the price elasticity of demand for food is low, less than one in absolute value, and it may be even smaller at higher levels of income. This "price-inelastic" characteristic of food demand means that, if agricultural productivity grows, prices received by farmers will fall by a higher percentage than the quantity demanded rises, creating incentives to remove resources from farming and transfer them to non-farm activities.

These two "demand-side" drivers cannot explain the transition in settings where farmers are selling their output at prices that are determined in a world market. In those cases, prices received by farmers depend little on local demand, so there must be "supply-side" explanations for the transformation as well.

A third, supply-side factor driving transformation is specialization. Even if the mix of activities in the economy remains the same, during economic growth the availability of capital and market opportunities allow people to expand production of what they do best, and then trade with others for the products they want to consume. Thus, farmers produce less of their own food, clothes, furniture, and so forth, and an increasing share of these kinds of activities is re-classified from "agriculture" to "industry".

Another supply-side factor that could drive transformation is the fact that land supply is fixed, while other forms of capital can expand. As people accumulate savings from year to year, they find fewer and fewer opportunities to add resources to their farms, and so prefer to invest their savings in non-farm enterprises. For example, the farmer who already has buildings, fencing, livestock, and equipment will tend to invest her savings in something else, such as a retail trade or services.

Does agriculture actually shrink?

The fact that having higher incomes leads to a smaller fraction of output and employment in agriculture does not mean that the absolute size of the farm sector declines. Indeed, as countries get richer, the level of farm production and consumer expenditure on farm goods usually keeps rising, and in countries with rapid farm productivity growth, output in the sector can grow as fast as non-farm output. As agricultural productivity and incomes grow, labor is gradually transferred from work on farms to work in other enterprises. Some of this work occurs in the same rural areas where the farms themselves are located – people find employment in small-scale manufacturing, in value-added processing of agricultural products, in transport and services, etc. Others, as noted in Chapter 4, migrate to cities and find work in the formal and informal sectors.

In most countries, the land area available for farm use is roughly constant over time, so any change in the number of farm workers translates directly into a change in number of acres available per worker. One might expect economic development to influence the number of people working on each farm, and it does, but in an unexpected way. Across countries and over time, the number of workers on each farm stays close to the number of workers in the family. Family farming dominates the sector, and so the number of workers per farm varies with family size, which tends to decline as the economy grows. Thus, poor countries may have five to eight workers per farm while rich countries may have only one or two, but that is mainly because of the declining number of workers per family. Furthermore, at every level of income, many family members work only part-time on the farm, and hire themselves out for off-farm work. A few do engage in hired farm work, but hired workers are less common in agriculture than in other sectors.

Family workers dominate farming until late in the development process for many reasons. Perhaps the primary one is that many field operations are difficult to supervise and monitor and are therefore done better by self-motivated workers. For example, a farm owner would have great difficulty ensuring that a hired worker plows, plants, or fertilizes appropriately, because these operations are dispersed across the field and many other factors intervene to determine that field's eventual yield.

Since family farming dominates the sector, any change in the number of farm families translates directly into a change in the average cropped area per farm. Figure 5.3 illustrates this process for the United States. The number of farms peaked in the 1920s, but as farm labor moved into cities, the land area per farm increased as exiting farmers rented or sold their land to the remaining operators. Note that the decline in the

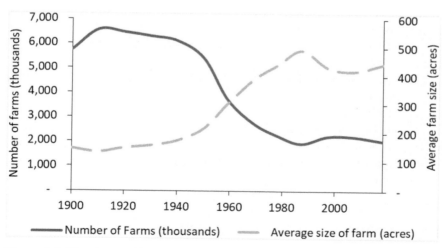

Figure 5.3 Number and average size of farms in the United States, 1900–2017
Source: Authors' calculations from U.S. Department of Agriculture, Census of Agriculture, various years

number of farmers cannot go on forever. In the United States, there has been relatively little decline since 1990, with roughly one-third the number of farms now as there were in the period from 1910 to 1920, and farm sizes are roughly three times as large. Similar patterns are found throughout the world as countries develop.

A great deal of difference in farm sizes over time exists across countries. Several middle-income countries in Asia are now in a period of rapid decline in the number of farmers, much like the United States in the 1960s. The poorest countries, however, have growing rural populations and fixed land bases. Some parts of Africa have experienced decades of decline in the available land per farmer, hindering the ability of farmers to feed themselves and slowing the economic transformation out of agriculture.

Implications of changes in the number of farmers

The key fact about the economic transformation presented thus far is that, as incomes rise, the share of agriculture falls, but the absolute number of farmers *rises and then falls*. The initially rising number of farmers in low-income countries translates directly into a rising number of workers per unit of available land. If output per unit of land cannot rise at least as fast as the number of workers, output per worker must fall. This downward pressure on farmers' income accounts for much of the deterioration in social conditions that we observe in the world's poorest regions.

An essential aspect of rural population growth is that it is temporary. If economic development continues, eventually non-farm employment becomes common enough to absorb the new workers, rural population growth slows, and any growth in output per unit of land translates directly into growing output per worker. Many of the people moving off the farm incur significant adjustment costs during the transition.

The fact that an economic transformation occurs with development does not explain the sources of economic growth and development. Understanding those sources of growth and how they contribute to development requires knowledge of a few basic economic principles related to production economics. In the next section, we introduce a set of principles that can be used to help explain the output and economic effects of input and technology choices.

EXPLAINING PRODUCTION CHOICES

Economic growth requires transforming a country's basic production resources into products and doing so in ever more efficient ways.

Economists have developed ways to characterize how that transformation occurs, utilizing the concepts of a *production function*, a *marginal product*, and *economic optimality*. These three basic production economic concepts are presented here and then used subsequently in models of economic growth and development.

Production functions

Production requires inputs – also called factors of production – such as labor, natural resources, and capital items. It also requires that these inputs be combined by a producing unit that can organize their use to obtain desired goods and services. A description of the way in which factors of production are combined to produce goods and services is commonly called a production function. A production function describes, for a given technology, the different output levels that can be obtained from various combinations of inputs or factors of production.

The relationship between the level of production that can be obtained when only one input is allowed to vary (say labor) while all other inputs are held fixed may look something like that shown in Figure 5.4. This relationship is also referred to as an *input response curve* or a *total*

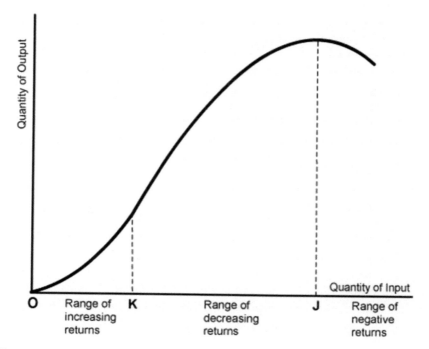

Figure 5.4 A production function with one variable input

product curve. In the case of labor, when no work is done the production level is usually zero, so the input response curve starts at zero. Output may then rise at an increasing rate, showing "increasing returns" to each additional unit of input. In farming, for example, the initial effort of planting is more productive if followed by additional effort spent weeding, so doubling labor time could more than double the resulting output. Eventually, however, all such opportunities will be exhausted and each additional hour of labor or unit of other input begins to offer "decreasing marginal returns": output continues to rise, but at a decreasing rate. Finally, at very high levels of input use, all opportunities to do *anything* productive may be exhausted, and additional inputs might actually reduce output (cause negative marginal returns).

On the particular production function drawn in Figure 5.4, the transition from increasing to decreasing marginal returns occurs at the input level marked K. Beyond that point, for each additional unit of labor, the *additions* to output become smaller and smaller, until eventually, at point J, additions to output may stop entirely. Beyond that point, additional units could actually reduce output, so the curve begins to slope downward.

The production function in Figure 5.4 shows the productivity of one input, when all the other inputs are held constant. Changing the quantity of this one input, perhaps labor, results in a movement along the curve. If other inputs were to change, that would be shown as a shift in the curve. We will see an example of such a shift later in this chapter.

If two inputs are allowed to vary simultaneously, the resulting production function can be illustrated as in Figure 5.5, with each curve (called an *isoquant*) representing a different level of output that can be achieved with different combinations of the two inputs. Curves higher and to the right represent greater output levels than curves lower and to the left. For example, point C represents a higher output level (200 units) than points A or B (100 units).

The isoquant that represents 100 units of output illustrates that the same level of output (100 in this case) can be produced with different combinations of labor and capital (combination A versus combination B). Thus, if a country has abundant labor and little capital, it might produce using the combination of labor and capital represented by A. If it has abundant capital and little labor, it might produce at B. The isoquant through points A and B shows the different combinations of labor and capital that can be used to produce 100 units of output. It also tells us how easy it is to substitute labor for capital in the production of that output. When isoquants are very curved, inputs are not easily substituted for each other. Straighter isoquants imply easier substitution

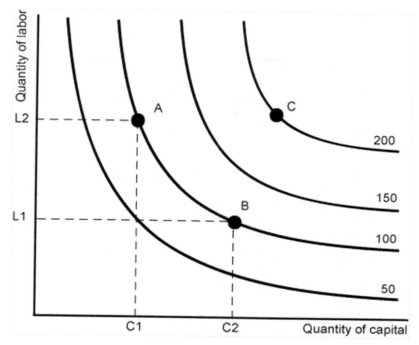

Figure 5.5 Production function with two variable inputs

Marginal product and the law of diminishing returns

The idea illustrated in Figure 5.4, that after some point, adding additional units of an input tends to generate less and less additional output, is known as the *law of diminishing returns*. Specifically, the law says:

In the production of any commodity, as we add more units of one factor of production to a fixed quantity of another factor (or factors), the additions to total output with each subsequent unit of the variable factor will eventually begin to diminish.

What is diminishing is the *marginal* output gain or *marginal product* of the factor (labor in Figure 5.4).[1] As discussed in what follows, the law of diminishing returns has important implications for countries experiencing rapid population (and labor) growth with a fixed land base.

A marginal product curve can be obtained (derived) from Figure 5.4 by examining *changes* in total output for each successive unit of input. The marginal product curve corresponding to the production function in Figure 5.4 is shown in Figure 5.6. To the left of K, the slope of the production function is increasing (Figure 5.4); thus, the changes in output are growing and the marginal product curve is rising (Figure 5.6). To the

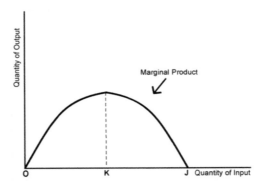

Figure 5.6 Marginal product curve derived from the slope of the total product curve in Figure 5.4

right of K, the changes are smaller and the marginal product curve falls. If total output eventually ceases to grow at all as more labor is applied, the marginal product goes to zero; this is point J on the production function and on the marginal product curve. Marginal productivity is important because it helps determine payments to factors of production, such as wages paid to labor. In addition, the marginal productivity of an input, together with prices of outputs and inputs, determines the demand for the input.

Economic optimality: what output and input levels will people choose?

All points along a production function are equally possible to achieve. But are they equally likely to be chosen? What factors motivate a farmer to choose one point as opposed to another? When people are asked what explains their choices, they mention a variety of factors, such as input scarcity, the need for output of particular products, traditions or habits, and a desire to minimize risk. Repeated studies have found that actual choices by large numbers of people over several years are best explained by *economic optimality*. Economic optimality means that farmers are rational and choose options that will give them the highest level of well-being attainable given the prices they face, the available resources and technology, and their ability to absorb risk.

Even in very low-income settings and across cultures, farmers generally attempt to optimize. They may consider cultural and risk factors as they optimize, but economic well-being plays an important role in their decision-making. Because farmers optimize, they will choose to produce somewhere along the production function and not below it. For any given level of input(s), they prefer to obtain as much output as they can attain. In other words, they prefer to be on the production function and not below it. But where along the production function would they decide to produce? Prices help determine the answer. Even for farmers whose production is largely for home consumption, some of their outputs and inputs are sold and purchased at prices set in markets off the farm. When markets set prices, farmers can often reach the highest-possible level of well-being by *maximizing profits*, subject to acceptable risk, and then trading those profits for goods they want to consume. This kind of economic optimality typically leads to a single point along the production function, as illustrated in Figure 5.7. In Figure 5.7, each level of profits can be represented by a straight line, whose slope is the price of the input divided by the price of output. This ratio of market prices is the rate at which the two goods could be exchanged in the market. In the left-hand panel in Figure 5.7, the highest such line, representing the highest attainable level of profits, occurs where the highest line is tangent to the production function. At this point, marginal revenue from the output equals the marginal cost of the input (MR = MC). On the right-hand panel in Figure 5.7, the slope of the profit line is the ratio of the two input prices and also represents the total cost of production. When farmers are producing on their production functions and employing the optimal amount of inputs to equate their marginal revenue to their marginal cost of obtaining the last unit of output (the price lines are tangent to the curves in Figure 5.7), they are said to have achieved *price or allocative efficiency*. This concept of efficiency can be an important source of economic growth.

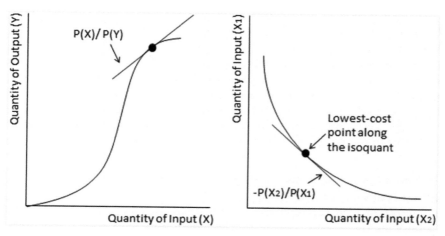

Figure 5.7 The economically optimal level of output and input choice

SOURCES OF ECONOMIC GROWTH

We can now use the production economics concepts described earlier to explore the possible sources of growth in an economy over time. One way that economic growth can occur is through increases in the amounts of inputs used in production. While production functions usually refer to a particular type of output (say corn), one can think of an aggregate production function relating total inputs to total output or total national product. Additional inputs can move a country out its aggregate production function to higher isoquants and higher levels of output. Therefore, three major elements in the development process are (1) *population growth* (which affects labor availability and cost), (2) *natural resource availability* (which affects the cost of environmental factors such as land with its associated soils, water, and forests), and (3) *capital accumulation* (which affects the availability of man-made inputs). These sources of growth cause movement along a given multi-factor production function.

A second means of spurring economic growth is to change the way in which a country uses its factors of production, increasing the amount of output produced by these inputs. These output increases can result from better organization of production or from shifts in the production function. For example, a new technology can shift the total product curve upward so more output is produced per unit of inputs. There are three primary ways to get increased output per unit of input: (1) increases in scale or specialization, (2) increases in efficiency, and (3) technological change. In many cases, markets can change, which in turn stimulates changes in these factors. Movements along a given production function versus shifts in the function are illustrated in Box 5.1.

A third means of stimulating economic growth is through increased *human capital* as embodied in people (e.g., improved education and health) and improvements in *social institutions* (the rules of the game). Increases in human capital can make labor more productive, contributing to technological progress and increased efficiency (especially when technologies and markets are rapidly changing). Social institutions help define property rights and costs of transacting for producers.

Let's examine more closely each of the sources of economic growth.

The demographic factor: effects of population growth on agriculture and the economy

For most of history, population growth was a major source of output growth in the world. People worked with primitive tools, and more

BOX 5.1 SOURCES OF GROWTH AND THE PRODUCTION FUNCTION

Growth in output can occur either from a change in market opportunities and relative prices, which leads farmers to add inputs using existing technologies, or because of an innovation that allows production of more output with given amounts of inputs.

The left-hand panel illustrates how profit-maximizing farmers would respond to increasing abundance and hence lower relative price of an input. For example, if rural labor becomes more abundant over time, there is a decline in wages relative to other prices, leading farmers to apply more labor in land preparation, weeding, etc. in an effort to obtain more output.

The right-hand panel shows how those same farmers might respond to a new invention, such as better-performing seeds or veterinary medicine for their livestock. Now the farmer can obtain more output at each level of input. This particular innovation was drawn so that the new profit-maximizing level of input use happens to be exactly the same as before: thanks to the innovation, the farmer has gotten more output for no change in the input.

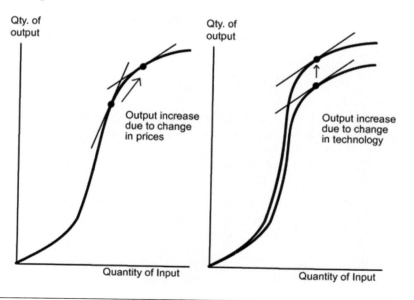

people meant more labor and output. Crop and pasture areas expanded with the rural workforce, although output per person remained roughly the same. A greater population density also reduced the distance between people and made it easier to develop cost-effective services such as transportation, communications, schooling, and so forth. Population growth, however, is a mixed blessing because, while there are more productive hands, there are more mouths to feed. As long as farmland is plentiful, land frontiers can be pushed back and growth continues in the agricultural sector, but in most areas of the world, the best farmland is already being used and rising numbers of farmers have no choice but to invest more time in each field. In this situation, diminishing returns to labor cause farm incomes to fall, unless farmers can turn to an alternative source of growth.

Population growth may also mean an increasing number of children relative to adults. If the number of consumers is growing faster than the number of producers, then the effect of population growth is also more likely to be negative. If population growth results from extending the productive life of workers, the odds of its effect being positive improve. Eventually, as incomes improve and birth rates decline, the number of available workers may also decline, especially in agriculture, where family members are a key source of labor. As a result, other sources of growth become increasingly important for sustaining economic growth.

Ecuadorian children

Natural resources: environmental influences on the location and pace of development

Natural resources – including land and its associated soil, water, forests, and minerals – have played an important role in economic development. The extension of the frontier in the United States brought additional land and mineral resources into production and helped create wealth. Similar expansions occurred in other countries. Extensive use of other types of natural resources has been important as well. For example, in the eighteenth and nineteenth centuries, one of the most important resources was coal, as countries with large and easily accessible coal deposits, such as Britain, used it to fuel the industrial revolution. In the twentieth century, oil became important in several countries. Will natural resources continue to be an important source of economic growth in the future, or will they limit it?

There is only so much land, and indeed, we see increasing problems with soil erosion, deforestation, and overgrazing. Increased combustion of fossil fuels releases carbon into the atmosphere, causing climate change while depleting their supply. Water resources are being exploited to their fullest potential (or overexploited) in many places. However, land expansion still contributes to overall output growth in a few countries in Africa and Latin America.

While technologies change, in essence creating new resources, there is no question that land is limited and that the opening of new uninhabited fertile lands will be much less important to future economic growth in most countries than it has been historically. Some minerals are being depleted in several countries and are thus becoming less available to stimulate growth than they once were. The real question for most countries is not whether exploitation of natural resources will be a significant source of growth, but whether natural resources will act as a constraint to growth, and the cost involved in transitioning from one natural resource regime to another. This issue is discussed in Chapter 9.

Accumulation of physical capital

Physical capital may be defined as a country's stock of human-made contributions to production, including buildings, factories, bridges, paved roads, dams, machinery, tools, equipment, and inventory of goods in stock. Physical capital, as we refer to it here, means human-made physical items and includes private physical goods and public infrastructure.

Capital accumulation is the process of adding to this stock of buildings, machinery, tools, bridges, etc. Another name for capital accumulation is investment. Capital investment is important because it can increase the amount of machinery and tools per worker, thereby increasing the

A plow and bullock can be a sizable investment in many developing countries

output or marginal product per worker. A higher marginal product per worker usually leads to a higher income per worker.

Capital accumulation is also related to the possibilities of making changes in the scale of production, for example when tractors are used to plow land. Furthermore, the process of capital accumulation involves a choice between consumption today and investing for future economic growth. The choices of how much to invest and in what types of capital have important implications for the rate and direction of economic development. As will be argued throughout this text, investment should be guided along an appropriate path by signals (prices) that reflect the true scarcity of resources.

Technological progress

Increases in input use (land, labor, and capital) accounted for much of the economic growth prior to the nineteenth century. However, evidence suggests that changes in how goods are produced have been the key engine of modern economic growth for many if not most countries.

The three sources of growth described earlier in this chapter involve increasing inputs with a given production technology. Economic growth can occur, but only through exploitation of natural resources and labor, or accumulation of costly resources through savings and investment from year to year. More important, this type of growth is subject to diminishing returns, as movements along the production function generate smaller and smaller increments of output for each additional unit of input (diminishing marginal product). Sustaining economic growth over time requires the constant invention of new technologies, to shift the production function upward and overcome diminishing returns (Box 5.1).

If technological progress allows the same or fewer resources to provide more output, the value of output per unit of resources rises, and this rise can lead to increases in per capita income. Resources can also be freed up to produce new types of goods. The phenomenon of technological progress is not new and has occurred for many years. What is new is the rapidity with which new technologies are now being developed. Modern technological progress is the result of both applied science and new knowledge in the basic sciences.

Specialization

As innovation occurs and capital is accumulated, increasing opportunities arise for people to specialize and trade with each other. Such *specialization and trade* can raise productivity and attract savings and investment. Specialization is related to scale as well. As firms increase in size, specialization is facilitated. "Division of labor" can make workers more efficient as they become proficient at just a few tasks. Adam Smith argued that this type of division of labor is at the heart of economic growth. In his famous book, *The Wealth of Nations* (1776), he noted that specialization is limited only by "the extent of the market", or the ease with which one person can trade with others, both within and across countries. As markets expand, the possibilities of mass-producing goods enable firms to gain efficiency in both production and marketing. Increased scale and specialization allow more output per unit of input and, hence, growth.

Efficiency improvement

Another type of organizational change that can lead to economic growth is improved production efficiency. Improved efficiency means getting more for the same inputs.

Efficiency in production can be divided into different types. *Technical efficiency* relates to whether producers are producing on the production function as opposed to below or inside it. Using the same number of inputs, some producers obtain higher output levels than others due to differences in management and effort. *Price or allocative efficiency*, mentioned earlier and illustrated in Figure 5.7 and Box 5.2, relates to the degree to which producers, operating on their production functions, employ inputs to equate their marginal revenue to their marginal cost of obtaining the last unit of output. By definition, producers who maximize profits are both technically and allocatively efficient.

Market efficiency is related to the type of economic system and the degree of market power within it. Improvements in resource allocation

BOX 5.2 NEW TECHNOLOGIES, INPUT USE, AND THE DEMAND FOR INNOVATION

Technological innovations can have different impacts on a farmer's input use and output levels, and changes in resource availability can lead to different kinds of innovation. The diagrams that follow illustrate how farmers' profit maximization affects their response to new technologies and the kinds of new techniques that are most needed in various countries.

The left-hand panel shows an innovation that, with no change in relative prices, would lead a farmer to increase input use. The most important examples of such technologies are "green revolution" crop varieties, whose growth habits and stress tolerance make it worthwhile for farmers to apply more labor, fertilizer, and water to the plant.

The right-hand panel shows another kind of innovation that, with no change in relative prices, would lead a farmer to cut back on input use. Most such input-saving innovations are mechanical devices such as bigger, faster implements, which take less capital and labor to do a given task.

"Input-using" innovations involve the discovery of new techniques *to the right* of existing input levels, whereas "input-saving" innovation involves discovery of new techniques to the left of them. Price changes, by leading farmers to look for new techniques in one direction or the other, help influence which kind of innovation is more likely to be discovered and adopted. Most notably, in poor countries where the farm labor force is rising, labor-using innovations are demanded. In contrast, once the farm labor force starts falling in richer countries, labor-saving mechanization is farmers' priority.

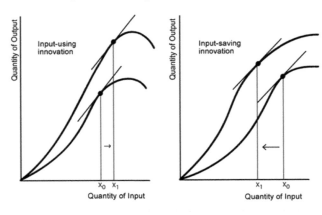

occur through market efficiency when increased competition or new technology lowers the margin between buyers and sellers. A country with a relatively free market with many buyers and sellers so that no producer or consumer can affect prices has greater market efficiency than one with a few producers who are able to influence prices. Access to good information affects market efficiency, and improved information flows can create growth due to more efficient allocation of productive resources.

Human capital

So far in this chapter we have explained economic growth without assuming any change in the people themselves. Much of economic growth is driven by changes in people's capabilities or their *human capital* as affected particularly by their education and health. The nature of these capabilities is easily misunderstood. Even the most illiterate, impoverished person is often intelligent and skilled, but educated healthy people can more easily contribute to the generation of new technologies and more readily utilize those technologies. Education is therefore an important source of economic growth inextricably linked with technological progress and, of course, with the productivity of labor, both male and female. Part of the economic benefits of education is derived from improved productivity of workers, part from improved quality of management, and part from education's contribution to producing new or improved technologies.[2]

Education is important, but in the lowest-income countries an equally important form of human capital is a person's health. Despite progress in improving health in most developing countries, undernutrition and preventable diseases remain among the world's biggest killers, and they sharply reduce the productivity of those who survive. Improvements in nutrition and disease control raise output directly, and make it easier and more worthwhile to keep children in school, leading to more education as well.

The term human capital is used in referring to education and health because education and health infrastructure are investments, in many ways similar to investments in physical capital that pay off over a long period of time and eventually depreciate. Human capital improvements due to investments in health have also been called improvements in physiological capital. Investments in female education and in basic health infrastructure have been major contributors to economic growth over the last 30–40 years.

Institutional change

Historical patterns of economic growth exhibit remarkable differences across countries and over time. Levels and rates of growth differ significantly even among neighboring countries. Many of these differences are attributable not solely to sources mentioned previously, but to institutions as well. Institutions include government policies, legal structures, and market structures. If markets exhibit distortions, efficient price signals will not be received by producers; if financial markets are incomplete or characterized by excessive risks, savings and capital accumulation will be constrained. If people are unsure about their ability to recover investments, due to political instability or ill-defined property rights, they will not undertake investments. The ability of institutions to adapt to new needs and demands can itself be a source of economic growth.

During economic growth, there is often explosive growth in many kinds of social and economic institutions. This new social capital may displace previous institutions, such as family or village networks, which might have been helpful but are not as well adapted to new circumstances. Some of these institutional changes are a result of economic growth, but in some they may play a causal role in economic development, so that a transformation of institutions could accelerate growth. For example, many countries benefit from the introduction of quality certification systems to enforce grades and standards, uniform procedures for contract enforcement and commercial law, and well-adapted property rights of various sorts.

SUMMARY

Economic growth involves a transition from low-income, agricultural-dependent economies to higher-income, non-farm employment. The process is driven by capital accumulation, technological innovation, and specialization in either sector. An economic transformation occurs for several reasons. First, demand for food is relatively fixed. It is "income-inelastic", so when incomes grow, demand for other things grows faster. Second, productivity increases in agriculture free up resources for nonagricultural production. Third, as people specialize and trade with each other, many tasks that were previously done on the farm are now classified as nonagricultural.

Although agriculture declines as a share of the economy, the sector does not shrink. Typically, total farm output continues to rise during periods of economic growth. Furthermore, when population is growing, the number of farmers tends to rise for many years, until the absolute size of the non-farm sector is large enough to absorb all those entering the workforce each year. The resulting change in land area per farmer will often place downward pressure on rural living standards during early stages of economic development, even as the rest of the economy grows.

To explain the causes and consequences of economic growth, we use production functions that describe, for a given technology, the different amounts of product that can be obtained from different amounts and combinations of inputs. An isoquant shows different combinations of two inputs that can be used to produce the same level of output, given a particular technology. The law of diminishing returns has important implications as population or capital increases with a fixed land base. To overcome diminishing returns and sustain growth over time, an economy needs technological change, increased specialization and trade, and improvements in efficiency that may be related to improvements in human capital and institutions.

IMPORTANT TERMS AND CONCEPTS

Capital accumulation	Natural resources
Economic efficiency	Non-farm job opportunities
Economic transformation	Population growth
Education	Production function
Input demands	Scale and specialization
Isoquant	Sources of economic growth
Law of diminishing returns	Technological progress
Marginal product	Input response curve
Human capital	Institutional change

LOOKING AHEAD

The sources of growth discussed in this chapter relate to whole economies, to sectors within economies, and to individual firms (including farms). Various theories have been proposed to explain how the sources of growth have been or could be combined to transform agricultural sectors and whole economies from low to higher standards of living. We examine these theories in the next chapter. In subsequent chapters, we consider how these growth factors can affect firms within the agricultural sector.

QUESTIONS FOR DISCUSSION

1 What is meant by the term factors of production?
2 What are the three major factors of production and how do they relate to the major sources of economic growth?
3 What is the law of diminishing returns and what might be its significance in relation to population growth?

4 At what point along the production function does the average product of labor begin to fall? Please illustrate graphically. What does this point imply for further use of labor to boost agricultural output?

5 Will natural resource limitations be a serious restriction to future economic growth or growth in food production?

6 What is capital accumulation and why is it important to development?

7 Why are specialization, efficiency, and technological progress important to agricultural and economic development?

8 What is meant by economic efficiency? What types of efficiency are there and how are they linked?

9 Why is an economic transformation inevitably associated with economic development?

10 What factors determine the rate at which an economy becomes transformed from an agricultural to a mixed economy with significant nonagricultural as well as agricultural activities?

11 If the total labor force were growing 2 percent per year and 50 percent of the labor force were in agriculture, how fast would nonagricultural employment need to expand in order to hold the number of people employed in agriculture constant? Why is this important?

12 What are the implications of the economic transformation for the agricultural sector?

13 What is meant by human capital and institutional change?

NOTES

1 The marginal product of an input is reflected by the slope of the total product curve, or $\Delta Y/\Delta X$, where Y and X represent output and input, respectively, and Δ represents a small change. Therefore, anything affecting this slope changes the marginal product.

2 Education can of course have other benefits associated with the capacity to develop new institutions and with many non-economic factors.

RECOMMENDED READINGS

Acemoglu, D., and J.A. Robinson, *Why Nations Fail: The Origins of Power, Prosperity, and Poverty* (New York: Random House, 2012), Chapter 3.

Mellor, J.W., *Agricultural Development and Economic Transformation* (New York: Palgrave Macmillan, 2017), Chapters 1–3.

Thirlwall, A.P., *Growth and Development* (New York: Palgrave Macmillan, 2011), Chapter 7.

6 Economic development theories and strategies

THIS CHAPTER

1 Reviews how economic development and development theories have evolved over time
2 Considers the interaction of technology and institutions and its implications for agricultural development
3 Considers the distinctive characteristics of agriculture as opposed to other sectors as the economy develops

EVOLUTION OF ECONOMIC DEVELOPMENT THEORIES

In the previous chapter, we identified potential sources of economic growth and the inevitable structural transformation that accompanies economic development. We turn now to theories that attempt to explain how these sources of growth can be integrated into transformation processes that lead to higher living standards. Theories of economic development have occupied economists for centuries. Different theories have led to diverse implications for what governments, private firms, or individuals might do to achieve development goals. One especially important contrast concerns the roles attributed to technology and productivity versus institutions and incentives. Emphases on technology and institutions in theories of growth and development have shifted over time because of changes in the constraints that limit economic growth, changing technological possibilities, and experiences with what has or has not worked. We consider in this chapter the historical evolution of agricultural and economic development and the progression of thinking among economists. Over time, a synthesis of ideas has emerged, with a focus on the interactions between technologies and institutions.

Mercantilism and colonialism

Prior to the 1500s, much of the world was a patchwork of agriculturally based, village-level economies with distances isolating people and production. During the subsequent 250 years, significant economic changes occurred, even if income growth rates remained relatively low around the world. Most of the Americas, Africa, and parts of Asia became colonized, while conventional wisdom held that wealth and economic development depended on the accumulation of gold and silver. According to this *mercantilist view*, exports were superior to imports at creating economic growth. Several European countries helped their merchants to accumulate wealth by using tariffs (taxes) to restrict imports and by granting monopolies over regional trade routes. For example, Britain granted a military-enforced monopoly to the East India Company for trade with Asia. The government gained from the tariffs and from taxes levied on the merchants. Farmers, laborers, and consumers paid a price.

Mercantilist trade was also tied to colonialism and led to diverse impacts on the colonized areas. The nature of the impacts depended on the policies of the colonizer and the initial population densities, resources, and institutions. Sparsely populated colonies where western Europeans settled and developed relatively inclusive institutions, such as protected property rights and broad participation in the economy, fared better than colonies that were more densely populated and ruled in a more extractive way. Areas where the land base and climate were suitable for slave-based plantation agriculture tended to fare worse over time than areas more suitable for family farms. In non-colonized areas, some nations such as Russia and China were feudal societies with peasants tied to estates of wealthy people. China was controlled by an emperor who gave peasants little freedom to invest.

In the late 1700s, economists such as **Adam Smith** began to challenge the mercantilist view, arguing that freer trade for imports and exports would improve standards of living more than just pushing exports, especially if combined with a competitive, equal-opportunity environment at home. Those arguments were extended by **John Stuart Mill** and **David Ricardo**, and their ideas about the benefits of division of labor and specialization, comparative advantage, and trade remain key concepts in modern economics. Their theories about the value of free trade were not easily accepted at the time, however, and many mercantilist ideas remain widespread today.

Emperor's gilded throne in China

Led by Britain, the eighteenth century was a period of economic expansion. Productivity gains in agriculture and food imports from the Americas allowed inexpensive labor and food to be supplied to a growing industrial sector. Agricultural technologies such as intensive crop rotations, green manure, forage-livestock systems, drainage, and irrigation were developed and applied, although organized agricultural research did not yet exist. Landlords earned higher returns, some of which were invested in industry. Profits were also extracted from colonies and from slave trade, enriching western European nations at the expense of indigenous societies. The introduction of property rights that protected innovators helped stimulate technological advances in industry, which led to an industrial revolution as labor productivity increased.[1]

Populations grew more rapidly, and many political leaders felt that having more people would make a country richer. In the early nineteenth century, this idea was challenged by **Thomas Malthus**, who argued that population was limited mainly by the food supply, and by a fixed supply of high-quality land. Ricardo agreed with Malthus and was pessimistic that economic growth could be sustained in the long run. They argued that as population grows, increments of labor are applied to a relatively fixed supply of high-quality land, with higher costs of production on lower-quality land. Agricultural growth is constrained by the law of diminishing returns. The increase in food demand would drive up food prices, driving living standards back to a subsistence level. If technological progress occurs, the situation may improve temporarily but not permanently. Ricardo's policy prescription was for Britain to free up trade. He pushed for the removal of Britain's *Corn Laws*, which would free up trade and allow food imports to keep the price of food from rising and choking off industrial growth.

History has shown that this *classical model* of economics underestimates the role of technological progress, especially in agriculture. The model also fails to consider factors that lower birth rates as economic growth occurs. It oversimplifies the forces influencing wages and the complexity of sharing arrangements that occur in many societies. Nevertheless, the classical model, with its emphasis on diminishing returns and the role of trade in facilitating economic development, significantly influenced later development theories.

Agricultural, industrial, and transportation revolutions
The agricultural and industrial revolutions spread from Britain to other countries in the 1800s. The industrial revolution contributed to and was influenced by a major drop in transport costs as a result of steam engines being placed on boats and wheels.[2] Railroads and ships radically reduced shipping costs on land and sea for nations positioned to take advantage. The telegraph also transformed communications. Britain, Belgium, France, Germany, Austria, Sweden, Spain, Italy, Russia, the United States, and Japan all experienced economic transformations in agriculture and industry that resulted in their incomes rising sharply.

Land-saving technologies were prevalent in western Europe and Japan. International migration of agricultural settlers from Europe to countries with broader expanses of available land such as the United States, Argentina, Chile, Uruguay, Australia, and New Zealand allowed for homesteading and per capita income gains through expanded use of land with rising labor productivity. Tropical countries were less able to take advantage of the improved agricultural and industrial technologies, due to institutional constraints, extractive policies of colonial powers, and in some cases diseases. Their incomes rose slowly, if at all.

Growth stages
By the late 1800s, there had been enough economic development in Europe, North America, and a few other temperate areas for observers to notice the sizable divergence in economic well-being compared to tropical regions and a clear shift in the mix of economic activities.

Industries, international trade, and international migration were all booming. Economists studied these patterns of change, with some noting how economies move through sequential growth *stages*. They summarized the stages in various ways, but most emphasized that economic development involves a structural (economic and social) transformation of a country.

Frederick List, a German economic historian, identified stages based on shifts in occupational distribution, such as pastoralism, agriculture, agriculture–manufacturing, and agriculture–manufacturing–commerce. Another German, **Karl Marx**, visualized and projected development stages based on changes in technology, property rights, and ideology. He felt that class struggles drive countries through stages, with industrial capitalism sowing the seeds for revolution and communism. One class possesses the land, capital, and authority over labor while the other possesses labor. Labor is never paid its full value because if wages rise during industrial capitalism, labor is replaced by machines, creating a "reserve army of the unemployed" that brings wages back down. Because capitalists derive their profits from labor, more machines and fewer laborers mean fewer profits. The pressure of lower profits leads to more exploitation, more unemployment, mass misery, and eventually revolution. Labor then gains control over the means of production under communism. Marx's ideologically based theory would influence political and development events in Russia, China, and other countries in the following century.

By the early twentieth century, other ways of thinking about growth stages emerged. **Alan Fisher** and later **Colin Clark** argued that a transition from agriculture to manufacturing and services occurs with development because of increases in output per worker and advances in science and technology. As workers shift out of agriculture, labor productivity rises because farming involves periods of down time both within and between seasons. At the time, public and private sectors had begun investing in research that was paying dividends in new technologies. Urbanization was increasing rapidly in Europe and the United States, and the number of farms peaked and began to decline.

Two world wars, the Great Depression, and nationalistic, inward-looking policies with respect to trade and immigration slowed economic development from 1914 to 1945. These major global events contributed to a rethinking of the role of government in economic development. Keynesian macroeconomic policies and the New Deal in the United States presaged a larger role for the state in developing countries in years ahead. So too did the Russian Revolution in 1917, which resulted from discontent by workers and peasants over poverty and inequality during a period of rapid industrial growth. State ownership of land and capital under communism and the use of central planning for allocating resources influenced subsequent thinking about the role of the state in some developing countries.

Colonial empires broke up during and after World War II, creating a new set of independent nations seeking strategies that would lead to more rapid industrialization and economic growth. Some new countries, such as India and Pakistan, and existing developing nations, such as Argentina, chose strategies of protecting domestic manufacturing through restricting imports and subsidizing exports of selected firms. The objective was to obtain industrial economies of scale. Many newly formed countries in Africa struggled in attempts to rapidly design new institutional structures for governing multi-ethnic populations. Other nations, such as China, Eastern European countries, and Ethiopia, implemented economic structures with heavy state involvement in all sectors.

Walt W. Rostow argued in the 1950s that countries go through stages in moving from a traditional to a modern economy, but that the secret to growth is to find and support emerging or "leading sectors". Growth in per-capita incomes would experience a "take off" into sustained growth once enough capital had been accumulated. He believed that an eventual slowdown in the rate of growth would be the normal path for any specific sub-sector in an economy, due to declining price and income elasticities of demand for the goods produced by the sub-sector. Therefore, leading sub-sectors must be identified and supported.

Capital accumulation and technology-driven growth

Many economists in the 1950s and 1960s emphasized the importance of capital accumulation for economic growth and development. One theory, developed by **Roy Harrod** and **Evsey Domar**, showed how the rate of output growth could be limited by the level of investment and the productivity of that investment. The Harrod–Domar model was simple and could be fitted to data on the observed capital/output ratio of an economy to project the productivity of additional investment. Its main insight was to identify the importance of domestic savings for financing capital investment.

When the model was applied to low-income countries, it was argued by **Hollis Chenery** and others that national savings was not the only possible source of capital. Borrowing from abroad or foreign aid could add to domestic savings, permitting faster growth of the capital stock. Each dollar of aid might have the same effect as a dollar of savings.

The Harrod–Domar–Chenery approach focused on the rate of national savings or external borrowing, with less attention to the efficiency with which additional funds were spent. In the 1950s, **Robert Solow** developed a mathematical model of an economy in which additional capital earns diminishing returns. In that case, the long-run rate of growth of per capita income is driven by the rate of technical change, not by savings. The model did not explain how technical change comes about: it treated new technology (and hence the growth rate of the economy) as exogenous to (outside of) the model. Later, a new generation of economists would posit growth models in which people choose how much to invest in new technologies, so that technical change and hence the growth rate is endogenous, explained by property rights and government policies.

Dual-economy models: "surplus labor" and unemployment

Early mathematical models of economic growth used a single sector to describe the economy and emphasized capital accumulation. Subsequently, economists developed two-sector models in which growth and poverty alleviation depend crucially on the allocation of labor between a traditional agricultural sector and more modern industrial sector. The most influential *dual-economy* (or two-sector) model was developed by **W. Arthur Lewis**. His model was subsequently modified by **John Fei** and **Gustav Ranis, Dale Jorgenson,** and others.

A simplified version of the dual-economy model can be illustrated using the total and marginal product curves shown in Figure 6.1. This version of the model is designed to relate most closely to the situation in large labor-surplus but relatively natural resource-poor countries in which domestic (as opposed to international) characteristics of the economy dominate.

The model includes several sources of growth discussed in Chapter 5 and illustrates the potential for using "surplus" labor and technological progress in agriculture to achieve economic growth. It assumes the existence of a large population in the traditional agricultural sector, for which the marginal product of labor is below the wage rate, which is determined by society's rules about sharing output. There is disguised unemployment ("surplus labor") in the sense that if the people who appear to be working in traditional agriculture were removed, production would not drop or would drop very little. In other words, labor is applied in the agricultural sector up to the point where it is in surplus in the upper left-hand panel in Figure 6.1; or to the right of N_3 or N_2 in the lower left-hand panel.

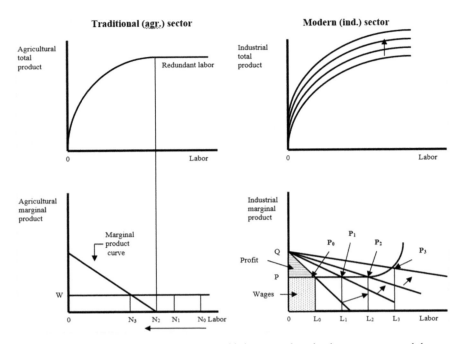

Figure 6.1 Graphical representation of labor-surplus dual-economy model

The wage rate in agriculture (W) is assumed to initially approximate the average productivity of labor in that sector (and eventually will be determined in an inter-sector labor market). Land is fixed. Wages in the modern industrial sector are assumed to be higher than those in the agricultural sector in order to attract labor from agriculture. Firms in the modern sector hire labor up to the point where the marginal product of labor equals the wage rate. Initially this is the point P_0 in the lower right-hand graph of Figure 6.1. Labor in industry is hired up to L_0 at the wage P.

In a "labor surplus" economy, the development process can be driven by transfer of labor from agriculture to the industrial sector, where it creates a profit that can be used for further economic growth. In the lower right-hand panel in Figure 6.1, total wages initially paid to labor in the industrial sector equal the area $PP_0 L_0 O$, while profits equal the triangular area QP_0P. This profit, or part of it, is reinvested in capital items such as equipment, machinery, and buildings – items that make labor more productive. This greater productivity shifts the total product of labor in industry upward (see the upper right-hand panel of Figure 6.1) and the corresponding marginal product of labor (demand for labor) out to the right (see the lower right-hand panel of Figure 6.1). Growing demand for labor is met by drawing more labor out of agriculture.

In the model, a shift of labor from agriculture to industry continues to drive economic growth as long as the marginal cost of labor to the modern sector remains constant (represented by the horizontal line between P_0 and P_2 in the lower right-hand panel in Figure 6.1). Once the supply of "surplus" labor from the traditional farm sector has been absorbed, the marginal cost of labor supplied to the modern sector turns upward (as it does to the right of L_2) and the growth in demand for labor by industry slows, because fewer profits are available for reinvestment.

Why might the wage rate in industry increase and the demand for labor stop shifting out? First, surplus labor in agriculture might be used up, so industry would have to offer higher wages to compete with agriculture for labor. Second, food production will start to decline if fewer than N_2 workers are employed in the agricultural sector. If population is increasing and incomes in the industrial sector are rising, then the demand for food will rise. Unless an increase in agricultural production occurs, agricultural prices eventually rise relative to industrial prices. This rise, in turn, raises the wage at which employers are able to obtain workers from agriculture for industry. The major implication is that economic growth becomes constrained unless there is technological improvement in both sectors.

The labor-surplus dual-economy model is a highly simplified view of the situation in countries with under-employed people. It has several limitations. First, evidence indicates that few if any situations exist where the marginal product of labor in agriculture is near zero. Few countries have excess labor in agriculture. However, Jorgenson and others have pointed out that the presence of an active labor market in which the two sectors compete for labor can generate the same implication of the need for technological improvement in both sectors. Second, the model ignores the possibility of international trade, although it could be added without much difficulty. Third, and more importantly, the model fails to recognize the cost of resources used in conducting research and educating farmers to produce more and facilitate adoption of new technologies. The issue of how to endogenize (build in the process for self-generating) the development of new technologies in a model of economic development was not addressed. Despite these limitations, it is a useful means of thinking about linkages between multiple economic sectors in a developing-country context and, importantly, shows why industrial development needs concurrent growth in agricultural productivity.

Dependency theory and trade protectionism

In the 1950s and 1960s, some development theorists saw international trade and investment as a cause of rather than a remedy for poverty in low-income areas, arguing that trade made the poor increasingly dependent and weak. **Immanuel Wallerstein**, for example, popularized the idea that prosperity of the "center" was linked to the impoverishment of the "periphery". *Dependency theory* encompassed a range of arguments, generally leading to the conclusion that the governments of low-income countries should protect their local economies from foreign trade and investment, pursuing self-sufficiency as a form of political and economic independence.

A few dependency theorists, notably **Andre Gunder Frank**, adopted a Marxist perspective that the income of wealthy countries was derived from the output of poor countries. In this view, wealthy countries use military and political power to limit poor countries' options, and thereby extract income that would otherwise belong to the poor. Expropriation of this type clearly did occur in the colonial period and through certain other interventions, although most economic historians believe it explains only a tiny fraction of the wealth in industrialized countries.

A more widely accepted set of ideas came from *structural* economists such as **Raul Prebish** and **Hans Singer**, who argued that market forces limit the degree to which poor countries can develop through trade with richer countries. In this view, the terms of trade (the ratio of prices of exports to prices of imports) tend to turn against developing countries over time, because they produce mainly primary products (agricultural and mineral) for which prices decline over time relative to the manufactured products they import. This deterioration in the *terms of trade* is believed to be generated by (1) low price and income elasticities of demand for primary products compared to manufactured products, (2) slow productivity growth in primary product production, and (3) monopolistic elements in the production of products imported by developing countries while primary products are produced competitively. To the extent that demand for poor countries' exports is price- and income-inelastic, then output expansion in the poor countries or in the world as a whole does indeed worsen poor countries' terms of trade, although this influence can explain only a fraction of the income gap between rich and poor countries.

The trade restrictions favored by dependency theorists could also be justified by much older arguments in favor of government intervention to protect domestic markets from foreign competitors, notably the idea that *infant industries* can get started only if they are temporarily protected from foreign competition, and the idea that a *big push* to expand many industries simultaneously could help countries take advantage of synergies among them. In the decades that followed, however, it became increasingly clear that industrialization aimed at replacing imports for the domestic market could generate only a temporary burst of economic growth. Countries that allowed freer trade generally grew more rapidly.

Growth versus poverty alleviation

The 1970s witnessed a shift in development thinking toward the importance of targeting poverty alleviation directly rather than relying on the benefits of economic growth trickling down to the masses. The economies of many of the newly independent countries in sub-Saharan Africa were stagnating, but also concerning was the high level of poverty still present in rapidly growing nations in East Asia and Latin America. It was clear that growth, while necessary, was not sufficient for poverty alleviation. Growth needed to be more *pro-poor*. Some development economists such as Chenery suggested taxing gains from growth and redistributing them to the poor. Others such as **Irma Adelman** suggested that redistribution was needed before growth, advocating for land reform, widespread education, support for small-holder farming in integrated rural development programs, and direct public support for societal safety nets.

The 1960s to 1980s also saw release of several improved rice and wheat varieties, with widespread adoption in Asia and Latin America, as part of the *green revolution*, described in more detail in Chapter 11. These varieties, combined with complementary irrigation and chemical inputs, raised yields and incomes significantly and reduced hunger in those regions. Agricultural growth combined with labor-intensive industrial growth and increased public spending contributed to overall economic growth and poverty reduction.

The period of rapid growth and pro-poor policies came to sudden stop for many countries in 1982, especially in Latin America, Africa, and some Asia countries, due to a massive external debt crisis, details of which are discussed in Chapter 18. These debts required countries to scale back public spending, liberalize trade, and privatize public enterprises. Austerity programs were implemented as part of this *structural adjustment* that helped to balance budgets but slowed economic growth and poverty reduction, especially in the 1980s, which has been called the *lost development decade* in Latin America and Africa.

Structural adjustment was viewed more as a macroeconomic rebalancing away from excessive public involvement in economies and toward increased roles for private markets. China had begun liberalizing its markets beginning in 1979, spurring rapid growth and poverty reduction. However, structural adjustment policies, supported or required by lenders as part of debt rescheduling, exacted a heavy cost in terms of foregone economic growth and rising poverty. Institutions were lacking in most countries for the private sector to respond rapidly, and already porous safety nets became sieves.

New growth theory

By the 1990s, statistics on national income across countries were available for researchers to test the basic predictions of the standard growth model, posited 30 years earlier by Robert Solow. The Solow model predicted that poor countries would eventually catch up to rich ones, because of diminishing returns to capital. Statistical tests showed that this type of "convergence" did indeed occur, but only among sub-groups of countries. The highest-income group of countries continued to grow with no sign of diminishing returns, while some poorer countries grew even faster to catch up, and other poor countries just stayed poor.

Economic theorists attempted to explain these results. **Robert Lucas, Paul Romer**, and others showed how rich countries' growth could be explained by a flow of new technologies, which help overcome diminishing returns. Their models hinge on the idea that new knowledge is a public good: once discovered, it can be used repeatedly in new technologies without being used up, and so technological innovations can accumulate without limit. But not all countries are able to generate or use these innovations.

What determines whether a country develops and applies appropriate new techniques? Knowledge itself is a public good, whose development and dissemination depend on public education and government-funded research. Individuals and private firms will never have enough incentive to invest as much in these resources as they are worth to society as a whole. But knowledge is economically valuable only when embodied in goods and services that meet consumer needs. Successful countries design institutions or societal rules that promote both public knowledge and encourage private enterprise.

A key question is the extent to which innovators should be given monopoly rights over the sale of new products, through patents and other forms of intellectual property rights. Government-enforced protection from imitators is a double-edged sword: it makes each invention more profitable than it otherwise would be, but it does so by restricting its use! The patent policies that are most economically successful limit the scope and duration of protection just enough to reward past innovators, while encouraging others to make use of the innovation. The British and U.S. patent systems were early pioneers in this regard, offering protection only to a specific product (to allow the entry of other, somewhat similar products), and limiting the time period of protection (to hasten the entry of other firms), while allowing competitors to challenge others' patents in the judicial system.

New institutional economics

It is clear that resource endowments and technologies are effective as sources of growth only if they operate in a conducive institutional environment. The importance of the rule of law, enforceable property rights and contracts, absence of serious government distortions to markets, and relatively low levels of corruption are crucial to economic development. In the 1980s, **Douglas North** stressed that the high costs of transacting prevent many countries from realizing improved levels of living. Improved information flows may help reduce the cost of transacting and make it more difficult for inefficient economic and institutional structures to survive. We return to the issue of how to reduce transactions costs in Chapter 11.

In the 1990s, **Mancur Olson** argued that a comparison of levels of living in countries with similar climates and natural resource bases, such as Haiti and the Dominican Republic, with similar population densities, such as Bangladesh and the Netherlands, and with similar cultures, such as North Korea and South Korea, makes it clear that climate, population density, and culture are not the primary determinants of why some countries develop economically and others do not. He argued that technological knowledge, if not technologies themselves, are transferrable across borders, so it is not the absence of technical knowledge that is most crucial for development. When someone from Haiti migrates to the United States, they earn on average more than a person in Haiti but less than a person already living in the United States. When a U.S. person moves to Haiti and takes a Haitian job, they typically earn more than a Haitian but less than when they were in the United States. Olson argued that the differences in wages stem from two factors: educational differences of the individuals and institutional differences in the countries, with latter being most important factor.

Daron Acemoglu and **James Robinson** subsequently expanded on these ideas and carefully documented the historical economic and political institutional structures for a large set of countries. They made a convincing argument that differences in economic development can be largely explained by the presence of inclusive economic and political institutions. They argued that pluralistic political institutions lead to inclusive economic institutions and incentives for entrepreneurial activity and economic growth. What nations can do to attain such pluralistic political institutions is the relevant question. Current institutions were shaped by history but are susceptible to change given the right circumstances and inducements.

The new globalization

The post-World War II period witnessed a gradual opening up of international trade, first in industrial products and then agriculture. The Global Agreement on Tariffs and Trade (GATT), initially signed by almost 100 nations, established basic rules for a world trading system and provided a forum for multilateral (multi-nation) trade negotiations. The goal was to implement rules for trade that would lead to mutually advantageous reductions in trade restrictions. The GATT grew in importance and success, although relatively little attention was paid to restrictions on agriculture, textiles, and clothing, sectors of importance for many developing countries. Negotiations in the late eighties and early nineties addressed these sectors, and many developing countries signed on to the new World Trade Organization, which replaced the GATT. Hundreds of smaller bilateral and regional agreements were also established. The North American Free Trade Agreement (NAFTA), which lowered trade restrictions between the United States, Mexico, and Canada, is an example.

Developing countries have also been affected by the revolution since 1990 in information and communication technology (ICT). Long distance information sharing has risen dramatically as computing power and telecommunications access have expanded exponentially and access to email and web-based platforms has become ubiquitous. ICT innovations have been adopted rapidly around the world. Combined with continued reductions in shipping cost and reduced tariffs, these innovations have contributed to a shift in the production share of manufacturing and services to developing countries.

These changes have contributed to a major restructuring of the global economy. Industries that can move, including most manufacturing, have shifted to areas of low-cost production. These shifts are dynamic as witnessed by the rise of clothing manufacturing in Central America and the Caribbean, followed by its subsequent movement to China and then to South Asia. The global restructuring has brought broad benefits to consumers, who pay less for food and manufactured goods than in the past. It has contributed to dramatically lower poverty rates, as people in lower-income countries benefit from income increases associated with employment in manufacturing and tradeable services. Shares of overall global income have risen substantially in countries such as China, India, Brazil, Indonesia, Nigeria, Mexico, Poland, and Turkey. Some developed countries, such as Australia and Korea, have experienced growth in their shares as well, but others, such as the United States, Japan, Germany, Italy, Great Britain, France, and Canada, have seen them shrink.

Globalization has not, however, been uniformly good. While average incomes have grown since 1990 in most countries, benefits have been unevenly distributed. In many developed countries, wages received by large shares of the population have stagnated, partly due to globalization and partly to technical change that has automated many manufacturing processes. While economic growth in some poorer countries has lowered global inequality, within many countries, inequality has reached unprecedented levels. Growing inequality and stagnating wages have led to popular discontent as political systems and other institutions have failed to adjust to the challenges created by wage stagnation and movement of manufacturing.

Increases in population and income are creating pressures on global resources and the environment. As a result, concerns have risen about the sustainability of economic development. The poor often suffer most from environmental damage, with livelihoods in farm households especially tied to the health of soil, water, and climate, but growing incomes have contributed to growing demands for products that place more stress on the environment. Development economists have turned increased attention to institutions related to property rights and policies that affect control over environmental resources. Theories and models address the multidimensionality of economic development, focusing on the roles of the state versus private markets in preserving the global commons while improving economic well-being (see Chapter 9).

DESIGNING A DEVELOPMENT STRATEGY

The concept of a *development strategy* implies a long-term road map that encompasses fundamental decisions with respect to: emphasis on agriculture versus the nonagricultural sectors, international market orientation (inward versus outward), focus on economic growth versus distribution and sustainability, and the appropriate roles for the public and private sectors. Many of these decisions present conflicting choices for countries when they design their development strategies. The appropriate path for a particular country depends on its starting characteristics and global economic conditions.

Sectoral emphasis

The issue of how much to invest in agriculture versus nonagricultural sectors is a recurring theme for policymakers in discussions about economic development strategies. In most countries, agriculture is initially the dominant sector, containing most of society's resources. It also contains the poorest and least politically influential people and so is often neglected by government. Investments in agriculture are slowed by this weak political base, but other factors inhibit such investments. Impacts of agricultural productivity growth can be difficult to observe. An increase in farm output generally leads to an increase in *other* activity, as farmers invest their resources in non-farm enterprises, and a lower cost of food helps non-farmers buy more of other things. So, agriculture appears to be a slow-growth sector, even as it drives the expansion of other sectors. Politicians generally want to please urban constituents and may adopt policies to lower food prices, which in turn reduce the profitability of investments in agriculture. Despite evidence that investments in agriculture lower poverty by more than investments in other economic sectors, there is usually stronger political pressure for urban investments and for policies that produce immediate, highly visible results.

The degree to which governments support agriculture also depends on world market conditions: in the late 1960s and early 1970s, the threat of food scarcity associated with Asian population growth led many countries to invest heavily in irrigation and crop breeding to raise agricultural productivity, especially within Asia. During the 1980s and 1990s, the payoff from those investments produced a relative abundance of food on world markets, which reduced demand for further investment, even in regions such as Africa where food was increasingly scarce. Agricultural markets tightened again in the mid-2000s, due in part to those lower investments in agriculture in the 1980s and 1990s, in part to increased demands in fast-growing countries in Asia, and in part due to growth in use of agricultural products for bio-fuels. The resulting higher prices for food once again stimulated public and private investments in agriculture. However, the last decade has seen steady reductions in these investments for many of the reasons previously mentioned.

Agricultural growth is a key contributor to industrialization and overall structural transformation in which the shares of employment and income in agriculture decline relative to other sectors. It is also essential for reducing poverty and hunger for the poorest segments of society and for delivering a host of environmental services. Agricultural growth is especially important in sub-Saharan Africa, where many of the rural poor are farmers and local economies depend on agriculture.

International market orientation

The debate persists among policymakers about the merits of an inward-(import-substitution, self-sufficiency) versus an outward-oriented strategy (relatively open trade, export promotion). Some observers have argued that developing countries are hurt by trade because they produce mainly primary products for which prices decline over time relative to the manufactured products they import. Proponents of an inward strategy argue that countries following an inward-oriented path suffer less from debt crises and protectionist policies in the developed countries. They also argue that protection from global competition may be needed until young industries are large enough to compete.

The impact of inward-directed strategies depends largely on the policies used to implement the strategy. Policies such as overvalued exchange rates, import tariffs, and explicit export taxes, which discourage exports and stimulate substitution of domestically produced goods for imports, have generally been shown to be counterproductive. They lead to distortions in resource prices and create monopoly profits, high government budget deficits, and inflationary pressures. Policies supporting production of foods for internal consumption via research, infrastructure, and other public investments can be called inward-oriented but are not associated with most of the distortions caused by measures typically used to promote import-substitution.

Proponents of outward strategies argue that by removing biases against exports, countries can achieve significant economic benefits from specialization and comparative advantage, from the import of products manufactured by highly capital-intensive industries abroad, and from the stimulus to employment provided by reduced pressures to concentrate capital in a limited number of capital-intensive industries. Economies of scale can be achieved due to enlargement of the effective market size. However, some countries that have been successful at promoting export-led growth, such as China, have, in fact, also relied on government support of exporting industries.

Theoretical arguments support either position. However, over the past four decades empirical evidence is weighted in favor of an outward-looking strategy that biases the economy neither for nor against exports. Evidence shows that policies often used to create an inward-looking strategy can lead to inefficiency. The economic efficiencies sacrificed in attempts to insulate a country from world market forces can be significant. Open markets expose a country to the effects of protectionist policies and interest rate fluctuations abroad. However, they also offer insurance against risks originating at home.

Many developing countries have a comparative advantage in exporting sugar, but face protectionist sugar policies in developed countries

Outward-looking strategies will be most successful if international markets are truly competitive and if access to markets is unrestricted. Until the last decade or so, international trade agreements, covered later in this book, moved world markets toward more transparency and fewer trade restrictions. Recently, trade restrictions have grown, in part arising from nationalist tendencies in developed countries and reciprocal actions by those affected.

Growth versus equity

The persistence of abject poverty even in some developing countries experiencing rapid economic growth, together with growing inequality in developed countries, has spurred a debate over the appropriate focus of development efforts. Most of us accept the goal of lifting as many people as possible out of extreme poverty, but ideas compete on how to do it. Essentially three general approaches have been suggested, sometimes in combination. The first is to make direct transfer payments (money, goods, services) from the more well-to-do to the poor. The second is to concentrate on growth as a goal, no matter who receives the income, in the expectation that some of the benefits will trickle down to the poor. A third is to direct specific efforts toward raising the productivity of the poorest segments of society during the growth process.

Direct transfer payments can be unaffordable for the poorest developing countries unless supported by international aid. The most important role of direct transfers may occur (1) during short-run weather-induced famines, unusually high food price spikes, pandemics, or other emergency situations and (2) among the perpetually disadvantaged elderly, orphaned, and handicapped.

The majority of the poor in most developing countries, however, are the unemployed and under-employed rural landless. Even unskilled urban workers are usually better off than the rural landless. The landless live close to the margin and may fall below it during bad crop years. Therefore, the important question is whether the benefits of growth will trickle down to the poor or whether development efforts must be directed at the poor.

During rapid growth, some benefits are captured by the poor. However, the income distribution often will worsen (become more unequal) during initial stages of growth unless specific efforts are directed toward incorporating the poor into productive activities. The poor can be bypassed by growth-oriented investments, especially when possession of assets, particularly land and education, is skewed. Countries that begin with a more equal distribution of assets tend to experience growth with equity more than others. Growth usually stagnates under conditions of extremely inequitable asset distribution. Growth itself can be affected by the wider spread of assets, institutional changes, and employment-creating activities.

The mere widening of the income distribution within a country as development occurs is not as much a concern as what happens to income *levels* of the poor. Neither the level nor the distribution of income will be improved for the poor in most countries unless they have improved access to assets such as land and education that can make their primary asset, labor, more productive during the growth process. Development strategies that increase employment opportunities and promote the supply of wage goods (mainly food) will have the best chances for reducing poverty under virtually all circumstances.

Sustaining the environment for future generations is another important distributional issue. Water pollution, soil erosion, and greenhouse gas emissions may impose economic, health, and environmental costs today, but result in even larger and in some cases massive costs for future generations. Many of the currently developed countries ignored these costs when they were rapidly growing, causing some developing countries to argue that they should as well if they hope to grow and escape poverty. The difficulty is that population densities are higher in many developing countries today and past pollution has accumulated to the point that all countries must contribute to their reduction or all will suffer the consequences. However, the case can made for financial support from rich countries to developing nations to compensate for past transgressions and to make it feasible for all to benefit in the future.

Private versus public

The appropriate mix of public and private involvement in an economy varies by country and by sector. Some services are almost always best provided using public funds, such as an independent judicial system and roads. These are *public goods*, whose provision is limited by *free rider* problems: people can benefit without paying, so government intervention is needed to force everyone to pay a share of their costs. Other activities can be funded voluntarily through private activity, but must be regulated by the public sector or they will be provided inefficiently.

Activities that are typically regulated by government, if not provided directly in the public sector, include *natural monopolies* such as water supplies, or services with *positive externalities* such as sanitation, health, and education. Too little of these services would be provided by private firms without government intervention. On the other hand, unregulated firms would provide too many goods that generate *negative externalities* such as pollution.

The outcome of interactions between the public and private sectors is often determined not by who does what, but by the degree of transparency and accountability in what they do. Private firms that can be held accountable to their investors and customers tend to work efficiently, as do public institutions that are accountable to voters and taxpayers. Either kind of institution can become corrupt and inefficient in the absence of appropriate checks and balances.

A useful way to explain the degree of accountability in the economy, over both public and private institutions, is through the relative size of *transactions costs* in the market or political system. Lower transactions costs typically make either system more accountable to a larger number of people. Easier transactions between customers and suppliers make the market more efficient, and easier transactions between citizens and their government usually make the public sector more efficient.

A range of institutional arrangements can keep transactions costs low and sustain checks and balances over time. Private markets should be regulated by public institutions, and the public sector must be kept accountable to private individuals. Otherwise, even if new technologies are available, growth can be hindered by inefficient institutions.

Many examples of inefficient institutional structures exist in the world. In developing countries, these inefficient institutions constrain economic growth, create incentives for strategic capture by favored groups, and can contribute to short-term economic crises. In developed countries, they also can cause periodic problems, such as the 2008 financial crisis, which was facilitated by lax financial regulations with limited oversight. Achieving the appropriate balance of institutional efficiency and accountability is difficult but critical for economic development.

SUMMARY

Early development theories followed a mercantilist view in which exports were superior to imports for creating economic growth. The classical model of economic growth stressed the importance of diminishing returns to labor as a constraint to growth, and the mid-twentieth-century Solow model stressed diminishing returns to capital. Contemporary experience, however, shows how countries with institutions that reward innovation can sustain rapid economic growth by breaking these constraints.

Growth-stage theories attempted to categorize the growth process into successive stages through which countries must pass as they develop. Dual-economy models focused on movement of labor out of agriculture and how the agricultural transformation can be smoothed by balanced growth in both sectors. Dependency theorists argued that developing countries become increasingly exploited as they become more integrated into world markets, and so should withdraw into self-sufficiency. Each of these classes of theories provides some insights into the development process but are not a comprehensive theory of growth and development.

Contemporary development strategies recognize the role of agriculture as an engine of economic growth. Agricultural growth, driven mainly by technical change with supporting institutions, frees up labor and other resources that can be used in other sectors. It helps alleviate poverty by improving food availability and stimulating broad-based employment growth. Most economists agree that international trade should be kept relatively open, and that governments should provide public goods, promote innovation, regulate monopolies, make markets more efficient, and ensure environmental sustainability. The exact development strategy for each country depends on its resource mix, stage of development, and institutional structure. New institutional arrangements need to be designed in many countries to enhance information flows and lower transactions costs, to make markets more efficient, and to promote accountability in the public and private sectors.

IMPORTANT TERMS AND CONCEPTS

Capital-led growth
Center and periphery
Classical model
Colonialism
Comparative advantage
Corn Laws
Dependency theory
Employment-led growth
Export-led growth
Growth stage theory
Growth versus equity
Harrod–Domar model

Import substitution
Income distribution
Institutional arrangements
Labor-surplus dual-economy
Mercantilism
Open versus closed economy
Public goods
Stage of development
Terms of trade
Accountability
Transactions costs

LOOKING AHEAD

In this chapter, the roles of agriculture in economic development were mentioned along with the need for countries to have development strategies. In much of the rest of the book, we will be examining how to develop the agricultural sector itself. Before we do that, however, it is important to discuss the nature of existing agricultural systems in developing countries. In the next chapter, we discuss the characteristics of traditional agriculture and agricultural systems.

QUESTIONS FOR DISCUSSION

1 What is the major factor that is hypothesized to constrain economic growth in the classical model?
2 What are the major features of the labor-surplus dual-economy model and what are its primary weaknesses?
3 Why might the wage rate eventually increase in the industrial sector in the labor-surplus dual-economy model?
4 What implications does technological change in the agricultural sector have in the labor-surplus dual-economy model?

5 What is the distinguishing feature of dependency theories? What are the policy implications of dependency theories?

6 Why might growing inequality in some countries endanger growth prospects?

7 Why is agricultural development important in most developing countries?

8 What is employment-led growth and why is employment important to development?

9 What are the arguments for and against inward- versus outward-oriented development strategies?

10 What are the three general approaches that have been suggested for alleviating abject poverty?

11 Why might both the private and public sectors have important roles to play in development?

12 Why are inclusive economic and political institutions important for development?

NOTES

1 Alain de Janvry and Elizabeth Sadoulet, *Development Economics: Theory and Practice* (New York: Routledge, 2016), p. 123.

2 Richard Baldwin, *The Great Convergence: Information Technology and the New Globalization* (Cambridge, MA: Harvard University Press, 2016), p. 49.

RECOMMENDED READINGS

Acemoglu, Daron, and James A. Robinson, *Why Nations Fail* (New York: Random House, 2012), Chapters 1–3.

Baldwin, Richard, *The Great Convergence: Information Technology and the New Globalization* (Cambridge, MA: Harvard University Press, 2016), Chapter 1.

De Janvry, Alain, and Elizabeth Sadoulet, *Development Economics: Theory and Practice* (New York: Routledge Press, 2016), Chapter 3.

Olson, Mancur, Jr., "Big Bills Left on the Sidewalk: Why Some Nations Are Rich and Others Are Poor", *Journal of Economic Perspectives*, vol. 10 (Spring 1996), pp. 3–24.

PART 3

Agricultural systems and resource use

Traditional farm in Nepal

7 Agriculture in traditional societies

THIS CHAPTER

1 Describes the common characteristics of traditional agriculture
2 Discusses how traditional farmers make decisions about their livelihoods
3 Discusses implications of characteristics of traditional farming systems for agricultural development

CHARACTERISTICS OF TRADITIONAL AGRICULTURE

Agricultural development has a key role to play in solving poverty, hunger, health, and environmental problems in the world. Before considering how to foster such development, it helps to consider the nature of agriculture in developing countries. It is difficult to design solutions that address agricultural development problems without an understanding of existing agricultural systems. This chapter focuses on traditional agriculture and Chapter 8 on a broader set of agricultural systems around the world.[1]

The term *traditional agriculture* conveys part of its own meaning. The word "traditional" means "to do things the way they have usually been done". Because natural resources, culture, history, and other factors vary from place to place, the way things have usually been done also differs greatly from one location to another. And, because conditions change, no type of farming system, no matter how traditional, is ever completely stable. A major challenge for agricultural development is to stimulate improvements in production practices and introduce higher value products that transform traditional farms into modernized farms with higher incomes. To do so, we need to understand the common characteristics found in traditional agriculture.

Livelihoods and the intermixing of farm and family decisions

Traditional agriculture takes several forms, but small farms predominate in most developing countries. Farm families have access to many types of assets, including human labor, land, physical capital such as equipment, financial capital, natural assets, and social and political assets. Farmers make decisions about how to use their assets in production, labor supply, consumption, and other activities, and these decisions reflect their "livelihood strategies". Production and consumption decisions are generally intermixed on traditional farms. For example, in remote areas in Bolivia, farmers produce a number of potato varieties, some for sale. However, some varieties are needed for families and guests during festivals; these varieties are often not available in local markets. The cultural requirement that such varieties should be available at these times affects household planting decisions. The importance of the family and the close relationship between production and consumption decisions occur because much of the labor, management, and capital come from the same household. A portion of the production is consumed on the farm and in the local community where it is produced. Farms may innovate using their resources, but the pace is slower without the use of modern inputs. Success in the farm enterprise may enhance nutritional status, which, can in turn lead to higher productivity, but production growth in traditional agriculture tends to track the rate of population growth.

Assets are often allocated to multiple activities, including on- and off-farm labor, with the latter coming inside and outside of agriculture. Households adopt diversified livelihood strategies in part to manage risks and partly to make up for missing markets. This intermixing of production and consumption decisions along with the low levels of income common among small-scale farms add elements of conservatism to family farming (see Box 7.1). A farm disaster usually means a family disaster. Consequently, traditional farms use crop varieties and breeds of livestock that have proven to be dependable under adverse conditions, such as low fertility or rough terrain, even if yields or productivities are modest.

For example, in some regions of the world cassava is grown on a portion of a farmer's land, with other portions devoted to more productive food or cash crops. Cassava grows slowly and has low value, but it grows on relatively poor soils and under a variety of weather conditions. It is a root

BOX 7.1 KEFA VILLAGE IN EASTERN ZAMBIA

The anthropologist Else Skjonsberg visited Kefa Village first in 1977 and several times since. Her book *Change in an African Village: Kefa Speaks* portrays a traditional agricultural system in Eastern Africa. Villagers in Kefa depend on land, which is controlled and allocated by the local chief. Some inherit cultivation rights from their parents, others request unused land from the chief, and others borrow land from relatives and neighbors. When land shortages arise, groups of villagers break away and search other areas for unused lands.

Households cultivate 1–4 hectares, with maize, groundnuts, sweet potatoes, and pumpkins produced for own consumption, and tobacco and cotton produced for sale. Fortunate farmers have access to wetland dambos, where they grow vegetables year-round. The agricultural year starts before the first rains in October, when the ground is broken by hand hoes. Maize, the most important food crop, is planted first, weeded first, and harvested first. Most villagers plant open-pollinated maize varieties, which have been used for generations. Maize is stored in granaries and in years of abundance it is used to brew beer or sell. Groundnuts are rotated with maize to maintain soil fertility and provide dietary protein. Hybrid maize varieties, with higher yields and shorter growing seasons, have been introduced, but most Kefa villagers are suspicious of their quality and only produce them for sale. Hybrids require purchased fertilizer, and in dryland farming, exposure to risk invites trouble. Many believe use of fertilizers will breed dependency and bring ruin to adventurous farmers.

Family members share work responsibilities. Women prepare meals, carry them to the fields, hand-cultivate all day, then return home with pots and pans, loads of firewood, and water. During December and January, the women take responsibility for weeding. It takes as long as three weeks to weed a hectare of maize, so family time is fully occupied. On rainy days, men make repairs around their huts, while women manage household affairs. When labor is scarce, some mobilize workers by throwing home-brewed beer parties; others trade labor and work together. During April through June, labor is in short supply and entire villages participate in harvests. Women are chiefly responsible for harvest, but men and older children assist. Women headload food crops in 50-kilogram bags from the fields to storage bins. In rare cases where oxen or motorized transport is used, men take responsibility for the task.

Although agriculture is the main source of well-being in Kefa, livelihoods are complex, and all households engage in nonagricultural activities. Some brew and sell beer, others practice crafts such as weaving or woodworking, many engage in petty trading, and others are healers, scribes, or have specialized skills. Cattle raising and off-farm incomes supplement farm incomes and help families buy farm and household equipment, clothes, and blankets and pay for services such as school fees. Off-farm activities are divided by gender; women brew and sell beer, trade, and weave, while men more often have specialized skills, work with wood, or do repairs. Incomes earned in these activities are held separately by men and women, and women are eager to engage in such activities because the money they earn provides them a degree of autonomy in decision-making.

Families in Kefa are structured in different ways. Only about half of the households are nuclear in the sense of two parents and children. About a third of households are headed by women, some divorced or widowed, some whose husbands are absent. Children participate actively in household economic life; by age 5 most contribute to household tasks and past 8 years, farm work increases. Boys are responsible for tending cattle, while girls assist their mothers in the house and care for younger siblings. Most children attend schools, but are excused during periods of peak agricultural labor. The elderly live with their families or are cared for by family members. The poorest of the poor have few relatives and depend on handouts from other villagers.

crop that can be pulled from the ground at different times when other foods may be short, and represents a form of informal insurance or savings.

Traditional farm households often consume many of their products at home, but the surplus they trade or sell connects them to the market as small commercial farmers. Surpluses traded or sold by traditional farms vary by country and by region, but few farms are entirely subsistence in the sense that they consume all they produce. Consequently, traditional farms are influenced by market price relationships in asset allocation decisions. Prices also affect choices of farmers to allocate their time to agricultural production versus other activities. If prices rise for their products, farmers earn additional income and may even choose to produce less, depending on their preferences for goods versus leisure.

The percentage of the total output that is marketed may be planned or unplanned and vary from year to year as production fluctuates with weather and other factors.

Labor and land use

Traditional farms are generally quite small, often only 1 to 3 hectares (about 2.5 to 7.5 acres). Labor applied per hectare planted, however, may be high and may increase with modernization as management intensifies. In many regions, land is a limiting factor and is becoming more limiting over time as populations continue to grow. Labor is often under-employed at certain times of the year. Much sharing of work and income occurs on traditional farms, so there is little open unemployment during slack times. This sharing means that the individual's wage may be determined by the average rather than the marginal productivity of labor, especially on farms with large families. However, there is little evidence that the marginal productivity of labor is zero or even close to it as posited by Lewis's dual-economy model discussed in Chapter 6. As a part of diversified livelihood strategies, family members often work off the farm part time, sometimes on neighboring farms, sometimes in other areas as they seasonally migrate. Petty trading, often carried out by women, is a common off-farm livelihood strategy.

Although family labor is important, traditional farms may hire some labor, at least during the busy times of the year. Low wages caused by under-employment in traditional agriculture create incentives to hire laborers. Traditional farmers can hire labor or buy a small amount of leisure and enhance their social status at relatively low cost. The people with the lowest economic and social status usually are not the owners of small traditional farms, but landless workers who are hired by those farmers.

Seasonality

Labor use in traditional agriculture varies seasonally along with agricultural cycles. During slack seasons, those immediately following planting or preceding harvest, labor may be abundant. However, during peak seasons, especially during weeding and harvest, labor can be in short supply. Wages often exhibit similar seasonal fluctuations. The seasonal nature of agricultural production can cause variations in consumption and nutritional status, particularly in African settings. Because storage facilities may be lacking and mechanisms for saving and borrowing may be incomplete, consumption patterns can follow agricultural cycles. It is common to find "lean seasons", when consumption is low and short-run malnutrition high, especially immediately prior to harvest (see Box 7.2).

BOX 7.2 SEASONAL MIGRATION:
A RATIONAL RESPONSE

Seasonal weather patterns cause traditional farmers to adopt production and consumption patterns to help smooth variations. Seasonality also induces migration as people search for employment opportunities and food. Other seasonal causes of migration are trade and marketing, cultivation of secondary landholding, and pasturing cattle. Seasonal migration is a worldwide phenomenon. In some rainfed areas of Africa, 30 to 40 percent of the economically active population migrates; in Guatemala, the annual coffee harvest induces widespread migration, while in rural Nepal as much as 30 percent of the households have at least one member who migrates.

Why does seasonal migration occur? During the lean season, labor demands on the farm are low, incomes are stretched, and food can be in short supply. Other rural regions may have crop conditions (due to environmental factors, technologies, or irrigation) that alter the agricultural calendar and create counter-cyclical demands for workers. Large plantations commonly producing many export crops also demand labor on a seasonal basis. Seasonal rural-to-urban migration involves workers migrating to towns, cities, and mines in search of work. These reasons combine to push migrants out of regions where their labor is temporarily in surplus and pull them into areas with high demands.

Seasonal migration is not inefficient nor is it caused by factors such as imperfect labor markets. It is a natural adaptation to highly seasonal agricultural cycles and can smooth family incomes and consumption. Seasonal migration also provides insurance; in the event of a crop failure, family income can be maintained in the short run by migration.

Seasonal labor flows have benefited countries by minimizing labor shortages in harvest times. Exports of cocoa and coffee from forest regions of Western Africa are largely made possible by seasonal migrants who provide labor during harvest. Other regions of the world have seen their total production possibilities shift outward as labor moves to fill seasonal gaps.

Source: Material was drawn from David E. Sahn (ed.), *Causes and Implications of Seasonal Variability in Household Food Security* (Baltimore: Johns Hopkins University Press, 1987)

Productivity and efficiency

Traditional farms are characterized by low use of purchased inputs other than labor. Yield per hectare is often high due to high rates of family labor use, but production per person and other measures of productivity tend to be low, although productivity varies substantially by year and by region. These factors do not mean, however, that traditional farms are inefficient. As T.W. Schultz points out, drawing on field research of David Hopper and others in India, traditional farms tend to be poor but efficient. Why?

The crop varieties, power sources, methods for altering soil fertility, and certain other factors available to traditional farms constrain productivity growth, and hence reduce returns to labor and traditional types of capital. Efficiency, as measured by equating marginal returns to resources in alternative uses, is often high. In other words, given the technologies available to traditional farmers, farmers are rational and tend to do a good job of allocating labor, land, and other resources. The implication is that just reallocating the resources they currently have will not have a major impact on output.

It makes sense that with relatively unchanging physical conditions, technology, and factor costs, traditional farmers would gradually become very efficient at what they do. When conditions change rapidly, many mistakes in resource allocation occur. Also, one must be careful not to equate limited education (another common characteristic in traditional agriculture) with lack of intelligence.

A situation with low use of certain inputs and low productivity but high economic efficiency under static conditions has important implications if productivity is to be increased. First, new technologies can help to change the production possibilities available to farmers. Second, investments to improve the quantity and quality of productive assets such as land can stimulate income growth. Third, education may be needed to help farmers learn to adjust resource use to changing conditions so as to maintain their high levels of efficiency. However, under the static conditions of traditional agriculture, education will do little to improve productivity, since peasant producers are already relatively efficient.

Rationality and risk

Traditional farmers are economically rational. They are motivated to raise their standard of living while, of necessity, they are cautious. Traditional farmers are not averse to change, but proposed changes must fit into their farming systems without altering too abruptly the methods they use to reduce risk and spread labor use. Traditional farmers face many risks, including weather-related uncertainty, agricultural pests and diseases, price and market-related risks, and human health risks. Decisions often reflect attempts to manage these risks. Because formal risk management mechanisms such as insurance are often not available, traditional households turn to informal mechanisms in response to a risky environment.[2]

One mechanism by which they spread risk is by exchanging labor and other resources through joint and extended families. Joint and extended families refer to relatives (and sometimes friends) beyond parents and their children. In many countries, substantial sharing of labor and goods occurs among friends and neighbors, which builds social networks and spreads risk. Reciprocal agreements to assist others in times of need can spread risk across space, through agreements with people facing other agro-ecological conditions or in different regions, across economic sectors, through migration and work choice, and across time, through intergenerational sharing. Some of these informal arrangements deteriorate as development proceeds, creating a need for new institutional arrangements to manage risk.

Another risk-spreading mechanism is reliance on diversified livelihood strategies. Traditional farmers frequently plant multiple crops on a single plot of land in a single season. For example, maize and beans are planted together throughout Latin America; in Africa, maize is intercropped with sweet potatoes, groundnuts, and other foods, depending on the location. Intercropping reduces reliance on success in a single crop and helps manage risk. Off-farm employment and seasonal migration further diversify income sources.

Off-farm employment

Because agriculture is so visible in developing countries, it is easy to assume that rural dwellers are only farmers. In reality, in most countries, off-farm income is an important source of earnings, especially for the rural poor. Many landless and near-landless families provide labor to other farmers; these agricultural labor markets are described in more detail in Chapter 13. Others work in nonagricultural enterprises; some are self-employed, producing goods and services for sale. Non-farm employment involves small-scale rural manufacturing, transport, services, and petty trading. Income from these enterprises helps offset fluctuations in earnings from agriculture, representing a risk management strategy. It can smooth intra-year variations in on-farm labor demands.

Rural non-farm employment accounts for about 25–30 percent of income across the developing world.[3] Non-farm income is particularly important for women, who can combine their household duties such as child care with income-generating work. The percentage of rural workers in the non-farm sectors varies from country to country, but generally is in the range of 20–50 percent. Off-farm employment is a higher proportion of total employment in Asia and Latin America than in Africa, but even in Africa, it exceeds 60 percent in countries such as Botswana and Swaziland.

THE ROLES OF LIVESTOCK

Livestock play many vitally important roles in traditional farming systems. Since about 60 percent of the poor in sub-Saharan Africa and Asia are dependent on livestock for some part of their livelihoods, there is need to improve animal productivity in developing countries. Livestock systems can place pressure on the environment, while environmental stress and change have important implications for traditional producers. When crops and livestock directly compete for the same resources, it is usually more efficient for humans to consume grain than it is to feed the grain to livestock and consume meat. However, in most traditional farming systems, livestock consume little grain. Let's consider several roles of livestock and some of the factors leading to change in livestock production systems.

Buffers and extenders of the food supply
Farm animals provide a special protection to farm families, acting as a buffer between the family and a precarious food supply. Animals are like a savings bank. Farmers can invest in them, they grow, and they can be consumed or sold during crop failures. In most traditional agriculture, livestock do not directly compete with crops because they eat crop residues, feed off steep slopes and poor soils, and consume materials. This consumption actually "extends" the food supply. Many are ruminants (e.g., cattle, goats, sheep, and buffalo) eating grass and other forages that humans cannot and converting them into products for human consumption. Livestock also make important contributions to dietary quality by providing meat, milk, and eggs. Small amounts of these high-protein, nutrient-rich foods can have a significant impact on human nutrition.

A cow is a type of savings bank in Kenya

Sources of fertilizer, fuel, hides, and hair

Animal manure is vitally important as a source of fertilizer and fuel in many countries. For example, from the remote hills of Nepal to the altiplano of Bolivia, it can be difficult to obtain chemical fertilizer. Animal manure increases soil fertility and adds organic matter. In countries where wood is scarce, animal dung is dried and burned for fuel. Often, these two uses of animal manure compete. Dung that is burned cannot be used to increase soil fertility. In India and other countries, methane digesters have been developed, and the gas produced is used for cooking. Use of a methane digester allows residual nitrogen to be applied to crops.

Few livestock products are wasted in traditional society. Clothing and blankets are made from animal hides and hair of not only cattle and sheep, but also buffalo, goats, and other livestock. Straps and harnesses are made from hides, feathers have different uses, and rennet for cheese production comes from animal stomachs.

Providers of power and transport

In many countries, livestock are a significant source of power. They plow the fields, transport products to market, and are used in processing. Large investments are needed to purchase tractors, making them prohibitively expensive for traditional farmers. In some cases, tractor services can be rented, but on steep slopes and rough terrain in parts of some developing

Farmer plowing with bullock in Thailand

countries it may be years before mechanical power completely replaces animal power.

Social and cultural symbols

Livestock, particularly cattle and goats, are highly valued in some societies for social and cultural reasons. A family's social status may be measured by the number of animals it owns.[4] Cattle are given as gifts during ceremonial occasions. While livestock serve major economic functions, they serve these other social and cultural functions as well.

Changes in livestock systems

Rapid urbanization and growing incomes in many developing countries have been associated with increased demands for animal proteins as a food source. Growing demand has supported meat prices and put pressure on global livestock systems.[5] While much of this demand will be met by industrial producers, traditional farmers can play a role. This role is probably strongest in the dairy sector as cheese can be produced on a small scale. Traditional farmers, particularly those with access to grazing land, can also benefit from increased prices of beef and other ruminants.

An additional strain on livestock systems comes from climate change, which is discussed in more detail in Chapter 9. Although impacts of climate change vary by location, it is likely that substantial temperature increases will occur in many areas, with especially harsh consequences on tropical drylands, where livestock grazing predominates. Feed resources in these areas will decline along with water availability, while increased temperatures will increase livestock consumption of already scarce water.

A final challenge to livestock systems is related to their adverse impacts on the environment. Livestock often feed on steeply sloped and low-productivity lands. As a result, they contribute to loss of soil cover, soil erosion, and nutrient-laden run-off that pollutes surface water. Livestock release methane gas, which contributes to climate change.[6] It is critically important that these challenges to traditional livestock producers be met through research and policy changes that increase productivity and reduce pressures on fragile environments.

IMPLICATION OF TRADITIONAL FARMS FOR AGRICULTURAL DEVELOPMENT

Despite the common features described thus far, a striking characteristic of farms in developing countries is their diversity. How land is organized and controlled within farms, gender roles, ties to markets, use of mechanical or animal traction, institutional relationships with respect to water rights and access to irrigation, and many other factors differ markedly across regions and sometimes within countries. Many farms in sub-Saharan Africa are still quite traditional, whereas farms in most of Asia and the Pacific have begun to modernize. In the next chapter, we discuss factors that cause livelihood strategies and farming systems to change over time.

Traditional farms are efficient on average, but poor. As population grows and less land is available per farmer, poverty increases unless agriculture changes. As noted in Chapter 5, unless agricultural productivity growth outstrips population growth, rural poverty will increase over time. But change brings additional risks and the danger of increasing income disparities. The distribution of income generated through new plant varieties or power tillers can be affected by asset distribution patterns and institutions that govern the rules of behavior in society. Risks must be managed, and institutions that substitute for the historical sharing arrangements must be created. Improved transportation systems are needed to improve information flows and build market linkages.

Several Asian countries face a need to alter their farming systems and diversify out of rice. While rice will remain the dominant food commodity in the region, vegetable and livestock production become increasingly attractive because of changing consumer demands as incomes grow. In coastal areas of Asia, aquaculture is replacing rice farming, introducing additional protein sources to the diets and diversifying income sources. Additional education and non-farm employment opportunities become key elements in an overall development strategy. Otherwise, the law of diminishing returns will keep traditional farmers in poverty in the years ahead.

As incomes grow in developing regions, consumer demands change and the global economy will respond to these changes in demand. Growth in meat and milk demand will put pressure on traditional livestock grazing systems, and policies may be needed to smooth the transition to more commercially oriented confinement and open-access grazing systems. Without such policies, market-based pressures may lead to social dislocation and environmental degradation in livestock-producing areas. The aquaculture revolution suggests that extension systems must adjust to new conditions in formerly agriculture-dominated regions.

Differences in crop yields and labor use across farms within traditional agriculture suggest the potential for raising production and incomes with proper incentives. Improving access by female members of farm households to technologies and credit, for not just agricultural production but also non-farm business development, can have a sizable effect on household incomes. Women are heavily involved in traditional agriculture, as discussed in Chapter 10.

Traditional farmer in his garden in Colombia

SUMMARY

Traditional agriculture is diverse, but traditional farms have many common characteristics. Traditional agriculture is generally characterized by small farms, with intertwined farm and family decisions. Traditional farm families consume, sell, or trade most of their products locally. Their land area per farm is small, but labor input per hectare is high. Hired labor is often important. Product and labor sales and purchases mean that farmers are, in general, closely linked to the economy and respond to market signals. Productivity and use of purchased inputs may be low, but efficiency is relatively high. Traditional farmers are rational but risk averse. They often live in extended or joint families. Livestock play many roles, including extending the food supply; providing a buffer against poor harvests; improving the quality of the diet; and generating fertilizer, fuel, hides, and hair. They also provide power and transport and meet social and cultural needs. Traditional farms differ by region, and as farms change some people, particularly the landless, may be left behind unless new technologies are accompanied by improved institutions and education.

IMPORTANT TERMS AND CONCEPTS

Assets and resources
Mixed cropping
Buffers and extenders
Diversification
Rational but cautious
Intermixing of farm and
    family decisions
Joint and extended families
Landless labor

Biological technologies
Traditional agriculture
Off-farm employment
Poor but efficient
Livelihoods
Role of livestock
Seasonality
Semi-subsistence farms

LOOKING AHEAD

A wide variety of agricultural systems are found in the world. These systems evolve over time. In the next chapter, we examine the factors that influence the type of farming systems found in a particular country at a point in time. The importance of technical, human, institutional, and political factors is discussed. Several common types of agricultural systems are described and the significant roles of women and children are highlighted.

QUESTIONS FOR DISCUSSION

1 Why might traditional farms be fairly conservative or slow to change from current practices?
2 Are traditional farms subsistence farms? What is meant by "semi-subsistence?"
3 Why are livestock important in many traditional farming systems?
4 Distinguish between productivity and efficiency. Why do traditional farms tend to have high levels of efficiency? Why do they tend to have low or high levels of productivity?
5 What factors influence resource allocation on traditional farms? If a farmer fails to adopt a new, apparently more profitable farming practice, is he or she irrational?
6 If traditional farmers use resources efficiently, why should we be concerned with raising productivity by increasing the use of new technologies?
7 Are many farmers who own 1 to 3 hectares usually the poorest people in rural communities in developing countries?
8 Why are joint and extended families still important in many developing countries?
9 Why are farm and household decisions often inseparably linked in developing countries?
10 Why are institutional changes often as important as technological changes for agricultural development?
11 Why do farmers practice mixed cropping? Are agricultural diversification and mixed cropping synonymous?
12 Why is hired labor often important in traditional or semi-subsistence agriculture?
13 Why are new biological technologies often more important than new mechanical technologies for fostering agricultural development?
14 Why is agricultural diversification becoming increasingly important in many Asian countries?

NOTES

1 Agricultural or farming systems include production practices, or *how* things are produced, as well as the types of enterprises, or *what* things are produced.
2 Paul B. Siegel and Jeffrey Alwang, *An Asset Based Approach to Social Risk Management* (Washington, DC: Human Development Network, Social Protection Unit, The World Bank, SP Discussion Series 9926, October 1999).
3 See Steven Haggblade, Peter Hazell, and Thomas Reardon, *Strategies for Stimulating Poverty-Alleviating Growth in the Rural Nonfarm Economy in Developing*

Countries (Rome: International Food Policy Research Institute, EPTD Discussion Paper No. 93, 2002).

4 In nomadic societies where no individual family owns the land, animal ownership is almost the only indicator of social status.

5 Scientists at the International Livestock Research Institute (ILRI) have identified three main livestock systems: agro-pastoral and pastoral systems where natural resources are constrained and people adopt strategies to meet these constraints, smallholder crop–livestock systems where natural resources may be managed to improve productivity, and highly intensive industrial livestock systems.

6 There is a wide variance from study to study, but a reasonable estimate is that 15–20 percent of global greenhouse gas emissions come from livestock.

RECOMMENDED READINGS

Dixon, John, Aidan Gulliver, and David Gibbon, *Farming Systems and Poverty: Improving Farmers' Livelihoods in a Changing World* (Rome and Washington, DC: FAO and the World Bank, 2001).

Ellis, F., *Rural Livelihoods and Diversity in Developing Countries* (Oxford: Oxford University Press, 2000).

Mellor, John W., *Agricultural Development and Economic Transformation* (New York: Palgrave Macmillan, 2017), Chapter 6.

Skjonsberg, Else, *Change in an African Village: Kefa Speaks* (West Hartford, CT: Kumarian Press, 1989).

8 Farming systems and their determinants

THIS CHAPTER

1 Identifies factors that influence the agricultural systems found in a particular country at a point in time
2 Explores the differences in farming systems found in various parts of the world
3 Presents economic concepts that help explain input and output choices in farming systems

MAJOR DETERMINANTS OF FARMING SYSTEMS

Farming systems around the world show considerable variety and are differentiated by how production is organized, by the technologies employed, and by the types of crops and livestock produced. Each system consists of a small number of dominant crops (or livestock) and numerous minor crops (or livestock). We must understand farming and the broader food and agricultural systems if we are to improve them. In this chapter, we examine the primary determinants of the prevailing systems before classifying and describing them.

Technical, institutional, and human factors affect the type of farming system that predominates in a region. These factors interact at each location and point in time to provide a unique environment for agricultural production (Figure 8.1). When these factors remain constant for several years, the farming system that evolves represents a long-term adaptation to that environment. Different farming systems have different needs for public support such as infrastructure, legal systems, and market-related

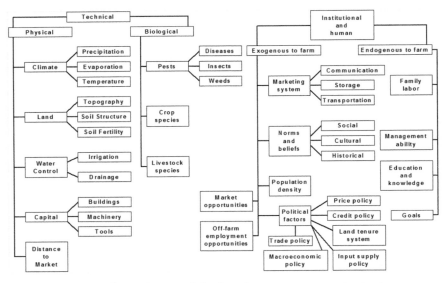

Figure 8.1 Major determinants of the farming system at a point in time

rules and norms. They also have different impacts on the natural environment and labor demand. Economic development can introduce rapid changes in underlying factors, thus placing pressure on a system.

Farming systems are the first layer of broader, often global, food and agricultural systems in the world. In addition to farming systems, the broader agricultural systems include traders, processors, retailers, policymakers, and consumers, among others. In this chapter, we focus on farming systems and in Chapter 15 on the broader food and agricultural systems.

Technical determinants of farming systems

Technical elements, including physical and biological factors, help determine the potential types of crop and livestock systems. Physical factors – including climate, land, water access, capital stock, and location relative to markets – are unique to each location, although water access and other capital stock can be altered through investments and new technologies. Similarly, investments in roads alter the relationship between physical distance and travel time. For example, nomadism, discussed below, which prevails in many arid regions, represents a long-term adaptation to harsh climates. However, the expansion of wells has encouraged more settled farming or ranching in many nomadic areas. Global climate change is likely to profoundly affect farming systems. We are already seeing adjustments to agricultural practices as weather patterns and temperatures change.

Biological factors such as pests and crop and livestock varieties are even more susceptible to modification. In the short run, however, these factors play a major role in defining the prevailing system. For example, the existence of the tsetse fly in areas of the African humid tropics has created farming systems that are dramatically different from those in similar climates where the fly does not exist. Animal traction is not an option in areas where the tsetse fly is common. Technologies to control the fly can help spread animal traction and alter traditional farming systems.

Institutional and human determinants of farming systems

Institutional and human elements influencing farming systems are characterized by exogenous (externally controlled) and endogenous (internally controlled) factors. Factors largely outside the control of farmers include social and cultural norms and beliefs, historical factors, population density, market opportunities and marketing systems, and off-farm employment opportunities. For example, high population densities in many South Asian countries are partly responsible for the very different farming systems there as compared to the systems found in the relatively low-density areas of sub-Saharan Africa and Southeast Asia. And as off-farm employment opportunities grow, some small farms evolve into part-time operations with crop and livestock activities chosen to facilitate the on- and off-farm activities.

Politically determined institutions such as pricing policies, credit policies, macroeconomic policies, trade policies, and land-tenure systems affect the farming system. Land ownership is highly skewed in many countries. In areas of Central America, for example, large commercial farms and plantations exist alongside small semi-subsistence farms. The farming practices used are largely determined by the distribution of land; plantations rely on landless and small-holding workers as suppliers of labor and the laborers mix off-farm incomes with food crops grown on their own holdings. These smallholders adopt diversified livelihood strategies within the overall context of their farming system. Prevailing patterns of land uses, crop mixes, and technologies on different-sized farms are affected by the distribution of landholdings. In many areas, people have only use-rights over the land they farm. For example, in much of Africa, under traditional tenure rules, families are given land to farm, but they cannot rent or sell it to others, and cannot use it as collateral for credit. Such land use institutions influence incentives for investments in land improvements, which, in turn, influence the prevailing farming system. The political system itself may dictate collectives, communes, or private property as the primary means of organizing land use in agriculture.

Endogenous or farmer-controlled determinants of agricultural systems include family labor, management ability, education, and knowledge, as well as the goals for which farmers are striving. Investments in education affect the value of time used on and off the farm, and as educational levels change, farming systems respond. Risk associated with agricultural production, particularly in arid, rain-fed regions, has forced farmers to adapt their practices to ensure survival. These adaptations are determined, in part, by the farmers' degree of risk aversion, which is affected by income, education, etc. Any of these factors can change over time. New technologies and population growth are two particularly important determinants of how and in what direction agricultural systems change over time.

MAJOR TYPES OF FARMING SYSTEMS

While the specific type of farming system in use depends on a large number of factors (Figure 8.1), many years ago Duckham and Masefield grouped farming systems into three basic types: shifting cultivation, pastoral nomadism, and settled agriculture (Figure 8.2).[1] Settled agriculture includes many subtypes. Let's briefly examine each of these systems.

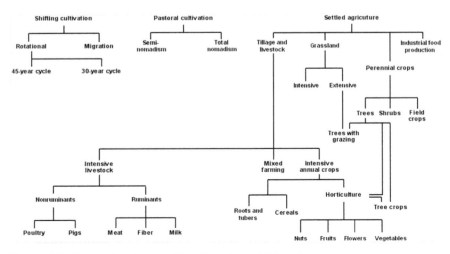

Figure 8.2 Example of a classification of world farming systems

Shifting cultivation

Shifting cultivation is an old form of agriculture still practiced in a few parts of the world. As the name implies, it involves shifting to a new piece of land when the fertility of the original patch runs out or when weeds and other pests take over. The movement may be fast or slow, and fertility-enhancing amendments such as animal manure may extend the use of one location. Migration from one piece of land to another may be random, linear, or cyclic. When cyclic, the rotation frequency can last as long as 30 to 45 years.

Shifting cultivation also has been called slash and burn because usually new areas are cleared by slashing the brush with a machete and burning it to clear the fields and release nutrients into the soil. Capital investment in the farm is low, with machetes, digging sticks, and hoes being the primary tools. Typical crops include corn, millet and sorghum, rice, and roots. Usually the crops are mixed or intercropped. Data on the extent of shifting cultivation are limited, but it appears to still be practiced on about 10 percent of the world's exploitable soils, particularly in Africa and Latin America. It is popular where population pressures are not too severe.

Shifting cultivation is frequently associated with insecure control over the land because of absentee, government, or unclear ownership status. It has been linked to soil erosion and other environmental problems in several developing countries, partly because there are few incentives to invest in practices that maintain soil fertility.

Pastoral nomadism

Pastoral nomadism involves people who travel, more or less continuously, with herds of livestock. Pastoral nomads have no established farms, but often follow well-established routes from one grazing area to another. Although there are probably only 30–40 million pastoral nomads in the world, they move through an area almost as large as the world's entire cultivated area. They are especially prevalent in the arid and semi-arid tropics. Examples include the Maasai of Kenya and Tanzania, the Hima of Uganda, the Fulani of West Africa, the Bedouin of the Eastern Mediterranean, and Mongolian nomads.

Pastoral nomadism can be total or partial. In the latter case, the nomads have homes and some cultivation for part of the year. Typically, five or six families travel together with 25 to 60 goats and sheep or 10 to 25 camels. Sometimes they own cattle as well. The livestock eat natural pasture and their productivity is low. Many partial nomads live near major cities, and it is not uncommon to see animals grazing in open lots in cities in the Middle East.

Nomads are common in the northern half of Africa
Source: Photo by Mesfin Bezuneh

Pastoral nomadism is associated with a variety of problems. Because grazing takes place on common land, there is a tendency for overgrazing because every individual farmer wishes to maximize their number of animals. As the animal population increases, grazing areas deteriorate and incomes shrink (see Box 8.1). This problem is known as the "tragedy of the commons", and ample evidence shows that traditional management systems have evolved in response to it. Little scope for technical improvement exists in pastoral nomadic systems, and serious problems arise in years of drought. From a social perspective, it is difficult to educate or provide health services to children of nomadic herders, making it difficult for them to undertake different occupations as they age. As the human population grows, additional pressures are placed on the resource base supporting the nomadic system. Global climate change presents an especially acute problem for pastoral nomad systems. Increases in temperatures will reduce pasture productivity and increase demand for water, and both factors will lower productivity. Accelerating desertification will also result lower productivity.

Settled agriculture
Settled agriculture includes a wide variety of agricultural systems such as mixed farming systems, intensive annual crops, intensive and

BOX 8.1 NOMADIC BEDOUIN IN JORDAN

In Jordan, "Badia" are rangelands generally receiving less than 200 mm of annual rainfall. The Badia cover about 80 percent of Jordan's area. Nomadic Bedouin tribes whose livelihoods were supported by animal production have occupied the Badia for centuries. Today, only about 5 percent of the Jordanian population lives in the Badia, and despite its apparent remoteness, it now houses settled populations with access to basic services such as roads, electricity, sanitation, schools, health care, and telecommunications.

Only about 5 percent of the Badia's population now lives through nomadic grazing, but the area still supports animal production; about 70 percent of Jordan's supply of animal proteins is produced there. Fertile areas are cropped, with barley being the main product grown under rain-fed conditions. Forage, vegetables, fruits, and wheat are produced under irrigated conditions in the most favorable sites. While much of the Badia's population is involved in agriculture and livestock production, residents also work in the civil service, commerce, the armed forces, and mining and prospecting industries.

Increasing population densities and poor livestock and agricultural management practices have led to serious degradation of the Badia. Overgrazing, unsustainable agricultural practices, and inappropriate water management techniques are contributing to degradation through water and wind erosion, declining soil fertility, and habitat degradation. These outcomes are driven by rapid population growth, spillovers from urban areas, and poverty, which pushes farmers and herders to adopt unsustainable practices. Agricultural policies have exacerbated some of these problems; for example, subsidized barley feed intended to mitigate dwindling vegetative cover creates incentives for higher animal densities than can be supported with natural growth, further spurring land degradation. The example of the transformation of the Badia shows the fluidity of traditional agricultural systems

Source: S. Akroush, K. Shideed, and A. Bruggeman, "Economic Analysis and Environmental Impacts of Water Harvesting Techniques in the Low Rainfall Areas of Jordan", *International Journal of Agricultural Resources, Governance and Ecology*, vol. 10(1) (2014), pp. 34–49, and T. Oweis, "Rainwater Harvesting for Restoring Degraded Dry Agro-Pastoral Ecosystems; a Conceptual Review of Opportunities and Constraints in a Changing Climate", *Environmental Reviews* (2016), doi:10.1139/er-2016-0069

extensive livestock systems, and perennial crops. The dominant farming systems result over time from an enormous amount of human experimentation. The systems we see most often produce a relatively high and certain return in storable products per unit of effort. They have spread from farmer to farmer, replacing less productive settled systems.

Mixed farming usually involves a mixture of crops and livestock. Few farming systems in developing countries consist of just one commodity. However, what is meant by mixed farming is the integration of crops and livestock production. As mentioned in Chapter 7, mixed farming is common in traditional agriculture because it produces relatively high returns while helping to manage risk, makes efficient use of labor and land, and helps maintain soil fertility.

Intensive annual crops are extremely important in the world. About 70 percent of the world's cultivated area is planted to the major grain crops, which include wheat, rice, and corn. Other important annual crops are barley, millet, sorghum, roots, tubers, vegetables, and pulses (such as beans, peas, and peanuts).

Perennial crops are grown and harvested over several years and include crops such as cocoa, coffee, bananas, and sugarcane. Some are grown in large plantations but others on very small farms as well, even in the same country. On small-scale farms, perennial crops are often *interplanted* with annual crops such as corn and beans. Perennial crops tend to be high-valued and are frequently exported. They also can help prevent soil erosion and preserve biodiversity in ecologically fragile areas.

Intensive livestock systems include both *ruminants* (for example, cattle, buffalo, sheep, and goats) that produce milk, meat, fiber, dung, and other products, and *non-ruminants* (for example, pigs and poultry) that are particularly important for their meat and eggs. These animals are often fed grains to supplement pasture and forage. In a few countries, intensive livestock systems involve carefully managed grasslands or pasture.

Extensive livestock systems include a variety of grazing systems on semi-arid range, high and cool mountain pastures, wet lowlands, and more. Livestock may graze on leaves as well as grass.

In summary, a large number of crop and livestock systems exist, many of which have been relatively productive or at least well suited to their environment. As populations, environments, technologies, incomes, and other conditions change, a particular system may no longer be adequate and is forced to adjust. Few systems are static for long today, and many offer the potential for improved productivity.

The influence of the political system

In Figure 8.1, political factors were listed as significant determinants of farming systems, including land tenure systems. The political system can dictate how property rights are allocated, including private, communal, and other types of land tenure arrangements. When collectives and communes have restricted individual farmers' responsibilities and rights to manage farm resources in response to market signals, as it did historically in Russia and China, the result was inefficiency and waste of resources. Political systems that allow independent family farms to operate in competitive markets have generally yielded higher productivity levels and faster growth rates over time. A good example of the potential benefits of reforming an inefficient land tenure arrangement was provided by China.

Beginning in 1979, China broke up its communal system and allowed individual farmers to respond more freely to market incentives on individual pieces of land. Since then, it has experienced significant increases in agricultural production (see Box 8.2). Adoption of new technologies and use of purchased inputs such as fertilizer have increased substantially. These changes occurred rapidly in China, causing important changes in world markets. Agricultural growth in China stimulated broad-based increases in income, with profound implications for food markets, such as increased demands for animal proteins.

Government policies other than rules governing land tenure also affect farming systems. Price policies that favor certain products over others or promote the use of different inputs can strongly affect the types of crops planted, how long they are grown, and even the degree to which traditional farmers interact with markets. Policies affecting the value of the land create incentives for additional or fewer investments in land. For instance, policies that discriminate against agriculture, such as export taxes, are quickly reflected in lower values of farmland. Population and family planning programs can affect population densities, with a large influence on the nature of the agricultural system.

In summary, the major types of farming systems in the world include shifting cultivation, pastoral nomadism, and several types of settled agriculture. These systems, particularly settled agriculture, can be affected in a major way by the political system in the country, which dictates private or public control over land use. Other government policies influence agricultural systems both directly and indirectly.

BOX 8.2 CHINESE AGRICULTURAL SYSTEMS

In rural areas of China prior to 1979, the agricultural production system was organized according to guidelines established in the national agricultural plan. Farming operations were organized into collective teams of 20 to 30 households; these teams were required to sell fixed quantities of output to the government at set prices. Quantities produced in excess of the quotas were also surrendered to the government. The collectives had some freedom to adjust inputs, but the acreage planted to each crop was determined by government planners.

This rigid system led to stagnation in agricultural output. Between 1957 and 1978, per capita grain production grew at a 0.3 percent annual rate, while soybean and cotton production per capita *declined*, respectively, by 3.0 and 0.6 percent annually. In 1978, rural incomes were virtually identical to levels of 20 years earlier. This poor performance of the agricultural sector had important implications in a country where 80 percent of the population resides in rural areas.

In 1978, the government decided to introduce the *Household Responsibility System*, which restored individual households as the basic unit of farm operation. Under this system, a household leases a plot of land from the collective, and, after fulfilling a state-set grain procurement quota, can retain additional output. This output can be consumed or sold to the government. The households have flexibility to determine acreage for individual crops. At the same time, the government prices of agricultural commodities were increased, and the prices paid for above-quota grain production were increased substantially above quota prices. Agricultural output began to grow rapidly following these reforms, and agricultural growth has averaged over 5 percent per year since the change in system. These reforms led to a wholesale change in the Chinese agricultural system, with almost all of the collective teams in China being converted to the new system.

Sources: Justin Y. Lin, "The Household Responsibility System Reform and the Adoption of Hybrid Rice in China", *Journal of Development Economics*, vol. 36(2) (1991), pp. 353–373; Ehou Junhua, "Economic Reform: Price Readjustment (1978–87)", *Chinese Economic Studies*, vol. 24(3) (Spring 1991), pp. 6–26.

ECONOMIC DETERMINANTS OF INPUT USE AND CROP AND LIVESTOCK MIX

As noted above, policies can influence the evolution of farming systems by changing relative prices of inputs and outputs. Let's examine more carefully how economic factors affect the choice of inputs and, more broadly, the type of farming system. In Chapter 5, we introduced the concept of an *isoquant* to illustrate that the same level of output can be produced with more than one combination of two inputs. The concept of *allocative efficiency* relates to how well farmers choose the correct amounts of inputs to apply and outputs to produce given the available technology, assuming they are trying to maximize profits. While farm and family decisions are inter-mingled, their success and even survival depends in part on how efficiently they allocate their productive assets. Efficient farmers are able to combine inputs in a way that reflects their relative prices. Efficient farmers also choose the most profitable output levels and mixes of outputs. The farming systems described in this chapter vary in intensity of input use and productivity, but they all represent long-term adjustments to prevailing conditions. As a result, we can conclude that on average they are efficient given prevailing institutions. As relative scarcity (and hence prices) of inputs and outputs change, these efficient producers adjust input mixes and amounts of output.

In Figure 8.3, the isoquant represents the combinations of labor and animal power that can be used to produce a specific amount of output,

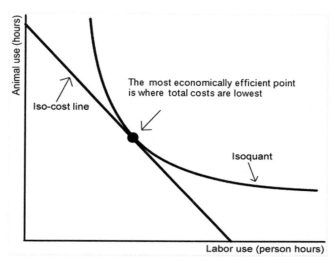

Figure 8.3 Input efficiency given relative input scarcity

with a given level of all other inputs; for example, two tons of corn on one acre of land. We expect all farmers to produce somewhere along this curve. Production to the right or above the curve would use more inputs than needed and would be technically inefficient. Production to the left or below the curve is technically impossible, given the other resources and technology available to the farmer. The slope of the isoquant is known as the *marginal rate of technical substitution* (MRTS) between the two inputs. In this case, the isoquant's slope is the additional labor input needed to save one unit of animal use, holding production constant. We expect farmers to adjust their use of animals and labor until the value of that labor time just equals the cost of adding animal time. In terms of the graph, we expect farmers to adjust until the slope on the isoquant just equals the price of labor relative to the price of animal power. That ratio is the slope of the relative price line, also called an iso-cost line because it traces a line of constant total cost. The economically efficient input combination is the point where the isoquant and the iso-cost curves are tangent or where the MRTS equals the input price ratio. If the price of labor goes down relative to the price of animal power, the iso-cost line would become flatter, tangency would occur at a point farther down the isoquant, and more labor and less animal power would be used. Thus, the drive to be efficient leads to changes in input mixes, and over time, this drive can alter the farming system. As an example, compare differences in farming systems between Africa, where labor is relatively scarce and land is relatively abundant, and South Asia, where labor is relatively abundant and land relatively scarce. Labor use per unit of land is far higher in South Asia as it is in Africa.

Similar trade-offs occur between different outputs. In Figure 8.4, the curved line represents the *production possibilities frontier* (PPF) or the combinations of corn and beans that can be produced with available resources. As with Figure 8.3, we expect farmers to produce somewhere along this curve. Production inside the curve would generate less output than is possible, and so be technically inefficient. Production outside the curve would be technically impossible, given these resources and the technology. The slope of the PPF is known as the *marginal rate of transformation* (MRT), the amount of additional corn that can be produced by reducing production of beans by one unit. The iso-revenue line reflects the price of beans relative to the price of corn, or the tradeoff in the market between corns and beans. The allocatively efficient combination of outputs depends on the relative prices of these two outputs. For example, if the price of beans rises relative to the price of corn, the iso-revenue line becomes steeper, and it pays to shift more resources into producing beans and away from corn.

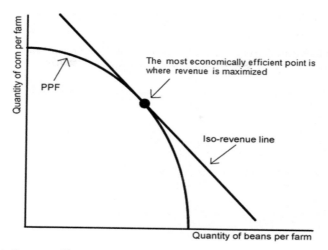

Figure 8.4 Output efficiency, given the technology and resource base

Input and output combinations observed in farming systems around the world are heavily influenced by technologies, resource bases, and relative prices. Farmers allocate resources to maximize their families' well-being in light of expected costs and revenues. Economic profitability is just one factor they consider in their decision-making, but usually an important one.

SUMMARY

Farming systems in the world exhibit considerable variability. Technical and human factors determine the types of farming systems. Technical factors include physical and biological factors. Institutional and human factors are characterized by externally and internally controlled forces. The major farming systems of the world can be grouped into three classes: shifting cultivation, pastoral nomadism, and settled agriculture. Settled agriculture includes many agricultural systems, such as mixed farming systems, intensive annual crops, intensive and extensive livestock systems, and perennial crops.

IMPORTANT TERMS AND CONCEPTS

Farming systems
Human determinants of farming
   systems

Perennial crops
Political determinants of farming
   systems

Intensive annual crops
Iso-cost and iso-revenue
Mixed farming system
Pastoral nomadism

Production possibilities frontier
Settled agriculture
Technical determinants of farming
systems

LOOKING AHEAD

In this chapter, we briefly examined the nature and diversity of existing farming systems in developing countries and their determinants. In the next chapter, we focus on environmental or natural resource problems that can influence the ability of a farming system to improve and achieve sustainable development.

QUESTIONS FOR DISCUSSION

1 What are the major technical determinants of farming systems?
2 Describe the major human determinants of farming systems. Be sure to distinguish exogenous from endogenous factors.
3 How might the political system affect the nature of the farming system?
4 What is shifting cultivation and why is it more commonly found in Africa and Latin America than in Asia?
5 What is pastoral nomadism and what problems might be present in this type of system?
6 Distinguish among the major types of settled agriculture.
7 How do the optimal quantities of inputs and outputs change as iso-cost and iso-revenue lines change their slopes and why?

NOTE

1 See Alec N. Duckham and G.B. Masefield, *Farming Systems of the World* (London: Chatto and Windus, 1970). Substantial variation is observed within these highly stylized farming system typologies.

RECOMMENDED READINGS

Duckham, Alec N., and G.B. Masefield, *Farming Systems of the World* (London: Chatto and Windus, 1970).Lin, Justin, "Agricultural

Development in China", in Carl K. Eicher and John M. Staatz (eds.), *International Agricultural Development* (Baltimore: Johns Hopkins, 1998), Chapter 31.

Loomis, Robert S., "Agricultural Systems", *Scientific American* (September 1976), pp. 98–105.

9 Resource use and sustainability

THIS CHAPTER

1 Examines the nature of environmental and natural resource problems that influence the sustainability of agricultural development in developing countries
2 Identifies the principal causes of environmental problems in developing countries
3 Discusses some potential solutions to environmental problems in developing countries

NATURE OF NATURAL RESOURCE AND ENVIRONMENTAL PROBLEMS

Sound management of natural resources is widely recognized as essential for sustainable agricultural and economic development. Yet, the effects of environmental degradation and poor natural resource management are evident throughout the world. The wide-ranging yet often interrelated problems of soil erosion, silting of rivers and reservoirs, flooding, overgrazing, poor cropping practices, desertification, salinity, waterlogging, deforestation, energy depletion, climate change, loss of biodiversity, and chemical pollution of land, water, and air are increasing problems in many developing countries. People in the poorest countries tend to be most dependent on their natural resource base for their livelihoods and thus are the most vulnerable to natural resource and environmental degradation. Poorer countries find environmental problems difficult to solve because population growth, outmoded institutional relationships, climate change, and a lack of financial resources conspire against solutions. The poorest people within these countries usually suffer the most from environmental degradation.

As agricultural and economic development occur, forces are set in motion, some reducing and others increasing pressures on natural resources and the environment. Changes in the rate of population growth, availability of new technologies, new social and institutional relationships, the increased value of human time, and shifts in the weight placed on future as opposed to current income all influence the relationship between human activity and the environment. Economic and environmental policies together with other institutional changes can either alleviate or aggravate natural resource problems. Specific environmental problems affecting developing countries are discussed in the following sections, followed by a description of causes and potential solutions.

Global versus local problems

Many natural resource or environmental problems are local in cause, effect, and potential solution. Others are regional or global. Problems such as soil erosion may be local, leading to lower productivity over time, but have wider implications if soil is deposited in rivers and transported to neighboring regions where the silt raises river levels, causing flooding. Others, such as deforestation, may appear to be local but affect the global climate as carbon is released into the atmosphere. Environmental problems affect every nation in the world, can hinder the long-run sustainability of farming systems, and are a growing concern. The following is a brief description of the more serious environmental problems facing developing countries.

Soil degradation, erosion, silting, and flooding

Topsoil is one of the world's most important natural assets. Its quality is defined by its structure, depth, nutrients, organic matter, acidity, salinity, and moisture-holding capacity. Farmers frequently invest in trying to improve soil through fertility amendments and by using soil conservation techniques. But these investments can be costly, and the poorest farmers are often unable to afford to undertake them and are less willing or able to wait for the future benefits they provide. As a result, we observe that the lowest-income farmers often draw down their "soil capital", applying insufficient soil amendments to fully replenish the nutrients removed at harvest or generated through natural processes. In effect, they are "mining" soil nutrients. The resulting soil degradation is usually reversible, if and when farmers find it profitable to apply more nutrients than plants withdraw.

An irreversible kind of degradation is excessive soil erosion due to the exposure of soil to wind and water runoff. The extent of the world erosion problem is difficult to assess because few nations have systematically surveyed their soil resources. Nevertheless, about 50 billion tons of soil are lost per year, with annual crops estimated to represent about 40 percent of global soil loss.[1]

Erosion rates of 50 tons per hectare are common in upland watersheds in many developing countries, and while this loss represents only about 3 millimeters from the top of the soil, the gullies and exposed bedrock from uneven erosion scar the landscape. Effects on productivity, especially over a longer period of time, are potentially serious. Eroded soils typically are at least twice as rich in nutrients and organic matter as the soil left behind so that, over time, fertility is lost due to erosion. Soil nutrient losses can be partially replaced by use of chemical fertilizers, but only up to a point, and fertilizer can be expensive. At any rate, the yields with fertilizers are lower than they would be in the absence of erosion, so that erosion reduces productivity below its potential.

Soils are deteriorating in the hills of the Himalayas, on the steep slopes of the Andes Mountains, in the Yellow River basin in China, in the Central American highlands, in the Central Highlands of Ethiopia, and on densely populated Java. The worst erosion in terms of average soil loss per hectare is found in the crescent from Korea to Turkey, in Eastern

Farming an erodible hillside in Ecuador

Houses flooded in Dhaka Bangladesh

Europe and the former Soviet Union, followed by the Central American highlands, and in the Sahel in Africa. Differences are due to the intensity of cultivation on highly erodible soils and availability of soil conservation alternatives.

The indirect or off-site effects of erosion through silting of rivers and reservoirs can be more serious than the on-site effects. When reservoirs fill with sediment, hydroelectric and irrigation storage capacity is lost, cutting short the useful lives of these expensive investments. When rivers silt up, flooding occurs during rainy seasons. For example, soil erosion in the hills of Nepal causes flooding in the plains of Nepal, India, and Bangladesh.[2] Flooding in the Yellow River basin in China is another example. In Ecuador, regular annual flooding in the Guayas River in the coastal plain causes hundreds of millions of dollars in damage and loss of lives. This flooding is directly tied to erosive farming practices in the Andean highlands.

Desertification

Excluding real deserts, potentially productive drylands cover about one-third of the world's land surface. About one-sixth of the world's population lives in dryland areas and produce cereals, fibers, and animal products. In arid regions, with under 300 mm of annual rainfall, vegetation is sparse and nomadic herding of animals like goats and cattle predominates. In semi-arid regions, with 300 to 600 mm of rain, dryland farmers grow cereals such as wheat, sorghum, and millet in more settled agriculture. The semi-arid regions are smaller in area but more densely populated than are arid regions.

The term *desertification* applies to a process occurring in arid and semi-arid regions. Desertification involves the depletion of vegetative cover, exposure of the soil surface to wind and water erosion, and reduction of the soil's organic matter and water-holding capacity. Intensive grazing, particularly during drought years, reduces vegetative cover; the loss of vegetation reduces organic matter in the soil and thus changes soil structure. After a rain, the earth dries out and becomes crusted, reducing infiltration of future rains. Then, even more vegetation is lost for lack of water; the surface crust is washed or crumbles and blows away, leaving soil that is less fertile and unable to support much plant life.

Cropping, particularly when very intensive and when combined with drought, is another major cause of desertification. If soil organic matter is depleted by intensive farming practices and not replaced, a process similar to that described earlier occurs. As supplies of firewood dwindle, people use dried manure for fuel rather than fertilizer. As the soil loses its fertility, crop yields fall and wind and water erosion accelerate. Eventually, the land may be abandoned.

Moderate desertification may cause a 25 percent loss of productivity, while severe desertification can reduce productivity by 50 percent or more. It is estimated that 65 million hectares of productive land in Africa have been abandoned to desert over the last 50 years. Desertification is particularly a problem in the Sahel region of Africa and in parts of the Near East, South Asia, and South America. In terms of people directly affected, approximately 50 to 100 million people are currently dependent on land threatened by desertification. Areas where desertification is a problem also tend to be areas with low and unpredictable rainfall. The ensuing periodic droughts create short-term severe food crises in those areas.

Salinity and waterlogging

Irrigation, one of the oldest technological advances in agriculture, has played a major role in increasing global food production. However, bringing land under irrigation is costly, and degradation of irrigated land through questionable water management practices causes some land to lose productivity or be retired from production completely. The major culprits are waterlogging and salinity.

Seepage from unlined canals and heavy watering of fields in areas with inadequate drainage can raise the underlying water table. Almost all water contains some salts. High water tables concentrate salts in the root zones and also starve plants for oxygen, inhibiting growth. Inadequate drainage also contributes to salinization when evaporation leaves a layer of salts that accumulate and reduce crop yields. A typical irrigation rate leaves behind about 2 to 5 tons of salt per hectare annually, even if the water supply has a relatively low salt concentration. If not flushed out, salt can accumulate to enormous quantities in a couple of decades.

Estimates are that between one-quarter and one-half of the world's irrigated land is affected by moderate to severe salinization. Some 20 to 25 million hectares are affected in India, 7 to 10 million hectares in China, and 3 to 6 million hectares in Pakistan. Other developing areas severely affected include Afghanistan, the Tigris and Euphrates River basins in Syria and Iraq, Turkey, Egypt, and parts of Mexico.

Deforestation and energy depletion

Forests play a vital role in providing food, fuel, medicines, fodder for livestock, and building materials. Tropical forests provide a home for innumerable and diverse plant and animal species. They protect the soil, recycle moisture, represent a sink for atmospheric carbon dioxide, and support livelihoods for millions of human beings. But forests are being cleared at a rapid rate. About 4 million hectares of tropical forest are cleared each year.[3] The earth's forested areas have declined by about one-half in the last century. Deforestation continues at a rapid pace in countries such as Brazil, Indonesia, Myanmar, Zambia, Tanzania, and Nigeria. These countries account for approximately 60 percent of the world's annual loss of tropical forests.[4]

Deforestation creates environmental problems on land and in the air. Forest clearing degrades soils and increases erosion in tropical watersheds. Soils in tropical forests tend to be fragile and unsuited for cultivation; their fertility is quickly depleted with ensuing erosion following tree clearing. In semi-arid areas, deforestation contributes to loss of organic matter, increases wind and water erosion, and speeds the rate of desertification. As forests are burned to clear land, carbon dioxide and carbon monoxide are emitted and contribute to climate change. It is estimated that more than 20 percent of the net increases to atmospheric carbon comes from deforestation.

In developing countries, seven out of ten people depend on fuel wood to meet their cooking and heating energy needs. The FAO estimates that three out of four people who rely on fuel wood are cutting wood faster

Deforestation has led to soil erosion in Nepal

than it is growing back. When people cannot find fuel wood, they turn to other sources of organic matter such as dung for fuel, thereby depleting soil fertility and aggravating soil erosion and desertification.

At the global level, bioenergy production in the form of liquid bio-fuels such as ethanol and biodiesel can provide substitutes for fossil fuels and fuel wood. However, bio-fuel production, most of which is based on maize, sugarcane, soybeans, rapeseed, palm, and sugar beets, competes with food production for land, water, and other inputs. This competition ties energy markets closely to food markets and leads to increased volatility in food prices.

Deforestation also threatens biological diversity. Tropical forests cover only 7 percent of the world's landmass, yet they contain more than half of all plant and animal species. In Madagascar, for example, there were, until recently, 9500 documented plant species and 190,000 animal species, most of them in the island's eastern forest. More than 90 percent of the forest has now been eliminated, along with an estimated 60,000 species.

Climate change

The earth's climate is undergoing change. Surface temperatures increased by almost 1° C during the past century. Recent projections of future increases range from 2.6° C to 3.9° C by 2100.[5] Strong consensus exists among the world's scientists that climate change is evident in shifts in ranges of flora and fauna, earlier onset and lengthening of growing seasons, and major changes in rainfall patterns. Observed changes in abundance of plants and animals and changes in ecosystem compositions have been attributed to climate change. As world temperatures rise, average sea levels rise, threatening coastal and low-lying lands. Climate change is associated with altered rainfall patterns and shorter growing seasons in some areas. Violent storms, monsoons, droughts, floods, and generally increased weather variability are likely. Global climate change could alter disease prevalence and be hard on certain animal species because their ecosystem may shift while the property-line boundaries of their preserves do not.

While there is some disagreement about the degree to which human activities affect the rate of climate change, it is clear that agricultural systems throughout the globe have begun to feel its effects. The effects vary substantially between regions. In higher latitude areas, agricultural productivity is improving with moderate temperature increases, while sub-Saharan Africa and coastal areas in Asia are feeling the strongest adverse effects. Semi-arid and arid areas are particularly vulnerable and will increasingly suffer a decrease in water availability, increased likelihood of drought, and growing heat stress. In these same areas, groundwater resources will decline so that moisture-related plant stress will lower productivity. Other areas will feel more mixed effects, but overall the most likely outcomes, which have already begun, are increased variability in weather patterns, including deeper and more prolonged drought, higher temperatures and reduced productivity in rain-fed tropical and sub-tropical agriculture, reductions in access to fresh water, and expanding populations of pests and diseases.

As climate change affects agriculture productivity, people respond to it by adjusting their farming techniques and their livelihood strategies. We are only now beginning to understand the degree of adaptation, but evidence shows that people in the most affected areas have started to change the way they farm and generate their livelihoods. In the short-run, farmers adapt by changing crop mixes, using water conservation measures, and adopting risk-management techniques to lessen the consequences of more frequent droughts. They adjust their livelihood strategies to include more non-climate-affected sources of income. For example, they work off the farm and migrate to earn incomes.

Over the longer run and as the change in climate increases, more options are needed to create opportunities to adapt. Governments may invest in and farmers may adopt technologies and production techniques that reduce the impact of climate change. Agricultural research systems can respond by producing shorter-season seed varieties that are more tolerant of drought, rice varieties that are more tolerant of salinity, and other germplasm resistant to environmental stress. Enhanced means of managing soil moisture such as water harvesting can be identified through research. Farmers may adopt conservation farming techniques that minimize disruption of the soils and increase the use of groundcover to reduce erosion and increase soil organic matter. All these steps should lessen vulnerability to rainfall shortages and increase productivity over time. Enhanced management of irrigation water through steps such as drip and micro-irrigation can improve the efficiency of water use. Conserving water is a particular concern because it is estimated that 70 percent of freshwater use is currently devoted to agriculture.

Developing-country agriculture can play an important role in slowing global climate change. Conservation agriculture and related practices to reduce erosion can help sequester carbon in soils and contribute to reductions in greenhouse gas emissions. Intensified agricultural production in currently cropped areas increases overall food availability and lowers rates of land clearing for new productive areas. Agro-forestry can aid in carbon sequestration. Perennial crop producers can plant trees and manage their existing woodlands to contribute to carbon retention. While most of the world's atmospheric carbon is being emitted by industrializing and industrialized countries, producers in less-developed countries can play an important role in mitigating their effects; the challenge is to create mechanisms whereby farmers can be compensated for improving the global environment.

It is important to recognize that if the projections of the scientific community are correct, the world is in a race against time. Adaptation will mitigate some of the ill effects of climate change, and some areas will likely prosper following adaptation. But adaptation will not ameliorate the ill effects of climate change in the most adversely affected regions. In low-lying coastal regions and some of the more arid areas, the imperative is to attain improvements in well-being over the short- to medium-term. Over the long haul, climate change is likely to alter the environment to such a degree that no adjustments in livelihood strategies will suffice. It is equally important, however, to recognize that climate change is just one of many stressors affecting agriculture in the developing world. As countries develop, labor costs rise, new technologies become available, and markets open to create new opportunities. These and other factors have dramatic implications for farming practices. They lead to larger farm sizes and major changes in how things are done. Farmers in developing countries need to continually adapt to changing circumstances, and, while climate change represents an important source of upheaval, adjustments to it are among many that must be made.

Chemical pollution

Misuse of chemical pesticides and fertilizers has contaminated the land and water in many developing countries, damaging the health of producers and consumers, stimulating the emergence of pests resistant to pesticides, eliminating natural pest enemies, and reducing fish, bird, and animal populations. Acute pesticide poisonings are common, and little is known about potential long-term health effects of over exposure to agricultural chemicals. Effective pesticide regulatory and enforcement systems are lacking in many developing countries.

Hundreds of pests have become resistant to chemicals, and the number is growing. Fertilizer runoff increases nitrate levels in ponds and canals, reducing oxygen levels and killing fish. Excessive pesticide levels often destroy fish in irrigated rice paddies.

Heavy use of pesticides and fertilizers tends not to hurt agricultural production in the short run. However, as resistance to pesticides builds up and natural predators of agricultural pests are reduced, future production potentials are jeopardized. And society bears the cost of off-farm pollution.

CAUSES OF ENVIRONMENTAL PROBLEMS

Environmental degradation can result from physical, economic, and institutional factors. Many environmental problems are interrelated; for example, deforestation, erosion, and silting of rivers and reservoirs are linked. Natural resource degradation usually has direct and indirect causes. For example, desertification can directly result from overgrazing and poor cropping practices, but indirectly result from poverty and population growth. Physical or technical causes of natural resource degradation are often the most visible. Land clearing for timber, fuel wood, cattle ranching, and farming can cause deforestation.[6] Deforestation results in loss of biodiversity, loss of soil, and diminished soil fertility as soil from recovered tropical forests loses its fertility quickly. If the forest is burned, carbon dioxide enters the atmosphere, contributing to climate change. If the area is semi-arid, loss of forests can lead to desertification. Desertification also results from overgrazing, which itself is caused by too many cattle feeding in an area subject to dry spells or droughts. Intensive cropping in semi-arid areas contributes to desertification.

Many other examples of physical causes of natural resource degradation can be cited. Salinity and waterlogging result from poorly managed irrigation systems. Chemical pollution results from excessive fertilizer and pesticide use. Silting of rivers and tidal surges during storms cause flooding. Agriculture, forestry, and other land uses contribute about a fifth of global greenhouse gas emissions that result from human activity, especially carbon dioxide, methane, and nitrous oxide.

The challenge in solving such problems, however, is in understanding what factors affect individual and group decisions about natural resource use. These factors are both economic and determined by institutions. Institutions include the legal system, cultural norms, market structures, and other rules of behavior affecting decision-making incentives. Once we understand how economic and institutional factors affect decisions about resource use, we can begin to formulate strategies to address the most serious environmental problems.

Economic causes of natural resource degradation

An important economic cause of natural resource degradation occurs when markets fail to reflect the true value of resources or the true costs of actions. Market failures emerge due to the presence of externalities, high costs of information, and in the provision of public goods. An externality is created when decision-makers impose costs on others without considering these costs when making the decision. Farmers, for example, may create off-farm costs associated with soil erosion or pesticide pollution without considering these external costs because they do not bear them (see Box 9.1).

A lack of information about or concern for environmental damage creates costs that lead to environmentally destructive behavior. For example, the farmer may be unaware that his farming practices are damaging long-term productivity or that cost-effective practices are readily available to improve the situation. In such cases, the market is failing to adequately transmit information to the farmer. Environmental quality is a public good, which means it is very costly to prohibit someone from benefiting from it, and one person's benefiting from it does not preclude another from benefiting from it. It is well known that markets, when left alone, undersupply public goods. All these forms of market failure contribute to natural resource problems.

Poverty is another economic condition associated with environmental degradation. Poverty drives people to farm marginal lands intensively, seek fuel wood, and follow other agricultural practices that produce food at the potential sacrifice of future production. As discussed in Chapter 4,

BOX 9.1 EXTERNALITIES AND PRIVATE DECISIONS

One market failure associated with environmental degradation is the divergence between private and social costs of actions. This divergence is caused by the presence of external costs. An external cost exists when an activity by one agent causes loss of welfare to another agent *and* the loss is not considered by the author. The effect of externalities on private decision-making is illustrated in the following figure.

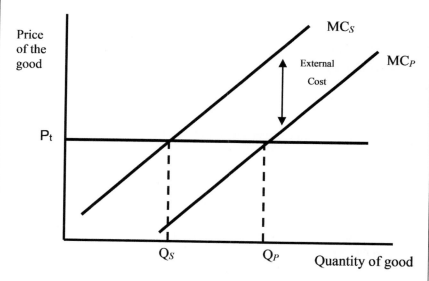

A farmer who cannot influence market prices will produce a good up until the point where the private marginal cost of its production (MC_p) equals the market price. In the figure, this point is shown where $MC_p = P_t$ and Q_p units are produced. An external cost is represented by the social marginal cost curve (MC_s), which exceeds the private cost curve. From society's point of view, the desirable production level is Q_s (where $MC_s = P_t$). The externality leads to more production of the good than is socially desirable. If the difference between the private and social cost is due to pollution, failure to account for the social costs contributes to environmental degradation. Notice that the free market alone will not reflect social costs – some action is needed.

poverty reinforces population growth, which is a contributor to many environmental problems.

The concern of the poor for the present, implying heavy discounting of future costs and benefits, is matched by the felt needs of governments in developing countries to stimulate industrial production. Governments follow policies that encourage natural resource-based exports to import capital goods. They also frequently lack financial resources to address environmental problems. Countries implementing economic development programs usually find high rates of return to many types of capital investment. High interest rates characteristic of these cases can encourage current consumption and may place demands on natural resources.

INSTITUTIONAL CAUSES OF NATURAL RESOURCE DEGRADATION

A major cause of environmental degradation is institutional failure, both private and public. Existing social structures and local customs may not be adequate to preserve the environment as economic development proceeds. Or, environmentally constructive social structures and customs may be destroyed by national policies or by increases in the costs of transactions and acting collectively. In some cases, inadequate institutions are the legacy of colonial interference or the result of more recent international influence.

Market institutions determine how well markets work and, as noted above, market failures are a chief cause of environmental degradation. These market failures mean that the market is not transmitting the true value of the resource to the decision-maker. Market failures can be due to inadequately defined property rights, costs associated with monitoring and enforcing property rights, and weak enforcement institutions. It may be unclear, for example, whether the farmer has the right to pollute the water or whether downstream users have the right to clean water. Even if these rights are legally clear, they may be difficult or impossible to enforce. Thus, uncertain property rights contribute to the market failure.

Inadequate property rights in forest, pastures, and ground and surface waters can undermine private or local collective incentives to manage resources sustainably. In some areas, the land or water resource was traditionally held in common. Under a common-property regime, people in the village or community had rights to use the resources but did not own or rent them privately. When the local society could maintain authority over the resource, or when population pressures were such that the resource was in abundant supply, then this common property could be managed in a socially optimal manner. However, as population increases and as national policies over-ride local authority, breaking down traditions and customs, incentives for resource preservation and traditional means of controlling access can be destroyed. If one person does not cut down the tree for fuel wood, another will. Or, if one person's goat does not eat the blade of grass, another person's goat will. Or, if one person does not use the water or catch the fish, another will. The result is that incentives exist for each individual to overexploit resources because otherwise someone else will.

Common-property regimes do not necessarily cause resource mismanagement if local institutions create incentives to efficiently manage the resource. In many areas of Africa, common-property institutions were said to cause overgrazing on rangelands. However, attempts by the government to replace these institutions with private ownership schemes were largely counterproductive, contributing to more rapid resource degradation. Efficient indigenous resource management institutions were replaced by less effective but more modern institutions. Common-property institutions are a viable means of managing resources.[7]

In areas of frontier colonization, poorly defined and inadequately enforced property rights can create incentives for overexploitation of natural resources. For example, the Peten region of northern Guatemala is undergoing high rates of deforestation, particularly in its western extremities. In the western Peten, the Guatemalan government established the Laguna de Tigre national park in 1990. It was hoped that the presence of a national park would slow settlement and help conserve the forest in its original state. However, the government does not have resources to adequately monitor and discourage settlement on these isolated public lands, and a weak legal system prevents enforcement of laws prohibiting illegal settlement. As a result, illegal settlers are deforesting the lands, leading to widespread environmental degradation.

Public policies are another major institutional cause of natural resource degradation. Agricultural pricing policies, input subsidies, and land use policies often discourage sustainable resource use. Governments in developing countries often intervene in agricultural markets to keep food prices artificially low. This causes land to be undervalued, reducing incentives for conservation. And, low incomes make the investment required for sustainable output difficult. On the other hand, higher agricultural prices raise the value of land, and, as a result, can contribute to increased deforestation. These competing impacts of agricultural prices on the environment make it important that policy impacts be explored as a part of government decision-making.

Governments sometimes subsidize fertilizer and pesticides to help compensate for policies that keep farm product prices low. If fertilizer or pesticide use causes an externality, then subsidies, because they increase input use, will increase the level of the externality. Subsidies may be indirect in the form of roads or export subsidies that encourage deforestation. Road access is strongly associated with deforestation in all regions of the world. Subsidized irrigation water can encourage its wasteful use.

Land tenure and land use policies may cause exploitation of agricultural and forest lands with little regard for future productivity effects. Short leases, for example, create incentives to mine the resource base in the short run, And, as just noted, it is an error to think that local incentive problems can be entirely corrected by national policies. In the 1970s and early 1980s, national policies on forests destroyed local conservation practices and incentives in Nepal.[8] A common policy in Latin America has been to require that in colonized areas land needs to be developed, which usually means cleared of trees, prior to receiving title to the land. Part of the deforestation in the Brazilian Amazon is associated with these types of titling rules.

Land use patterns are sometimes affected by colonial heritage or other international influences. In parts of Latin America and the Caribbean, large sugarcane, coffee, and banana plantations, or even cattle ranches, are found in the fertile valleys and plains, while small peasant farms intensively producing food crops dot the eroding hillsides, Low labor intensity of production in the valleys depresses job opportunities and forces the poor to rely on fragile lands to earn incomes. These patterns are the legacy of colonialism. Colonial powers in Africa changed cropping system to cash cropping in areas where cash cropping could not be supported by the natural resource base. Peasants have been forced onto marginal lands, reducing lands for nomads. Traditional nomadic trading patterns were also disrupted.

These and other institutional policies have contributed to natural resource problems. Institutional change is therefore one of the potential solutions to these problems.

POTENTIAL SOLUTIONS TO NATURAL RESOURCE PROBLEMS

Solutions to environmental problems contain technical, economic, and institutional dimensions. Technical solutions are needed to provide the physical means of remedying natural resource degradation, while economic and institutional solutions provide the incentives for behavioral change.

Technical solutions to natural resource problems

A variety of technical solutions are available to solve many environmental problems. Where technical solutions are lacking, government-sponsored research and education can develop new natural resource-conserving practices and facilitate their adoption.

Windbreaks, contour plowing, conservation agriculture, legume fallow crops, alley cropping, deferred grazing, rotational grazing, well-distributed watering places, and re-vegetation or reforestation are all examples of physical practices which could help reduce soil erosion, silting, and desertification. Solar pumps, biogas generators, and more efficient cooking stoves can provide or save energy, thereby reducing fuel wood consumption, deforestation, and desertification. Embankments can provide protection from flooding for limited areas, and dams can be built on rivers to control water flows.

Irrigation canals can be better lined to reduce waterlogging and salinity and to conserve water resources. Drip irrigation systems make more efficient use of irrigation water and can be widely adopted, particularly in vegetable-production systems where flooding or open canals were used in the past. Integrated pest management techniques can be developed that involve increased biological and cultural control of pests to reduce pesticide pollution. Germplasm banks can be used and conservation reserves established to preserve endangered plant species.

These are just a few of the potential technical or physical solutions to environmental problems. In many cases, these technical solutions are already known, but in others additional research is essential for success. In the pest management area, for example, much work still needs to be completed on biological controls for major pests in developing countries. Integrated pest management (IPM) is a family of pest management techniques that lowers dependence on toxic pesticides; in many countries, these techniques are technically feasible, but have not been widely spread to farmers due to limited extension and agricultural outreach services and to competition from chemical sellers.[9]

Technical solutions to natural resource problems are essential for reducing environmental degradation. In almost all cases, however, these solutions must be combined with economic and institutional changes that create incentives for behavioral change. Without these incentives, it is unlikely that the technologies will be widely adopted, since they usually imply increased costs to their users.

A brush fence in Kenya being used to facilitate rotational grazing

Economic and institutional solutions to natural resource degradation

International and natural agricultural research systems can generate new technologies to increase food production and incomes. As incomes grow, population pressures are reduced, and the demand for environmental protection increases. New institutions may be formed (or existing institutions may evolve) in response to this demand and incentives for resource conservation can be created.

As countries develop, the major source of growth is not the natural resource base but rather new knowledge (see Chapter 5). This knowledge can, to some extent, substitute for natural resources and is less subject to the diminishing returns associated with more intensive use of natural resources. Increases in agricultural productivity resulting from the new knowledge or technologies not only raise incomes, but also the value of human time. As the value of human time increases, population growth rates decline with favorable implications for natural resource problems.

The most immediate way to solve natural resource problems, however, is through reforms of economic policy, institutional changes to reduce market failures, and reform of property right regimes to encourage decentralized management solutions.[10] Increasing returns from agriculture by reforming input and output pricing policies should help. However, increased returns to agriculture can also put additional pressure

Spraying pesticides in the Philippines

on forest resources, so institutional mechanisms to reduce deforestation must accompany changes in agricultural pricing policies.

Several means are available for addressing the underlying market failures associated with environmental degradation. Subsidies and taxes can be used as "carrots" or "sticks" to reduce externalities or off-site effects associated with agricultural production and forest use. An example of a conservation subsidy (i.e., a "carrot") might be a program in which the government shares the cost of building terraces, windbreaks, and fences, or of planting trees to reduce erosion. In some cases, workers can be paid in-kind with food from internationally supplied food aid. An example of a "stick" is a sales tax on chemical pesticides. Such subsidies are designed to "internalize" the externality, so that the economic actor considers the social costs associated with his or her decisions.

Institutional change that creates secure property rights will help address some problems of environmental degradation. Ownership of land titles increases returns to long-term investments in land. Removal of rules that guarantee land titles only if forests are cleared will slow deforestation by reducing individual returns to it (see Box 9.2). Provision of property rights does not necessarily imply privatization. There are numerous examples of common-property regimes managed in environmentally sound fashions. Institutional changes that reinforce these common-property management schemes are likely to be more effective than privatization.

Many successful examples of assigning property rights and creating markets for environmental quality can be found. In eastern Peten, Guatemala, community organizations were granted contracts for sustainable use of forest resources. These organizations, because they have the rights to the natural resources, control access to the forest and "police" extractive activities, such as timber harvest by outsiders. As a result, the eastern Peten is still heavily forested, especially in comparison to the western Peten, where inadequate property rights and high enforcement costs have contributed to illegal settlements and deforestation (see previously). In Zimbabwe, villagers were given rights to harvest elephants and sell these rights to hunters. The money from these sales is kept and used for development purposes in the villages. The villagers now see the elephants as a valuable resource and protect them from poachers. As a result, elephant populations are growing rapidly in areas where 15 years ago the elephant was practically extinct.

Certification is a process whereby international markets recognize and reward products that are sustainably produced. For example, wood in the eastern Peten is harvested in an environmentally sustainable manner and is certified as "green" by Smartwood, an international organization. The wood is favorably received in international markets and receives a price premium. Other products, such as coffee and cocoa, can also be certified as being produced in an environmentally and socially sustainable manner. Such certification creates incentives for enhanced resource management.

Certification is just one element of an emerging family of mechanisms to create markets for environmental goods. Payments for environmental services (PES) are schemes whereby demanders of environmental goods are brought together with suppliers so that both can benefit. A global example is the Clean Development Mechanism (CDM) established by an international environmental agreement called the Kyoto Protocol, which allows countries that are committed to greenhouse gas emission reductions to pay for carbon emission-reducing projects such as reforestation

BOX 9.2 INSTITUTIONS AND DEFORESTATION IN THE BRAZILIAN AMAZON

Brazil contains 3.5 million square kilometers of tropical forests, some 30 percent of the world's total. Most of the forests are found in the Brazilian Amazon basin. Continued deforestation of this rich reserve of plant and animal species has raised concerns for its effects on atmospheric carbon and on the maintenance of global biodiversity.

The Brazilian government made a conscious decision in the 1960s to develop the Amazon as a means of relieving population pressures, providing territorial security, and exploiting the region's wealth. Ambitious road-building programs, other infrastructure development, agricultural colonization projects, and policies providing tax and other incentives for agricultural and industrial development were begun. These projects had the effect of opening access to the Amazon and promoting environmentally unsound development.

Tax exemptions and cheap credit spurred the creation of large-scale livestock projects, whose economic and environmental suitability to the region was questionable. The National Integration Program established a network of villages, towns, and cities and cleared lots for in-migrating settlers. The plans for these settlements were made without regard for soil fertility or agricultural potential, and the cleared forest lands were quickly eroded and otherwise degraded.

Environmentally destructive settlement practices were promoted throughout the Amazon by the Brazilian government's practice of awarding land titles only for deforested lands. A migrant in either an official settlement project or an invaded area could obtain title to the land simply by clearing the forest. Once the title was granted, the owner could sell or transfer it to someone else, and proceed to clear additional lands. Speculators often buy or seize the land, sell the timber, graze cattle on it for a few years, and then sell it to soybean farmers. Estimates are that ranching accounts for 80 percent of deforestation In the Amazon.

The rate of deforestation in Amazonia is directly influenced by government policies and other institutional arrangements. Policy reform and other institutional adjustments can slow, or even reverse, this process if there is a will to do so.

in developing countries as an alternative to more expensive emission reductions in their own country. The United Nation's REDD (for Reducing Emissions from Deforestation and Forest Degradation in Developing Countries) is an example of multiple mechanisms to create value for the carbon stored in forests. Examples of PES schemes are found throughout Central America, where water-using towns and cities pay upstream farmers to adopt practices that reduce damage to water quality. These schemes create a market for the environmental good and induce producers to consider the value of the resource when making decisions.

Regulation is an alternative institutional mechanism for influencing environmental behavior. Although difficult to enforce, regulation can play a role when combined with other economic incentives. For example, burning of crop stubble, farming of particularly erosive lands, or logging in certain areas can be prohibited in conjunction with a program that also provides other benefits to farmers or forest owners. Families can be restricted from settling in flood-prone areas, perhaps with the provision of funds for resettlement. Experience shows that without incentives for changing behavior, regulations tend to be ineffective, since enforcement is costly and there are private incentives to cheat.

Physical restrictions on grazing, land reform programs that distribute land to small-scale farmers, revised leasing arrangements, and many other government-sponsored institutional changes can improve natural resource sustainability if certain principles are followed. First, there is a need for careful assessment of the economic benefits and costs, including externalities, resulting from the policies and the expected reactions to them. Second, local input is needed in the decision-making process. Third, compensation often is required for any losers. That society as a whole will be better off following these institutional changes is not enough. Losers may need to be compensated or they may oppose any change. PES schemes can be exploited in such instances and those who benefit from the change can "bribe" producers to adopt it.

These three principles hold for institutional changes at various levels – local, regional, national, and international – and they are not always easy to apply. If developed countries want developing countries to reduce carbon-dioxide emissions, developed countries must be willing to foot part of the bill. The Kyoto Protocol for climate change, adopted in 1997, reflected this need for mutual sacrifice to limit greenhouse gas emissions. It was the product of several years of intense negotiations and reflected developing country energy needs for economic development. The agreement, although not ratified by the U.S. government, entered into force in early 2005 and sparked creation of markets for trading emission allowances under the CDM. New markets for formerly unvalued environmental goods (such as carbon sequestration) represent opportunities for producers in developing countries. The REDD program, which started in 2008, is another example of international collaboration. The challenge is to overcome institutional barriers and information and administrative costs at the local level.

Policymakers need to consider what factors affect individual decisions. Solutions to environmental problems do not just emerge from changes in the legal environment. If society wants deforestation reduced, it cannot just pass a decree. It must involve local decision-makers in designing an institutional solution that provides incentives for appropriate behavior. Someone may need to estimate the costs and benefits associated with alternative institutional mechanisms. Enforcement mechanisms need to be fair and have teeth.

The presence of transactions costs and collective action has created institutional environments that are destructive to the natural resource base. The absence of new institutional arrangements to replace previous social and cultural norms is a serious problem.

Improvements in information flows and creation of markets to reflect environmental values are essential. Education also becomes vitally important; throughout the developing world, school curricula focusing on environmental sustainability are having visible impacts. Young people are increasingly involved in solutions to environmental problems because they recognize the value of environmental improvement.

SUMMARY

Sound environmental management is essential for sustained agricultural development. Yet, environmental degradation is evident throughout the developing world. Climate change, soil erosion, silting of rivers and reservoirs, flooding, overgrazing, poor cropping practices, desertification, salinity and waterlogging, deforestation, energy depletion, loss of biodiversity, and chemical pollution have become major problems. Poverty, high rates of return to capital, rapid population growth, inadequate information, and misguided public policies conspire against solutions. Environmental problems are interrelated, and understanding their causes requires sorting out complex physical, economic, and institutional linkages. Technical solutions are needed for each of these problems, but economic and institutional changes must provide the incentives for behavioral change; the solution to environmental problems requires many changes in behavior. As incomes grow, population pressures are reduced, and the demand for environmental protection increases. Economic development can mean more resources for addressing environmental problems, but short-term movement toward development can increase pressure on the environment. Changes in taxes, subsidies, regulations, and other policies can influence local incentives for conservation. Balancing benefits with costs, obtaining local input in the decision-making process, and compensating losers are needed for effective solutions to local and global environmental problems. Because transactions costs must be reduced for natural resource conservation to occur, information flows must be improved and human capital must be developed. Environmental issues that are global in nature, such as climate change, will require international cooperation and agreement. Unless such cooperation is achieved, the environmental and economic health of the world is in jeopardy. Time is running out faster than many are will admit.

IMPORTANT TERMS AND CONCEPTS

Biodiversity

Chemical pollution

Climate change

Common property

Deforestation

Desertification

Discounting of costs and benefits

Environmental degradation

Externalities

Flooding

Global warming

Greenhouse effect

Institutional change

Market failure

Natural resource management

Overgrazing

Payments for environmental services

Public goods

REDD

Regulations

Salinity and waterlogging

Soil erosion

Subsidies and taxes

Sustainable resource use

LOOKING AHEAD

In this chapter, we examined the nature and causes of environmental problems in developing countries. Potential technical, economic, and institutional solutions were considered so that agricultural development can be sustainable. In the next major section of the book, we consider what it takes to improve agriculture more generally from both a technical and institutional perspective to contribute to sustainable development. However, first, in Chapter 10, we consider how human resources, including family structure and gender issues, influence standards of living in developing countries.

QUESTIONS FOR DISCUSSION

1 What are the major natural resource problems facing developing countries?
2 Are the poorest countries the most vulnerable to environmental degradation? Why or why not?
3 How are flooding and soil erosion related?
4 What is desertification?
5 How are waterlogging and salinity problems interrelated?
6 How are deforestation and energy problems interrelated?
7 What are the major technical or physical causes of natural resource degradation?
8 What common market failures lead to environmental degradation in developing countries?
9 What is a public good? Why might the free market undersupply a public good?
10 How is climate change related to market failure? What efforts to address the market failure might have major impacts on carbon emissions?
11 What are some of the technological solutions to natural resource problems?
12 What are some of the economic and institutional solutions to natural resource problems?
13 How does a PES scheme help correct for market failure?
14 What are three key principles that must hold if institutional changes are to successfully solve environmental problems?
15 Why are reductions in transactions costs important for sustainable natural resource use?
16 How do property rights affect incentives for resource use?
17 Why might local institutions better manage common-property resources than centralized government?
18 What effect would a high discount rate have on incentives to conserve the environment?

NOTES

1 Pasquale Borrelli, David A. Robinson, Panos Panagos, Emanuele Lugato, Jae E. Yang, Christine Alewell, David Wuepper, Luca Montanarella, and Cristiano Ballabio, "Land Use and Climate Change Impacts on Global Soil Erosion by Water (2015–2070)", *Proceedings of the National Academy of Sciences*, vol. 117(36) (September 2020), pp. 21994–22001.

2 While flooding is a serious periodic problem in many countries, not all or even most flooding is due to silt. Low-lying countries like Bangladesh and parts of Egypt, Indonesia, Thailand, Senegal, the Gambia, and Pakistan are particularly vulnerable to flooding due to high river levels during the rainy season and sea surges during storms. About 80 percent of Bangladesh, for example, is a coastal plain or river delta. In 1998, approximately two-thirds of the land in this country of 130 million people was flooded. While a certain amount of normal flooding can have a positive effect on agricultural production, excessive flooding results in substantial loss of life from disease as well as drowning.

3 M.C. Hansen, P.V. Potapov, R. Moore, M. Hancher, S.A. Turubanova, A. Tyukavina, D. Thau, S.V. Stehman, S.J. Goetz, T.R. Loveland, A. Kommareddy, A. Egorov, L. Chini, C.O. Justice, and J.R.G. Townshend, "High-Resolution Global Maps of 21st-Century Forest Cover Change", *Science*, vol. 342 (November 15, 2013), pp. 850–853, http://earthenginepartners.appspot.com/science-2013-global-forest.

4 Food and Agricultural Organization of the United Nations, *Global Forest Resources Assessment 2010 – Main Report* (Rome: FAO, Forestry Paper No. 163, 2010), www.fao.org/docrep/013/i1757e/i1757e00.htm.

5 See Paul Voosen, "Earth's Climate Destiny Finally Seen More Clearly", *Science*, vol. 369 (July 24, 2020), pp. 354–355.

6 It is estimated that as much as 80 percent of worldwide deforestation is caused by land clearing for agriculture (D. Boucher, P. Elias, K. Lininger, C. May-Tobin, S. Roquemore, and E. Saxon, *The Root of the Problem: What's Driving Tropical Deforestation Today?* [Cambridge, MA: Union of Concerned Scientists, 2011]).

7 Elinor Ostrom, "The Challenge of Common-Pool Resources", *Environment: Science and Policy for Sustainable Development*, vol. 50(4) (2011), pp. 8–21; Elinor Ostrom, *Governing the Commons: The Evolution of Institutions for Collective Action* (Cambridge: Cambridge University Press, 1990).

8 See Daniel W. Bromley and Devendra P. Chapagain, "The Village Against the Center: Resource Depletion in South Asia", *American Journal of Agricultural Economics*, vol. 68 (December 1984), pp. 868–873.

9 See George W. Norton, E.A. Heinrichs, Gregory C. Luther, and Michael E. Irwin (eds.), *Globalizing Integrated Pest Management: A Participatory Research Process* (Ames, Iowa: Blackwell Publishing, 2004).

10 See, for example, Elinor Ostrom, "Reflections on 'Some Unsettled Problems of Irrigation'", *American Economic Review*, vol. 101(1) (2011), pp. 49–63.

RECOMMENDED READINGS

IPCC, *Climate Change and Land: Summary for Policymakers, Special Report* (Geneva: IPCC, 2020), p. 41.

World Bank, *Future of Food: Shaping a Climate-Smart Global Food System* (Washington, DC: World Bank, 2015), p. 32.

10 Human resources, family structure, and gender roles

THIS CHAPTER

1 Discusses the role of human resources in agricultural and economic development
2 Examines differences in family structure and gender roles in farm households in developing countries
3 Considers determinants of gender roles in farm households

Poor agricultural households in developing countries have few assets. Some own small parcels of land and a few animals, but all households have human assets. The productivity of human assets helps determine prospects for accumulation of other assets and improved well-being over time. Labor productivity can be enhanced through investments in education, health care, nutrition, and acquisition of skills. Decisions about investments in education, how household labor is deployed, and the size and structure of families are made within families. These decisions depend on policies and other incentive structures, cultural norms, and gender roles. They have major impacts on productivity, asset accumulation, and household well-being. In some societies, for example, girls are less likely than boys to attend school; in others, women are less likely to receive health care and have shorter life expectancies than men. We examine the role and determinants of investments in education, how human resources affect household well-being, and the roles of men, women, and children in making decisions and participating in household activities. Significant strides in education have been achieved over the past three decades. In 1990, about 100 million primary school-aged children in the world were out of school. By 2020, prior to COVID-19, that number had been cut in half, although about a fifth of primary school-aged children in sub-Saharan Africa remained unenrolled.

ROLE OF EDUCATION

Overall productivity of the economy depends on the quantity and quality of inputs into production. Better education, health care, and acquisition of skills are clear means of improving labor productivity; accumulation of these factors is called investment in human capital. Better-educated individuals earn higher incomes, and these higher incomes reflect more productivity. Education can be an important contributor to greater agricultural productivity, and low productivity of human resources in agriculture is a serious problem in many developing countries. Better-educated farmers are more able than less-educated farmers to adopt new technologies, understand price and market information, and access credit and other productive assets. Educated care-givers can prepare more nutritional meals, reduce diseases through improvements in basic sanitary practices, and assist their children in learning at a younger age. Countries that fail to improve the human capital of farmers and their families find it difficult to develop anything else.

Objectives and benefits of education

Rural education is an investment in people with the following objectives: (1) increasing agricultural productivity and efficiency, (2) preparing children for non-farm occupations if they leave farming, and (3) enhancing the quality of life by enabling better decision-making. Education may help motivate farmers toward change, teach improved decision-making and farm-management methods, provide farmers with technical and practical information, and lead to better marketing of higher-valued farm outputs. Agricultural extension complements other sources of information because it speeds the spread of knowledge about new technologies and other research results (see Chapter 12 for more details on extension systems).

A country with a literate people in rural areas will have better information flows than one without, simply due to better communications. Communications help reduce the transactions costs that hold back development; they smooth the flow of information to improve on-farm management and lower risk. Education helps farmers acquire and understand technical, institutional, and market information.

Investments in education yield returns not just for the farmer, but for society as a whole – educational attainment is a public good. As education levels increase in a village, all villagers gain from more productive neighbors, better information flows, and more experimentation and innovation. Because it results in a more productive and efficient agriculture and in a more productive labor force for non-farm employment, and because of its public good characteristics, education, particularly at the primary and secondary levels, is financed by government in most countries. Nobel prize winning economist T.W. Schultz noted that education helps people to deal with economic disequilibria. Thus, as agriculture in a country shifts from a traditional to a more dynamic, science-based mode, the value of education increases.

Education is important not just for farmers and for children who will continue farming, but also for those who leave agriculture. Education for non-farm jobs is particularly important for agricultural development if the youth acquire jobs as agricultural extension agents, managers of cooperatives and other business firms supplying inputs to farmers or marketing their products, agricultural scientists, or government officials who administer agricultural programs. Educated children who do not choose agricultural occupations often send remittances back home; these remittances are an important source of investment capital for farmers. Education represents an investment in human beings, and these investments reap returns inside and outside of agriculture. If a child of a farmer becomes educated and decides to leave agriculture and migrate to a city for a job, the individual and society as a whole gain from the investment.

Education of girls can be particularly important for development. As women become more educated, they live longer and healthier lives, the value of their time increases, the health and nutrition of family members improves, and total fertility declines. They have fewer, healthier, and better-educated children. They also earn more in farming and off the farm. Payoffs to women's education are found in the short run through improved productivity, and long-run payoffs include reductions in intergenerational poverty. Although progress has been made in improving girls' access to schooling, gaps remain, but overall in the poorest countries, 48 percent of children in school are girls, up from 37 percent in 1970. The largest gaps in girls' schooling are in Afghanistan, Pakistan, and several of the poorest sub-Saharan Africa countries.

Major types of education

Three basic types of education exist: (1) primary and secondary education, (2) higher education, and (3) adult education. Most countries have a goal of almost universal primary education and eventually secondary education as well. Primary education provides the basic literary and computational skills. Secondary education provides training for students going on to higher education, and technical education for those who seek immediate employment.

The need for higher education related to agriculture depends in part on the growth of employment opportunities in agricultural research, extension, agribusiness, and government. Undergraduate agricultural programs have expanded in many African, Asian, and Latin American countries in recent years. Some of these colleges, such as the Pan-American Agricultural School in Zamorano, Honduras, require a mix of academic and practical training and draw students from multiple countries.

Postgraduate programs also have expanded in several larger developing countries, such as India, the Philippines, Brazil, and Mexico. The quality of these programs is variable, but the programs have a better track record of their students returning home after completing their degrees than do graduate programs in developed countries. Foreign academic training in developed countries also has the disadvantage that the training and research may be less relevant to the home country of the student.

In adult education, often called *extension* education in agriculture, farmers are the primary clientele and programs are mostly oriented toward production problems facing them. Extension accelerates the dissemination of research results and, in some cases, helps transmit farmers' problems back to researchers. Extension workers provide training on a variety of subjects and must have technical competence, economic competence, farming competence, and communication skills. Thus, extension workers require extensive training and retraining to maintain their credibility with farmers. As information requirements for farming increase, adult literacy is gaining importance for understanding agricultural innovations. Technology and extension information are increasingly being transmitted through electronic means, so basic cellphone and computer literacy are also important. Basic adult literacy and the ability to absorb new messages about productivity-improving technologies are highly complementary, so that adult education in rural areas has been broadened to include basic skills.

Issues in education in developing countries

Because education is critical for development prospects, several interrelated issues must be addressed by education policymakers. These issues include barriers to participation in primary school; steps to improve school quality; finance questions, such as use of measures to recover costs; retention of students through higher grade levels versus expanding basic coverage to all; and decisions about educational curricula, such as providing technical versus more general education. Research shows that relatively minor steps can have large impacts on school attendance and student learning. For example, low-cost measures to improve health by removing intestinal worms have reduced absenteeism and improved attendance in rural Kenyan schools. Providing free school uniforms and modest cash transfers at key times during the school year also boosts attendance. Cash transfers to poor families, which provide school lunches and payments conditional on keeping children in school and complying with basic health screening, have been shown to boost school attendance in many settings. Promising low-cost reforms to improve school quality include performance-based incentives to teachers, increased parental involvement in local committees, and proactive remedial education. These changes are important because evidence shows that simply injecting additional resources into schools does not improve outcomes without structural changes in how education is delivered.[1]

Cost recovery measures such as school fees were introduced in many developing countries in the 1980s. They are based on the idea that because some of the benefits of education are private and are captured by the individual, the beneficiary (the student or his or her family) should bear some of the costs. The measures also broaden the financial base of the educational system and provide resources to cash-poor local school districts. Increasing evidence shows that such fees represent major barriers to participation in schooling, especially to the poorest, and countries that have abolished fees have seen significant growth in school participation. Many one-time proponents of cost-recovery in basic education now oppose such fees. Elimination of fees helps reduce gender and economic barriers to participation in education.

Developing countries face choices about the design of their educational curricula in rural areas. While most schools provide basic literacy and mathematics, choices need to be made about technical content. The experience has been mixed relative to agricultural education at the K–12 level in developing countries. While some argue that rural schools need to provide useful skills and thus should focus on training in agriculture, evidence shows that design of an effective agricultural curriculum is difficult and costly. Often, training methods do not correspond to conditions faced by poor farmers, and time spent in such training reduces time available for other subjects. When rural schools focus too closely on rural-specific skills, graduates face disadvantages when seeking higher education or obtaining work in urban areas.

Female education is as important as male education, yet it is often neglected

FAMILY STRUCTURE AND GENDER ROLES

Family structures vary around the world, and that variation implies differences in specific roles played by individual family members in household affairs, agricultural production and marketing, and income generation in and out of agriculture. In many West African countries, families live in compound households that include more than one generation, and individual family members are assigned specific parcels of land to farm. In much of Latin America, the basic household is a nuclear family with parents and children, and family members have specific responsibilities within the household and in farming. In Asia, nuclear families predominate, and in some cases family members work side by side in fields, but in some countries men and women undertake different tasks. Regardless of the region, women have key roles to play in farming systems. Women are involved not only in household chores and child rearing but are a major source of labor for food production and account for a large proportion of economic activity.

Gender roles

The term "gender" refers to non-biological differences between women and men, and roles in farming and household decisions in developing countries differ by gender. With the notable exception of strongly Islamic

Women harvesting wheat in India

societies, women play two major roles in the rural areas of most developing countries. They have household responsibilities for child rearing, food preparation, collecting water and firewood, and other chores. They are also paid or unpaid workers in agriculture or off the farm. They produce, process, preserve, and prepare food. They work in fields, tend livestock, thresh grain, and carry produce to market. In many areas, women manage the affairs of the household and the farm. They sell their labor to other farms and sometimes migrate to work on plantations. Involvement in farm production may be seasonal, particularly in Asia, where, in many countries, women assume major responsibilities for weeding and harvesting, both on their own farms and as paid labor on other farms. Women also work in small industries and in the informal sector, producing goods and services for sales locally or beyond.[2]

Women are important to agriculture in most of the world. In many African countries, most tasks connected with food production are left to women. Men may tend livestock or produce cash crops, but food crops are generally the purview of women. In some areas of Africa where men migrate to work elsewhere, the household administration is left to women. In Nepal, over 80 percent of women are employed in agriculture, due in part to job-related male out-migration (Box 10.1).

Similar cases exist in the Central American highlands, where men migrate seasonally to participate in coffee harvests and to coastal plantations. Households headed by women make up 20 to 35 percent of rural

BOX 10.1 GENDER ASSESSMENT
OF AGRICULTURE IN NEPAL

In Nepal, agriculture contributes one-third of the gross domestic product (GDP) and about three-quarters of the population work in the sector. The role of women in the sector is crucial given that over 80 percent of women are employed in agriculture. Yet, the conditions of employment for the majority of rural women are perilous, since they mainly work as subsistence agricultural producers. Shifts in the traditional division of labor are noted, with many women taking on additional responsibilities such as ploughing and marketing, due to job-related out-migration of rural men. The shortage of labor has also caused the abandonment of rural agricultural land, contributing to a decline in agricultural production. Yet, women's ownership of land is increasing: female-headed households accounted for about one-fifth of total agricultural landholders in 2011, which represents a rise of 10 percent compared to 2001. This is an important development, as land-ownership rights remain a major constraint for most women.

Studies have shown a persistent gender-biased wage gap throughout the country that is especially visible in agriculture: women receive wages about 25 percent lower than men, despite legal provisions for equal pay between the sexes. The entrepreneurial potential of women still remains largely untapped. Evidence shows that in Nepal, farms managed by women produce less value per hectare than those managed by men, suggesting the existence of gender inequalities, particularly in accessing, adopting, and using technologies. Women and men agricultural producers have often very distinct sets of agricultural knowledge, skills, and criteria for choosing crop varieties and performing activities, such as selecting seed, cultivating, harvesting, and processing crops. Rural women are constrained by their weak decision-making and bargaining power, triple-work burden (productive, reproductive, and community work), and limited knowledge about market demand and supply, as well as restricted opportunities for setting up micro-enterprises and agriculture businesses.

Source: Food and Agriculture Organization. *Country Gender Assessment of Agriculture and the Rural Sector in Nepal* (Kathmandu: FAO, 2019), p. ix. www.fao.org/3/CA3128EN/ca3128en.pdf

households in developing countries, excluding China and Islamic societies.[3] In Latin America, women milk cows and care for animals, while tending garden vegetables and other food crops. In sugar- and fruit-producing areas, especially in the Caribbean, women work as cash laborers on plantations, contributing a substantial proportion of household income. In Asia, many examples of female farming systems are found.

Even though they tend to work much longer days than men, the true extent of involvement of women in agriculturally related activities is often underestimated and misunderstood by policymakers. In the past, when surveys were taken, men would respond as heads of households and would frequently describe the woman's principal occupation as housewife. In many societies, women do not view themselves as "farmers", even when they work long hours on the farm and have large influences over farming-related decisions. As a result, in many surveys, women were counted as economically inactive. This "invisibility" of female employment led to policies and programs that ignored women and sometimes adversely affected them. Much has been done in the past two decades to better measure women's participation in economic activities and in household decision-making, and this problem of "invisibility" is disappearing.

A continuing gender-related problem in developing countries is lack of empowerment of women. Without empowerment, women's status has been lowered. Within the household, this lower status may mean less power to make decisions, less food, fewer health and education-related investments in women and girls, and a heavier work and disease burden. In times of household crisis, women and girls may bear a heavier burden; in southern Ethiopia, for example, research shows that women suffer more from shocks to income and health.[4] Lower status of females has been associated with weaker control over household resources, less access to information and public services such as education and health, discrimination in employment, and unequal rights to land and other important assets.[5] Lower status can prevent access to agricultural support services, resulting in potentially lower productivity on women's lands (discussed later in this chapter).

DETERMINANTS OF GENDER ROLES IN AGRICULTURE

Social, cultural, and religious factors, population pressures, farming techniques, off-farm job opportunities, colonial history, income levels, disease and health conditions, and many other factors determine the role of women in farming systems. Sometimes in areas with apparently similar physical conditions, women assume very different roles. As off-farm job opportunities, population pressures, income levels, and farming techniques change, so too does the role of women (see Box 10.2).

Shifting cultivation with hand hoeing lends itself more to female labor than does settled cultivation with a plow. For countries with low population densities, adequate food could be raised without using male labor in farming. Men used to spend their time felling trees, hunting, and in warfare. In most areas, agriculture has changed from shifting cultivation to settled agriculture and cash crops. This has resulted in a greater role for men, but often the role of women in farm work still dominates.

BOX 10.2 TANZANIA: CONSERVATION AGRICULTURE FOR SUSTAINABLE DEVELOPMENT

The Conservation Agriculture for Sustainable Agriculture and Rural Development project, which began in 2004, promotes conservation agriculture (CA) for small-scale and resource-poor farmers, especially women. In the project, energy-efficient agricultural production technologies, combined with participatory methodologies, enable farmers to adopt practices that reduce labor and raise yields and incomes. Women are the main providers of agricultural labor in Tanzania and will benefit most from the reduced labor requirements of CA.

The project was centered in Arumeru District in the Arusha region of Tanzania, a highly agricultural, rain-fed area. The primary conservation techniques are ripper tillers, which reduce tillage by cutting furrows into the soil rather than inverting it completely, and the jab planter, which allows for planting operations to be done through the soil cover with no tillage. Farmer Field Schools, discussed later in this book, were the main means of training. Participants in the schools were taught in a hands-on manner about CA techniques. Because CA was expected to have a strong impact on women, women represented the majority of field school participants, and women participants were followed carefully to see how CA affected them.

Adoption of CA has three main impacts: reduced demand for household labor, increased food security through higher yields, and increased household income. The labor effects are especially important: in addition to saving labor for planting – predominantly a women's activity, CA requires better coordination of the land preparation and planting, so women and men work together more frequently. Lower labor requirements associated with CA practices affect women and other family members differently. Poor women-headed households benefit from lower labor demands, because a decrease in labor pressures frees family members from working in the field. Children can pursue their education uninterrupted by sudden labor shortages. Women in landless households have fewer opportunities to sell their labor, but higher crop yields – and thus higher labor requirements for harvesting – could cushion the reduction in hired labor opportunities. Additional employment opportunities for rural women laborers as a result of higher yields would have an immediate effect on household livelihoods.

Source: World Bank and International Fund for Agricultural Development, *Gender in Agriculture Sourcebook* (Washington, DC: The World Bank, 2009)

The shift to the plow and draft animals has made a difference in the amount of male labor used in some areas, and long-standing differences in farming techniques undoubtedly account for many of the regional gender differences in farming activities.[6] In regions of intensive cultivation on small, irrigated farms, for example in several Asian countries, men, women, and children must work hard to generate enough production on a small piece of land. Work is mostly done by hand. In contrast, on larger farms, more tasks may be mechanized, and women devote a higher percentage of their time to housework. In some cases, mechanization has displaced female labor and lowered their status as a result, since housework is often under-appreciated. In other cases, especially sub-Saharan Africa, mechanization has increased the amount of land that can be cultivated by men and put additional strain on women who are responsible for planting and weeding.

Integration of small-scale farmers into the labor market has increased women's role in agriculture, because it is often the males who work off the farm. In some countries, males work away from the household for several weeks or months at a time, increasing the labor burden on remaining women. As economic development progresses, incomes grow and the value of time increases; these factors raise wages and may increase the burden on unpaid farm workers, such as women and children. New communications technologies, such as ubiquitous cellular telephones, now found throughout the developing world, also affect gender roles. For example, in Andean countries, women have traditionally marketed potatoes, but as information on market conditions becomes more freely available due to cellular phones, the roles of women in potato marketing are being affected.[7] Telecommunications technologies are altering gender roles and women's status throughout the world.[8] Diseases such as HIV/AIDS have further complicated men and women's roles; as sick people can no longer work in agriculture, women increasingly assume productive roles while still being the primary care-giver to the ill.

Policy implications

Why is it important to address gender inequities in society? First, as a normative concept, gender equality is important in its own right. Women ought to have equal legal and social status because social justice is an important indication of development. Second, many studies have shown that gender inequities slow the process of economic development. Less empowerment of women is associated with less schooling, lost earnings, inefficient allocation of labor, and poor health of them and their children.[9] Over time, gender inequities lead to lower nutritional and health status of children, less educational attainment, and slower growth. In agriculture, gender is important as one of the several socioeconomic characteristics that influence the adoption of new technologies.

Since women are important in agriculture, their opinions must be sought when designing new technologies. The impact of these technologies on the relationship between men and women should be considered during the design. Fortunately, many agricultural research systems now regularly conduct participatory assessments to guide technology development. In such assessments, stakeholder inputs are sought and research programs are modified based on this input. If women are making production decisions, they should receive education and guidance from extension services. Most international aid agencies such as the World Bank and the United States Agency for International Development now recognize that without considering the roles and responsibilities of women and receiving inputs during project development, these projects are much less likely to succeed. Much has been done to measure women's empowerment and the impacts of projects and policies on empowerment.[10]

Third, an increasing body of evidence shows that as women's participation in the economy grows, family well-being improves. Income earned by women is more frequently used for purchases that broadly benefit the family, such as for health care, school fees, and food for children.[11]

One means of improving income-earning opportunities for women is to take steps to provide them with inputs such as credit and new seeds. Women often have inadequate access to credit for a number of reasons. First, in many societies, women lack legal status necessary to enter into contracts. Second, only very infrequently do women hold title to land, often necessary as collateral for loans. Third, there seems to be a bias against women in the administration of credit programs.

It is likely that most new agricultural technologies are relatively gender neutral, and we see efforts on the part of certain public extension systems to increasingly reach women farmers. However, lack of access to credit and purchased inputs may continue to keep women farmers at a disadvantage. Furthermore, women often grow food crops that are minor in terms of value of production but are important in the diets of families. Agricultural research often neglects these crops, and this neglect may have adverse effects on nutrition. Because extension services are still highly staffed by males in most countries, communication with female farmers can be inhibited. Even in Africa, where women represent the majority of farmers, male farmers have greater contact with extension services. Some studies have found that productivity on women's plots lag behind those of men. Lower yields are not because of inherent differences in productivity, but because women farmers have less access to inputs. As a result, addressing problems of women's access to technology, information, and inputs can have a major impact on overall productivity of developing country agriculture.

The impacts of credit, technology, and other agricultural policies on women have been altered by discriminatory land reform and settlement policies. In Latin America, where land reform and settlement schemes often have been designed to benefit "heads of households", women have, by convention, been largely excluded. In Ethiopia and Tanzania, rights to lands have been bestowed on men. In Asia, specifically the settlement schemes in Indonesia, Papua New Guinea, and Sri Lanka, land was only given to male heads of households. Inadequate access to land, worsened by government policies, when combined with problems of access to credit can hinder women's ability to participate in agricultural development. Given the large role that women play in developing country farming systems, efforts that ignore or discriminate against them have distorting effects and diminish chances of success.

Economic development itself can have positive impacts on gender equality. The process of development expands job opportunities and the presence

Colombian women receiving instructions on how to vaccinate a chicken

of more capital raises productivity. These changes raise the value of time – women's time as well as men's. Development also is typically accompanied by investments in infrastructure such as water, roads, and electricity. As development occurs, access to telecommunications, such as cellular telephones and the internet, makes information more accessible, and improved accessibility often benefits women and children. The costs of acquiring information fall and barriers to empowerment shrink. These changes can lower work burdens of women, leaving more time for other activities. Higher incomes leave more resources for investments in assets such as human capital. As incomes grow, gender disparities in education and health status tend to shrink. Public investments in schools and health facilities lower the cost of investing in human capital and help shrink gender inequalities. In fact, gender disparities in education are most acute in the lowest income countries and almost nonexistent in high-income countries.[12]

Despite strong empirical links between economic growth and gender equality, equality is not an automatic by-product of growth, and the path of development can have important implications for gender relations. Governments that encourage equal participation and foster rights of women often find growth and greater gender equality march hand-in-hand. Gender equality has beneficial growth effects, and growth reinforces women's rights. Governments can be proactive by reforming institutions to establish equal rights and opportunities for women and men, they can strengthen policy and institutional incentives for more equal access to resources and participation, and they can take active measures to confront disparities.[13] At a minimum, they should take steps to monitor these disparities by measuring women's conditions.

Role of children

Children represent the future human resource base of a country. Economic growth and development over time depend on how resources are invested in children. As noted in Chapter 4, children represent current sources of pleasure for parents, and they are a source of investment for future income gains and security in old age. Children are a major source of farm labor in every region of the world, and their tasks expand with each year of their age. They typically begin by following a parent or sibling into the field and rapidly become involved in hoeing, weeding, harvesting, and other tasks. They feed and otherwise care for animals. They, particularly boys, may work as low-paid farm laborers on other farms. Young girls often care for younger brothers and sisters to free their mother for other work. Farm children throughout the world take on major farm responsibilities at a very young age.

At times, conflicts occur between the use of children in farm duties and providing income to the family and longer-term investments in their education. For example, in times of household crisis, such as drought or crop failures, children may be pulled out of school to lower expenses (such as school fees) or increase incomes. Such informal risk management techniques can have long-term adverse consequences because the child's lifetime productivity is being compromised by reduced access to education. Gender inequalities in investments in children have long-term consequences, but depend on social norms and other factors. For example, in many societies, in time of crisis, decreased spending on girl's education and even health care and food is a common means of coping with household financial stress. Such actions lower the status of girls and their quality of life, but are the product of long-standing cultural norms.

As adults become ill from diseases such as HIV/AIDS and malaria, children are called upon to assume a greater share of farm work and other household responsibilities. Increased disease burdens, especially in sub-Saharan Africa, are changing the roles of children and altering social structures in rural areas. In fact, some argue that AIDS has increased the vulnerability of entire villages and regions to crop failure and famine by lowering food production and increasing the work burden on children. These factors subvert livelihood coping strategies and mean that in time

Teenage girls making Trichoderma compost in Bangladesh

of need, fewer assets are available to households to help them manage risks.[14] HIV/AIDS, malaria, and other epidemics put immense burden on children.

Governments recognize the long-term adverse consequences of withdrawing children from schools. Recent experiments with conditional cash transfers are showing these programs to be very effective at promoting continued schooling. An example was the PROGRESA program (also called Oportunidades and then Prospera) in Mexico, whereby families received regular but modest cash allotments on the condition that their children remain in school and receive regular nutrition and health interventions. The program has proven to be so successful in increasing children's education participation, reducing drop outs, reducing child labor burdens, and improving child welfare that the Mexican government expanded its coverage so that more than 40 percent of the rural population was once covered.[15] Other similar programs now exist in more than 30 developing countries, including virtually every country in Latin America, and major programs in Bangladesh, India, Indonesia, Turkey, and Pakistan. However, despite its success, the Prospera program was terminated by the Mexican government in 2019 due to political objections and doubts about its targeting. It was viewed by many as an expensive program that did not provide benefits to the people who needed it most.

SUMMARY

The productivity of the economy depends on the quantity and quality of human capital. Better-educated individuals are more productive and earn higher incomes. Low productivity of human resources in agriculture is a serious problem in many developing countries. Better-educated farmers are more able to adopt new technologies and understand price and market information, and have more access to credit and other forms of capital. Education also prepares children for non-farm occupations.

Women and children play important roles in agriculture, and these roles vary by region, stage of development, and other factors. Social, cultural, religious, historical, technological, and other factors, as well as off-farm employment, determine the role of women in farming systems. Women's roles in agriculture have implications for credit and input policies, for the generation and extension of new technologies, and for land reform policies. Gender inequities can have adverse implications for long-term development inside and outside of agriculture. Compelling evidence shows that governments should take proactive steps to lower gender inequalities.

IMPORTANT TERMS AND CONCEPTS

Impacts of education on
  development
Human capital
Determinants of the role of
women in agriculture
Multiple roles of women
Regional differences in the
  roles of women

Implications of the role of
  women in agriculture
Constraints faced by women
  farmers
Role of children
Impacts of diseases and disease
  epidemics

LOOKING AHEAD

In this chapter, we briefly examined the role of human resources, family structure, and women and children in the process of agricultural and economic development. In the next part of the book, we consider means for improving those systems to increase agriculture's contribution to human welfare. We begin in Chapter 11 by providing an overview of agricultural development theories and strategies before exploring in detail the individual components of those theories and strategies.

QUESTIONS FOR DISCUSSION

1 How do investments in human capital affect productivity inside and out of agriculture?
2 What is the purpose of education for the farmer and his or her family?
3 Why should farmers support education if it just means their children will move out of farming and do something else?
4 Why might education be considered a public good?
5 What are the major types of education?
6 What roles do women and children play in agriculture?
7 In which region of the world is the role of women in agriculture the greatest?
8 What factors determine the roles of women in agriculture?
9 What are some important implications of the roles of women in agriculture?
10 Why might census statistics and other data undercount female participation in farming?
11 Why do women from near-landless and smallholder households participate more in agriculture relative to those from larger farms with more land ownership?
12 How might gender inequality slow the process of development?
13 What steps might governments take to address problems of gender inequality?
14 How does disease pressure affect the roles of children in farming?

NOTES

1 Michael Kremer and Alaka Holla, "Improving Education in the Developing World: What Have We Learned from Randomized Evaluations?", *Annual Review of Economics*, vol. 1 (2009), pp. 513–542.
2 Lynn R. Brown, Hilary Feldstein, Lawrence Haddad, Christina Peña, and Agnes Quisumbing, Chapter 32, p. 205 in Per Pinstrup Andersen and Pandya-Lorch (eds.), *The Unfinished Agenda: Perspectives on Overcoming Hunger, Poverty, and Environmental Degradation* (Washington, DC: International Food Policy Research Institute, 2001).
3 Food and Agriculture Organization, *The State of Food and Agriculture: Women in Agriculture: Closing the Gender Gap for Development* (Rome: Food and Agriculture Organization of the United Nations, 2011).

4 Stephan Dercon and Pramila Krishnan, "In Sickness and in Health: Risk Sharing Within Households in Rural Ethiopia", *Journal of Political Economy*, vol. 108(4) (August 2000), pp. 688–727.

5 Agnes Quisumbing and Lauren Pandolfelli, "Promising Approaches to Address the Needs of Poor Female Farmers: Resources, Constraints, and Interventions", *World Development*, vol. 38(4) (2010), pp. 581–592.

6 Alberto Alesina, Paola Giuliano, and Nathan Nunn, "On the Origins of Gender Roles: Women and the Plough", *Quarterly Journal of Economics*, vol. 128(2) (2013), pp. 469–530.

7 Nadezda Amaya and Jeffrey Alwang, "Women Rule: Potato Markets and Access to Information in the Bolivian Highlands", *Agricultural Economics*, vol. 43(4) (2012), pp. 403–413.

8 See, for example, Robert T. Jensen and Emily Oster, "The Power of TV: Cable Television and Women's Status in India", *Quarterly Journal of Economics*, vol. 124(3) (2009), pp. 1057–1083.

9 World Bank, *Engendering Development* (New York: Oxford University Press, 2001).

10 Sabina Alkira, Ruth Meinzen-Dick, Amber Peterman, Agnes R. Quisumbing, Greg Seymour, and Ana Vaz, "The Women's Empowerment in Agriculture Index", *World Development*, vol. 52 (2013), pp. 71–91.

11 See Norbert Schady and José Rosero, "Are Cash Transfers Made to Women Spent Like Other Sources of Income?", *Economics Letters*, vol. 101 (2008), pp. 246–248; Cheryl Doss, "The Effects of Intrahousehold Property Ownership on Expenditure Patterns in Ghana", *Journal of African Economies*, vol. 15(1) (2005), pp. 149–180.

12 See World Bank, *Engendering Development*.

13 See World Bank, *Engendering Development*, particularly chapter 6.

14 A. de Waal and A. Whiteside, "New Variant Famine: AIDS and Food Crisis in Southern Africa", *The Lancet*, vol. 362 (October 11, 2003).

15 See International Food Policy Research Institute, *PROGRESA – Breaking the Cycle of Poverty* (Washington, DC: IFPRI, 2002).

RECOMMENDED READINGS

Doss, Cheryl, "Men's Crops? Women's Crops? The Gender Patterns of Cropping in Ghana", *World Development*, vol. 30(11) (2001).

Food and Agriculture Organization, *The State of Food and Agriculture: Women in Agriculture: Closing the Gender Gap for Development* (Rome: Food and Agriculture Organization of the United Nations, 2011).

Meinzen-Dick, Ruth, Agnes R. Quisumbing, Julia Behrman, Patricia Biermayr-Jenzano, Vicki Wilde, Marco Noordeloos, Catherine Ragasa, and Nienke Beintema, *Engendering Agricultural Research*. IFPRI Research Monograph (Washington, DC: International Food Policy Research Institute, 2011).

Quisumbing, Agnes R., Lynn R. Brown, Hillary Sims Feldstein, Lawrence Haddad, and Christina Peña, *Women the Key to Food Security*

(Washington, DC: International Food Policy Research Institute, August 1995).

Quisumbing, Agnes R., Ruth Meinzen-Dick, T. Raney, A. Croppenstedt, J.A. Behrman, and A. Peterman (eds.), *Gender in Agriculture and Food Security: Closing the Knowledge Gap* (New York: Springer, 2012).

World Bank and the International Fund for Agricultural Development, *Gender in Agriculture Sourcebook* (Washington, DC: The World Bank, 2009).

11 Theories and strategies for agricultural development

THIS CHAPTER

1 Describes how the sources of agricultural growth tend to change as development occurs and how agricultural development theories have evolved over time
2 Presents the theory of induced innovation as applied to agriculture and its implications for the types of technologies generated and for institutional change
3 Discusses how transactions costs and collective action may alter the direction of technical change, with implications for asset distribution

THEORIES OF AGRICULTURAL DEVELOPMENT

We have discussed the importance of agricultural development for solving the world food–income–population problem. We have considered the nature and diversity of existing agricultural systems in developing nations. We now consider means for improving these systems to strengthen agriculture's contribution to human welfare. In this chapter, we provide an overview of agricultural development theories and strategies. In subsequent chapters, we examine in more detail the individual components of the strategies outlined here. Our over-riding concern is to identify strategies that facilitate sustainable growth with equity. We explore why agricultural development has occurred in some countries and why it has not (or has proceeded very slowly) in others.

Many theories have been suggested to explain how the basic sources of economic growth (labor, natural resources, capital, increases in scale or specialization, improved efficiency, education, and technological progress) can be stimulated and combined to generate broad-based and sustainable agricultural growth.[1] It is clear from historical experience that the relative importance of alternative sources of growth changes during the development process and has changed over time for the world as a whole. It is also clear that institutional arrangements such as marketing systems, price and credit policies, a well-functioning legal system, and transparently enforced property rights play an important role in stimulating or hindering development. Let's examine agricultural development theories and evidence to see what lessons they provide for operational strategies.

Expand the extensive and intensive margins

One means of generating increased agricultural production is to expand the use of land and labor resources. The development of agriculture in North America, South America, Australia, and other areas of the world during colonization was based on using new lands. In some of these cases, indigenous labor or slaves were also exploited. The opening up of forests and jungles in parts of Africa, Latin America, and Asia provides additional examples of expanded resource use. Economists call this increased use of land and labor *expanding or exploiting the extensive margin*.

In many historical cases, sparely populated lands were combined with labor to produce commodities for both local consumption and export. Reductions in transportation costs facilitated exports. In Thailand, for example, rice production increased sharply in the latter half of the nineteenth century, and much of the increased production went to export markets. In many colonies, exports of primary production were extracted for use in more-developed countries, and often a large share of the benefits of these exports was not realized by the producing countries but was instead transferred to the developed countries.

Expansion of unutilized land resources provides few opportunities for substantial growth in developing countries today. In areas of Latin America and Africa where additional land does exist, disease, insect, and soil problems conspire against its use in agriculture. Abundant labor is available in some countries, and continued growth of the labor force will generate increases in total agricultural output. However, most growth in

Agriculture in Asia is intensive even in hilly regions

per capita agricultural output will have to come from more *intensive* use of existing resources.

Various methods can be used to achieve more intensive resource use. Early efforts in England, Germany, and other European countries included more intensive crop rotations, green manure, forage–livestock systems, drainage, and irrigation. In many developing countries, these same factors increased land productivity. Terracing is an effective means of conserving soil productivity in hilly areas of Asia. In the mountainous regions of Central America, grass strips have been used to create terrace-like structures that conserve soil and enhance productivity. Crop rotations can enhance soil productivity and control pests. Minimum tillage and cover crops can reduce erosion and help soils capture carbon through increased organic matter content. Hayami and Ruttan estimate that agricultural development based on similar types of "conservation" has been responsible for sustaining growth rates in agricultural production in the range of 1 percent per year in many countries, including developing countries, for long periods of time.[2]

While scientists are gaining knowledge of technical and institutional innovations to lower the cost of conservation efforts, population pressures are creating a need for better ways to sustain the natural resource base. Hence, conservation will play an increasingly important role in maintaining if not expanding agricultural production in the future. Conservation agriculture involving minimum tillage, cover crops, and improved rotations has expanded over the past decades, especially on large farms in Brazil and in parts of Asia and Africa.

Another means of intensifying agricultural production is to produce more crops per unit of time through altering cropping patterns or using shorter season varieties so that two and three crops can be produced per year where one or two were produced before. Such production changes usually require scientific input to develop the required seeds, tools, or other inputs to make the double or triple cropping possible. Access to irrigation or surface water sources can facilitate this intensification.

Diversification and production of higher-valued commodities represents another means of intensifying production. These become more important as development proceeds and incomes grow, creating increased demand for higher-valued vegetables and animal proteins. Production can also be intensified by improving transportation systems to bring higher-valued commodities to urban centers. Closeness to cities and markets lowers marketing costs, increases access to labor and capital markets, lowers the cost of obtaining new and more productive inputs, and facilitates the flow of information. One implication of this "location" theory of agricultural development is that countries should encourage decentralized industrial development. Strong linkages between agriculture and markets for farm inputs and outputs can help stimulate local economies. Developing nations should improve transportation infrastructure in rural areas to increase linkages to larger markets.

Develop high-payoff inputs

Agricultural development can be accelerated through generation and diffusion of new and improved inputs and technologies (such as seeds, fertilizers, pest management practices, and irrigation systems). This approach, articulated several years ago by Schultz in *Transforming Traditional Agriculture*, is based on the idea discussed in Chapter 7 that farmers in traditional agriculture are rational and efficient given their current resources and technologies.[3] What these farmers need are new, high-payoff inputs and technologies to increase their productivity.[4] The process of spread of new technologies is technical change.

The need for technical change in agriculture has been widely accepted because of the success achieved by modern wheat, corn, and rice varieties beginning in the 1950s and 1960s. These varieties are highly responsive to fertilizer, pesticides, and water management, and their widespread adoption resulted in substantial growth in agricultural output in many developing countries. Some have argued that failure to generate technologies appropriate for conditions in Africa contributed to lagging agricultural development there compared to other developing regions. The distributional or equity effects and environmental impacts of these inputs, however, have been the subject of much debate.

Hayami and Ruttan argue that the high-payoff input theory is incomplete because it fails to incorporate the mechanism that induces the appropriate types of these new inputs and technologies to be produced in a country. The theory also fails to explain how economic conditions stimulate the emergence and growth of agricultural research and educational systems. It does not identify the process by which farmers organize collectively to support change in institutions and in investments in public infrastructure such as irrigation and drainage systems. In the next section, we explore the induced innovation theory proposed by Hayami and Ruttan to address these issues.

THEORY OF INDUCED INNOVATION

Induced innovation theory helps explain the mechanism by which a society chooses an optimal path of technical and institutional change in agriculture. The theory says that technical change in agriculture represents a response to changes in resource endowments and to growth in product demand. Changes in institutions are induced by changes in relative resource endowments and by technical change.[5]

Induced technical innovation

Technical change in agriculture can follow different paths. Technologies can be developed that facilitate the substitution of relatively abundant and low-cost factors of production for relatively scarce and high-cost factors. A rise in the price of one factor relative to others will induce technical change that reduces the use of the more expensive factor relative to others. For example, if the price of land goes up relative to labor and fertilizer, indicating that land is becoming relatively scarce, technologies such as improved seeds will be developed that can be combined with labor and fertilizer to increase production per unit of land.

This process of induced technical change is illustrated in Figure 11.1. The range of possible technologies given the state of scientific knowledge in time period 0 can be represented by what Hayami and Ruttan call the *innovation possibilities curve*, I_0^*. The specific technology employed in that time period is represented by the isoquant I_0. Production occurs at point A with N_0 units of land and L_0 units of labor, the least-cost combination of those resources given the input price ratio P_0. Now, if labor becomes more

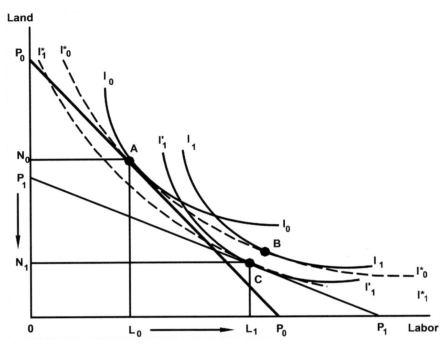

Figure 11.1 A model of induced technical change
If the ratio of the price of land to labor changes from P_0 to P_1, incentives are created not only to substitute labor for land and to move from technology I_0 at point A to technology I_1 at point B, but also to develop a new technology I'_0 at point C. Innovation possibility curves I^*_0 and I^*_1 represent the range of potential technologies that can be applied in period 0 and period 1.
Source: Yujiro Hayami and Vernon W. Ruttan, *Agricultural Development: An International Perspective* (Baltimore: Johns Hopkins University Press, 1985)

abundant relative to land so that the price of labor is reduced relative to the price of land (the new price ratio is represented by P_1), the farmer will substitute labor for land on the current isoquant. If the labor price change is expected to last, incentives are created to adopt a more labor-intensive technology and production might occur at point B on isoquant I_1. However, the theory of induced innovation says that incentives are created not only to select a new technology from the current technology set (that is, move to point B on I_1), but also to conduct research to develop new technologies. These new technologies save scarce resources and use abundant resources more intensively. Following agricultural research, the new technology set is represented by the new innovation possibility curve I_1^*. As the innovation possibility curve moves toward the origin, the same quantity can be produced at lower cost by using relatively less expensive inputs more intensively. Following the generation of this new technology set, farmers can adopt the new least-cost technology I'_1 and employ N_1 of land and L_1 of labor at point C.

Hayami and Ruttan compare the agricultural development histories of Japan and the United States to illustrate the validity of the theory. Japan experienced increasingly higher priced land compared to labor and stressed the development of biological technologies such as improved seeds and fertilizers. These technologies tend to save land and use labor more intensively. The United States, on the other hand, has approximately two times as much land per worker as does Japan. As the U.S. frontier expanded to the west, land became relatively abundant compared to labor, and innovations such as mechanical technologies to save labor emerged. The result was successful agricultural development in both countries, but agricultural output per worker is ten times greater in the United States than in Japan, while output per hectare is ten times greater in Japan than in the United States).[6]

Changes in output price relative to an input price also can induce technical change, as illustrated in Figure 11.2. The curve U represents

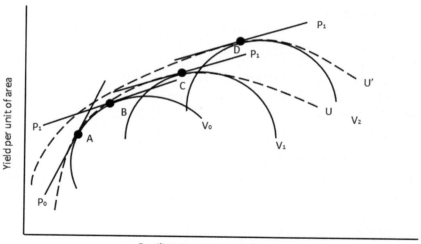

Figure 11.2 Shift in fertilizer response curve as price ratio changes
If the output/fertilizer price ratio changes from P_0 to P_1, incentives are created not only to apply more fertilizer and increase output from A to B using the traditional variety V_0, but to develop and adopt a new variety V_1 and to move to point C. Curve U represents the "envelope" of a series of available and potential crop varieties. Production of new (basic science) knowledge may also be induced so that curve U may shift up to U', and farmers move to point D and adopt new variety V_2.
Source: Yujiro Hayami and Vernon W. Ruttan, *Agricultural Development: An International Perspective* (Baltimore: Johns Hopkins University Press, 1985)

the range of current and possible production technologies in a given time period. Hayami and Ruttan call this the *meta production function*. Specific production technologies are represented by V_0, V_1, and V_2. At the initial fertilizer-output price ratio (P_0), producers use technology V_0 and produce at point A. If the price of fertilizer falls relative to the price of output (P_1), then incentives are created to move to point B on the existing technology. If the price ratio P_1 is expected to continue, farmers press scientists to develop a more fertilizer responsive variety, V_1, if it does not already exist. Farmers adopt the new variety and move to point C. In the long run, the meta production function itself may shift up (shown in Figure 11.2 as U') as more basic scientific advances are made. Farmers may then shift to a new technology represented by V_2 and move to point D.

Induced institutional change

Incentives are created for technical change, but where do these new technologies come from? How do farmers acquire them? What determines whether technologies are developed that are suitable for all farmers or only for *some* of the farmers? These questions are addressed by the theory of induced *institutional* change.

Farmers demand new technologies from private input suppliers and from the public sector. Hayami and Ruttan argue that public research scientists and administrators are guided by price signals and by pressures from farmers. The more highly decentralized the research system, the more effectively these pressures work. Research systems that welcome and facilitate inputs from farmer groups and that engage in participatory planning and research are also more responsive. The formation and growth of the research systems themselves can be the result of pressures from farmers who are responding to market forces.

Induced innovation also occurs in the economy as a whole. For example, as energy and gas prices rise, producers and consumers not only switch to existing, more energy-efficient vehicles, but also press for new types of vehicles that are even more fuel saving. The public sector may also respond with laws that require more fuel-efficient cars.

Many other types of institutions (rules of society or organizations) affect technical change and agricultural development. The rights to land, marketing systems, government pricing and credit policies, and laws governing contracts are just a few. The theory of induced institutional innovation recognizes that institutions can become obsolete and in need of adjustment over time. It says that new technologies and changes in relative resource endowments or price changes provide incentives for a society to demand new institutional arrangements (see Box 11.1 for an example).

BOX 11.1 INDUCED INSTITUTIONAL INNOVATION IN JAVA

In Java, customary rules have governed both land rights and labor exchange for many centuries. With traditional technologies, these rules have helped allocate resources so that subsistence levels of foods have been available to all village members. These communal institutions have been put under stress by modern technologies that increase the productivity of labor and the returns to landowners. These changes induce changes in the institutions governing resource allocation.

An example of an institutional innovation is the disappearance of the *bawon* rice harvesting system. This traditional system allowed everyone, whether they were from a particular village or not, to participate in the harvest and share the output. As population grew with traditional technologies, this purely open *bawon* system gradually evolved into various forms, some of which limited harvest rights to village residents, while others limited harvest rights to a set number of participants, or to people who were invited by the farmers.

Widespread diffusion of fertilizer-responsive rice varieties created sharply higher returns to harvest labor and induced a remarkable change in harvest-contract institutions. One such innovation was the introduction of the *tebasan* system, in which standing crops are sold to middlemen, who hire contract labor for harvesting and thus reduce the harvester's share while increasing returns to the landowners. Another institution is the *ceblokan* system, which limits harvesting rights to those workers who perform extra services such as transplanting and weeding without pay. A study shows that in a village where *ceblokan* was first adopted in 1964 by seven farmers, by 1978, 96 out of 100 farmers had adopted the system.

These innovations in harvest-labor institutional arrangements were largely spurred by increased incomes and higher wages accompanying technological innovation. Increased incomes and wages created incentives for farmers to change their labor-contracting system. These changes are now widespread in Java.

Source: Masao Kikuchi, and Yujiro Hayami, "Changes in Rice Harvesting Contracts and Wages in Java", Chapter 6, in Hans P. Binswanger and Mark R. Rosenzweig (eds.), *Contractual Arrangements, Employment and Wages in Rural Labor Markets in Asia* (New Haven, CT: Yale University Press, 1984)

Examples of institutional changes induced by technological change can be found in the shift from share tenure to more fixed-payment leases, which has occurred in several countries as new varieties and irrigation systems have increased yields while reducing risks.[7] An example of an institutional change due to a change in relative resource endowments is the switch from communally owned land to more private forms of property rights as population pressures increase land scarcity.

In some countries, we observe what appear to be socially desirable institutional changes, technical changes, and relatively rapid and broad-based agricultural development. However, in others we observe what seems to be perverse institutional change, agricultural stagnation, or agricultural growth with the benefits received by only a small segment of the population. Of course, many countries fall between these extremes or may move from one group to the other over time. Why do we see these differences in institutional changes that influence agricultural performance, and how do they relate to the theory of induced innovation? The answer lies partly with transactions costs and with the incentives for and effects of collective action by groups of people with common interests.

IMPLICATIONS OF TRANSACTIONS COSTS AND COLLECTIVE ACTION

The induced innovation theory presented above implicitly assumes well-functioning markets for products and factors. Prices are assumed to convey all the relevant information to decision-makers, and resources are allocated efficiently and independently of the distribution of assets (such as land) in society. Price-responsive producers are assumed to possess knowledge about alternative technologies and be able to lobby agricultural scientists to create the improved technologies that save scarce resources. Assuming no economies of scale in production, there is one optimal path for technological change.

Transactions costs
Unfortunately, transactions costs affect both factor and product markets, creating the possibility of differing optimal paths of technical or institutional change depending on farm size or other factors. Transactions costs refer to the costs of adjustment, of information, and of negotiating, monitoring, and enforcing contracts.[8] These costs arise because assets are fixed in certain uses in the short run, because information may

be costly, because there are differences in the ability to use information, and because people are willing to benefit at the expense of others.[9]

The presence of transactions costs may mean, for example, that the cost of credit falls as farm size increases, that labor costs per hectare increase as farm size increases (because of supervision costs), and the cost of land transactions declines as farm size increases. Therefore, as farm size grows, labor use per hectare may decline while machinery use per hectare and the demand for capital-intensive technologies may increase. Owners of large farms also may be quicker to adopt new technologies because they have fewer credit constraints affecting input purchases.

Transactions costs might mean that the distribution of assets matters for the direction of technical and institutional change.[10] Because the demand for particular types of technical and institutional changes will vary by farm size, the potential is created for conflicting demands on the public sector. Politicians and other public servants respond to the demands of competing groups by considering their own personal gains and losses. Consequently, a change that would benefit society as a whole may not occur if a politician receives greater private gain from an interest group that does not want the change than from a group that does.

Collective action

When producers of a commodity are few, economically powerful, and regionally concentrated, they may find it easier to act collectively to influence public decisions in their favor than if these conditions do not hold. Even if the conditions do not hold, if a commodity is very important in the diets of people in urban areas or if it earns substantial foreign exchange, the public sector still may act to help its producers. However, if producers are neither organized into a powerful collective lobby nor producing an important commodity for urban consumption or export, they will seldom receive support for the agricultural research they need. This fact may explain why peasant farmers with small landholdings are often neglected when agricultural research priorities are set.

Policy implications

The concern over the existence of transactions costs and collective action is not just a concern over the distribution of the benefits of agricultural development. Rather, it is a concern that the rate of economic growth itself will be diminished, as the most appropriate mix of technologies and institutions to maximize economic efficiency will not be produced. Although the theory of induced innovation provides an optimistic view

of how market forces can work, almost like an invisible hand to stimulate technological and institutional change, the presence of transactions
costs and collective action sounds a cautionary note that there is an
invisible foot out there eager to stomp on that hand. The reality that
agricultural and overall economic development has progressed steadily
in some countries while stagnating in others demonstrates that development is neither automatic nor hopeless. An operational agricultural
development strategy is needed that recognizes (1) the role that relative
prices can play in guiding technical and institutional change and (2) that
imperfect information and other transactions costs can sidetrack development unless domestic and international institutions are proactively
developed to constrain inappropriate collective action. Inappropriate
here is defined as actions that impose inefficiencies or fail to meet the
equity goals of a society. Several of these institutions are briefly mentioned and discussed more thoroughly in subsequent chapters.

Domestic and international institutions

Land, credit, pricing, marketing, and research policies are all crucial to
generation and adoption of appropriate technologies and for agricultural development in general. Sources of agricultural growth change
over time, and few countries today can achieve substantial production
increases by expanding their land bases. In addition, land currently
in production is being degraded due to pressures on a fragile natural
resource base. Ownership of land and other assets is highly unequal in
many countries and fragmented in others. Hence, one institutional component of an operational agricultural development strategy is to reex-
amine the arrangements governing land ownership and use and to make
any needed adjustments.

Improved transportation, marketing, and communications systems
also become crucial as economic development proceeds. Lower transportation, marketing, and communications costs can reduce transactions
costs, improve information flows, and thereby facilitate broad-based
agricultural growth. Isolated regions tend to be poor regions.

Provision of modern inputs and credit to finance their purchase are
additional components of a successful agricultural development strategy.
Farmers are rational and relatively efficient given their current resources.
Consequently, new inputs combined with improved technologies are
needed to raise the productivity of farmers in developing countries.
Research and technology transfer policies can facilitate the creation and
adoption of these technologies. Pricing policies should be designed so as
not to discourage the use nor encourage the abuse of improved inputs.

Improved transportation to reduce transactions costs becomes crucial as development proceeds

Enhanced farmer education will improve ability to recognize the benefits of and to use the technologies. Education improves capacity to assimilate and use information and thus can help reduce transactions costs.

Agricultural development is affected by macroeconomic and trade policies that arise outside the agricultural sector. The levels and types of taxes, spending, and government borrowing can dramatically influence farm prices and input costs. Exchange rates, or the value of the country's currency relative to currencies in other countries, can have major effects on domestic agricultural prices and trade.

In some countries, foreign debt repayments significantly constrain growth and reduce domestic consumption. Internationally influenced interest rates and prices vary substantially over short periods of time, adding an additional measure of unpredictability to debt levels and national incomes. International labor markets for agricultural scientists mean that high salaries draw some of the brightest and most educated scientists to more-developed countries and international agencies. Foreign aid is a source of capital and technical assistance for a few countries but is often unreliable and usually comes with strings attached. Developing countries must carefully design macroeconomic and trade policies that do not discriminate against their agricultural sector if they expect it to grow.

Operational strategy

Any operational agricultural or economic development strategy must (1) recognize individual behavioral incentives, (2) consider the presence of imperfect information, and (3) include institutional arrangements to improve market efficiency and offset market imperfections. Individuals must feel it is in their self-interest before institutional changes will occur or technologies will be adopted.

Information is valuable, imperfect, and costly to acquire, and can exhibit economies of scale in acquisition. These attributes provide the incentives and the means for some people to use the advantage they have from asset ownership, power, or willingness to engage in unscrupulous behavior to acquire information before others.

In fact, even if all assets were initially distributed equally, unless information were available equally to all or unless enforceable rules were instituted to constrain dishonest behavior, the willingness of some to gain "unfair" advantage would eventually lead to unequal distributions of assets. In primitive societies, information is basically available to all, and inappropriate activities are constrained by social and cultural norms. However, as societies become more complex as they develop, information becomes more imperfect and new institutions are needed to replace the rules that no longer constrain socially undesirable behavior.

People must feel it is in their interest to design and enforce particular institutional changes, and they need to know the implications of those changes. Institutional change involves costs because some people benefit from current arrangements and will fight any change.

The following suggestions can help lower the cost of institutional change:

- In countries where asset ownership has become so skewed that inequality is slowing agricultural development, asset redistributions (particularly land) are needed.
- Improvements in education, communications, and transportation can improve information flows and the ability of people to act on information.
- Decentralized industrial growth should lower labor adjustment costs (and facilitate employment), reduce externalities associated with urban crowding, improve market performances in rural areas, and help stimulate agricultural growth.
- Social science research can help lower the cost of designing and examining the implications of alternative institutional changes affecting agriculture. It can increase our understanding of farmer behavior,

particularly of limited resource farmers in developing countries and why they do or do not adopt new technologies.

- A government structure is needed that includes enforceable laws to protect citizens from each other and from government failures. Policies and regulations can also be used to reduce market failure. Well-functioning and transparent legal systems with independent judiciaries can help facilitate transition toward enhanced institutions.
- Improved international laws and other institutions are needed to reduce incentive problems created by international market failures.

SUMMARY

Several theories of agricultural development have been proposed over time. Expansion or conservation of resources, diffusion, use of high-pay-off inputs, and induced innovation are some of the major ones. Technical and institutional changes are key components of any operational agricultural development strategy. These changes may be induced by relative price changes resulting from change in resource endowments and product demand – up to a point. Because of transactions costs, collective action, and the realities of human behavior, the agricultural sector may not follow an economically efficient development path. The distribution of assets has important implications in the presence of transactions costs and collective action. If land is unequally distributed, then, because of transactions costs, the demands (for technologies, inputs, policies, etc.) of one group of producers are likely to be very different from those of others. Collective action can then pull the development process from its optimal path. Institutional changes to improve information flows and constrain exploitive behavior are crucial to agricultural development.

IMPORTANT TERMS AND CONCEPTS

Agricultural research and
  extension
Asset distribution
Asset fixity and adjustment costs
Collective action
Communications
Enlightened self-interest

Innovation possibilities
  curve
International factors
Invisible hand
Location theory
Market failure
Meta production function

Externalities
Farmer behavior
High-payoff inputs
Induced institutional innovation
Technical change
Induced technical innovation

Perfect information
Resource conservation
Resource exploitation
Transactions costs

LOOKING AHEAD

In this chapter, we considered theories of agricultural development and suggested a broad framework for operational agricultural development strategies. In the following four chapters, we consider sector-specific means of generating particular technical and institutional changes to stimulate agricultural growth. In later chapters, we consider macroeconomic and international factors. We begin in Chapter 12 by focusing on agricultural research and extension.

QUESTIONS FOR DISCUSSION

1 Contrast the resource exploitation and resource conservation theories of agricultural development.
2 Why is the resource exploitation theory of agricultural development less useful today than it was historically?
3 Why has the importance of resource conservation increased in recent years?
4 Why has the high-payoff input theory become widely accepted?
5 What criticisms do Hayami and Ruttan make of the high-payoff input theory?
6 Describe the theory of induced technological innovation. Be sure to identify both the importance of relative input price changes and changes in the relative prices of inputs to outputs.
7 Describe the induced institutional innovation theory.
8 What are transactions costs? What is meant by collective actions?
9 What are the implications of transactions costs and collective action for institutional innovation?
10 How might information be made more accessible to farmers?
11 What are the implications of a grossly unequal asset ownership pattern for economic growth?

12 Why are improved international institutions needed for agricultural development?

13 Why does Japanese agriculture have much higher output per hectare than U.S. agriculture, but much lower output per worker?

NOTES

1 Yujiro Hayami and Vernon W. Ruttan, *Agricultural Development: An International Perspective* (Baltimore: Johns Hopkins University Press, 1985) characterized agricultural development theories into six approaches: (1) resource exploitation, (2) resource conservation, (3) location, (4) diffusion, (5) high-payoff input, and (6) induced innovation. The first part of the chapter draws on their ideas.

2 Hayami and Ruttan, *Agricultural Development*, p. 52.

3 Theodore W. Schultz, *Transforming Traditional Agriculture* (Chicago: University of Chicago Press, 1964).

4 Hayami and Ruttan have labeled Schultz's approach the "high-payoff input" model. A recent description of this approach in the context of Kenyan agriculture is found in Roger Thurow, *The Last Hunger Season: A Year in an African Farm Community on the Brink of Change* (New York: Public Affairs, 2013).

5 Hayami and Ruttan (*Agricultural Development*, p. 94) define institutions as the rules of society or of an organization that facilitate coordination among people by helping them form expectations that can reasonably hold in dealing with others. They reflect the conventions that have evolved in different societies regarding the behavior of individuals and groups relative to their own behavior and the behavior of others.

6 Hayami and Ruttan, *Agricultural Development*. Many developing countries, particularly in Asia, are finding the Japanese path of technical change more appropriate than the U.S. path, given their relative resource endowments and the nature of changes in those endowments.

7 Share tenure is an arrangement whereby a farmer who is renting land pays the rent with a fixed percentage of the farmer's output.

8 A succinct discussion of transactions costs is found in Douglas C. North, "Institutions, Transactions Costs, and Economic Growth", *Economic Inquiry*, vol. 25 (1987).

9 William J. Baumol, "Williamson's The Economic Institutions of Capitalism", *Rand Journal of Econometrics*, vol. 17 (1986), p. 280, points out that if there were no fixed or sunk costs in land, capital, or labor, resources could easily be transferred to optimal uses. If information were perfect or if people could always figure out how to design contracts to cover any contingency, fixed costs would not matter. If people did not try to profit at others' expense, contracts could be drawn loosely and adjustments made as conditions change.

10 See Alain de Janvry, Marcel Fafchamps, and Elisabeth Sadoulet, "Transaction Costs, Public Choice, and Induced Technological Innovations", in Bruce M. Koppel (ed.), *Induced Innovation Theory and International Agricultural*

Development: A Reassessment (Baltimore and London: Johns Hopkins University Press, 1995).

RECOMMENDED READINGS

Fuglie, Keith O., and Nicholas E. Rada, *Resources, Policies, and Agricultural Productivity in sub-Saharan Africa* (Washington, DC: U.S. Department of Agriculture, Economic Research Service, Report 145, February 2013).

Hayami, Yujiro, and Vernon W. Ruttan, *Agricultural Development: An International Perspective* (Baltimore: Johns Hopkins University Press, 1985), Chapters 3–4.

Koppel, Bruce M. (ed.), *Induced Innovation Theory and International Agricultural Development: A Reassessment* (Baltimore and London: Johns Hopkins University Press, 1995).

Thurow, Roger, *The Last Hunger Season: A Year in an African Farm Community on the Brink of Change* (New York: Public Affairs, 2013).

PART 4

Getting agriculture moving

International Rice Research Institute in the Philippines

12 Agricultural research and technology transfer

THIS CHAPTER

1 Discusses the role of public and private agricultural research in generating improved technologies and institutions and the effects of those technologies on income growth, income distribution, and food security
2 Describes the major types and sources of agricultural research innovations
3 Examines the role of agricultural innovation transfer mechanisms

THE ROLE OF AGRICULTURAL RESEARCH

A major determinant of growth in agricultural production is the effectiveness of agricultural research and the spread of improved technologies and institutions. Through research and activities that extend innovations to farmers, the productivity of existing resources is increased, new higher-productivity inputs and sustainable ways of producing food are developed and disseminated, and new or improved institutional arrangements are designed and instituted. Examples of research outputs include higher-yielding plant varieties, sustainable methods for controlling insects and diseases, increased knowledge about methods for manipulating plant or animal genes, and designs for improved agricultural policies. Research creates the potential for increased agricultural production, improved food security and nutrition, increased foreign exchange, reduced pressure on the natural resource base, and many other positive results. Let's consider in more detail the nature of these effects and the possibilities for negative as well as positive outcomes.

Over time, agricultural research has been associated with improvements in incomes and reductions in poverty. It is estimated that without the productivity improvements generated through agricultural research, an additional 40 million hectares of land, about the size of Germany, would have been needed to feed the world's population growth since 1960. Productivity gains have saved highly erosive fragile soils and reduced deforestation, and helped preserve biodiversity. Specific research successes include a new African rice variety that is more productive and better suited to harsh environmental conditions, cassava varieties that are resistant to cassava mosaic virus and raise yields by 10 tons per hectare, and enhanced strains of tilapia fish that grow 60 percent faster than traditional strains.

Impacts on agricultural productivity

Productivity increases generated through agricultural research imply a shifting upward of agricultural production functions. The simple example of increasing the output per unit of an input, say fertilizer, is illustrated in Figure 12.1. If a more responsive seed variety is made available through research, output produced per kilo of fertilizer may increase. The research that produced that higher quality seed may be either public or private or both. Public research is conducted in national research institutions, public universities, or government-sponsored research in private entities. Private research is financed by private companies.

Research and subsequent technical change in agriculture raises productivity. The value of agricultural production added per worker is shown in Table 12.1 for India, China, Indonesia, Nigeria, and Brazil (five of the more populous countries of the world) for 2000 and 2016. Despite population growth, which might be expected to push production onto more marginal agricultural lands, agricultural productivity per worker rose substantially in each of these countries, roughly tripling in China and Nigeria and doubling in India, Indonesia, and Brazil. This same pattern is found in most other developing countries, although value of agricultural output per worker has declined in several sub-Saharan Africa countries, including Uganda, Kenya, Malawi, Burundi, Liberia, Zambia, and Zimbabwe, where population growth has outpaced slow productivity improvements. In cases where value added per worker is rising, we would expect to find increasing wages among farm workers; as a result, benefits from productivity growth are diffuse in the rural economy.

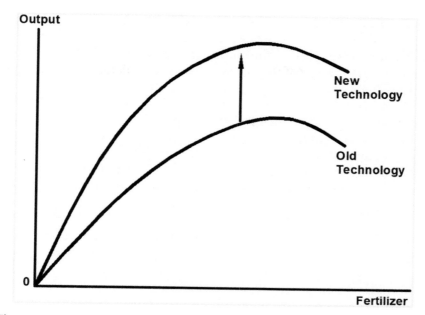

Figure 12.1 The effect of research on input productivity: new technologies generated through research can shift the production response function upward

Table 12.1 Agricultural Value-added Per Worker (2010 USD)

Country	2000	2016
India	965	1,702
China	1,073	3,450
Indonesia	1,785	3,473
Nigeria	1,661	5,881
Brazil	5,235	11,051

Source: World Bank, World Development Indicators Online Database

The examples shown in Figure 12.1 and Table 12.1 are oversimplified in the sense that most new technologies require different mixes of inputs; not all other inputs are held constant. Measurement of total productivity gains due to research requires netting out the cost of any additional inputs employed with the improved technologies. The resulting total net cost reduction per unit of output produced can then be used to summarize the total productivity effect. This total productivity effect is illustrated in Figure 12.2. New or improved technology shifts the original commodity supply curve (S_1) downward to S_2 because the supply curve is a marginal cost curve and the new technology has reduced the cost per unit of production. The new, lower cost of production means that more output is supplied to the market at a lower price. This lower price is good for consumers of the product, but producers might be hurt.

Many studies have estimated the economic returns to society from public research investments aimed at achieving these productivity increases. One study found more than 1,700 distinct estimates of the returns to various research programs around the world and a median economic rate of return of 44 percent.[1] Individual programs and projects vary widely in their estimated returns, but on the whole, agricultural research has been a highly profitable investment for the societies that undertake it. Returns are well above government cost of capital or earnings on many alternative investments. National leaders have a responsibility to invest scarce public resources in activities that yield high returns.

Increased agricultural productivity not only creates the potential for higher real incomes to producers through lower costs and to consumers through lower food prices but can also help a country's agriculture become more competitive in world markets. Efficiency gained through

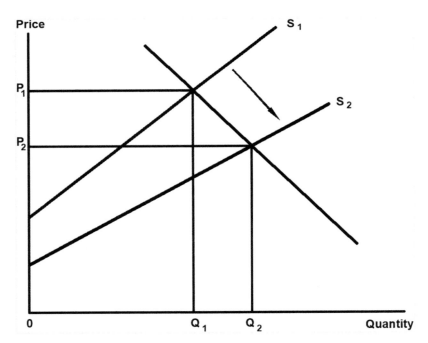

Figure 12.2 Effect of research on supply: agricultural research reduces the cost per unit of output, causing the supply curve to shift to the right

higher agricultural productivity can be turned into foreign exchange earnings or savings as a result of additional exports or reduced imports.

The fact that agricultural research has yielded high returns in many countries in the past does not imply that these returns are guaranteed for all research systems or types of research. Each country must carefully consider the appropriate type of research organization and portfolio of activities, given its resource base and special needs (see Box 12.1 for an example of a research portfolio).

BOX 12.1 MAJOR TYPES OF RESEARCH IN THE NATIONAL AGRICULTURAL RESEARCH INSTITUTION IN ECUADOR

The listing here of the major types of agricultural research activities in Ecuador provides an example of a typical applied research portfolio for a small developing country. Given its limited research budget, the country must decide which commodities to concentrate on and how much to emphasize each type of research.

1 **Plant breeding:** development of new lines and varieties that yield more and are resistant to insects and diseases; maintenance of a germplasm collection
2 **Cultural practices:** determination of optimal planting densities, improved harvesting methods
3 **Crop protection:** improved methods for control of insects, diseases, weeds, and nematodes, including biological, cultural, and chemical methods
4 **Soils and fertilizers:** development of improved soil conservation methods, chemical analysis of soils including macro- and micro-element analysis, toxicity studies, economic analysis of soil conservation and fertilization practices
5 **Water management:** studies of water needs, improved irrigation methods, salinity control
6 **Mechanization:** design of improved agricultural implements
7 **Socioeconomics:** diagnosis of constraints to technology adoption, monitoring and evaluation of research, analysis of farm management practices and opportunities
8 **Technology validation:** on-farm transferring, testing, and validation of new technologies

9   **Seed production:** basic and registered seed production, tech-
     nologies for seed production, improved vegetative propagation

10   **Post-harvest technologies:** improved methods for storage,
     drying, cleaning, packaging, and transporting agricultural
     products

11   **Agro-forestry:** improved systems of agro-forestry and of pas-
     turing forests

12   **Animal improvement:** animal breeding, introduction and
     selection of animals from outside the country, adaptation of
     animals to different climates

13   **Animal health:** prevention and cure of diseases and external
     and internal parasites

14   **Animal nutrition:** improved forages, analysis of concentrates
     and other supplementary feeding programs, evaluation of
     nutritional deficiencies, nutritive value of feeds

Source: Julio Palomino, Planning Director, National Agricultural Research
Institution, Ecuador

Distributional and nutritional effects

Agricultural producers at different income levels, with different farm
sizes, in different locations, and with different land tenure arrangements,
can gain or lose as a result of new technologies and institutional changes
generated through research. These gains and losses depend on market
conditions, among other factors. Consumers are major beneficiaries of
agricultural research due to falling product prices, but the benefits they
receive differ by income level and are influenced by the nature of the
research portfolio. Returns to land versus labor are also influenced by
research. Nutritional implications follow from these differential producer, consumer, and factor-income effects.

Farm size and tenure

The issue of whether improved agricultural technologies benefit large
farms more than they do small farms has been the subject of substantial debate. Farm size is not a major impediment to adoption of
new biological technologies such as improved seeds, which are a significant focus of developing country agricultural research. However,
larger farms do tend to be among the first adopters of many new

technologies, probably because it pays large farms more to invest in obtaining information about the technologies. Owners of large farms may have more formal education that helps them process the information and a greater ability to absorb risk. Large farms often have better access to credit needed to purchase modern inputs. Most small farms in the same region as large farms do eventually adopt the technologies, but the first adopters typically receive greater income gains from adoption. Late adopters may be faced with lower producer prices because overall production increases as early adopters expand their output. Even if all producers in a given region adopted a scale-neutral technology at the same time, absolute income differences would widen because the increased returns per hectare are spread over more hectares on larger farms.

As noted in Chapter 11, not all technologies and institutional changes are scale-neutral. For example, certain types of mechanical technologies can be used profitably on large but not small farms. With differences in transactions costs, large farmers may press research systems for research results suitable for them even if the country's resource base on average would dictate a different type of technology. Also, while many technologies are scale-neutral and some are biased toward large farms, it may be difficult to generate technologies biased toward small farms. All this implies that reducing transactions costs through improved information is important, but it also implies that research may not be the best policy tool for achieving distributional objectives.

Tenant farmers represent an important producer group in many countries. It is difficult to generalize about the effects of research on the incomes of tenants versus landlords. One might expect that improved biological technologies would make labor more productive and thus help tenants, but the distribution of income gains is influenced by other factors as well. If each landlord has several tenants, so that the average size of landlord holdings is greater than the average size of tenants' farms, then the average landlord would gain relative to the average tenant if each received equal shares of income gains per hectare. Still, tenants are likely to see absolute growth in their incomes with productivity-enhancing innovations.

Contractual arrangements influence the distribution of research benefits, and the arrangements may change as well as a result of new technologies. If the tenant pays the landlord a fixed *share* of the output, the division of any income gains after adopting the new technology depends on the sharing mechanisms for both output and production costs. But if the tenant pays a fixed *amount* to the landlord, the tenant can keep the income gains until the landlord raises the rent. Often, increases in land productivity are bid into land rents (i.e., the value of land increases), and landowners are able to capture these rents by changing tenancy agreements.

Regional disparities

Regional differences in resource endowments and basic infrastructure can influence the distribution of research gains among producers. In fact, disparities in the net benefits from research between regions tend to be larger than disparities within regions. Data from India indicate that the new rice and wheat varieties that increased production so dramatically in the late 1960s through the mid-1970s primarily benefited the more productive wheat and rice states. Productivity increased sharply in the country's northern region. From 1967 to 1976, the central and eastern regions actually had decreasing rice yields. These interregional yield differentials diminished over time, but the technologies clearly benefited certain regions more than others. The introduction of modern crop varieties exacerbated interregional disparities in many countries because those technologies often required irrigation and greater use of farm chemicals. Producers in dryland areas and regions with poor infrastructure for transporting fertilizer were disadvantaged. Broadening the scope of agricultural research and decentralizing the research structure can help reduce regional disparities, although rates of return on research aimed at more productive regions are consistently higher than those for marginal areas.

Producers and consumers

The distribution of benefits from technological change between producers and consumers depends largely on the degree to which quantity demanded responds to price changes. If producers face an elastic demand for their output, increased supplies will place little downward pressure on prices so producers rather than consumers capture most of the benefits of the innovation. Export crops, for example, tend to have relatively elastic demands, and thus new technologies for the production of these commodities tend to favor producers. Basic staples in the diet have relatively inelastic demands, as discussed in Chapter 3. The benefits of research on these commodities flow largely to consumers through lower prices.

The poor spend a higher proportion of their income on food and so benefit relatively more than others from any decline in food prices due to research-induced increases in food supplies. This benefit is received by both the urban and the rural poor. The rural poor are often landless laborers who purchase food or small owner-operators or tenants who retain a large part of their output for home consumption. A study in Colombia, for example, found that the lower 50 percent of Colombian households received about 15 percent of total national household income, but they captured nearly 70 percent of the net benefits of the rice research program.[2] Benefits to consumers flow across regions, especially where adequate transportation exists, and dampen the interregional disparities to producers mentioned earlier.

Land, labor, and capital

New technologies allow the same output to be produced with fewer resources, thus freeing up those resources for use elsewhere in the economy. The dual-economy model described in Chapter 6 illustrated the potential for labor released from agriculture to become a fundamental source of industrial growth. However, the effect of technical change on the demand for resources is influenced by the nature of the technology and by the nature of product demand.

Some new technologies result in proportionate savings of all inputs, while others save labor and use land or vice versa. For example, a new machine to cultivate the land may save labor and require a farmer to use more land to justify the cost. A higher-yielding rice variety may require more labor but produce more per unit of land. If a technology is neutral with respect to its effect on land and labor use, and if the demand for the product is elastic, the demand for both land and labor may grow proportionately following adoption of the technology. The reason is that, with elastic demand, total revenue increases with a shift out in the supply curve, providing increased returns to all resources. On the other hand, if product demand is inelastic, a neutral technical change can reduce the demand for all inputs proportionately.

Most new technologies are biased toward the use of one resource or another. Many of the higher-yielding varieties that comprised the "green revolution" (see Box 12.2) require significantly more labor input per unit of land. As a result, strong poverty-reducing impacts of the green revolution were transmitted through labor markets. In countries where markets are highly competitive and input prices reflect true input scarcity, the induced-innovation model presented in Chapter 11 predicts that new technologies will be developed to save the relatively scarce resources. However, if input prices are distorted, externalities exist, or transactions costs are high, technical change will not necessarily be biased in a direction that saves the scarcest resources; this "inappropriate" bias will thus reduce the rate of overall agricultural growth below its potential.

BOX 12.2 THE GREEN REVOLUTION

The term *green revolution* was coined in 1968 by William S. Gaud, former Administrator of the U.S. Agency for International Development, to describe the dramatic wheat harvests that had been achieved in 1966 to 1968 in India and Pakistan. The term gained further publicity in 1970 when Norman Borlaug was awarded the Nobel Peace Prize for his research that produced the high-yielding, semi-dwarf Mexican wheats that had performed so well in Asia and Latin America. As the semi-dwarf wheats were making their dramatic entry, the International Rice Research Institute released new semi-dwarf rice with the same dramatic effect.

The big innovation of the green revolution was developing varieties of wheat and rice that would not fall down (lodge) when nitrogen fertilizers were applied. These new lines of plants also tended to be earlier maturing, to produce many shoots (tillers), and to be less sensitive to day length.

Because so many factors influence the effect of new technologies on resource use, it is difficult to generalize about the effect of research on employment, on the long-run returns to land, and so on. One implication is that agricultural research is a relatively blunt instrument for implementing a policy of distributing income to particular resources.

Nutritional implications

Agricultural research can influence human nutrition through several mechanisms. First, if new technologies are aimed at poor farmers, a high proportion of the resulting income streams will be spent on improving the diet. If the technologies are aimed at commodities produced and consumed at home, the effect will be direct. If the technologies affect export crops produced by small farms, the extra income may be spent on buying food from others. Even if the new technologies are suitable only for large farms producing export crops, the influence on nutrition of the poor may be positive if the demand for labor increases. However, this employment effect is not at all certain and depends on the factor biases discussed earlier.

One nutritional effect of research comes from the increased availability of food at lower prices. As supply shifts out against a downward sloping demand curve, all consumers benefit from lower food prices that increase real wages and raise purchasing power throughout society.

Research can be used to reduce fluctuations in food supply, prices, and income and thereby alter nutrition. Some of the severest malnutrition occurs in rural areas during years of low incomes due to lower than normal production. Research on drought-tolerant varieties can help reduce production fluctuations and help lower malnutrition. Research can be used to directly fortify crops such as rice, beans, sweet potatoes, and cassava with micronutrients such as iron, zinc, vitamin A, and vitamin B. Micronutrient deficiencies can be as detrimental to human health as protein and energy deficiencies.

It is difficult to draw conclusions about the nutritional implications of a particular portfolio of research activities because the sources of nutritional impacts identified previously can act counter to one another. For example, a labor-saving technology used to produce export crops might lower wages and not induce changes in food supply, thus making landless laborers worse off. Some concern has been voiced about the nutrition effects of research devoted to export-crop production. If numerous producers switch from food crops to export crops, then there is potential for domestic food prices to rise, and such a rise would hurt the urban and landless poor. However, there is little empirical evidence of this switch, and nutritional levels are perhaps most influenced by research that generates the largest income gains, particularly if those gains are realized by low-income producers. Therefore, focusing research disproportionately on commodities with high nutritional content may result in less income than if the research were focused on other commodities. For example, improving the productivity of a vegetable export crop in Guatemala may improve the family's nutrition more than improving the productivity of its maize crop, because the former will lead to a greater increase in farm income and therefore the family's ability to buy food.

Environmental effects of research

Concerns over environmental degradation in developing countries were discussed in Chapter 9. Deforestation, soil erosion, climate change, desertification, pesticide pollution, and loss of biodiversity have become serious problems in many countries, and research can play a major role in their solution.

First, new technologies for mitigating soil erosion, providing alternative energy sources, sequestering carbon, and substituting for chemical pesticides can be generated through research. Second, research can be used to design improved policies, providing increased incentives to adopt management practices and help sustain the integrity of the natural resource base. Third, the higher incomes generated through research-induced productivity increases will put downward pressure on population growth in the long run. Fourth, higher income streams will also reduce the pressures to abuse the environment in the short run just to obtain food and fuel. Finally, income growth will create more demand for environmental quality. Thus, agricultural research is critically important for encouraging environmentally sound and sustainable agricultural growth.

Research organizations have been criticized in the past for devoting too many resources to research related to modern inputs such as fertilizer, pesticides, and irrigation. Excessive and improper use of these inputs can cause environmental damage. An additional criticism has been that too little research is aimed at resource-conserving technologies, such as integrated pest management and methods for reducing soil erosion. There is some truth in these claims, although research on sustainable farming practices has accelerated over time (see Box 12.3). Also, market failures tend to cause an undervaluation of environmental services, as discussed in

BOX 12.3 RESEARCH AND THE ENVIRONMENT: THE CASE OF THE CASSAVA MEALYBUG

The cassava mealybug was accidentally introduced from Latin America into Africa in the early 1970s and soon began causing severe damage to cassava crops. Because some 200 million Africans depend on cassava as a staple food, this damage became a deep concern.

Researchers at the International Institute of Tropical Agriculture (IITA) in Africa, in collaboration with those at the International Center for Tropical Agriculture (CIAT) in Latin America, found a means of biological control. Importation and distribution of the parasitic wasp *Epidinocasis Iopez*, a natural enemy of the mealybug from Latin America, led to dramatic reductions in African mealybug populations with biological methods. No pesticides are required, and small-scale African farmers are freed from a damaging pest by nature itself.

Source: J. Zeddies, R.P. Schaab, P. Neuenschwander, and H.R. Herren, "Economics of Biological Control of Cassava Mealybug in Africa", *Agricultural Economics*, vol. 24(2) (2001), pp. 209–219

Chapter 9. Because of this undervaluation, producers and consumers often do not demand resource-conserving technologies. In the long run, one of the best ways to combat forces leading to environmental degradation is to raise incomes and reduce poverty. Research can be an effective means of raising incomes, though in the short run, more agricultural research should, perhaps, be aimed at conserving environmental resources.

Other research issues

Institutional change

Much agricultural research results in new or improved technologies that are embodied in inputs or methods of production. However, agricultural research can be directed toward the design of new or improved policies or institutional changes. In other words, agricultural research can help lower the cost of adjusting institutions to the changing physical, natural resource, economic, and biological environments. A static or distorted institutional environment can be as great a hindrance to agricultural development as can a static technology base.

Credit policies, marketing and pricing policies, land tenure rules, crop insurance, and natural resource policies are examples of institutional arrangements that can be improved through research. Institutional changes that improve the flow of market information and reduce externalities are particularly important.

Public versus private sector research

Just because agricultural research is important to development does not imply that the public sector must conduct it. Both the public and private sectors are heavily involved in research. Why does the private sector not provide all the needed agricultural research? For many types of research, it is difficult for one firm to exclude other firms from capturing the benefits from the research; many types of research are public goods. In other words, a firm may incur substantial costs in conducting research but, once the research is completed, other firms can make use of the results without incurring much cost. Thus, the firm has little incentive to do the research in the first place. In addition, many types of research are highly risky, so that firms are hesitant to take the risk for fear of incurring a substantial loss.

Certain types of research, particularly applied research related to mechanical and chemical innovations, are less risky and potentially patentable and thus attract sizable private research activity. Some types of biological and soils research, on the other hand, have historically been more difficult to patent and have thus been primarily conducted in the public sector. However, the patentability of biological research has grown over time and has played a major role in the development of new genetically modified crops and animals. As a country develops, the research role of the private sector typically increases in developing and marketing improved seeds as well as in mechanical and chemical innovations. However, there is often a time lag between the development of public sector research and the establishment of substantial private sector research activity. One action that a country can take to promote private research is to establish enforceable property rights (patents, licenses, etc.) over research results, not just for mechanical and chemical technologies but for biological technologies as well.

Intellectual property rights

Intellectual property rights (IPRs) refer to legal protections, granted for a defined period of time, to scientific, technological, and artistic inventions. Copyrights, trademarks, patents, plant breeders' rights, and trade secret laws are examples of ways that intellectual property rights are granted. Legal systems differ by country, and hence the types, extent, and duration of rights granted vary as well. Patents and plant breeders' rights are the most important forms of intellectual property protection for agricultural research results and technologies. Over time, copyrights have become more important as well because the databases that contain information about plant genes can often be copyrighted.

Patents are the strongest type of intellectual property, as the patent holder can exclude all others from making, using, selling, or offering to sell the invention in the country while the patent is in force (unless others purchase a license to use it). To be patentable, an invention must be new, useful, not obvious, and be disclosed so that others can pay a license to use and replicate it. Plant breeders' rights (PBRs) grant protection to crop varieties that are new, distinct, uniform, and stable. Patents and PBRs give a monopoly on commercializing the invention or variety for a defined period of time, which allows the inventor or breeder to recover their costs and, often, far more than their costs. This protection therefore gives them incentives to invent or breed that they otherwise would not have, but can lead to long-term monopoly profits that may, in fact, be economically inefficient.

Many developing countries are still in the process of designing and implementing an intellectual property protection system for plants and animals. Details of IPR systems vary from country to country, but countries that lag behind run the danger of private firms and individuals being reluctant to develop or sell products with new technologies embedded in them. Developing countries have grown fearful that as more and more technologies are covered by intellectual property rights, their people and firms will be discouraged from using the technologies and resulting products because of the high costs of licensing the technologies or paying for the higher-cost products. This issue has been a topic of discussion and action in multilateral trade negotiations since the early 1990s and is discussed more in Chapter 17.

NATURE, ORGANIZATION, AND TRANSFER OF RESEARCH

Some agricultural research is very "applied" and yields immediate practical results. Others are more "basic" or fundamental and may not yield results for many years. Agricultural research systems themselves are organized in a variety of different ways. Let's consider the major categories of agricultural research and organizational arrangements.

Categories of agricultural research

Agricultural research can be categorized into basic research, applied research, adaptive research, and testing. *Basic* research develops knowledge with little or no specific use in mind. Studies of evolution, genetics, biochemical processes, and so on may discover fundamental principles of substantial significance to more applied researchers, but the specific end use of the research results are often difficult to identify prior to the research. Most basic research is carried out in developed countries or in the largest of the developing countries.

Applied agricultural research is aimed at solving particular biological, chemical, physical, or social science problems affecting one or more countries or areas in a state or region. Development of new plant varieties, methods for controlling specific insects and diseases in plants or animals, and animal nutrition research are examples of applied research. Applied research may take place at international research centers or in national research systems.

Adaptive research takes the results of applied research and modifies or adapts them to local conditions within a country or region. A plant variety developed for a broad area may need to be modified for a specific microclimate. Fertilizer recommendations, methods for controlling soil erosion, and many other technologies require adaptation to the local setting. Most of this research takes place at local experiment stations or on farms.

Testing research is conducted at local experiment stations or on farms to assess whether research results from other locations are suitable for solving local problems. Improved pesticides, management practices, or plant varieties are examples of research results that may be tested. All countries conduct some testing research, but for very small countries with limited resources, testing may represent a large portion of total research. Much testing is conducted by farmers themselves.

These categories of research are linked and dependent on each other. A research center may be involved in several categories.

Ecuadorian scientists recording disease data in an applied pest management experiment on plantain

Biotechnology

Much applied and adaptive agricultural research involves what has been called *biotechnology* research. *Traditional biotechnology* research includes well-established techniques in plant breeding, biological control of pests, conventional animal vaccine development, and many other types of research. *Modern biotechnology research* includes use of recombinant DNA, monoclonal antibodies, marker-assisted breeding, gene editing, and novel bio-processing techniques, among others.

Modern biotechnology provides new tools and strategies for increasing agricultural production. The tools for improving agricultural output range from novel approaches to cell and tissue culture to the genetic manipulation of biological material. Modern biotechnology is based on several new technologies. One of them, recombinant DNA, often called *genetic engineering*, enables the essential genetic material in cells, DNA, to be manipulated. It offers the possibility of transferring genetic material from one species to another, thereby transferring a useful genetic trait. Such a transfer is also called *transgenics* and produces genetically modified organisms (GMOs).

Another biotechnology technique, monoclonal antibodies, is used to detect individual proteins produced by cells, thereby providing a method for rapid and specific diagnosis of animal and plant diseases. A third novel bio-processing technique involves new cell and tissue culture technologies that enable rapid propagation of living cells. These techniques provide improved methods for large-scale production of useful compounds by the microbial or enzymatic degradation of various substrates.

Modern biotechnology is also used to map the location and functions of genes in individual species. By identifying whether "markers" on a chromosome exist for a specific gene or genes that control a trait of interest, a process called *marker-assisted breeding* can be used to speed up the breeding process to incorporate a useful trait in a new variety.

Gene editing refers to using techniques to insert, modify, replace, or delete DNA in the genome of a living organism at predetermined locations.[3] Gene-editing techniques are used in plants, animals, and humans to detect and repair genetic diseases.

Modern biotechnology can potentially produce new plant and animal traits, plant and animal growth hormones, bio-pesticides, bio-fertilizers, diagnostic reagents for plant and animal diseases, and enzymes and food additives. They may improve the tolerance of plants and animals to particular pests and stresses such as drought and increase the efficiency with which plants and livestock utilize nutrients, or increase a plant's nutritional quality (for example, rice or cassava with increased vitamin A or iron). They may reduce the need for agrichemicals.

Modern biotechnologies are on the cutting edge of science, and if developing countries are to be successful in developing their own modern biotechnologies or adapting technologies produced elsewhere, they will need scientists trained in microbiology and biochemistry. These countries will need to integrate modern biotechnology into traditional biotechnology research programs. They will need to put in place or refine bio-safety rules and resolve rules on intellectual property rights, as the rights to many aspects of the technologies are patented and owned by private companies.

Benefits and costs of modern biotechnology

Concerns have been expressed by some about the health and environmental safety of modern biotechnologies, especially for those technologies that involve transferring genes across species. All technologies involve some risks, and each country needs to develop and implement a regulatory system that allows it to test and monitor the safety of its new agricultural technologies. The risks associated with modern biotechnologies are thought to be relatively low, and many of the technologies can have positive effects on health and the environment through effects on reducing pesticide use. However, there can be no certainty that adverse health and environmental effects will not occur. Consumers, especially in Europe, have expressed reservations about consuming foods produced with the use of genetic engineering. One concern has been the possibility that genes, say, from an herbicide-tolerant crop, might transfer through pollen to another species, creating perhaps a super-weed that would be difficult to control with an herbicide. Gene transfer across species does occur frequently, although odds of creating a super-weed are slim. Another concern is whether people may have an allergy to a transgenic crop. A third concern is whether people should be attempting to alter nature, although many types of agricultural research in addition to genetically modified organisms could be subject to this same concern.

Economic concerns have also been raised with respect to whether a few companies might end up controlling the intellectual property rights associated with the genes and to the transformation processes, thereby gaining some monopoly power. If they did gain such power, they might charge farmers a high price for their seeds. Countries, however, can regulate companies and have their public research systems enter into joint ventures with the private sector to ensure freedom of access to seeds at reasonable prices.

Biotechnologies are just one of many potential means of increasing agricultural productivity in developing countries, and perhaps the greatest danger is that developing countries forgo the food and income growth that the technologies may afford them. In 2018, approximately 192 million hectares of transgenic crops – about 14 percent of the total crop area in the world – were grown in 26 countries. More than half of the biotech crops planted were grown in developing countries, with Brazil, Argentina, India, and China leading the way. However, not all of those countries plant biotech food crops, as opposed to say cotton, and planting of transgenic crops in sub-Saharan Africa has been limited to South Africa, Sudan, and Burkina Faso to date.[4]

Some fear that the new seeds will cost too much for farmers in developing countries, as private firms attempt to capture their research costs through only selling seeds of crops that are hybrids or that have a "terminator gene" embedded in them. Hybrids or terminator genes would force farmers to purchase new seeds each time they plant or the seeds will not grow. Due to the concerns being raised on this issue, seed companies have not employed the terminator gene, although they have emphasized hybrids to protect their investment. The public sector has also been involved in biotechnology research in many countries to help ensure that transgenic seeds are available at a reasonable price or for open-pollinated varieties for which seeds can be saved and replanted. Modern biotechnology, including GMOs, has been widely used and consumed for more than 25 years with no harm to human health or unexpected environmental effects.

Several studies have documented potentially large economic benefits that would accrue from increased use of biotechnologies in developing countries.[5] These benefits would be realized by consumers through lower food prices and through increased nutritional quality. Producers might also gain through lower costs of production. If developing countries do not pursue agricultural biotechnologies, they may be placed at a competitive disadvantage compared to countries that do pursue them. However, transgenic technologies are certainly not the only means of improving crop productivity, and many others, such as marker-assisted breeding, have become even more important, both because they are less controversial and because regulatory costs related to ensuring bio-safety are lower.

Organization of agricultural research

Public agricultural research systems in developing countries have a variety of organizational structures. Often there is a central research station with substations located in different geo-climatic zones. Research may be conducted at universities, but the proportion of agricultural research conducted at colleges and universities tends to be much less than in developed countries such as the United States.

The structure of the research system is influenced by historical forces including, among others, colonial history and major foreign assistance projects. Some agricultural research in developing countries is organized along commodity program lines: for example, a maize program, a rice program, a wheat program, or a sheep and goat program. Other cross-cutting or systems research areas such as soil fertility, socioeconomics, and even plant or livestock protection may have separate programs.

Some agricultural research systems have a mandate to publicly spread their research results to farmers. Even if such spread, often known as extension, is not included in the mandate of the national research institution, a mechanism is still needed to obtain information on current problems facing farmers and for testing new technologies under actual farm conditions. This mechanism may involve on-farm research. Experiment station research is needed so that experiments can be run under controlled conditions that enable particular components of new technologies to be developed and tested without the confounding of possibly extraneous factors. However, the real-world robustness, profitability, and cultural acceptability of new technologies cannot be assessed without testing under actual farm conditions. Frequent contact between scientists and farmers increases the likelihood that constraints and problems facing farmers will be included in the development and evaluation of new technologies.

International agricultural research centers

The 1960s saw the emergence of a group of international agricultural research centers (IARCs) that now includes a network of 15 institutions located primarily in Africa, Asia, Latin America, and the Middle East, as shown in Figure 12.3. The funding and operation of these "Future

CENTERS   ■ REGIONAL OFFICES OF CENTERS   Placement markers are approximate and indicate city locations

Figure 12.3 The "Future Harvest" international agricultural research centers (see table on page 255)

Research center (see Figure 12.3)	Research coverage
Africa Rice (formerly WARDA)	Rice and rice-based cropping systems in Africa
Bioversity* (formerly IPGRI)	Conservation of plant genetic material; bananas and plantain
CIAT* – Centro Internacional de Agricultura Tropical	Phaseolus beans, cassava, rice, tropical pastures
CIFOR – Centre for International Forestry Research	Forest systems and forestry
CIMMYT – Centro Internacional de Mejoramiento de Maiz y Trigo	Wheat, barley, maize, high-altitude sorghum
CIP – Centro Internacional de la Papa	Potato, sweet potato, other root crops
ICARDA – International Center for Agricultural Research in Dryland Areas	Crop and mixed farming systems research, with emphasis on sheep, wheat, barley, broad beans
ICRISAT – International Crops Research Institute for the Semi-Arid Tropics	Sorghum, pearl millet, pigeon pea, chickpea, groundnuts
IFPRI – International Food Policy Research Institute	Food policy
IITA – International Institute for Tropical Agriculture	Farming systems: cereals, grain legumes, roots and tubers
ILRI – International Livestock Research Institute	Livestock diseases and production systems
IRRI – International Rice Research Institute	Rice
IWWI – International Water Management Institute	Irrigation
World Agroforestry	Agro-forestry
World Fish Center	Fisheries and other living aquatic resources

* In 2020, Bioversity and CIAT merged into a single center called "The Alliance". The CGIAR has undergone many restructurings over time and membership has changed over time.

Harvest" centers are coordinated through the Consultative Group for International Agricultural Research (CGIAR), headquartered at the World Bank in Washington, DC. Although the first center, the International Rice Research Institute (IRRI), was founded in 1960, the international center model drew on the historical experiences of the colonial agricultural research institutes that were effective in increasing the production of export crops such as rubber, sugar, and tea. The model also drew on the experiences in the 1940s and 1950s of the Rockefeller Foundation's wheat and maize programs in Mexico and the Ford and Rockefeller Foundations' rice program in the Philippines. The results of the research and training programs of the centers are aimed not just at the country where the center is located, but at the neighboring region or even the world.

The first IARCs, IRRI and CIMMYT (International Center for Maize and Wheat Improvement), produced new varieties of rice and wheat that substantially increased yields, especially for rice in Asia. The first of several rice varieties, IR-8, released by IRRI and coop-erating national programs, responded to high rates of fertilizer and water application by producing more grain and less straw. Subsequent research has focused as well on improving grain quality, incorporat-ing disease and insect resistance, and adapting to submergence and drought. The substantial yield boost experienced in parts of Asia in the late 1960s resulting from these new technologies was termed the green revolution (Box 12.2).

The success of the green revolution in increasing yields and incomes led to the expansion of the international agricultural research center concept to the other commodities and regions identified in Figure 12.3. Maize, millets, tropical legumes, cassava, livestock, potatoes, and many other commodities have received emphasis. The research results from these newer centers have not been as spectacular as the early gains in rice and wheat, but these centers, too, have made significant contribu-tions. For example, disease-resistant beans, cassava, and millet varieties are now being grown in several countries. These centers also provide a public link between research being undertaken in the private sector on modern biotechnology and national agricultural research systems in developing countries to help ensure that these national systems are not left behind.

CGIAR members include the World Bank, the Food and Agricultural Organization of the United Nations (FAO), the United Nations Devel-opment Program (UNDP), and several national governments, regional banks, and foundations. These institutions provide the funds for the centers. The CGIAR, founded in 1971, is headquartered at the World Bank. The total budget for the 15 Future Harvest Centers was $900 mil-lion in 2020 with work in more than 70 countries. In addition to these centers, there are a few related international research centers that play a similar role, such as the World Vegetable Center in Taiwan and the Inter-national Center for Insect Physiology and Ecology in Kenya.

Transfer of research results

The discussions of research categories and of national, regional, and international agricultural research centers imply that at least some research results may be transferred from one location to another. These transfers may occur internally in a country or across national boundaries. Prior to the 1960s, little attention was focused on the importance of indigenous agricultural research in developing countries. It was thought that the possibilities for transferring technologies from developed countries were substantial and that programs were therefore mainly needed to assist in this transfer. The relative lack of success with direct transfer of machinery, plant varieties, and other materials from developed to developing countries led to the realization that improved developing-country research capacity was essential. However, many research results are regularly transferred from one country to another. What types of research results are transferable and what determines their transferability?

Materials such as improved seeds, plants, and animals; scientific methods, formulas, and designs; genes; and basic research output are all potentially transferable to some extent. Each country must decide whether to simply screen these items and attempt to directly transfer them, to screen them and then modify and adapt them to their own environment, or to undertake a research program that is comprehensive enough to produce its own technologies.

The choice among these transfer and research options will depend on the relative costs of direct transfer of technologies and other research results. Transfer of research results involves costs of information, screening, or testing. There may also be license costs or fees for patented items. Many transfer costs increase with the size and environmental diversity of the country. A country's own research costs are somewhat independent of size; for that reason, it can be more cost-effective for larger countries to conduct their own research than for smaller countries.

If the natural resource base in one developing country is similar to that in another country where the new technology is produced, then the chances of transfer will increase. For example, new wheat varieties are often transferred from Argentina to Uruguay because those countries have similar wheat-growing regions. Some technologies are more environmentally sensitive than others are. The international agricultural research centers attempt to produce plant and animal materials that have broad environmental suitability. In many cases, the receiving country can then adapt these materials more specifically to its microclimates.

Table 12.2 Global Public Spending on Agricultural R&D by High-income Countries and by Low- and Middle-income Countries, 2008

Region/country	Percent of total spending on agricultural research
High-income countries	51
sub-Saharan Africa	5
China	13
India	7
Other Asia & Pacific	5
Brazil	4
West Asia & North Africa	6
Eastern Europe & former Soviet States	6

Source: Nienke Beintema, Gert-Jan Stads, Keith Fuglie, and Pail Heisey, *ASTI Global Assessment of Agricultural R&D Spending, Developing Countries Accelerate Investment* (Washington, DC: IFPRI, 2012)

Agricultural research spending

Agricultural research occurs in the public and private sectors. In developing countries, the public sector often undertakes most agricultural research, and the bulk of public sector agricultural research occurs in the Asia and Pacific region. The highest levels of spending occur in China, India, and Brazil. In 2008, $32 billion was spent in developed and developing countries on public agricultural research, roughly half of those expenditures occurring in developing countries (see Table 12.2). Only about 5 percent was spent in sub-Saharan Africa, and the percentage spent there has been declining since 1980. Total spending on agricultural research in Africa has increased only about 1 percent per year over the past several years despite increased malnutrition in the region.[6] If private support for agricultural research is included, these disparities in funding identified are even sharper, with Africa accounting for less than 1 percent of total funding on agricultural research.[7] These numbers place increased importance on the technology transfer issues raised above.

ROLE OF EXTENSION EDUCATION

Countries unable to develop the skills and knowledge of their farmers and their families find it difficult to develop anything else. The utilization of new technologies and institutions is critically dependent on a workforce that is aware of and understands how to use them. Agricultural extension education can help motivate farmers toward change, teach farmers improved decision-making methods, and provide farmers with technical and practical information. Extension is complementary to other sources of information because it speeds the transfer of knowledge about new agricultural technologies and other research results. It helps farmers deal with technological and economic change. Thus, as agriculture in a country moves from a traditional to a more dynamic, science-based mode, the value of extension education increases.

In extension education, farmers are the primary clientele and the programs are mostly oriented toward production problems they face. Extension accelerates the dissemination of research results to farmers and, in some cases, helps transmit farmers' problems back to researchers. Extension workers provide training for farmers on a variety of subjects and must have technical competence, economic competence, farming competence, and communication skills.

Many public extension systems are poorly funded and managed. Some countries have eliminated them completely and rely only on private and non-governmental organizations (NGOs) to spread the latest research results and technologies to farmers. Private firms that sell products such as improved seeds and chemicals are heavily involved in technology transfer associated with specific products. NGOs exist on outside financial support from governments and from private individuals and groups in other countries or on private local support. Reductions in support for public extension have been caused by budgetary pressures and perceptions that the extension services have not been particularly effective. Extension systems that survive have sought improved means to reach farmers cost-effectively. Such means usually include increased use of mass media and carefully crafted mixes of technology diffusion methods. They utilize the latest information and communication technologies to reach farmers with timely information.

Extension methods

A variety of methods are employed to transfer research knowledge and technologies to producers: individual farm visits, regularly scheduled group meetings, technology demonstrations that may involve a field day when hundreds of farmers are invited to observe the latest research results, and transfer of information through cellphones and other mass media methods such as radio, TV, and internet. Some types of technologies and information are transferred more effectively through intensive methods such as in-person meetings. Others are amenable to transfer through less intensive (and usually less expensive) methods such as field days and mass media. Much has been learned about mass media transfer of information, and internet- or cellphone-based transfer now occurs in many countries, even some of the poorest. Each country must decide what is most cost-effective for its public extension system, and each NGO will decide which approach allows it to best achieve its objectives. No one method works best in every situation, and extension costs and effectiveness depend on the type of technology, topography of the country, access to cell service and mass media, cultural and social factors, and many other variables. Evaluating effectiveness of alternative measures helps inform decision-makers about which methods are most appropriate given their resource bases, extension messages, and intentions.

Organization of extension

Many organizational structures for extension exist in developing countries. A common extension structure is the village agent model that assigns extension "agents" to live in villages and provide individual and group training of farmers on a variety of agricultural topics. Village extension agents are supported by regional or national subject matter specialists. Unfortunately,

Extension field day in Ecuador

too often extension agents are poorly trained and little motivated. They may be spread thin, diverted to non-extension activities, or politicized and unconnected to research. A well-functioning system needs clear lines of authority, adequate training, modern information and communication technologies, and financial rewards for personnel, or the system becomes relatively ineffective. Research and extension linkages are essential and are facilitated if research and extension are linked in the same institution. Unfortunately, often they are not. These factors have led many developing country governments to eliminate the public extension system. Such actions may make sense in the context of poorly functioning systems, but efforts to transform the extension system into a modern service-oriented program can be effective means of promoting agricultural development.

SUMMARY

Agricultural research generates new or improved technologies and institutions that increase agricultural productivity, moderate food prices, generate foreign exchange, and reduce pressures on the natural resource base. Studies have found the economic returns on public agricultural research investments to be high. Agricultural research can have distributional effects by farm size and tenure, by region, by income level, by factor of production, and so forth. Consumers, particularly low-income consumers, are major beneficiaries of agricultural research, as the poor may spend 80 percent of any income increases on food, and food prices tend to fall as agricultural productivity increases. Agricultural research can influence nutrition by raising farm incomes, lowering food prices, and reducing the variability in food production. Agricultural research can generate technologies, institutional changes, and higher incomes that lead to reduced pressures on the environment. The public sector has a role to play in agricultural research because the private sector has inadequate incentives to conduct a sufficient amount of socially beneficial research, in part because often private firms conducting research cannot capture enough of the benefits. Intellectual property rights can help in creating incentives for private research investment.

Agricultural research can be classified into basic, applied, adaptive, and testing research. These categories are linked and dependent on each other. Since 1960, a system of international agricultural research centers has provided, in partnership with national research organizations, new technologies and institutional changes suitable to several developing countries. These institutions helped to produce a green revolution that greatly increased the production of maize, rice, and wheat. Research can be transferred across national borders, but the ease of transfer depends on the type of research, the relative cost of transfer and indigenous research, the natural resource base, and other factors. Use of modern biotechnology has grown around the world in recent years but is yet to be widely adopted in developing countries. Well-functioning extension systems can help speed up the spread of improved technologies.

IMPORTANT TERMS AND CONCEPTS

Adaptive research
Agricultural education
Agricultural extension
Agricultural productivity
Agricultural research
Applied research
Basic research
Biotechnology
Experiment stations

Gene editing
Genetically modified organisms
Green revolution
Intellectual property rights
International agricultural research
  centers
Non-governmental organizations
Scale-neutral technology
Technology transfer
Testing research

LOOKING AHEAD

This chapter considered technical factors that can influence development of the agricultural sector. The following several chapters address a set of institutional issues that are equally important if agriculture is to progress in developing countries. We begin in the next chapter discussing land and labor policies.

QUESTIONS FOR DISCUSSION

1 What is the purpose of agricultural research in developing countries?
2 How does research influence agricultural productivity and food prices?
3 Under what conditions might research on a non-food export crop have as much or greater positive effect on nutrition than research on a food crop?
4 Why might agricultural research tend to benefit large farms more than small farms?
5 Why might agricultural research increase the regional disparity in income in a developing country?

6 Why are consumers, especially poor consumers, often the major beneficiaries of agricultural research?

7 What factors influence the returns to particular factors of production following research?

8 How might agricultural research help improve the environment?

9 How might research result in institutional change?

10 Why should the public sector get involved in research? Why not leave it to the private sector?

11 Distinguish among basic, applied, adaptive, and testing research.

12 What is modern biotechnology? Genetic engineering? Gene editing?

13 What are the international agricultural research centers and how does their work tie into the agricultural research systems in developing countries?

14 What is the "green revolution", when did it occur, and where?

15 What role does extension play in agricultural development?

16 How might research, education, and extension be complementary activities?

17 How can intellectual property rights influence production of agricultural technologies?

NOTES

1 See Julian M. Alston, Connie Chan-Kang, Michele C. Marra, Philip G. Pardey, and T.J. Wyatt, *A Meta-Analysis of Rates of Return to Agricultural R&D* (Washington, DC: International Food Policy Research Institute, IFPRI Research Report 113, 2000).

2 Grant M. Scobie and Rafael Posada, "The Impact of Technical Change on Income Distribution: The Case of Rice in Colombia", *American Journal of Agricultural Economics*, vol. 60(1) (February 1978), pp. 85–92.

3 Matim Qaim, "Role of New Plant Breeding Technologies for Food Security and Sustainable Agricultural Development", *Applied Economic Perspectives and Policy*, vol. 42(2) (2020), pp. 129–150.

4 In 2018, GMOs were planted on 192 million ha, equivalent to 14 percent of the total worldwide cropland. These 192 million ha were grown by 17 million farmers in 26 countries. Most of these countries are located in North and South America, followed by Asia. In Europe and Africa, very few countries have adopted GMOs, which is mostly due to limited public acceptance in these regions and unfavorable regulatory environments (Qaim 2016). The countries with the biggest shares of the total GMO area in 2018 were the USA (39%), Brazil (27%), and Argentina (12%), followed by Canada (7%), India (6%), Paraguay (2%), China (2%), Pakistan (1%), South Africa (1%), and a number of other countries (ISAAA 2018). *Source:* ISAAA, *Global Status of Commercialized Biotech/GM Crops: 2018* (Ithaca, NY: ISAAA Brief No. 54, 2018).

5 See, for example, Matim Qaim, "Role of New Plant Breeding Technologies for Food Security and Sustainable Agricultural Development", *Applied Economic Perspectives and Policy*, vol. 42(2) (2020), pp. 129–150; Guy Hareau, George W.

Norton, Bradford Mills, and Everett Peterson, "Potential Benefits of Transgenic Rice in Asia: A General Equilibrium Analysis", *Quarterly Journal of International Agriculture*, vol. 44 (2005), pp. 229–246.

6 CGIAR Science Council, *Science for Agricultural Development: Changing Contexts and New Opportunities* (Rome: Science Council Secretariat, 2005).

7 See Philip G. Pardey, Nienke Beitema, Steven Dehmer, and Stanley Wood, *Agricultural Research: A Growing Divide* (Washington, DC: IFPRI, 2006), p. 1.

RECOMMENDED READINGS

Alston, Julian M., George W. Norton, and Philip G. Pardey, *Science Under Scarcity: Principles and Practice for Agricultural Research Evaluation and Priority Setting* (Ithaca, NY: Cornell University Press, 1995).

Masters, William A., "Paying for Prosperity: How and Why to Invest in Agricultural Research and Development in Africa", *Journal of International Affairs*, vol. 58(2) (2005), pp. 35–64.

Pardey, Philip P., Nienke Beitema, Steven Dehmer, and Stanley Wood, *Agricultural Research: A Growing Divide* (Washington, DC: IFPRI, 2006).

Qaim, Qaim, "Role of New Plant Breeding Technologies for Food Security and Sustainable Agricultural Development", *Applied Economic Perspectives and Policy*, vol. 42(2) (2020), pp. 129–150.

13 Land and labor markets

THIS CHAPTER

1 Discusses the meaning of land tenure and land reform
2 Explains why flexible land tenure systems enhance agricultural development, yet are difficult to achieve, and what the requisites are for a well-functioning land market
3 Describes the nature of agricultural land and labor markets in developing countries

MEANING OF LAND TENURE AND LAND REFORM

Land and labor are fundamental inputs into agricultural production, and land is often distributed unequally. Therefore, we see large farms with land concentrated in the hands of a few, and small farms with excess labor. Typically, in these cases, a market develops in which labor is hired to work on larger farms or land is leased to small-scale landholders for rent or for a share of the output. An alternative is to subdivide large holdings through land reform or market-based redistribution efforts. In this chapter, we consider determinants and consequences of alternative land tenure systems and labor market structures. Well-functioning land and labor markets are crucial to agricultural development because land is a major input into production and poorly functioning markets will lead to misallocation and inefficient use of this resource. Evidence shows that the rural poor, particularly those with little or no land will benefit more from an additional unit of land than do the rich: mechanisms to reallocate land can increase productivity and reduce poverty.

Land rights determine social and political status as well as economic power in developing countries. Secure access to land can enhance incomes, provide an important insurance function, and increase access to financial and non-financial services. *Land tenure* is a term used to refer to those rights or patterns of control over land. Land rights include rights to use and to exclude use, rights to output from the land, and rights to transfer the land or its output to others.

As population density increases, farming techniques change, and markets for agricultural products grow, pressures often build to change existing land tenure arrangements. In societies where land has been held in common, permanent and enforceable individual rights to land may evolve. In countries where ownership patterns are highly skewed, with a few people owning much and many owning little or no land, pressures often are exerted on the government to undertake a land reform or eliminate constraints to more equal land distribution by establishing well-functioning land markets. These pressures may arise from the rural poor who desire increased economic well-being or from those in power who hope that minimal concessions to the poor will diffuse political unrest. A land reform is a dramatic attempt to change the land tenure system through public policies. Land reform may change not only rights and patterns of control over the land resource but also the mode (organization) of production (whether semi-feudalistic, capitalistic, or socialist) and the agrarian class structure. Consequently, few subjects related to agricultural development are as controversial. In recent years, more attention has been focused on rights to land and how secure rights facilitate development of functioning land markets. Market-based measures have supplanted administrative approaches to land reallocations.

Land ownership and tenure systems

A wide array of land ownership and tenure systems exists in the world. These systems reflect differences in historical influences, levels of income, culture, political and legal systems, climate, and other factors. The systems vary in size and organization of landholdings. They affect incentives to produce and invest, and they influence the distribution of benefits from agricultural growth. Examples of average size of landholdings from around the world are presented in Table 13.1. The larger holdings in Latin America compared to Asia and Africa are particularly evident. However, information on *average* landholdings masks important difference within countries; these differences are shown in Table 13.1 as Gini coefficients.[1] While average holdings, for example, in Latin America are quite high, many landless and near landless families can be found in

Table 13.1 Landholding Sizes and Distribution, by Region

Region	Median Landholding Size (ha)	Gini Coefficient
East Asia	2.07	.51
sub-Saharan Africa	2.18	.49
South Asia	2.32	.59
Mideast and North Africa	6.05	.66
Eastern Europe	8.69	.62
Latin America	17.70	.81
High-income countries	20.83	.56

Source: Dietrich Vollrath, "Land Distribution and International Agricultural Productivity", *American Journal of Agricultural Economics*, vol. 89 (February 2007), pp. 202–216

the region. Latin America has the most unequal distribution of land in the world, while the distribution in Asia and Africa is relatively equal (Table 13.1). In Latin America, as elsewhere in the world, the colonial past still influences land ownership patterns today (see Box 13.1).

Family farms, corporate farms, state farms, and group farms are major types of farm ownership, but organization of farm enterprises within these types can vary substantially. Often, the owner is also the operator. Sometimes, those who operate or work on the farm may earn a fixed wage or pay rent in cash or as a share of the farm output to the owner.

Small subsistence or *semi-subsistence family farms* are common in developing countries. Families often provide most of the labor, and cultivation is labor-intensive. Much of the output is consumed on the farm where it is produced. However, not all small family farms are subsistence or semi-subsistence farms; many are commercial farms producing substantial surpluses for sale. Those farmers that do consume most of what they produce are usually very poor. Often, family members work on other farms or in non-farm employment. When assets are few and risks are high, it is important to diversify income-earning opportunities. The latter can lead to the small farms becoming part-time operations, especially as development proceeds over time with job opportunities growing in the non-farm sector.

Large-scale commercial family farms sell most of what they produce. While in developed countries these farms are highly mechanized and often use only a small amount of non-family labor, in developing countries the operations are usually more labor-intensive and use a high proportion of hired labor. The owner frequently does not live on the farm, but pays a manager to oversee day-to-day operations.

BOX 13.1 COLONIALISM AND
LAND OWNERSHIP

Many of the land ownership patterns found in developing countries are the vestiges of colonial rule. The *latifundia* or extensive
large-scale farms that currently exist in Central and South America
alongside *minifundia* or very small farms are a direct descendent
of colonial rule. The Spanish and Portuguese colonizers allocated
large tracts of land to elites who formed tropical plantations or
large haciendas. Both types of landholding were made possible
through the direct enslavement of indigenous populations, the
importation of slaves from Africa, or the *encomienda* system that
gave indirect control over local populations to certain elites.

Some of the richest agricultural lands in Africa have land ownership patterns that were established during European colonization.
Because European countries coveted exotic tropical products, such
as cocoa, coffee, tea, and tropical fruits, agricultural production
in Africa was reorganized under colonial powers to help ensure
production of these products. Large landholdings were allocated
to European settlers, such as the tea and coffee plantations in eastern Africa; rarely were the land's original inhabitants compensated.
In many instances, the land's original inhabitants were resettled
to areas with lower agricultural potential, poor rainfall, and inadequate infrastructure. Areas that had been self-sufficient in food
production became exporters of goods to Europe, while much of
the indigenous population relied on rain-fed agriculture in marginal areas. An adequate labor supply was maintained sometimes
through enslavement and sometimes through economic coercion.

In Asia, colonial rule led to similar forms of plantation agriculture. Japanese colonies in Korea and Taiwan produced for export
to Japan; the Dutch colonized Indonesia; Spanish plantations
existed in the Philippines; the British colonized much of the Indian
sub-continent and other regions.

Following the end of colonial rule, many of these land ownership
patterns persisted, because of the political powers of the landed
elite. Some land reforms undertaken prior to 1970 were designed
to remove the less desirable aspects of these landholding patterns.
Implicit forms of enslavement of labor, such as through the maintenance of indebtedness, were prohibited. In many countries, the

result of these reforms has been to reduce labor use, increase mechanization, and leave the distribution of land largely unchanged. The legacy of colonial landholding patterns has been pervasive for rural poverty in many regions of the world.

Corporate farms often produce a limited number of commodities in large-scale units. These farms may have their own processing and marketing systems. This type of farm is more prevalent in developed than in developing countries, but there are numerous examples of large corporate farms in developing countries. The fruit plantations found in Central American countries, banana plantations of the Philippines, and cocoa plantations of West Africa are a few examples.

State farms are usually large, owned and operated by the government, and run by hired labor. Managers are responsible to a government-planning agency that may set targets for production and direct the timing and method of key farming operations. Examples have existed in the past in China and the former Soviet Union. State farms usually suffer from inadequate incentives and poor management.

Group farms are communes, kibbutzim, collectives, or other types of farms that are operated by a group of people who work and manage the farm jointly. These group operations may also involve nonagricultural activities. Often, collectivized farms are characterized by over-investment in labor-saving, capital-intensive technologies, since individuals do not receive the full returns from their labor. Special arrangements may be devised (for example a point system) to provide incentives for individual members to work harder. The kibbutzim of Israel are an example of a group farm system. *Cooperative* farms exist in some parts of the world, but cooperative purchase of inputs and marketing of outputs is a more common organization. The Mennonite communities in the Paraguayan Chaco are an example of privately held land whose owners organize cooperatives for input purchases and product marketing.

Farms are also differentiated by types of tenancy or leasing arrangements. Farm families may lease all or a part of their land for cash or for a share of the production from the land. A farmer may be allowed to farm a piece of land in exchange for his or her labor on another part of the owner's land. In some countries, the village, tribe, or national government may own the land and grant use rights to individual families. This system is common in Africa, where traditional leaders allocate land to individuals who maintain control over it and its output as long as they cultivate it.

Tenancy, risk, and efficiency

Tenancy arrangements affect the distribution of risk and transactions costs among tenants and landlords. They also influence incentives to work or apply inputs. A share lease, for example, spreads production risk between the landlord and tenant, while a cash lease concentrates the risk on the tenant. A cash lease implies lower transactions costs for the landlord than a share lease, since production has to be monitored under the latter. A tenant may have less incentive to apply fertilizer or even labor under a share lease than under a cash lease. To circumvent this disincentive, the landlord may share the cost of the fertilizer or place conditions on labor applied. In such cases, the landlord bears the transactions costs associated with monitoring input use and measuring output. Thus, the use of a particular land- or labor-contracting mechanism may be a response to the presence of risk or transactions costs. These factors can explain why the land market may not dictate a single type of tenancy system even within a single country.

Types of land tenure reform

As development proceeds, pressure may grow to change fundamental tenancy relationships by altering the legal system or through administrative fiat. Changes in land relationships can take many forms. *Land*

Livestock at a Mennonite cooperative in Paraguay

redistribution is an effort to modify the distribution of land ownership or possession/use. *Land tenure reform* involves steps to change the legal and institutional framework related to land administration. *Land reform* encompasses both redistribution and tenure reform.[2] Prior to the 1970s, many if not most land reforms involved a movement away from feudalistic and semi-feudalistic land tenure arrangements toward capitalist or socialist ownership modes.[3] Feudalism was characterized by large-scale estates controlled by the traditional landed elite with labor bonded to the estates through different forms of coercion.

Anti-feudal land reforms have eliminated feudalism in most of the world, and the farm types described above have replaced feudal models. In many countries, however, this post-feudal order has resulted in some large capitalist farms or estates controlled by an elite well-to-do class and a coexisting small-farm sector. In a few countries (for example, South Korea and Taiwan), the post-reform agricultural sector consists primarily of small family farms. And in a few, such as Cuba, socialist farms still predominate. The form of the post-reform agrarian structure depends largely on the motivation and political ideology behind the reforms (see Box 13.2).

Land tenure reform today generally does not refer to the types of anti-feudal reforms instituted in many countries prior to the 1970s. In those reforms, prohibition of bonded labor and reductions in labor exploitation were achieved, but in many cases a significant redistribution of land was not. As de Janvry notes, countries like Colombia and India had successful anti-feudal land reforms but very little redistribution of land.[4] Land tenure reform as a policy issue today usually relates to seeking a shift in the distribution of lands from large to medium-sized and smaller landholdings. It also involves creation of more secure rights to land and creation of conditions for functioning land markets. Improved tenure security empowers people to make better decisions, more effectively manage risks, and participate on a more equal basis in markets. Land tenure reform often involves market-based efforts to increase access to land, and secure rights to land are needed for a well-functioning land market.

Land tenure rights in rural China have evolved since the early 1950s, when collective ownership was adopted as a form of socialist public ownership of land. The original structure created communes, which were centrally controlled collective entities where communal leadership made all farming decisions. Incentives were misaligned under this system, and the failure of the communes contributed to mass starvation from 1959 to 1961. Multiple gradual reforms have occurred since 1978, and the government adopted a system of public ownership that gives farmers an option to separate land contract rights from operation rights. That

BOX 13.2 LAND REFORM IN EASTERN EUROPE

Following the collapse of Soviet-style models of central economic planning and control and the movement toward democracy in the late 1980s, governments in Eastern Europe were faced with the problem of how to reform their agricultural sectors. The organization of the agricultural sectors in these countries was rather similar: approximately one-third of the farms were state farms and two-thirds were collectives (cooperatives). Most farm employees managed a household plot of about one-half hectare, while the state farms and collectives were large, about 2000 to 3000 hectares. Two paths of reform are illustrative of general trends in the region: Romania and Bulgaria.

In both countries, the rights of landowners prior to collectivization were recognized by parliamentary decree in February 1991. These decrees also established procedures for reclaiming these property rights. In Romania, land redistribution proceeded quickly. Local land commissions were established to hear household claims for up to 10 hectares. Some proof of the claim was needed. Whenever possible, claimants were given back the land actually owned, and when not, an alternative of equal size and quality was returned. Once in possession, the owner could sell it immediately, or purchase more land. Thus, a market for titled land, with very few institutional restrictions, was established. There was not an attempt to create farms of optimal size.

The Bulgarian redistribution proceeded much more slowly. Administrative delay hindered progress, and local commissions were very slow in forming. The laws implementing the distribution were very rigid, and the construction of "appropriate size holdings" through administration was attempted. The local commissions adjudicated claims, but a planning team reassigned plots. The law prohibited purchase and sale of land for three years, hindering development of a land market.

Most new landowners in both countries remained integrated into the collective management system. In Romania, the formation of a land market opened a period of holdings consolidation and resale, but actual exit from the collective was delayed until the infrastructure for individual management was developed. The slowness of the redistribution in Bulgaria guaranteed the existence of collective systems for many years.

Source: Karen Brooks, J. Luis Guasch, Avishay Braverman, and Csaba Csaki, "Agriculture and the Transition to Market", *Journal of Economic Perspectives*, vol. 5 (1991), pp. 149–162

is, farmland in rural China can now be rented by individuals, corporate farms, and other entities as long as it remains in agricultural use. Land rental has loosened central control and been associated with gradual increases in agricultural productivity, especially since the early 2000s.[5] Even establishing rental rights to land is complicated when ownership is vested in the state.

Transactions costs and the agrarian structure

No form of land tenure is universally efficient. Differences in natural resource endowments and in institutional arrangements all influence risk, transactions costs, and the farmer's opportunity to exploit his or her managerial ability. If there were well-defined private property rights and a reasonably equitable distribution of land, perfect information, and zero transactions costs (especially the cost of enforcing contracts), markets would work perfectly and economic efficiency would not depend on the agrarian structure. Bargaining would occur among landowners, renters, and laborers; neither the returns to labor nor the overall economic efficiency of the agricultural system would depend on the type of agrarian structure.

In the real world, however, risk varies from country to country. Markets are not perfect. Costs of acquiring information and of negotiating, monitoring, and enforcing contracts can be high. People are willing to exploit others, labor hired on a time-rate basis may shirk (increasing the cost of supervision), the price of land may decline as farm size grows, and larger landowners may have better access to markets and information.

Many of these factors confer an economic advantage to large farms. Owners of larger holdings can gain additional political advantage through collective action and can reinforce their advantage through the tax laws and pressures on the types of new technologies produced by the public research system. Owners of larger holdings have easier access to agricultural credit because the costs of administering a loan can be spread over more land, thus making the cost per hectare of large-scale loans lower than small-scale loans. The result can be additional gains for the elite, but reduced economic efficiency for the agricultural sector and the country as a whole. Land tenure reform may be needed in these cases.

LAND REFORM AND REDISTRIBUTION IN PRACTICE

A country can desire land tenure reform for economic, social, and political reasons, yet land reform, whether it involves change in land tenancy or ownership, is always difficult to achieve. Let's examine briefly why land redistribution may be desired, why it may be difficult to achieve, how a country can measure whether a reform has succeeded, and what factors improve the chances of achieving successful land tenure reform.

Need for more equitable access to land

The broad goals of most societies include desires for improved income growth (efficiency), equity (income distribution and poverty reduction), and security (political and economic stability). A more equitable access to and more secure rights to land can contribute to all of these goals.

A skewed distribution of landholdings can hamper economic efficiency for several reasons. Large landholdings may not be farmed intensively, even in very densely populated countries; in fact, an *inverse* relationship between farm productivity and farm size has been found in many developing country settings.[6] Some hold land for speculative reasons. Others are absentee landlords who provide little supervision of those working on the farm. If the farm is owned by the government, planning and management may be centrally and poorly controlled, and individual incentives may be stifled. Large farms may substitute machinery for labor, exacerbating an unemployment problem. Large farmers facing labor supervision problems often demand capital-intensive innovations from the agricultural research system. As a result, new technologies generated through publicly supported research may not reflect the true scarcity values of land, labor, and capital in the country.

Countries with large landholdings often have a coexisting sector of farms that are too small to provide an adequate living. These smallholdings of one or two hectares or less may employ labor to the point at which its marginal product is low. Thus, reducing the size of large farms and increasing the size of very small farms may be one way to raise the marginal product of labor in agriculture and thereby raise income per worker.[7]

Other land tenure problems may have to be solved to improve entrepreneurial incentives and to reduce risks facing farmers. Establishment of land markets may increase the efficiency with which land is used. Share or cash rents may need to be changed as new technologies become available. Lease lengths may need to be more securely established to encourage capital investment.

Apart from growth or efficiency concerns, land redistribution often is needed for equity reasons. The number of landless laborers is growing in many countries, along with associated poverty and malnutrition. The principal resource these people control is their labor, the value of which is depressed by under-use of labor on large farms. Providing land resources to the landless can be one means of raising incomes. As large farms are broken up, even those poor who do not receive land can benefit due to increased economy-wide demand for labor. Large farms convey political power to a small group. This group may distort economic policies in a direction that hinders overall economic growth and creates severe hardship on the poorest segments of society. Thus, to achieve development as defined in Chapter 1, addressing the land distribution problem may be necessary.

In addition to growth and equity concerns, land redistribution can enhance political and economic security or stability. Expropriations of land and partial land reforms experienced in many countries in the past have probably occurred primarily for purposes of political stabilization. This stabilization can have positive and negative impacts on economic growth and equity. To the extent that land redistribution dampens political unrest and reduces violence, it reduces the death and suffering that can accompany the violence. However, if a partial land reform achieves political stability without redistributing enough land or economic power to stimulate widespread growth and fundamentally reduce economic hardship and hunger, it may only perpetuate a status quo of chronic suffering.

Why land redistribution is difficult to achieve

Because of the political and economic power that accompanies land ownership in many countries, it is difficult to conduct a meaningful redistribution of land. Historically, land reforms have often been made possible only after significant social upheaval caused by revolution, the overthrow of colonial powers, or war. In the former Soviet Union and China, social revolutions destroyed the power of the landed elite prior to commencement of collectivizing land reforms. An army of occupation enforced the socialist reforms in Eastern Europe following World War II. The extreme economic, political, and social turmoil of the 1970s in China and of the 1980s and 1990s in the Soviet Union and Eastern Europe created conditions for land reforms. In capitalist countries such as Japan, the Republic of Korea, and Taiwan, defeats in war or occupation were followed by redistributive reforms.

In countries with capitalist forms of social and economic relationships, land reforms are difficult to achieve because those holding land rights also have strong political power (see Box 13.3). Interests of urban consumers often align with those of landowners. Because large farms frequently have large marketed surpluses, consumers fear that food price increases may follow a redistribution to smaller management units.

BOX 13.3 LAND RESETTLEMENT
AND REFORM IN ZIMBABWE

Prior to its invasion in 1890, land in Zimbabwe was held under communal tenure, and tribal leaders allocated use rights to members of the tribe. Mercenaries in Cecil Rhodes' Pioneer Columns were promised 3,000-acre holdings in exchange for assistance in colonizing the area. During the colonial period, Native Africans were relocated to low-rainfall, low-productivity land and were barred from land ownership outside these tribal reserves. Large-scale resettlement without compensation continued through the early 1950s.

In 1965, the minority white government declared independence from Great Britain and continued enforcing restrictive land-tenure rules against Native Africans. The subsequent war of independence used the "land question" as a uniting principle. Overcrowding and dwindling production on communal lands were associated with widespread rural poverty, and independence was viewed as the best alternative.

The Lancaster House Agreements, which paved the way for independence in 1980, formed a basis for post-independence land reform. The British government allocated £44 million for purchase on a "willing seller, willing buyer basis". Robert Mugabe won the first free election and promised to resettle blacks on purchased white lands. Resettlement reduced civil conflict, provided opportunities for war victims and the landless, and relieved some population pressures on communal lands.

Between 1980 and 1990, the Zimbabwe government obtained some 3 million hectares for resettlement and resettled roughly 54,000 households. The pace of resettlement slowed through the 1980s as attention moved toward providing agricultural services to communal areas. Farms in resettlement schemes had variable performance. The Lancaster House Agreements expired in 1990, effectively ending donor support of resettlement. Through the mid-1990s, few farms were resettled. Following currency devaluation in late 1997, unrest grew and independence war veterans began to demand access to land. Government responded by listing some large-scale commercial farms for "compulsory" resettlement. Although owners would be compensated, the method of compensation was unclear and abandonment of the "willing buyer, willing seller" principle caused unease among landowners. Between 1997 and 2000, resettlement became more contentious as rural interest groups increased pressure on the government through protests and forced seizure of white farms. In response, government began a "fast track" resettlement process, and between 2000 and 2003, it acquired more than 75 percent of the nearly 4,500 white-owned commercial farms. Since 2000, around 8 million hectares were transferred to over 165,000 households. Evidence shows that while the resettlement was violent and relatively chaotic, over time, recipient households have done rather well. New investments in land have occurred and agricultural support services have emerged.

The Zimbabwe experience provides a number of lessons. Inequitable land access can create strong political forces, especially when few opportunities are available outside agricults. As internal political pressure and the economic crisis grew, the Mugabe government felt increasing urgency for resettlement while resources to finance land purchase became scarcer. Land reforms of the type practiced in Zimbabwe can have huge unsettling effects. It is important that the emerging smallholder sector be provided support services and access to markets. The upheaval was socially destructive and led to declines in production of maize and export crops, but, over the past few years, production of food crops and the sector as a whole have begun to stabilize, and many poor farmers have improved their situations.

Sources: William A. Masters, *Government and Agriculture in Zimbabwe*. (Westport, CT: Praeger, 1994); Ian Scoones, Nelson Marongwe, Blasjo Mavedzenge, Jacob Mahenehene, Felix Murimbarimba and Chrispen Sukume, *Zimbabwe's Land Reform: Myths and Realities* (Suffolk, UK: Boydell and Brewer, 2010)

Small changes may be supported to achieve political stabilization, but large-scale restructuring of property rights is difficult. Occasionally, governments support redistributive land reforms in response to revolutionary pressures, such as Mexico (1940 to 1977) or the Philippines (1972 to 1975). Or, land reforms result following military overthrows of the government, such as in Peru (1969 to 1975). Land reforms within capitalist agriculture are usually slow to occur because compensation is required if they are to be accepted by those losing land. Unless the government has a large fiscal surplus, which is rare in developing countries, or access to substantial foreign aid, gainers cannot compensate the losers sufficiently for the land reform to be politically viable.

A successful land tenure reform should alter the incentive structure in rural areas. Whether this structure has been altered can be measured by evidence of increased and continuous capital accumulation by small farmers in the form of livestock, farm buildings, equipment, and other improvements. Because these investments are gradual, it may take a generation, perhaps 25 to 30 years, to truly evaluate the success of a change in land tenure or redistribution.

Agricultural productivity should increase in the long run. However, in the initial years following a land reform, productivity may stagnate. The mix of commodities produced may change and disruptions may occur to input and output marketing channels, credit flows, changes in technologies needed from the agricultural research system, and so forth. Marketed surpluses may also decrease in the short run because the poorer segments of the rural population, who benefit from the land redistribution, have a high income elasticity of demand for food. As their incomes increase they consume more, and the aggregate marketed surplus may decline. Thus, short-term increases in agricultural productivity or marketed surpluses are not good measures of the success of land reform.

Producer associations and other farm groups also are likely to be formed after a successful land reform. These associations can play an important role in promoting development and adoption of new technologies for agriculture, improving marketing channels, and so forth. Emergence of these associations is therefore another test of a successful land reform.

Alternatives to land reform
The cost and political difficulty of attaining an effective land reform have led to alternatives to large-scale, administrative redistribution of lands. An increasing body of evidence now shows that market-based reforms are effective at increasing investments, increased productivity, and more equitable outcomes.[8] Examples of market-based land redistribution efforts include fortification of sales and rental markets, encouraging cooperatives to redistribute lands to their members, sales or transfer of government lands, and creation of land banks. These efforts generally require three complementary steps: (1) legal definition and assignation of property rights, (2) creation of a legal framework for efficient functioning of the markets themselves, and (3) insuring that complementary

markets, particularly finance and insurance, function efficiently. These steps can be costly and difficult, and a market-based reform that does not address all will likely fail in its objectives – to redistribute land toward more efficient users.

Assignment of property rights involves surveying lands, titling them, and creating a land registry so that prospective participants can examine the land's history of transactions, including liens and competing claims. Legal reforms include determining who can participate in transactions, means of contract enforcement, removal on implicit or explicit restrictions on rental and transfer, etc. Implicit restrictions to rental, for example, may occur because without an adequate legal framework, squatters may possess strong claims to ownership. Land owners may be reluctant to rent to others because they fear losing claims to ownership. Weak legal systems make it difficult to enforce property ownership rights and may slow the development of land markets. Issues such as women's rights to own and transfer lands can have efficiency and equity effects of subsequent market processes.

Finally, while land markets have the potential to efficiently redistribute lands, in the presence of distortions in credit and insurance markets, creation of land markets alone may not solve the problem of inequitable distribution. For example, if banks or other creditors are unwilling to lend money in relatively small amounts due to transactions costs associated with such loans, then the poor may not be able to finance purchase or rental of the small amounts of land they seek (see Box 13.4). Unequal distribution of productive assets such as capital can exacerbate such problems because the poorest may not have collateral to support a loan. Insurance markets are important because the poorest of the poor may be less willing to risk their assets as collateral.

BOX 13.4 REFORM OF CAPITALIST AGRICULTURE IN COLOMBIA

Colombia presents an example of some of the pitfalls associated with land reforms. In the 1930s, there was a public outcry, mostly by urban consumers who desired cheaper foods, over the lack of productivity on the large landholdings of the rural elite. In 1936, Law 200 was passed that said that potentially productive but poorly cultivated or abandoned large holdings were to be expropriated by the government. This threat caused land productivity to rise for a short time, and virtually no land was confiscated. During the 1950s, there was a long period of civil conflict known as "La Violencia" that hastened the destruction of traditional social relations and weakened the political powers of the old agrarian oligarchy.

Following a peace pact, a new phase of land reform began. Law 135 of 1961 set forth an ambitious reform package that included full compensation to existing landholders. The gradualist approach doomed the package from the start. Political pressure from landed groups allied with urban consumer interests successfully diverted inputs, often with substantial subsidies, to large-scale farms. Land values on favored farms increased dramatically, making compensation financially impossible. By 1972, only 1.5 percent of all land in large farms had been redistributed.

Law 4 in 1973 declared an end to this redistributive reform and returned the country to the principles of Law 200. At the same time, a political coalition between large-scale farmers, a small but substantial family farm sector, and urban consumers formed and created pressure for a rural development program that favored the first two groups. Landless and marginal farmers were politically and economically excluded.

The conditions for a successful land reform never really existed in Colombia. Shifting alliances between urban and rural power groups diminished the political will. A lack of clear conviction for redistribution, combined with the slow pace of reform, further inhibited the efforts. Policies favoring large farms, largely intended to diffuse political opposition, had the effect of destroying any prospects for real reform.

PRIVATE LAND PURCHASES AND "LAND GRABBING"

Large-scale acquisitions of farmland in Africa, Latin America, and Asia by foreign interests have received wide attention since the early 2000s. Reports showed that as much as 50 million hectares of land in developing countries had been transferred to foreign investors by the end of the decade.[9] Discussion of the impacts of these acquisitions is highly variable: some denounce them as "land grabs" and highlight the negative repercussions in less-developed countries; others are more sanguine, noting that such acquisitions can boost investments and lead to greater agricultural productivity. The evidence is mixed, and the impact depends on the nature of the transfer, motives of the contracting parties, and institutions.

Land transfers take different forms, including private foreign entities seeking investment opportunities and foreign governments motivated by food security concerns or other potential returns. Some involve outright purchases, some are long-term leases, and some are business partnerships between foreign entities and domestic investors.[10] The global commodity price spikes in 2008 helped stimulate interest in investments in primary sectors such as agriculture and energy, and relatively high commodity prices since then have sustained this interest. Policy reforms in many African and Latin American countries have lowered risks to potential investors associated with such investments. Foreign direct investment can benefit the recipient country by increasing agricultural productivity (especially on previously under-used lands), generating employment, and stimulating investments in infrastructure. They also can provide injections of capital and necessary foreign exchange.

Evidence about the long-term impacts of increased international purchases of productive lands is limited. As the name "land grabbing" implies, substantial criticism of these transfers has emerged. Some argue that land acquisitions can hurt vulnerable populations by denying them access to farmland for their own use. Others protest that the lack of transparency in negotiations, contracting, and monitoring opens the door for exploitation and capture of illicit income by the elite. Still others note that legal protections for local stakeholders may be weak, and exposure to powerful foreign interests may lower welfare and lead to environmental degradation or other costs that will eventually be borne by locals. In fact, many of the contracting mechanisms used for land investments are relatively simple and do not adequately address the complexities of the transactions.

Land investments by foreign entities stir emotions but are not themselves inherently bad. Part of the negative press land investments have received focuses on the supposed goals and motivations of the countries from which the investments originate. In fact, the largest country actors (renters or purchasers) are from the United Kingdom, the United States, and India, and their motivations are widely divergent. When properly designed and administered, foreign investments can provide many benefits to the receiving country. Mechanisms are needed to ensure that these deals do not expropriate lands from local owners and that they benefit local stakeholders. Due diligence is required to ensure that the investor's business plan is solid, and contingencies have adequately been considered. Investments in large-scale agricultural production activities imply complications that are not always recognized. For example, in many parts of Africa, rights to land are determined locally. If local actors are not engaged in the negotiations, long-term viability of a land-transfer deal may be compromised. Receiving governments should carefully consider the types of investments they desire and how these investments will complement other actions in the rural sector. The capability to monitor and enforce contracts is essential, and mechanisms to assess environmental, social, and economic impacts will strengthen transparency and acceptance. Efforts to reform tenure arrangements prior to implementation of such contracts will help ensure transparency and respect for the rights of local stakeholders.

AGRICULTURAL LABOR MARKETS

Labor is often the most valuable resource the rural poor possess. This labor can be used to cultivate their own lands, to process and market products after harvest, to produce nonagricultural goods, some for own consumption and others to be sold in markets, for child-care, cooking, and other household activities. Alternatively, this labor can be used to work for others, both farm and non-farm employers. In most less-developed countries, agriculture accounts for upwards of 60 percent of total employment, and more than one-half of this labor is unpaid work on the family farm. Unlike industrial economies where firms employ the vast majority of workers, farm-households in developing countries both supply and demand labor, and rural labor market outcomes depend on the distribution of land, agricultural technologies, and decisions of many small-scale producers. Where land is unequally distributed, small-scale landowners and the landless supply labor to large-scale landowners who need additional labor to carry out their farming operations. Labor markets help them allocate resources into their most valuable uses by transmitting signals about resource scarcity across space and time. As labor is an important input to production and a key asset held by the poor, the conduct and performance of labor markets are especially important for broad-based agricultural growth.

Farm-household decisions and labor markets
Profit-maximizing farmers apply an input up to the point where its value of marginal product equals its price (see Chapter 5). The demand for labor on a farm thus depends on the production technology, the price of output, and the wage rate. This simple relationship explains many phenomena related to labor use in developing-country agriculture: (1) labor use varies seasonally and within the growing season; (2) timing of labor-intensive operations such as planting and harvesting is associated with more

intensive work; (3) access to other productive inputs such as land or mechanical traction alters on-farm operations and labor use; and (4) as opportunities off the farm (such as in nearby urban areas) increase and drive wages up, labor use on the farm decreases. During periods of peak operations, even relatively poor farmers engage workers to supplement family labor, and labor sharing is commonly found in many societies.

Casual versus permanent labor

Labor may be hired on a *casual* or temporary basis by the day or for some other short period of time, such as for the harvest or weeding period. Alternatively, labor may be hired on a more permanent or longer-term basis, perhaps for months or years. Casual labor is usually paid in cash and in kind (for example, food; many day labor wages include a meal for the worker). Workers may be paid daily or on a piece-rate basis for certain tasks. Women are often paid less than men, even for the same task. Casual labor is characterized by strong *seasonality*; workers are hired during planting and harvest, when farm labor demands are highest. Longer-term workers may have supervisory responsibilities or perform tasks requiring special care or special skills, such as applying farm chemicals. Formal or informal contracts may be developed to handle seasonal fluctuations and risks associated with agricultural production.

Seasonal farm workers in India

Transactions costs, asset inequality, and labor markets

Labor markets in developing countries often contain imperfections due to power imbalances, imperfect information, and transactions costs. Power imbalances emerge when a single or small number of employers are in an area. In such cases, the employers may exercise monopsony (single buyer) power over their employees and use fewer workers at lower wages than would exist in a competitive labor market. Large-scale plantations, such as those existing in Central America and in cocoa-producing areas in West Africa, may exhibit such power. Imperfect information and transactions costs also constitute major sources of labor market imperfections. Labor must be hired, with corresponding costs of search and contracting, and supervised. Supervision involves costs of monitoring and enforcement. Such costs may distort incentives for hiring and use of different types of workers.

Information imperfections mean that employers may be unaware of the reliability of workers, some of whom shirk their duties. As a result, costly supervision or other contractual mechanisms must be undertaken to ensure the worker performs his or her duties as expected. Share-cropping and piece-work contracts are two such mechanisms commonly found in less developed countries. One study of the effectiveness of such contractual arrangements conducted in the Philippines found that piece-rate and shared cultivation were associated with significantly higher worker effort than wage-only contracts.[11] Contracts that tie labor, land use agreements, credit, and other inputs together often represent responses to imperfect information, transactions costs, and risk sharing.

Wages in agriculture, whether on a casual or a full-time basis, are relatively low. This is partly a result of high fertility in rural areas; growing populations exert downward pressure on wages. Throughout the developing world, people who rely on agricultural employment as their main source of income tend to be poor. Poverty rates are high among tobacco-estate workers in Zimbabwe and Malawi, day laborers on the Indian sub-continent, and among coffee and other plantation workers in Central America. Government interventions into labor markets are often justified based on this observed poverty. Because labor is one of the few assets the poor possess, efforts to increase productivity and returns to labor can represent a clear means of benefiting the poor. However, interventions in rural labor markets are complicated, and many view these markets, particularly the agricultural labor market, as the last refuge of the rural poor. While one avenue of escape from rural poverty is to migrate to urban areas, it is also important to understand what kinds of interventions might strengthen rural labor markets so that employment can represent a pathway out of poverty.

Administrative measures to increase returns to rural employment include minimum wage legislation and creation and enforcement of labor standards, such as child labor laws and maximum work weeks. Unfortunately, administrative measures have not been overly successful in rural areas. Minimum wages for farm workers have been tried in a number of countries, including Zimbabwe, South Africa, and several Central American countries. These tend to be difficult to enforce because of high transactions and other costs. Other labor market interventions include establishment of labor enforcement standards, provision of labor market information, investments in education and schooling to increase worker productivity, and promotion of nonagricultural job opportunities that compete with agricultural employment. Non-farm employment constitutes a large and growing share of rural labor markets. As agriculture develops over time, it must compete with alternative employment opportunities in rural labor markets.

Increasing wages for farm work are now evident in many corners of the developing world. In rural China, widespread migration to coastal cities for work in factories has tightened labor markets leading to wage increases. Similar patterns are observed in Latin America, the Middle East, and throughout Asia, where out-migration, whether temporary or permanent, is diminishing the supply of working-age adults. In many parts of Africa, growth of industry in rural hubs has created employment opportunities for people who would otherwise work on farms. In some cases, the increase in wages is related to changing demands for skills in an increasingly commercial farm sector. For example, in Senegal, rapid growth of the export horticulture sector has created demands for semi-skilled farm workers. The gradual spread of new technologies such as micro-irrigation, conservation agriculture, integrated pest management, and use of tunnels for vegetable production has changed the skills profile of the hired worker on many farms. The skills-mix change is associated with growing compensation.

More fundamentally, success in improving living conditions and reducing poverty has lowered fertility rates in many developing countries, so that labor is no longer as abundant as it was in the recent past. The forces leading to wage increases in farming areas are likely to continue into the future, meaning that wages too are likely to continue their growth. These trends have profound implications for the reduction of rural poverty moving forward.

SUMMARY

Land tenure refers to the rights and patterns of control over the land resource. Land rights determine social and political status as well as the economic power of a large proportion of the population in developing countries. A land reform is an attempt to change the land tenure system through public policies. Land tenure systems vary in farm size and organization, affect incentives to produce and invest, and influence the distribution of benefits from agricultural growth. Family farms, corporate farms, state farms, and group farms are major types of farm ownership. Many types of tenancy or leasing arrangements also exist.

The post-feudal order has resulted in some large capitalist farms and a coexisting small farm sector in many countries. No form of land tenure is universally efficient. Land tenure reform is difficult to achieve because those holding the land rights have political power. Land tenure reform, including more secure rights over land, is needed for improved economic efficiency, equity, and political and economic stability. Unless there is evidence that incentives have been created for farmers to undertake hard work and increase their capital investment, and unless poverty has been reduced and social status improved for the rural poor, a successful land tenure reform has not occurred. Changes in land tenure and more secure property rights should be accompanied by credit, marketing, and other services, and new landowners should be taxed to support development. Market-based land redistribution efforts include fortification of sales and rental markets, encouraging cooperatives to redistribute lands to their members, reduced government ownership, and creation of land banks.

Labor is often the most valuable resource the rural poor possess. Labor markets in developing countries often contain imperfections due to power imbalances, imperfect information, and transactions costs. Many of the oddities found in agricultural labor markets, such as share-cropping, piecework, and labor sharing, are responses to the imperfections. Government interventions into labor markets are often justified based on observed market failures, but these interventions tend to have limited effectiveness. Out-migration, commercialization of agriculture, and lowered fertility rates associated with economic development have increased agricultural wages in the recent past. These forces are likely to continue into the future.

IMPORTANT TERMS AND CONCEPTS

Capitalistic agriculture	Permanent labor
Casual labor	Political stabilization

Compensation	Property rights
Corporate farms	Public capital formation
Family farms	Semi-feudal land tenure
Group farms	Socialist agriculture
Land grabbing	State farms
Land redistribution	Successful land reform
Land reform	Tenancy reform
Land tenure	Transactions costs
Marketable surplus	

LOOKING AHEAD

In this chapter, we considered institutional changes related to land and labor. In the next chapter, we consider institutional changes related to inputs, insurance, and finance. Governments often intervene in input, insurance, and credit markets. We will examine the nature and advisability of these interventions.

QUESTIONS FOR DISCUSSION

1 What is land tenure?
2 What are the major ways farms are organized?
3 What are the major types of tenancy arrangements?
4 Why might certain forms of tenancy organization be more economically efficient than others?
5 What is land reform?
6 How does an anti-feudal land reform differ from land reforms within a capitalist or socialist agrarian structure?
7 Why is a land redistribution program often necessary?
8 What social goals might be achieved through land redistribution?
9 Why is a land reform difficult to achieve?
10 Why are large landholdings in a densely populated country bad?
11 What are the requisites of a successful land reform?
12 What pressures might population growth or new technologies place on existing land tenure arrangements?
13 What alternatives exist to administrative land reforms?
14 How can more secure land rights improve agricultural productivity?
15 What distinguishes casual labor from permanent labor and why do both exist?
16 Why are transactions costs a problem in labor markets?

NOTES

1 The Gini coefficient is a widely used measure of inequality that ranges from 0 (complete equality) to 1 (complete inequality).

2 See Hans P. Binswanger-Mkhize, Camille Bourguignon, and Rogier van den Brink (eds.), *Agricultural Land Redistribution: Toward Greater Consensus* (Washington, DC: The World Bank, 2009).

3 See Alain de Janvry, "The Role of Land Reform in Economic Development: Policies and Politics", *American Journal of Agricultural Economics*, vol. 63 (May 1981), pp. 384–392.

4 de Janvry, "The Role of Land Reform in Economic Development".

5 Liu Shouying, Xiong Xuefeng, and Long Tingyu, "Rural Land Rights in China: Evolution and Case Studies", *China Economist*, vol. 15 (March–April 2020), pp. 109–120; Klaus Deininger and Songqing Jin, "Securing Property Rights in Transition: Lessons from Implementation of China's Rural Land Contracting Law", *Journal of Economic Behavior and Organization*, vol. 70 (2009), pp. 22–38.

6 Leah Bevis and Christopher Barrett, "Close to the Edge: High Productivity at Plot Peripheries and the Inverse Size-Productivity Relationship", *Journal of Development Economics*, vol. 143 (2020).

7 Vollrath, Dietrich, "Land Distribution and International Agricultural Productivity", *American Journal of Agricultural Economics*, vol. 89 (February 2007), pp. 202–216.

8 See Klaus Deininger and Songquing Jin, "Tenure Security and Land-Related Investment: Evidence from Ethiopia", *European Economic Review*, vol. 50 (July 2006), pp. 1245–1277; Klaus Deininger and Songquing Jin, "Land Sales and Rental Markets in Transition: Evidence from Rural Vietnam", *Oxford Bulletin of Economics and Statistics*, vol. 70 (February 2008), pp. 67–101 for examples.

9 Lorenzo Cotula, Sonja Vermeulen, Rebeca Leonard, and James Keeley, *Land Grab or Development Opportunity? Agricultural Investment and International Land Deals in Africa* (London and Rome: IIED/FAO/IFAD, 2009).

10 See Joachim von Braun and Ruth Meinzen-Dick, *Land Grabbing by Foreign Investors in Developing Countries: Risks and Opportunities* (Washington, DC: IFPRI Policy Brief 13, 2009).

11 See A. Foster and M. Rosenzweig, "A Test for Moral Hazard in the Labor Market: Contractual Arrangements, Effort, and Health", *Review of Economics and Statistics*, vol. 76 (1994), pp. 213–227.

RECOMMENDED READINGS

Binswanger-Mkhize, Hans P., Camille Bourguignon, and Rogier van den Brink (eds.), *Agricultural Land Redistribution: Toward Greater Consensus* (Washington, DC: The World Bank, 2009).

Cotula, Lorenzo, Sonja Vermeulen, Rebeca Leonard and James Keeley, *Land Grab or Development Opportunity? Agricultural Investment and International Land Deals in Africa* (London and Rome: IIED/ FAO/IFAD, 2009).

Deininger, Klaus, and Songquing Jin, "Tenure Security and Land-Related Investment: Evidence from Ethiopia", *European Economic Review*, vol. 50 (July 2006), pp. 1245–1277.

Vollrath, Dietrich, "Land Distribution and International Agricultural Productivity", *American Journal of Agricultural Economics*, vol. 89 (February 2007), pp. 202–216.

14 Inputs, finance, and risk

THIS CHAPTER

1 Explains the importance of inputs and credit and other financial services to developing-country agriculture
2 Describes the nature of rural financial markets and the determinants of rural interest rates
3 Discusses why governments may be tempted, usually inadvisably, to subsidize credit and financial services

IMPORTANCE OF NEW INPUTS

Successful agricultural development requires increased output per hectare and per worker. This agricultural intensification depends in part on the availability and financing of new, often manufactured, inputs. Fertilizers, new seeds, irrigation systems, mechanical power, and supplemental minerals and nutrients for animals are examples of these inputs. Input purchases link farmers with national and international markets and expose them to the associated rewards and risks. As energy prices vary and demands for food grow over time, the cost of production and relative returns of different input mixes are affected by internationally determined forces. Governments must address a series of policy and regulatory issues related to production, distribution, pricing, financing, and regulation of farm inputs, and to the encouragement of optimal input usage given the risks faced by farmers.

Role of manufactured inputs

Manufactured inputs play an important role in agricultural development because the potential for expanding the land resource is limited in most countries. This scarcity or inelastic supply of land means that its price tends to increase over time, both absolutely and relative to the price of labor. The induced-innovation theory described in Chapter 11 indicates that farmers will seek new technologies that enable them to substitute lower cost inputs for those whose scarcity and price are rising. Agricultural research, described in Chapter 12, will create the plant varieties that are responsive to these inputs. Higher-productivity inputs include new seeds, fertilizer, irrigation systems, and pesticides, some of which will be produced domestically, but with prices that are affected by international markets.

Seeds, fertilizer, irrigation, and pesticides tend to be highly complementary inputs. To be more productive than traditional varieties, new varieties of wheat, rice, corn, and other food crops require more fertilizer and better water control than would be used under traditional practices. Water and fertilizer induce lush plant growth and an environment favorable to weeds and other pests, thus raising the profitability of pesticides and other pest management inputs. If this package of inputs is available to farmers together with the necessary financing and information on usage, land and labor productivity can be raised (see Box 14.1). The result is an increase in output per hectare and per unit of labor applied, at least in those areas where the new inputs are suited and adopted. When the new inputs are adopted, it is likely that production cost per unit of output is lower than before. A description of the inputs will help better define their potential and limitations.

Seed

Seeds of high-yielding varieties are usually a relatively low-cost input. However, seed of superior varieties must be developed or identified, tested, produced, and multiplied, monitored for quality, and distributed to farmers. The government often has a role to play in the development, testing, quality monitoring, and production of basic seed. Private firms can be involved in seed multiplication and their distribution to farmers. The exact roles of public and private bodies may change as the seed industry matures. As hybrid seeds continue to spread for crops such as maize and rice, the importance of the seed industry grows, as farmers planting hybrids need to purchase new seeds if they expect to maintain

---

BOX 14.1 MODERN INPUTS AND ECONOMIC GROWTH

New technologies and inputs help achieve increases in agricultural output and income in rural areas of developing countries. This income is spent by the households on goods and services, some of which are produced locally and others which are imported into the region. These expenditures induce income growth in the non-farm economy, the so-called *multiplier effects*. By far, the largest portion of these multipliers is caused by household expenditures on consumer goods and services, though the effects resulting from increased use of farm inputs and in processing, marketing, and transportation of farm output are substantial contributors to regional growth.

Linkages between farms and suppliers of inputs also create spillovers into the local economy. Though seeds, agrichemicals, irrigation supplies, and farm machinery usually are not produced in agricultural regions, input supply services, including technical advice, machinery repair, and a large proportion of irrigation construction and maintenance, can be produced locally. These activities create opportunities for non-farm employment and income that is in turn spent locally. The creation and deepening of backward linkages from agriculture are important contributions to rural economic development.

---

productivity. Recycled seeds of hybrid varieties are less productive than fresh seeds. Even land-races or seeds from traditional varieties lose productivity over time due to disease infections. One of the concerns with genetically modified crops is that one or a few seed companies may own the intellectual property rights associated with the new seeds and therefore may charge a significant premium (see Chapter 12 for further discussion). The government can play a role in ensuring no undue exercise of monopoly power by seed companies.

Fertilizer
Higher-producing varieties require additional fertilizer, particularly nitrogen, phosphate, and potash. These nutrients can be obtained from natural fertility in the soil, animal and plant wastes, and leguminous

plants that can fix nitrogen from the air. These natural sources often, but not always, must be supplemented by chemical fertilizers to provide the necessary quantities and precise mixtures required. In areas where the supply of natural fertilizers is relatively inelastic, as commercial fertilizers become less expensive and are available in relatively elastic supply, their use can be expected to increase.

Water

Availability of irrigation water is a major determinant of planting intensity, inputs used, and hence production. Higher fertilizer application rates require more and better-timed water input. Drainage is also important because few crops can tolerate excessive standing water or salinization. Several important factors complicate irrigation decisions. Irrigation infrastructure requires large financial investments and governments often provide funds or encourage private entities to provide funds for such endeavors. Efficient water management requires proper pricing mechanisms: private users of water might over- or under-use irrigation water if it is not properly priced. Proper pricing is complicated by difficulty in measuring the amount of water used.

Development and management of irrigation and drainage systems often require a combination of public and private initiatives. Governments can seek to expand and modernize irrigation and drainage facilities. They can design pricing rules to encourage economically sound water use. Farmers and farmer groups can develop smaller, often well-based, systems and the necessary canals for distribution among farms.

Efficient water use is likely to grow in importance in many areas of the world as looming water shortages result from over-use of aquifers, damming of major river systems, and climate change, which affects rainfall patterns and temperature-based rates of evaporation. Water danger zones are emerging in the Sahel region of Africa, the Horn of Africa, the entire Middle East, the Indo-Gangetic Plains in India and Pakistan, and the North China Plain. In these areas, growth in demand or dwindling supplies or both will likely be associated with water shortages. Competition with alternative water uses for human consumption or industrial production creates further demand on water resources. Unless solutions are found, water will increasingly constrain agricultural production in the future. Solutions include better management of existing supplies and new efficiency-enhancing technologies such as drip irrigation, supplementary irrigation, fertigation systems, and water-harvesting techniques.

Micro-irrigation system in Nepal

Pesticides

Farmers often find using pesticides (insecticides for insects, fungicides for diseases, and herbicides for weeds) profitable, as agricultural production intensifies through increased use of new seeds, fertilizer, and water. Sometimes these pesticides are applied as a preventative treatment and other times after a major pest problem develops.

Pesticides can have serious drawbacks, however. Some pesticides are toxic to humans and animals and result in poisonings in the short run or chronic health problems in the longer term. Applications with improper equipment or inadequate protective clothing exacerbate health problems. Improper storage and handling can create adverse health consequences. Chemical pollution can spread beyond the area where the pesticide is applied, with particularly deleterious effects on fisheries. Some pesticides kill insects that are beneficial to agriculture. When pesticides are applied over a period of time, the target insects, diseases, or weeds can develop resistance, making increased applications necessary to maintain the same level of effectiveness. Rotation of pesticides with different active ingredients can also manage resistance in pests.

Pesticides, despite these problems, will likely be used for some time until additional pest-resistant varieties, biological and cultural practices, and other substitute methods for pest control can further be developed. Several of these methods, called integrated pest management or IPM, have already been developed and implemented for certain pests on certain crops in certain locations. Additional research is needed, however, to make these practices more widely available.

Animal inputs

As discussed in Chapter 7, livestock play an important role in farming systems in developing countries. Animal productivity is often low, and new inputs related to disease control, feed supplements, improved shelter, and, in some cases, improved breeds can make a difference. Inputs for controlling diseases and parasites are particularly important; the significance of feed supplements, shelter, and new breeds varies from country to country and by type of livestock. Because indigenous livestock have been adapted to their specific environments, the transfer in of new breeds is complex, except perhaps for poultry.

Mechanical inputs

Tilling, planting, cultivating, and harvesting are still done by hand in parts of the developing world, particularly in sub-Saharan Africa and in hilly regions on other continents. In many areas of Asia and Latin America, animals are an important source of power. Even in countries where farming is more mechanized, power tillers and tractors are often restricted to tillage and a few other operations. In many developing countries, labor is abundant and its cost is low. Employment opportunities outside agriculture are limited in many cases, so labor displacement can be undesirable. Mechanization is most profitable in countries where land is abundant, labor is scarce, and capital is cheap. This situation used to exist in relatively few countries, but economic growth, increased urbanization, and increased agricultural productivity has, in recent years, led to upward pressure on labor prices in most developing countries.

The types of mechanization that occur will differ by farm size. Highly productive cropping systems, whether on small or large farms, can benefit from more precise planting depths and fertilizer placement, mechanically pumped irrigation water, mechanical threshing, transport, power spraying of pesticides, and tilling when timing is critical for multiple cropping. Even where labor is usually abundant, shortages can occur in certain seasons, which, if relieved through mechanization, could increase the overall demand for labor.

Individual farmers consider the private profitability when deciding whether to invest in a machine. If very large farms exist in countries with abundant labor in agriculture, some farm operators may still prefer labor-saving machinery because it allows them to deal with fewer employees. Given the transactions costs and capital subsidies that may exist, it may be more privately profitable to follow large-scale mechanization even if society as a whole would be better off without it. Such behavior is one of the reasons that land reform is important in some developing countries (see Chapter 13).

Input markets

Developing countries often subsidize the purchase of seeds, fertilizers, irrigation water, and pesticides. Such subsidies can lead to losses in economic efficiency for the country as a whole, can be costly to the government, and, particularly in the case of pesticides, may lead to environmental damages from over-use. Governments occasionally become involved in multiplying and selling improved seeds to farmers at or below cost, competing with the private sector.

Fertilizer subsidies can be used in select situations in which governments desire to stimulate food production and evidence shows that fertilizer use is lagging. Prior to the mid-2000s, evidence had accumulated that blanket fertilizer subsidies were economically inefficient and cost far more than the social benefits they provide. They also tended to benefit large-scale producers the most. In some countries, these subsidies had been used to compensate for artificially low prices imposed on agricultural outputs for the purpose of keeping food prices down for urban consumers. While this combination of policies can have the desired effect, at least in the short run, high costs to the government and potential fiscal problems can result, making the policies non-sustainable. Also, economic efficiency losses associated with these policies can be substantial. Studies show that from the farmer's perspective, access to inputs can be more important than their prices. Subsidy policies and government involvement in input markets often lead to input shortages and rationing, which are harmful to long-run growth.

In a few cases in sub-Saharan Africa, such as in Zambia and Malawi, targeted fertilizer subsidies may have been useful. Fertilizer uptake in these countries has historically been very low, and agronomists and soil scientists agree that traditional fertility management practices such as fallows have not adequately promoted growth in food production. Behavioral economists have shown that farmers sometimes need a "nudge" to adopt new seeds and fertilizers, even if there is good evidence that they are profitable. Some subsidy programs use vouchers to reduce the cost to producers while others distribute small packets of seeds and fertilizers to targeted producers. A voucher program has the advantage that it can be designed to promote simultaneous growth of private input supply networks. While the jury is still out on many of these programs, all of them recognize the dual importance of lowering costs of input deliveries, mainly by relying on private suppliers, and the broad benefits from more intensive use of modern inputs where these inputs are appropriate.[1]

In summary, with some exceptions, input subsidies are inadvisable. The government can play a more constructive role by ensuring the availability of the inputs (including the improvement of rural roads), publishing price information to encourage competition, setting quality standards for seeds and fertilizers, requiring and enforcing labeling of input containers, and regulating use of toxic pesticides and transgenic seeds.

FINANCE, RISK, AND INSURANCE

Two universal features of agriculture are the temporal gap between planting and harvest and the inherent riskiness of production. These features are especially important in developing countries. The delay between application of inputs and harvest means that farming requires investment: labor, seeds, fertilizer, and other inputs are applied and paid for long before returns are realized. Even when planting and weeding use household labor and seeds are saved from the prior harvest, use of these factors implies a cost. Food must be paid for, and seeds saved for future planting imply less to eat now. Production risk can be more pronounced in developing country agriculture because many such farmers depend on rain; poorer quality soils common in some developing areas store less water and fewer nutrients; and plant diseases and pests are more prevalent in tropical countries. Growing evidence indicates that climate change is raising risks faced by farmers due to higher temperatures, more erratic rainfall, more extreme weather events, and shifting pest populations.[2] In coastal areas, rising sea levels increase salt water intrusion, lowering productivity and sometimes leading to complete crop failure.

These pervasive risks magnify the importance to developing-country agriculture of financial services. These services include credit (borrowing and lending), savings, and insurance. The different financial services overlap, as savings can be used for input and capital purchases (and hence substitute for credit), and as a safety net (through precautionary savings) that can substitute for insurance. Developing-country households use complex strategies to purchase inputs and food, to invest in the future, to manage risk, and to ensure that day-to-day finances are in order. Access to financial services helps determine the suitability and effectiveness of these strategies. Understanding rural financial markets requires consideration of the three components, and efforts to strengthen one component may be compromised by weaknesses in others.

Types of financial service providers

Financial service providers can be *formal* or *informal*. Private commercial banks, government-controlled banks, cooperative banks, and credit societies are formal sources. Public or private, these financial institutions usually are regulated by the government and are open to audit and inspection. In addition to credit, they can provide other services, such as savings and insurance. Historically, formal financial institutions have generally not served the needs of small-scale farmers in developing countries. As a result, many developing-country governments have intervened to promote access to formal financial services, primarily credit. These programs were largely unsuccessful for many reasons, one of which was that they did not recognize alternative, informal financial arrangements found throughout the developing world.

Informal financial service providers include moneylenders, merchants, pawnbrokers, landlords, friends, and relatives. Some sources – e.g., landlords and merchants – combine other economic activities with lending. Except for absentee landlords, the relationship between borrower and informal lender is generally marked by personal contact, simple accounting, and low administrative costs. Many informal insurance arrangements can be found throughout the world. These include burial societies, common in much of the world, particularly in Southern Africa. Burial society members voluntarily contribute to a communal pot that is used to pay funeral costs of members and their families. In Zimbabwe, the "Zunde raMambo" system, named for the Shona phrase "the king's granary", is used as informal crop insurance, particularly for the poor or disabled. Villagers contribute labor to a common field or donate maize to a common pool with the idea that the stock will be distributed to those in need – for example, in the event of a crop failure. These types of institutions function well because members know each other and social pressures can be used to discourage cheating.

Some financial service providers cross the boundary between informal and formal. Examples are rotating credit and savings associations

(ROSCAs) found throughout the world, which are essentially informal, but many are linked to the formal financial system. ROSCAs are groups of people who meet regularly, pay into a common pool at meetings, and allow one member to take home the entire pool at least once over the lifetime of the ROSCA. Many micro-finance institutions start informally and evolve over time into formal sector institutions. Micro-finance refers to small loans to individuals or groups that are paid back over time. In addition to loans, micro-finance institutions can offer savings facilities and insurance to members.

The variety of financial institutions found in developing countries demonstrates the strong demand for such institutions (financial services are necessary) and specific weaknesses in rural financial markets that hinder entry of formal sector institutions. The structure of successful rural institutions reflects adaptation to these weaknesses.

Weaknesses in rural financial markets

Despite the importance of financial services to agriculture, developing-country farmers rarely have access to formal credit, savings, or insurance. The main reason for this absence is market failure. Market failure results from factors such as transactions costs and imperfect (or costly) information. It means that competitive markets will not supply *Pareto optimal* quantities of rural financial services. Examples of transactions costs are easy to come by. In a lending market, lenders may not have full information about the credit-worthiness of a borrower, the borrower may lack collateral, or claiming collateral may be difficult in the event of a default. Lack of information about clients hampers credit and insurance markets; *adverse selection*, where lenders do not know attributes (such as willingness to take on risk) of potential clients, means that reliable clients can be priced out of formal markets. When reliable clients do not participate, the institutional sustainability is fraught. In insurance markets, *moral hazard*, where an insured person acts recklessly, makes insuring farm production difficult. If a crop failure results from a decision of the insured, the insurance mechanism will not work. Widespread risk (called *covariate risk*) leads to multiple defaults at one time, which can tax the resources of even the best-funded insurance schemes. In many contexts, the concept of insurance is not well understood and potential clients may be discouraged from entering into insurance contracts. Savers need some assurance that their deposits will be repaid (with interest), but institutions guaranteeing savings are not common in developing countries.

Rural credit in developing countries

Access to credit becomes important as a country's agriculture begins to develop. Credit helps farmers purchase inputs, facilitates purchase of durable productive inputs such as machinery, and helps households manage their resources. Without credit, even high-return investments would be infeasible for many farmers. Loans facilitate risk management since farmers can borrow during bad years and pay back loans during good years. Even within cropping seasons, short-term credit is used to smooth consumption and provide cash at times of acute needs.

Rural credit markets in developing countries suffer from scarce collateral, widespread risk, and underdeveloped complementary institutions. Collateral is scarce because borrowers are poor; land, an important form of collateral, is often held without title, and, in cases of default, social pressures make it difficult for a lender to collect. Formal credit programs can be politicized, and well-connected borrowers often refuse to repay loans; loan forgiveness is commonly found in politically sensitive government lending programs. In many countries, women farmers do not hold title to land and are thus excluded from formal credit markets. In fact, evidence holds that limited access to credit for women farmers leads to fairly substantial efficiency losses in developing-country agriculture.[3] Widespread risk and the absence of complementary institutions, such as insurance, make lending riskier and create disincentives for formal credit. If a borrower faces a catastrophic loss, loans are not repaid and credit markets are weakened. The presence of moral hazard and adverse selection also slow formation of formal lending institutions in rural areas: information about the reliability of potential borrowers is scarce and costly.

Informal lenders are important sources of funds in many rural areas. These lenders usually know the borrowers personally, require little collateral, make consumption as well as production loans, are accessible at all times, and usually are flexible in rescheduling loans. They do not face the information and other transactions costs characterizing formal-sector lenders. However, these informal lenders also tend to charge high interest rates and are frequently accused of exploitive activities. In cases where lenders are landlords, merchants, or both, they have been accused of using their position to coerce borrowers and force their clients to rent from, borrow from, buy from, and sell to them. Thus, these agents are said to earn monopoly profits. Are borrowers consistently being exploited? It is important to examine this question because it has important implications for the role of more formal private and public credit institutions.

Do informal lenders exploit borrowers?

The issue of borrower exploitation revolves around the existence of usury or monopoly profits earned by lenders. It is important to consider factors determining the interest rates charged by these lenders. The major components of interest rates on loans are: (1) administrative costs, (2) the opportunity cost of lending, (3) a risk premium due to the probability of default in repayment, and (4) monopoly profit.

Administrative costs should not be too high for moneylenders, given simple contracting procedures and personal knowledge of clients. Opportunity costs of lending are low in rural areas because interest rates offered by banks tend to be low. Therefore, the critical factor in determining whether interest rates are generating monopoly profits in the informal money market is the risk premium or the probability of default. The risk premium for loans to small-scale, particularly tenant, farmers can be high. These farmers are close to the margin of subsistence, and a streak of bad weather or a serious illness can spell disaster. Without formal collateral, the risk of default grows. Covariate weather risk means that a spell of bad weather creates potential for simultaneous default of many borrowers. Therefore, one would expect relatively high interest rates just to cover the risk factor. Exploitive situations do exist in which moneylenders extract monopolist gains. However, careful empirical studies seem to indicate that monopoly profits may not be as widespread or large in informal credit markets as is often believed. The reason is competition. The amount lent is usually small, and start-up costs required to become a moneylender are low. This ease of entry serves to keep interest rates at an appropriate level given the level of risk, administrative costs, and the opportunity cost of capital. If profit margins become large, incentives are created for new moneylenders to enter the business and compete away those profits.

High risks associated with loans to subsistence farmers, however, mean that lenders have incentives to maintain tight control over borrowers. Moneylenders who are also landlords or merchants have means of controlling their clients through leases, consumer credit, and others. Other moneylenders may be hesitant to lend to someone who already owes substantial sums or who has defaulted to another. In summary, it appears that some exploitation by moneylenders does occur, particularly if the moneylenders control the land or the market. However, the magnitude of this exploitation may not be as great as is often believed. Evidence of high interest rates on rural loans alone is not sufficient to conclude that moneylenders are exploitive, since there are high costs associated with making these loans. Informal sources of credit serve a vital function in most developing countries because, without them, most small farmers would not have access to credit.

Formal credit and transactions costs

Why are small-scale farmers in developing countries not better served by formal sources? Formal financial institutions find that transactions costs are high. Loans, savings, and insurance needs are small, and the paperwork and time spent evaluating potential clients, collecting payments, and supervising loans in order to reduce risks of default are costly. Often, the government regulates the maximum interest allowed and that rate will fail to cover administrative costs and risk. Thus, where private and public sources of finance exist, they tend to serve larger-scale farmers to reduce administrative costs and risk of default (Box 14.2).

The magnitude of these transactions costs is illustrated by a relatively successful bank that has provided credit for many years to the rural poor in Bangladesh. The Grameen Bank of Bangladesh targets households owning less than 0.5 acres of cultivable land.[4] The bank organizes its clients into groups and associations, provides credit without collateral, and supervises utilization of the loans. A maximum amount (the equivalent of about $150) is lent to individuals within a group of five members. Nearly three-fourths of the borrowers are women. Peer pressure together with close supervision ensures repayment rates of more than 90 percent. The interest rate charged is roughly 16 percent a year, and the default rate has historically been less than 2 percent. The bank is subsidized, however, by the Government of Bangladesh, which lends

---

BOX 14.2 ADMINISTRATIVE COSTS AND LOAN SIZE

The cost of lending to farmers includes relatively large fixed costs to pay for administration and bookkeeping. To cover these costs, interest rates must be higher for smaller loans, even if all borrowers have equal risk of default. For example, if the variable cost of capital is 10 percent but the bank incurs a fixed cost of $10 to administer each loan, for the bank to break even on each loan it must charge a total of 20 percent interest to those who want to borrow $100 for repayment after one year. In contrast, those who want to borrow $1000 would have to pay only 11 percent.

Bangladesh families have benefited from Grameen Bank loans

it money at subsidized rates and insures Grameen bonds, which have been used to raise capital. The interest on the loans would be around 5 to 10 percent higher than if the bank had to break even to borrow at the same rate as the other financial institutions in the country.[5] Because the default rate and the opportunity cost of capital are low, it is clear that most of the interest charged is to cover administrative cost. The bank could lower this cost with less supervision, but the default rate would likely rise and offset the cost saving.

The Grameen Bank also lends very little money for activities associated with crop production. In general, this type of *microcredit* lending serves mostly for livestock and poultry, for small-scale processing and manufacturing, and for trading and shopkeeping. These activities are less risky than crop production. The Grameen Bank model has been improved upon through sequential experimentation, and micro-finance organizations around the world are now flourishing without subsidization. These organizations and some of their organizing principles are discussed below.

Government-assisted credit programs

Governments use credit programs to stimulate agricultural development and compensate for failures in other markets. International donors sometimes support subsidized credit programs. Government-supported credit is based on the notions that (1) credit is critical to the adoption of new technologies, (2) moneylenders exploit farmers and public credit can provide them with competition, (3) credit can be combined with supervision and education to increase the capacity of farmers to use modern inputs, (4) subsidized credit can offset disincentives to production created by other policies that discriminate against agriculture, and (5) government-supported credit programs can lessen inequities in the rural sector.

Subsidized credit provides an easy vehicle for transferring public funds to the rural sector, but it can compromise the viability of the rural financial system. Subsidized credit creates excess demand for credit by lowering interest rates. It erodes capital availability in financial markets and undermines rural financial institutions. Private banks cannot cover expenses at low interest rates, yet they are forced to lower interest rates in order to remain competitive with public credit sources, even if not required to lower them by law. Thus, the survival of private institutions can be threatened. An equally important effect of subsidized loan rates is that they lower all interest rates and, hence, discourage private savings. If agricultural development is to be able to generate capital, then viable rural financial institutions are needed both to provide loans and to mobilize savings.

Because subsidized credit generates excess demand for loans, credit is rationed and almost inevitably goes to the larger farms, for which the administrative costs are lower. Because the subsidized loans are valuable, the credit system can become politicized as large landowners offer favors to bank managers to obtain loans or financially support politicians to encourage continuation of the program. In addition to these distributive effects, default rates on subsidized loans tend to be high.

Innovations in rural finance

As countries have learned from their failures with subsidized credit programs, and as experience has grown with targeted small, group-loan programs such as the Grameen Bank in Bangladesh, provision of small loans to low-income people has expanded. More than 10,000 micro-finance institutions (MFIs) now serve more than 140 million members[6] worldwide. The Grameen Bank, however, while demonstrating that poor people can be good credit risks given a credit program structured with proper incentives, has remained somewhat constrained by its inability to operate entirely without subsidy. Since the late 1980s, the *poverty lending* approach of banks such as the Grameen Bank has been challenged by a more commercially oriented *financial systems* micro-finance approach. While both approaches focus on the poor, the latter emphasizes savings services to the poor as well as loans. A financial systems approach enables banks to generate sufficient resources to be sustainable and to provide opportunity for the economically active poor to save and invest at a decent return during times when they are able to save. Some are experimenting with innovative ways of "nudging" their clients toward increased savings. These innovations build off the simple insight that people are rarely able to save the amounts they intend to. Examples of microcredit banking systems that have proven profitable are found in countries as diverse as Bolivia and Indonesia. Micro-financial institutions are also experimenting in offering the third component of the finance trinity: micro-insurance. Micro-finance institutions have incentives to help their clients manage risks, since a poor outcome may lead to default on loans.

New experiences in providing finance to small-scale and poor farmers have been built on a number of principles. The first principle is recognition that credit, savings, and insurance are interlinked and efforts to provide one component should consider impacts on the others. Second, funds are fungible and can be used for things other than input purchases, such as consumption and emergency needs. By better enabling risk management, access to financial services can improve income generation over time. Third, for sustainability, credit providers should charge what the loans cost, which is usually more than is charged to large commercial borrowers because of transactions costs on many small loans. Some of those costs arise from the necessity of screening credit applicants. A key innovation of micro-finance is use of joint group liability; loans are made to groups and if one member of the group defaults, the entire loan is considered to be in default. Using group liability, groups use local knowledge to screen members and moral suasion to enforce repayment. These factors reduce transactions costs and improve loan repayment rates. Commercially oriented micro-finance provides formal competition for informal money lenders, and hence is most likely to succeed in precisely those areas where moneylender profits are excessive due to local monopoly power.

Careful studies that have examined the impacts of micro-finance on poor clients provide evidence that micro-finance is a positive factor, albeit just one of the tools necessary for economic development.[7] Problems with micro-finance include rigid repayment rules, reliance on borrowing groups, which can exclude the poorest of the poor, and other factors that contribute to very low default rates.

Risk and insurance

Farming is a risky occupation and developing-country farmers have adapted to risk for eons. Sources of risk include market-related fluctuations in prices and employment and health risks, but possibly the most serious risks facing farmers are weather-related. These hazards include drought, heat stress, floods, and storms. Many of these are becoming increasingly severe over time as carbon loading in the atmosphere exacerbates global climate change.

Risk has *intrinsic* and *instrumental* impacts on farmers. Intrinsic impacts work through current well-being: people are better off when income and consumption are stable. The greater deviations are from normal, the larger the adverse impact on well-being. Evidence of this intrinsic effect is that household surveys regularly show that consumption variability is lower than income variability: people use different tools to smooth consumption. The drive to avoid consumption fluctuations (particularly losses) is the basic behavioral motivation for formal insurance – people pay money to avoid unanticipated losses because such losses hurt.

The instrumental impacts of risk are evident in the short-run, but their real consequences are felt in the long run. In response to risk, farmers adjust their behavior and operations. For example, farmers tend to use familiar technologies and inputs because losses are so disruptive. As a result of risk avoidance, developing-country farmers under-invest in modern technologies perceived to be risky. They diversify their production with the hope that if one crop fails perhaps others will survive; they spread production over spatially separated fields to overcome localized weather shocks like flooding or hail; they grow traditional crops. All these actions imply costs as diversified operations fail to benefit from scale economies, spatially separated fields are less efficiently farmed and bring increased costs of monitoring and moving inputs and equipment, and traditional crop varieties usually yield less than new varieties. Weather-related risks have the potential to slow productivity growth due to avoidance of new technologies, new practices, and specialization.

Like credit, risk management tools can be formal and informal. Insurance is the primary formal risk management tool, and involves subscription payments before the hazard occurs and receipt of compensation after a loss. Formal weather insurance is not common in developing countries, partly because lack of information creates problems of adverse selection and moral hazard. Because formal insurance providers do not have good information about the trustworthiness of potential clients, farmers who take more risks are more likely to enroll in insurance. With crop insurance, farmers may underapply inputs or completely abandon their crop, and insurers face high monitoring costs to ensure this behavior does not occur. These and other manifestations of the high cost of information make it difficult to provide actuarily sound weather insurance. In addition, because weather shocks are highly covariate, weather events affecting large swaths of the agricultural population can bankrupt an insurance scheme.

Formal crop insurance has never gained much traction in the developing world for the reasons previously mentioned. Costs of monitoring and assessing losses are high and lead to premiums that are high and unaffordable to the poor. Information asymmetries and covariate risk, both of which are particularly pronounced in developing countries, compromise the viability of traditional indemnity-based crop insurance programs. Because risk can have such a pernicious effect on agricultural development, a viable alternative – index-based crop insurance – has emerged. Index-based insurance reduces the influence of information asymmetries by making the insurance payout dependent on an area-based trigger, not on actual losses suffered by farmers (the trigger is usually an index of adverse weather events crossing a threshold, but the idea is also applicable to price and other insurance). In this way, the actions of the individual farmer are de-linked from the insurance payout, minimizing adverse selection and moral hazard. Despite their theoretical appeal, index-based insurance programs have not been uniformly successful in developing countries and take-up at actuarial fair prices has been low. Advocates of such insurance products have experimented with contract designs, better measurement of weather (adjustments to the "trigger"), and pairing insurance with complementary risk-management tools such as risk-tolerant varieties and other financial products such as savings and credit.

While formal weather insurance is contracted before a hazard occurs, informal weather risk management can occur *ex-ante* – before the shock is realized – or *ex-post*. Ex-ante actions, such as intercropping or spatially spreading fields and others mentioned earlier, can smooth income in the face of weather shocks but lead to long-term inefficiencies. They are like an insurance product in that they only pay off when crops fail. Risk acts like a bully, inducing farmers to opt out of high-return endeavors, engage in relatively low-return activities, and invest in low-return but liquid assets.[8] Farmers can react after realization of a loss by selling assets; borrowing or seeking aid from relatives, friends, and other sources; or adjusting consumption patterns. These ex-post adjustments can be especially pernicious. Liquid assets such as livestock are difficult to accumulate, have generally low returns, and emergency sales often fetch "fire sale" prices. Emergency loans can imply high interest costs.

Coping mechanisms, such as reduced food consumption, switching to lower-cost sources of calories, or withdrawing children from school, have obvious consequences. With large covariate risks, informal insurance is almost always inadequate.

Because of the increasing frequency and intensity of droughts and flooding due to climate change, modern plant breeding programs at international and national agricultural research systems are increasingly looking to produce drought- and flood-resistant varieties. These varieties, which have been disseminated throughout the world, are like an insurance policy as they only really pay off when there is a drought or flood. They generally do not have a yield advantage over other improved varieties, but the production stability they afford enables better planning and the payoff they afford if the hazard is realized can be quite substantial (see Box 14.3).

Lessons for finance policies

Several lessons emerge from the applied research on risk, credit, and insurance. First, adoption of new technologies often requires purchase of modern inputs. Consequently, credit availability is more important to development than the interest rate charged, and a tradeoff exists between credit availability and subsidized interest rates. Second, the viability of

---

BOX 14.3 FLOOD-TOLERANT VARIETIES "CROWD IN" BETTER MANAGEMENT PRACTICES

Reduced risk can have many beneficial effects on farmers and their decision-making. One example is found in Odisha state in eastern India, where flood-tolerant rice varieties have been introduced. Flood tolerance is very similar to insurance, but it is embedded in the seed technology itself. Researchers found that use of these varieties not only protected farmers from flood risk but also caused them to invest more heavily in beneficial labor-intensive practices and fertilizers, uptake more fertilizer, and plant more area. The "insurance" component, by reducing risk, "crowded in" more beneficial practices, leading to more stable and higher incomes.

Source: Kyle Emerick, Alain de Janvry, Elisabeth Sadoulet and Manzoor H. Dar, "Technological Innovations, Downside Risk, and the Modernization of Agriculture", *American Economic Review*, vol. 106 (2016), pp. 1537–1561

rural financial institutions can be jeopardized by subsidized credit. This weakening can constrict the supply of and demand for financial services. Third, risk is an important factor affecting farmer decision-making, and both formal and informal means exist for managing risks. Fourth, formal lenders and insurers face high transactions costs in gathering information about potential clients. Many innovations in rural finance have involved means of designing institutions to mitigate problems related to asymmetric information. Enhanced information and communications technologies can help reduce transactions costs.

SUMMARY

Successful agricultural development requires increased output per hectare and per worker. This intensification depends on the availability of new, often manufactured, inputs. Seeds, fertilizer, pesticides, irrigation, mechanical power, and supplementary minerals and feeds are examples of these inputs. Manufactured inputs can substitute for inelastic supplies of land to increase production at a lower per unit cost, but several issues must be resolved by each country with respect to externalities associated with chemicals and the role of the government in producing, distributing, and financing inputs. Government input subsidies can discourage private competition for input supply, can be costly to the government, and may encourage over-use of inputs such as pesticides. However, targeted subsidies and input supply programs show some promise as evidence grows that subtle obstacles inhibit adoption of new technologies.

Access to financial services is essential as a country moves from traditional to modern agriculture. Credit from informal sources such as moneylenders is often viewed as oppressive. However, risks and administrative costs of loans to small farms are high and monopoly profits may not be as prevalent or as high as often portrayed. When moneylenders are also landlords or merchants, the chances of exploitation are greater. Formal private and public lenders do not serve a high proportion of the farmers because risks and transactions costs are high. Because governments frequently subsidize interest rates, rationed credit tends to go to the larger farms. The subsidies erode the capital in the financial system and, thus, the number of farms served. Low interest rates also discourage deposits and reduce the ability of formal private banks to compete. Farmers manage pervasive risks using formal and informal tools. The main formal tool is crop insurance, which has not spread widely in developing countries. Credit and insurance programs for developing countries can be designed to mitigate effects of adverse selection and moral hazard.

Credit, savings, and insurance are interlinked, and efforts to provide one component should consider impacts on the others.

IMPORTANT TERMS AND CONCEPTS

Adverse selection
Covariate risk
Fertilizers and pesticides
Fungibility
Grameen Bank
Group lending
Index insurance
Informal financial management
Input subsidies
Integrated pest management
Irrigation systems
Mechanical power

Micro-finance
Moneylenders
Money-markets
Moral hazard
New seeds
Opportunity costs of lending
Organized credit sources
Purchased inputs
Risk of default
Subsidized credit
Vouchers

LOOKING AHEAD

Food chains lengthen as food systems develop and governments often intervene in agricultural markets. In the next chapter, we examine why governments intervene and the effects of the interventions. Efficient marketing systems are essential for agricultural development.

QUESTIONS FOR DISCUSSION

1 Why are manufactured agricultural inputs usually necessary for agricultural development?
2 What are some of the key manufactured inputs needed?
3 In what manner are agricultural inputs complementary in nature?
4 What are the advantages and disadvantages of pesticides?
5 Why is mechanization a controversial issue?
6 Why do governments subsidize the purchase of manufactured inputs?
7 Why is credit important to agricultural development?
8 How do organized and informal sources of credit differ?
9 Why might bankers be biased against small farmer loans in developing countries?

10 What are subsidized interest rates? Are they a good idea for getting agriculture moving? Why do governments subsidize interest rates?

11 How does risk affect farmer decision-making?

12 What types of information asymmetries are most problematic for rural finance in developing countries?

13 Please provide an example of a moral hazard affecting crop insurance.

14 How might transactions costs associated with rural financial markets be reduced?

NOTES

1 See Nicholas Minot and Todd Benson, *Fertilizer Subsidies in Africa: Are Vouchers the Answer?* (Washington, DC: IFPRI Issue Brief 60, 2009).

2 World Bank, *Agricultural Risk Management in the Face of Climate Change* (Washington, DC: World Bank, 2015), https://openknowledge.worldbank.org/handle/10986/22897 License: CC BY 3.0 IGO.

3 Diana Fletschner, "Women's Access to Credit: Does It Matter for Household Efficiency?", *American Journal of Agricultural Economics*, vol. 90 (2008), pp. 669–683.

4 See Mahabub Hossain, *Credit for Alleviation of Rural Poverty: The Grameen Bank of Bangladesh* (Washington, DC: International Food Policy Research Institute Research, Report No. 65, February 1988), for an excellent discussion of the Grameen Bank; see also David Roodman, *Due Diligence: An Impertinent Inquiry into Microfinance* (Washington, DC: Center for Global Development, 2011) for information on the impacts of such programs.

5 Hossain, *Credit for the Alleviation of Rural Poverty*, p. 11.

6 International Labor Organization, *Facts on Microfinance for Decent Work* (Geneva: ILO, 2010).

7 Abhijit V. Banerjee, Dean Karlan, and Jonathan Zinman, "Six Randomized Evaluations of Microcredit: Introduction and Further Steps", *American Economic Journal: Applied Economics*, vol. 7 (2015), pp. 1–21.

8 Travis J. Lybbert and Michael R. Carter, "Bundling Drought Tolerance and Index Insurance to Reduce Rural Household Vulnerability", in Arsenio M. Balisacan, Ujjayant Chakrovarty, and Majah-Leah V. Ravago (eds.), *Sustainable Economic Development: Resources, Environment and Institutions* (Oxford: Academic Press, 2015), pp. 401–414.

RECOMMENDED READINGS

Banerjee, Abhijit, and Esther Duflo, *Poor Economics: A Radical Rethinking of the Way to Fight Global Poverty* (New York: Public Affairs, 2011).

Carter, Michael, Alain de Janvry, Elisabeth Sadoulet, and Alexandros Sarris, "Index Insurance for Developing Country Agriculture:

A Reassessment", *Annual Review of Resource Economics*, vol. 9 (2017), pp. 421–438.

Karlan, Dean, and Jacob Apple, *More Than Good Intentions* (London: Dutton, 2011).

Robinson, Marguerite, *The Micro Finance Revolution: Sustainable Finance for the Poor* (Washington, DC: The World Bank, 2001).

Zeller, Manfred, and Richard L. Meyer, *The Critical Triangle of Microfinance: From Vision to Reality* (Baltimore: Johns Hopkins University Press, 2003).

15 Pricing policies and marketing systems

THIS CHAPTER

1 Discusses the nature of markets, how and why governments tend to intervene in agricultural markets, and the results of those interventions
2 Explains the importance of efficient marketing systems and describes how marketing systems have changed over time in developing countries
3 Considers the role that government can play in providing marketing infrastructure, market information, marketing services, and regulations

PRICING POLICIES

Food and agricultural prices are major determinants of producer incentives and real incomes in developing countries. These prices are influenced by policies and by the efficiency of marketing systems. Pricing policies and marketing systems have changed significantly in recent years, especially in response to domestic budgetary and global market pressures. Direct government control over agricultural markets has diminished in many countries. The roles of government, processors, wholesalers, and retailers are changing. Governments in some developing countries continue to adopt pricing policies that reduce food prices for urban consumers even if farmers are forced to bear the costs. In other developing countries, increased integration into global markets has resulted in freeing up of prices and in new approaches to adding value through processing, marketing, and regulating farm commodities and products.

Ironically, in many developed countries where farmers are a small proportion of the population, government price interventions often support agricultural prices at the expense of taxpayers and consumers, and in some cases with deleterious effects on producers in developing countries. Why do we observe these policies? How are they implemented, and what are their short- and long-run effects? These questions are addressed in the next sections, followed by a discussion of the roles of agricultural marketing systems and how those systems have changed over time.

Reasons for price intervention

Governments intervene into agricultural price formation for two major reasons: to change the outcomes in agricultural markets and to raise revenue to pay for roads, police, and other public services. These interventions have a large influence on the welfare of both producers and consumers. Sometimes government policies reflect the long-run interest of society as a whole, helping to stabilize and raise incomes, but often they reflect more narrow or short-run political objectives.

The long-run interest of most societies includes policies that (1) contribute to economic growth, (2) improve income distribution or at least meet minimum needs of citizens, and (3) provide a certain measure of food security or resiliency over time. Governments vary widely in what they actually do, and their choice of policies helps explain the wide differences in economic outcomes across countries and over time. The choice of which policy to use is influenced by how governments respond to key interest groups. Urban consumers want lower food prices, particularly the poor, who spend a large fraction of their income on food. Employers also prefer low food prices, which allow them to pay lower money wages. But low food prices hurt farmers and reduce investment in agriculture, which lowers farm productivity over time.

In many developing countries, the balance of political power favors urban consumers and employers. Although farmers may be in the majority, they are usually poorer, are often illiterate, and are geographically dispersed across the countryside. Thus, political power with respect to food prices is centered in urban-industrial areas.

As development proceeds and incomes grow, several factors may cause the balance of political power within countries to shift toward helping farmers, often at the expense of consumers. First, food prices become less important in household budgets because the proportion of income spent on food declines with higher incomes. Second, the declining relative size of the agricultural sector makes it less costly for the government to succumb to pressures from farmers, while at the same time the reduced number and increased specialization of farms improves the ability of farmers to organize for collective action. Third, governments in richer countries have easier access to other sources of tax revenue beyond the farm sector.

The form of government interventions into agricultural commodity markets also shifts as development proceeds. In the poorest countries, interventions often focus on international trade because that is easiest to control. Governments typically tax imports and exports, and since poor countries often export farm goods and import manufactured goods, the result is a tax on farmers and protection for local industries. In somewhat higher-income developing countries, governments often introduce food price subsidies and increasingly try to support farm income as well. They also focus on public goods such as roads, market information, and market regulations. At the highest levels of economic development, perhaps the most important transition is toward targeted government programs that attempt to meet political objectives with fewer side effects. For example, food price subsidies may be restricted to benefit only the poorest consumers, while farm subsidies may be made less distorting.

During early stages of development, agricultural policies are often highly inefficient, partly because governments have limited administrative capacity, but also because citizens who lose from bad policy may be unable to organize against them. Inefficiencies remain over time, but policies can improve as development proceeds, due partly to the structural transformation of the underlying economy but also to improvements in political accountability. Countries at all levels of development can also backslide in their agricultural policies, particularly when international trade is involved, as discussed in Chapter 17.

Methods of price intervention

Governments intervene to influence agricultural prices in many ways. They may attempt to set price ceilings or floors and enforce them with commodity subsidies or taxes, manipulation of foreign exchange rates, commodity storage programs, restrictions on quantities traded, and/or other policy instruments. Let's examine how a few of these instruments work.

Suppose the government wants to lower the price of rice to consumers because it is an important food in the diet. The supply of rice must therefore be increased in the market relative to demand. Additional supplies can be created by increasing imports or by stimulating domestic production. In either case, government revenues must be used to bridge the gap between the initial price and the desired *price ceiling*. Figure 15.1 presents an illustration of how the price ceiling and subsidy might work.

The supply and demand schedules would intersect at price P_0 and quantity Q_0 if there were no trade in rice. However, the country in this example is assumed to be a rice importer, so the world price of rice, P_w, is below P_0. Initially, at P_w and without government intervention, quantity Q_1 is produced domestically, Q_2 is demanded by consumers, and the difference, $Q_2 - Q_1$, is met by imports. If the government desires to artificially create a domestic price for rice, P_d, below the world price, it must pay a subsidy per unit of rice equal to the difference between the world price and the desired domestic price $(P_w - P_d)$. This subsidy could be paid on a per ton basis to commercial importers to cover their losses for importing rice at a price below what they pay on the world market, or it could be paid to a government agency that imports rice.[1] In either case, the direct cost to the government of the subsidy is $(P_w - P_d)$ times $(Q_4 - Q_3)$, which equals area *adeh* in Figure 15.1. This kind of price ceiling program has been used in several African and Asian countries. Consumers benefit, but domestic rice producers are hurt by the lower price of rice.

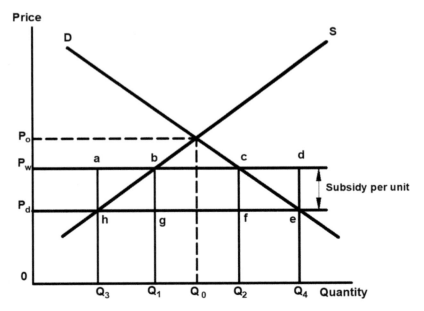

Figure 15.1 Economics of a price ceiling and consumer subsidy to lower agricultural prices

Sometimes the government prefers not to allow scarce foreign exchange to be spent on increased imports. In this case, farmers may be legally forced to sell their commodity to the government at a low price. For example, the government might force farmers to deliver Q_3 units of rice at P_d. Although nothing is imported, the demand for rice (Q_4) exceeds its supply (Q_3). The government must then ration rice to consumers. The shortage in the market provides incentives for farmers to sell their crop illegally on the *black market* for a higher price. Even if the government allows adequate imports to meet the projected demand at the lower price, if the price of the product is higher across the border, farmers will (usually illegally) sell in a neighboring country, thus further reducing domestic supplies.

One means to avoid reducing domestic production and illegal sales while at the same time supporting farm incomes is for the government to administer a two-price scheme in which producers are paid the world price, but consumers pay only the subsidized price. This type of system is illustrated in Figure 15.1. Rather than paying *adeh* to importers, the government would pay $P_w bgP_d$, or a subsidy of $(P_w - P_d)$ times $(Q_1 - 0)$ to producers and a subsidy of *bdeg*, or $(P_w - P_d)$ times $(Q_4 - Q_1)$, to importers. Producers would still receive P_w, while consumers would face a price of P_d, thus the name *two-price scheme*. An even higher subsidy could be paid to producers to further reduce imports and increase the producer price. The obvious difficulty with this scheme is its impact on the government budget. The subsidy costs have to be paid for by some means. Because of the cost, few major commodities are subsidized this way in developing countries, although related schemes have been used in the past in Brazil, Egypt, and Mexico as well as in a few other low-income countries. Table 15.1 lists examples of past food subsidy programs in developing countries.

Developing countries often have food subsidy programs that are targeted toward the poor or to nutritionally vulnerable groups. These subsidies can be implemented through ration shops, ration cards, food stamps, or other means. Usually only the very poor are eligible, to keep the cost down, but in some cases ration shops, which sell basic grains and other staples, are located in poor neighborhoods under the theory that only the poor will frequent them. Alternatively, self-targeting can be achieved by subsidizing foods that the poor tend to buy, such as starchy staples or maize. The impact of targeted subsidies on agricultural prices and incentives depends on how they are financed, but food subsidies need not have adverse effects on agricultural incentives.

Another common price-policy instrument in developing countries is the export tax. The purpose of an export tax is to raise government

Table 15.1 Examples of Existing or Previous Consumer Price Subsidy Programs in Developing Countries

Country	Principal foods subsidized	Type of program	Food distribution	Actual coverage (implicit targeting)
Bangladesh	Wheat and rice	Price subsidy	Targeted and rationed	Mostly urban
Brazil	Wheat	Price subsidy	General	Total population
China	Rice	Price subsidy	General	Mostly urban
Colombia	Selected processed food	Food stamps	Targeted and rationed	Poor households with preschoolers or women who are pregnant or lactating
Egypt	Wheat	Price subsidy	General	Total population
Egypt	Rice	Price subsidy	Rationed	Mostly urban
Egypt	Sugar, tea, frozen meats, fish, and certain other foods	Price subsidy	Rationed	Total population
India	Wheat and rice	Price subsidy	Rationed	Total population
Mexico	Maize and certain other foods	Price subsidy	General	Mostly urban
Morocco	Wheat	Price subsidy	General	Total population
Pakistan	Wheat	Price subsidy	Rationed	Mostly urban
Philippines	Rice and oil	Price subsidy	Targeted and rationed	All households in areas selected for high level of poverty
Sri Lanka (up to 1977)	Rice	Price subsidy	Rationed	Total population

Country	Principal foods subsidized	Type of program	Food distribution	Actual coverage (implicit targeting)
(from 1979)	Rice	Food stamps	Targeted and rationed	50 percent of population, biased toward the poor
Sudan	Wheat	Price subsidy	General	Mostly urban
Thailand	Rice	Price subsidy	General	Total population
Zambia	Maize	Price subsidy	General	Mostly urban

Source: Per Pinstrup-Andersen, *Food Subsidies in Developing Countries* (Baltimore: Johns Hopkins University Press, 1988), p. 6

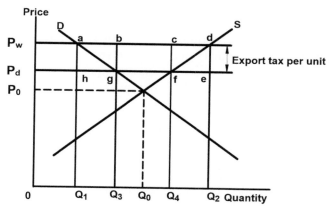

Figure 15.2 Economics of an export tax to raise revenue

revenues or reduce domestic commodity prices. The effects of the tax are illustrated in Figure 15.2. Because the country exports the commodity, the world price, P_w, is shown above the price, P_0, which would have prevailed domestically if there were no trade. If exports were freely allowed, this world price would prevail in the domestic market, and a total quantity of Q_2 would be produced domestically, Q_1 would be demanded by domestic consumers, and the difference $(Q_2 - Q_1)$ would be exported. Then, if an export tax equal to $P_w - P_d$ were imposed, the domestic price would fall to P_d, consumers would increase consumption to Q_3, producers would reduce the quantity supplied to Q_4, exports would decline to $Q_4 - Q_3$, and the government would earn an export tax revenue of $(P_w - P_d)$ times $(Q_4 - Q_3)$ or the area *bcfg* in Figure 15.2. Poor countries may impose export taxes because they lack an alternative source of revenue. In the Figure 15.2 example, the country is unable to influence the world price P_w, because it is a small producer in the world market for the commodity. Domestic producers pay the cost of the tax through lower prices. If the country is a large producer, such as Brazil in the coffee market, its exports and any export tax influence the world market price. Therefore, part of the burden of the export tax can be passed on to consumers in other countries.

Governments follow many types of pricing policies; those previously described are among the most common and direct pricing instruments employed in developing countries. Another direct-pricing policy is the attempt to stabilize commodity prices through a *buffer stock* program. With such a program, supplies are purchased by the government if the price drops below a certain minimum floor level and then dumped on the market if the price rises above a certain ceiling level. The purpose of the program is to stabilize short-run prices rather than alter the long-run price. Buffer stock programs can be costly because they require investments in storage capacity and losses in storage can be substantial. However, in cases where prices may spike quickly or global markets might appear to be unreliable, they may provide benefits over reliance on short-term purchases of commodities to stabilize prices. For example, when global food prices spiked upward in 2008, several rice-exporting countries prohibited exports and short-term price increases were exacerbated in rice-importing countries. Hardships caused by rice price spikes in the Philippines and other importing countries might have been ameliorated through a modest buffer stock program.

A common indirect pricing policy in developing countries is to overvalue the foreign exchange rate. The foreign exchange rate is the value of the country's currency in relation to the value of foreign currency: for example, the number of Mexican pesos that equal one U.S. dollar. If the official foreign exchange rate implies that the local currency is worth more than it actually is, and if exports occur at the official rate, then this overvalued exchange rate acts as an implicit export tax. However, it does not provide tax revenue to the government. More discussion of the trade effects of direct and indirect pricing policies is found in Chapters 16 and 18.

Interventions to shift either the supply of, or demand for, agricultural products also affect prices. Income transfer and employment programs are examples of policies to shift demands. Policies that steer investments into different sectors, credit programs, agricultural research, and land reforms all affect agricultural product supplies. The net effect is to change equilibrium prices in markets. Governments can examine price trends and shifts and treat them as indicators of an underlying problem. In some cases, the problem is induced domestically, but in other cases, it is driven by international forces. For example, the rapidly increasing food prices experienced by most developing countries in 2008 were driven more by international than domestic supply and demand factors.

Prices provide important indicators of sector performance. However, policies that attack the symptom – such as rapidly rising prices – by, perhaps, directly imposing price controls, can create long-run damage to economic growth. A preferred price intervention would be to address the causes of the problem by either investing in productivity enhancing technologies or by making more imports available. If demand lags behind supplies, then programs to stimulate demands, such as food stamps, might be contemplated. In general, it is preferable to address the causes of undesirable price trends rather than to directly intervene in the price formation process for reasons discussed later.

Short- and long-run effects of pricing policies

A few of the direct, short-run effects of food and agricultural pricing-policies are illustrated in Figures 15.1 and 15.2. As producer and consumer prices are raised or lowered, changes in production and consumption occur. Producer incomes, margins between the price to the producer and that paid by the consumer (the "marketing margin"), foreign exchange earnings, price stability, and government revenues are also directly influenced by price policies. These and other direct and indirect, short- and long-run effects of pricing policies are summarized in Table 15.2.

An important short-term effect of many price policies is to transfer income between producers to consumers. Within consumer groups, the poor tend to be the most sensitive to food prices, since they spend proportionately more income on food. The poor are usually targeted either indirectly because a food they eat is subsidized or directly by being provided food stamps or access to ration shops. However, studies show that even well-targeted price subsidy programs are associated with large "leakages" to the non-poor. These leakages imply higher program costs to the government and create distortions.

A major feature of direct and indirect effects of many price policies is the influence of those policies on efficiency of resource allocation. In the short run, resources are diverted to less-productive uses because of the intervention. Additional indirect or long-run misallocation of resources can result as investments and structural changes occur that expand less

Table 15.2 Summary of Price Policy Effects

Direct short-run effects of price policies

1 Changes in consumer and producer prices
2 Changes in quantities produced and consumed
3 Changes in exports, imports, and foreign exchange earnings
4 Income transfers between and among consumer and producer groups
5 Government budget effects
6 Price stability effects
7 Changes in marketing margins and their effects on efficiency of resource allocation

Indirect and long-run effects of price policies

1 Employment changes
2 Incentives for capital investment
3 Incentives for technical change
4 Changes in health and nutrition
5 Long-run changes in allocation of resources in production, storage, transportation, and processing

efficient sectors of the economy at the expense of more efficient ones. In addition, efficiency losses occur due to the resource costs associated with collecting taxes or administering the policy. Food stamp and ration shop programs have fewer distortionary impacts because they shift food demands among recipient groups rather than working through price signals.

Distortions in the normal price differences for a commodity across locations, between points in time, and at different levels of processing can influence storage, transportation, and processing of the commodity. For example, urban prices are normally expected to be higher than rural prices for the same food commodity because of transportation costs. If the government sets a ceiling price that is equal in both rural and urban areas, transporting the good from the rural to the urban areas may no longer be profitable. In fact, in some cases governments have been known to set urban food prices lower than rural prices, with the result that food, supplied by imports, is transported from urban areas to rural areas. The disincentive effects on local producers are obvious.

Likewise, ceiling prices can discourage the normal seasonal storage of a crop if prices are not allowed to rise to cover storage costs. Also, if a government reduces the price margin allowed between farm and retail levels, processors and marketers can be forced out of business.

Pricing policies may be implemented through government procurement agencies with *monopsonistic* (single buyer) power. Thus, opportunities are created for illegal garnering of rents by government employees, and inefficiencies can arise that may force additional reductions in farm prices. These often unintended results of pricing policies can be particularly severe in countries with poor communications and underdeveloped legal systems.

Other indirect effects of pricing policies include employment changes, incentives to develop and adopt new technologies, and changes in health and nutrition. If total revenues for one sector or commodity are raised through pricing policies, more people may be employed. Also, producer incentives to press private firms or public research agencies for new technologies as well as incentives to adopt technologies may be enhanced. Consumer price subsidies can have important impacts on health and nutrition. In cases where they are financed through government tax revenues and not by depressing producer prices, they can be an effective means of transferring income to targeted groups.

Once price policies are instituted, they are difficult to repeal. Urban consumers in numerous countries have reacted in negative and sometimes violent manners to government attempts to lower consumer subsidies. In summary, price-policy effects are pervasive and influence the efficiency of the production and marketing systems.

MARKETING FUNCTIONS AND SYSTEMS

Marketing transforms products over time, space, and form through storage, transportation, and processing. Through marketing, goods are exchanged and prices are set. Markets communicate signals to producers, processors, input suppliers, and consumers about the costs of buying, selling, storing, processing, and transporting. These major marketing functions and their linkages to price policies are summarized in Figure 15.3.

In the earliest stages of development and in remote areas, a high proportion of the population lives on farms and is relatively self-sufficient. The demand for agricultural marketing services is limited. As development proceeds, with resulting increased living standards and urbanization, the size and efficiency of the marketing system become more important. Unless marketing services are improved concurrently with the development and spread of new technologies, improvements in education and credit, and the other factors discussed in this section of the book, economic development will be hindered. An inefficient marketing system can absorb substantial private and public resources and result in low farm-level and high retail-level prices.

FUNCTIONS OF MARKETS AND MARKETING

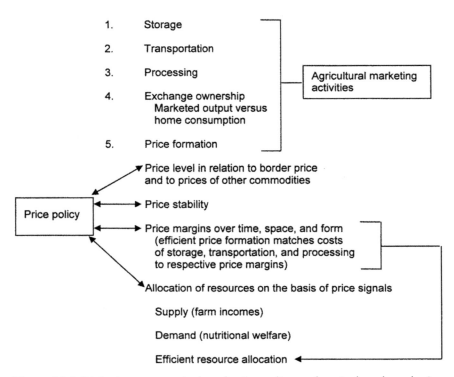

Figure 15.3 Links between agricultural price policy and agricultural marketing
Source: C. Peter Timmer, "The Relationship Between Price Policy and Food Marketing", in J. Price Gittinger, Joanne Leslie, and Caroline Hoisington (eds.), *Food Policy: Integrating Supply, Distribution, and Consumption* (Baltimore: Johns Hopkins University Press, 1987), p. 294

Marketing system deficiencies in developing countries

Private marketing systems in many developing countries operate relatively well, in that prices are influenced by underlying supply and demand conditions. Products are stored, transported, processed, and exchanged in roughly the amounts expected given prevailing costs, except where governments have intervened with price policies. Price rigging by opportunistic marketing agents is generally not a serious problem. However, because marketing and transactions costs can be high and some price distortions do occur, marketing system deficiencies may slow the rate of agricultural growth and influence the distribution of the benefits of that growth. Let's consider the nature of these deficiencies before turning in the following section to the possible public role in solving them and the rapid changes we see occurring in some markets.

The principal weaknesses in marketing systems in developing countries are: (1) infrastructure deficiencies that raise the cost of transport and storage, (2) producers' lack of information, and (3) government-induced market distortions. The magnitude of each of these deficiencies differs across regions and by country, and is changing for the better in many countries, but severe problems are found in some nations, particularly in sub-Saharan Africa. One effect of these weaknesses is to create a large spread between prices producers are paid for their products and retail prices. Marketing system deficiencies also create wide variations in producer prices within countries and within years. sub-Saharan African countries have larger price spreads than Asian and Latin American countries, indicating more deficient marketing systems.

Good communications (e.g., roads, railroads. telephones, postal services) and storage infrastructure are crucial to a well-functioning agricultural marketing system. The availability and quality of rural roads, in particular, have a strong influence on marketing costs and on the willingness of farmers to adopt new technologies and sell surplus production. A farmer who has only a few hectares may still have to market several tons of output to generate revenue needed to apply new seeds, fertilizers, and other modern inputs. Cellphones, internet services, postal services, radio stations, and so on increase access to information. Modern storage facilities are important to minimize rodent, insect, and water damage while commodities are being held. Most storage occurs on the farm or at facilities owned by private traders. Storage may also be provided by the government for buffer stocks and food distribution programs.

Producers require information to improve market efficiency and reduce transactions costs. Unequal access to information can give a competitive advantage to particular groups of farmers or traders who have more information. When roads, basic telecommunications, and news services are lacking or are available only to a few, those with better information on market prices, crop prospects, prospective changes in international forces, and so on can earn higher profits and, in some cases, gain political power as well. Thus, access to information is of fundamental importance for agricultural development. The wireless communications revolution is having a profound effect on information availability and, hence, marketing efficiency. Low-cost cellphones are widely available in developing countries, even in relatively remote rural areas. Vegetable producers from China to Brazil now receive price information through cellphones. Likewise, coffee producers in the Guatemalan highlands can receive up-to-the-minute price information by cellphone. These innovations lower the cost of attaining information, enable farmers to retain more value, and enhance planning for deliveries, lowering waste and improving efficiency.

The structure of agricultural markets is usually such that the number of middle agents is smaller than the number of producers. Economists hold differing views on whether relatively fewer such intermediaries result in monopolistic power on the part of the intermediary and an unfair bargaining advantage. One needs to be cautious in drawing conclusions. Because more efficient traders and processors tend to deal in large volumes, there are naturally fewer of these than there are producers. On the other hand, in most countries with private marketing systems, ease of entry is such that there are still enough processors and other middle agents to provide competition for each other. Examples of collusion and monopolistic power, however, undoubtedly exist for certain products, particularly in isolated areas, where information is costly and social and cultural factors play a contributing role. This form of market power is under pressure from the telecommunications revolution described earlier; enhanced information can be a powerful countervailing force to market power.

A marketing problem for producers of major commodities in some developing countries is a situation in which government-controlled

Vegetable market in India

marketing organizations (often called *parastatals*) are given monopoly power and legal authority to purchase all of a product while setting its price as well (Box 15.1). As discussed in the price-policy section, the tight controls that characterize these markets can have negative effects on producer incentives and market efficiency. Agricultural marketing

---

BOX 15.1 COMMODITY MARKETING BOARDS IN SUB-SAHARAN AFRICA

In a few sub-Saharan African states, publicly sanctioned monopolies still purchase, and in some cases export, agricultural goods. These marketing boards serve as the sole buyers, purchasing crops at administratively determined prices and selling them at prevailing world market prices. State marketing agencies are vestiges of the colonial period, and their origins and histories vary considerably. Many were established during the Great Depression of the 1930s or World War II. Their official mandates were almost invariably to benefit producers by reinvesting revenues in agriculture and, especially, stabilizing producer prices.

As the colonial governments were confronted with growing needs for revenues, they quickly found ways of diverting marketing board funds away from agricultural development and into general revenue coffers. Following independence, African governments continued to use the commodity marketing boards as extensions of their normal revenue-generating arms, and the initial purposes of the boards were ignored. Examples are found in Ghana and Nigeria immediately following independence.

Since colonial times, these boards have been used to transfer resources from agriculture into "modernizing" and mostly urban development. They have served political objectives by raising revenues, increasing employment of favored groups, and keeping primary commodity prices low to benefit urban and industrial concerns. The boards never really fulfilled their mandate to improve and stabilize conditions in agriculture. In combination with other policy distortions, they contributed to the stagnation and decline of agriculture in many African countries. Fortunately, most of the boards were eliminated during the 1980s and 1990s as countries went through economic structural adjustments, but vestiges remain in countries such as Zimbabwe, Zambia, and Kenya.

systems are inherently complex. Markets transmit a large amount of information from diverse sources, and decisions made by centralized agencies can create serious market distortions. Fortunately, use of agricultural marketing parastatals has declined in recent years, which generally has increased prices received by farmers. In some cases, price volatility has risen as well.

THE ROLE OF THE PUBLIC SECTOR IN AGRICULTURAL MARKETING

The primary role of the government is to provide the infrastructure required for an efficient marketing system, particularly roads, a market information system, a commodity grading system, and regulations to ensure the rights of all participants. The underlying rationale for government involvement is the presence of public goods and market failures creating externalities. Public goods provide benefits to society as a whole but would be supplied in less than the socially desirable amounts by the private sector alone. Externalities involve often unintended positive or negative effects of the actions of one person (firm) or persons (firms) on other people.

Provision of infrastructure
The private sector can be expected to build many of the required storage facilities, processing plants, and so on, but investments in roads, seaports, airports, and, in most cases, telecommunications will require government involvement. One firm, or even a small group of firms, will lack the incentives to build sufficient roads, not just because of their high cost but also because of the difficulty of excluding others from or charging for their use. Roads are a public good that serve all industries, consumers, and national defense.

Several studies have estimated the economic benefits of roads to agriculture in developing countries. For example, Fan and Chan-Kang found that even low-quality rural roads in China have a 5–1 benefit cost ratio.[2] The evidence in numerous countries suggests that investments in infrastructure have greatly narrowed farm–retail margins.

Provision of information
Provision of accurate crop and livestock reports requires investments in data collection and dissemination. Production and consumption data may be poor quality, but accurate data on marketed quantities, qualities,

and prices can give essential information for formulating agricultural policies and for decisions by individual economic agents.

To ensure equal access to information, data need to be collected in major markets and disseminated on a regular basis. Information on market prices, crop prospects, and factors influencing demand can be spread through radio broadcasts and newspapers once market reports are released. An efficient, competitive market requires widespread access to information. Otherwise, a small group of large-scale farmers, traders, or processors can gain market power at the expense of small-scale farmers, particularly those in remote areas. These agents can then use the resulting profits to influence political and economic policy to favor themselves. The result is both efficiency losses (reduced economic growth) and distributional inequities.

In economies highly oriented toward subsistence production, markets offer few premiums for higher-quality products. As interregional communication, and particularly as export trade, develops, quality standards increase in importance because buyers need to compare the products of many different sellers, often without seeing the product before the sale. In markets using modern technology, purchases are often made electronically or over the phone, something that can only happen with a recognized system of grades and standards.

Threshing, drying, cleaning, storage, and processing practices for crops and feeding, slaughtering, storage, and other practices for livestock influence the quality of the final product. Unless grades and standards are established with corresponding price differentials, then producers and processors have little incentive to incur the costs of producing higher quality goods.

Regulations

Market regulations are important to a well-functioning marketing system. These regulations relate to factors affecting health and safety, to weighing practices, and to other legal codes that influence the enforceability of contracts. The purposes of many of these regulations are to ensure basic honesty and reduce transactions costs in marketing. As discussed in Chapter 11, development brings with it a reduction in personal exchange and associated social and cultural constraints on behavior. Increased impersonal exchange requires new institutional arrangements to substitute for the rules of behavior that had been imposed previously by a more personal society.

The importance of market regulations does not imply a need for heavy involvement of government marketing boards or other public trading agencies. Banning private marketing activities does not improve the welfare of either farmers or consumers. While there is a role for the government in the activities discussed earlier and perhaps in implementing a price stabilization scheme, more extensive public monopolization of domestic marketing functions tends to produce high marketing costs and large market distortions.

THE CHANGING STRUCTURE OF FOOD MARKETS

A restructuring of food markets in developing countries began about 30 years ago and has involved a movement toward large-scale wholesalers and supermarkets. In a few cases, the supermarkets are owned by multinational companies, and in most cases, the result has been higher quality products and more efficient (lower-cost) marketing. These markets are, however, increasingly forcing small-scale food retailers out of business, just as they did in many developed countries. Before the advent of supermarkets, local brokers or small-scale wholesalers brought relatively undifferentiated commodities from the rural areas to small shops or central markets in the urban areas. In most of the developing world, this structure still predominates. However, large and often specialized wholesalers increasingly bring products from rural areas to larger processors, supermarkets, and food service chains in urban areas.[3]

As market structures change, they do so unevenly in the developing world, with urban retail markets changing before rural markets, and certain geographic areas undergoing a more rapid transformation than others. The degree of transformation is greatest in South America, East Asia, and North-central Europe. It is next greatest in Central America and Mexico, Southeast Asia, South-central Europe, and South Africa. A third wave of market transformation is now occurring in South Asia, Eastern Europe, and parts of Africa.[4] In some cases, supermarkets contract with farmers directly to ensure consistent and high-quality supply. Farmers in all income groups can benefit from such contracting, although richer households may benefit more than poorer ones in absolute terms. In one study in Kenya (see Box 15.2), supermarket contracts were found to cause the strongest reductions in multidimensional poverty among the poorest households.[5]

The market transformation taking place in developing countries tends to include the following set of changes: (1) a shift from raw commodities to more specialized products, (2) rapid organizational change involving consolidation in the processing and retail segments of the food system with the rise of supermarkets, (3) institutional change in the markets with the rise of contracts and private grades and standards for food quality

BOX 15.2 SUPERMARKETS AND SMALLHOLDER FARMERS

Modern retailers are increasingly replacing traditional markets and shops, with implications for consumers' food choices and nutritional outcomes. Modern retailers also influence the way agricultural produce is sourced from farmers, with implications for farmers' marketing choices and livelihoods. For fresh fruits and vegetables, supermarkets serving high-value markets often contract farmers directly to ensure consistent and high-quality produce. Contracts can benefit farmers by reducing market risk and overcoming credit constraints. However, companies often prefer contracting with larger-sized farms, raising the question of whether smallholder farmers can also participate successfully in these contract schemes. Ogutua and others analyzed the effects of contracting with supermarkets on smallholder farmers' income and poverty, using survey data from small-scale vegetable growers in Kenya. Using quantile regression analyses, they found significant reductions in income poverty and in multidimensional poverty. Farmers in all income groups benefited, with richer households benefiting more than poorer ones in absolute terms, but supermarket contracts caused the strongest reductions in multidimensional poverty in the poorest households. On average, supermarket contracts increased household incomes by over 40 percent.

Source: Sylvester Ochieng Ogutua, Dennis O. Ochieng, and Matin Qaim, "Supermarket Contracts and Smallholder Farmers: Implications for Income and Multidimensional Poverty", *Food Policy*, vol. 96 (August 2020), pp. 1–11

and safety, (4) technological and managerial change among suppliers, wholesalers, and retailers, (5) distributional and technological impacts of the wholesale and retail market changes on farmers and other market participants, and (6) opening of opportunities to export fresh vegetables, fruits, and specialized products to higher-income countries.

Efforts are needed to prepare poor and small-scale producers to access these new marketing channels and value changes: improve quality, adhere to size and other standards, and develop organizational and contracting skills. Supermarkets demand a regular supply of food products through the year, and often farm operations need to be coordinated to smooth supply over seasons. Off the farm, impacts of this retail revolution on participants in traditional supply and retailing channels are not always well-understood but may be substantial. Reardon and Timmer provide a synopsis of what has occurred in food markets in developing countries since the 1950s and the reasons for those changes.[6]

The growth in demand for horticultural products that has occurred as incomes have grown over time, especially in Asia, has produced opportunities for small-scale producers if they can organize intermediate level assembly of high-quality products to fill contracts with wholesalers and even retailers. Efforts to organize small-scale vegetable and fruit producers into cooperatives and other group associations for this purpose have the potential to significantly raise incomes. The public sector can assist by providing information to meet the demands in the market chain for these relatively high value products (see Box 15.3).

BOX 15.3 DEVELOPMENT OF VEGETABLE MARKET INTERMEDIARIES IN NEPAL

Marketing of horticultural products is a major challenge in Nepal because of the large number of smallholder producers in geographically isolated areas with poor infrastructure. High transactions costs in aggregating production to marketable volume and limited market information constrain efficient and competitive marketing. The large number of small producers hinders quality control and coordinated production scheduling. Abundant family labor reduces labor supervision costs, but a mechanism is needed to coordinate product marketing beyond the farm level. With public support, a series of local marketing and planning committees (MPCs) have been established to manage community market collection centers. Through these collection centers, produce is sold to traders who have access to larger, more lucrative markets than are available locally. This institutional mechanism has been highly successful and grown rapidly over the past decade. The MPCs provide information to help their members plan market-led production and they provide loans for agricultural inputs. They also lobby the government to influence policy. Each MPC has representatives from 5 to 12 farmer groups, each of which has 15–20 members. When an MPC is well established, it can register as a cooperative and gain legal backing that makes available more attractive financing options.

SUMMARY

Food and agricultural prices are major determinants of producer incentives and of real incomes in developing countries. Governments in those countries often adopt pricing policies to reduce food prices for urban consumers at the expense of producers. Political leaders devise policies to meet society's objectives and the demands of interest groups, to generate revenue, and, in some cases, to line their own pockets. Governments can influence agricultural prices by setting price ceilings or floors and enforcing them with subsidies, taxes, manipulation of exchange rates, storage programs, quantity restrictions, and other policy instruments. These interventions influence producer and consumer prices and incomes, production and consumption, foreign exchange earnings, price stability, government revenues, the efficiency of resource allocation, employment, capital investment, technical change, health and nutrition, and marketing margins.

Marketing refers to the process of changing products in time, space, and form through storage, transportation, and processing. Goods are exchanged and prices are determined in markets. The importance of these functions increases as markets become more commercialized. Developing countries often have marketing systems characterized by deficient infrastructure, inadequate information, weak bargaining position for producers for certain commodities, and government-induced distortions. The government can help solve certain marketing deficiencies, particularly the lack of roads and information. The public sector can provide a system of grades and standards as well other regulations. These contributions can help reduce transactions costs that rise as markets become less personal. Governments should avoid the larger parastatal marketing agencies that tend to introduce marketing distortions.

Private marketing systems have gradually evolved over the past 50 years in developing countries, with many countries currently experiencing a shift from raw commodities being sold in small shops to more differentiated food products being assembled and processed by larger wholesalers. Supermarkets have opened in many urban areas of developing countries with increased product contracting from farmers. This market consolidation is likely to continue at a fast pace in the future and will have profound impacts on producers, consumers, and middle agents. Exports of fresh fruits, vegetables, and other specialized products have grown, and small-scale farmers in some developing countries are able to fit into these highly complex value chains.

IMPORTANT TERMS AND CONCEPTS

Buffer stock programs
Competitive market
Export tax
Externalities
Foreign exchange rate
Grading system
Infrastructure
Interest groups
Market information
Market regulations
Marketing board
Marketing functions
Marketing margin

Middle agents
Monopsony
Parastatal
Price ceiling
Price distortions
Price floor
Price formation
Pricing policies
Resource allocation efficiency
Supermarkets
Two-price program
Time, space, and form
Value chains

LOOKING AHEAD

This chapter concludes the discussion of technical and institutional factors that can influence development of the agricultural sector. The following set of chapters moves beyond the agricultural sector and considers international trade, macroeconomic forces, international capital flows, and other policies that feed back on agricultural development. We begin in the next chapter by considering the importance of international trade. Problems faced by developing countries with respect to agricultural trade, and potential solutions to those problems, are explored.

QUESTIONS FOR DISCUSSION

1 Why do developing country governments frequently set agricultural prices below market levels?
2 Why do governments get involved in stabilizing prices?
3 What are the direct short-run effects of price policies in agriculture?
4 What are the indirect and long-run effects of price policies in agriculture?
5 Draw a graph to illustrate the effects on supply and demand of a price ceiling set above the market equilibrium price.
6 Draw a graph to illustrate the effect of a price support to farmers set above the market equilibrium price.

7 What are the major food marketing functions? Why are these functions necessary to get agriculture moving in developing countries?

8 What are the major deficiencies in agricultural marketing systems in developing countries?

9 What role might the government play in improving an agricultural marketing system?

10 Discuss the potential role of buffer stocks in an agricultural development program in a developing country.

11 Why might government marketing boards and parastatals create inefficiencies in resource use?

12 Why do governments in developing countries use export taxes on agricultural commodities more frequently than do governments in more-developed countries?

13 Why does the increasing impersonal exchange that accompanies development imply a need for increased government regulation?

14 Why are marketing grades and standards important?

15 Why does increased market information improve marketing efficiency?

16 What has happened to the growth of supermarkets in developing countries over the past few years and why?

17 What is the likely impact of supermarket growth on producers, markets, and consumers?

NOTES

1 C. Peter Timmer, *Getting Prices Right: The Scope and Limits of Agricultural Price Policy* (Ithaca, NY: Cornell University Press, 1986), p. 36.

2 See Shenggen Fan and Connie Chan-Kang, *Road Development, Economic Growth and Poverty Reduction in China* (Washington, DC: International Food Policy Research Institute, Research Report No. 138, 2005). Chapter 4 in this research report contains an extensive review of research findings about infrastructure and income growth in developing countries.

3 See Thomas Reardon and C. Peter Timmer, "Transformation of Markets for Agricultural Output in Developing Countries Since 1950: How Has Thinking Changed?", in R.E. Evenson, P. Pingali, and T.P. Schultz (eds.-), *Handbook of Agricultural Economics, Volume 3: Agricultural Development: Farmers, Farm Production, and Food Markets* (Amsterdam: Elsevier, 2006), Chapter 13.

4 Reardon and Timmer, "Transformation of Markets for Agricultural Output in Developing Countries Since 1950".

5 Sylvester Ochieng Ogutua, Dennis O. Ochieng, and Matin Qaim, "Supermarket Contracts and Smallholder Farmers: Implications for Income and Multidimensional Poverty", *Food Policy*, vol. 95 (August 2020), pp. 1–11.

6 Reardon and Timmer, "Transformation of Markets for Agricultural Output in Developing Countries Since 1950".

RECOMMENDED READINGS

Amaya, Nadezda, and Jeffrey Alwang, "Women Rule: Potato Markets and Access to Information in the Bolivian Highlands", *Agricultural Economics*, vol. 43(4) (2012), pp. 403–413.

Fan, Shenggan, and Connie Chan-Kang, *Road Development, Economic Growth and Poverty Reduction in China* (Washington, DC: International Food Policy Research Institute, Research Report No. 138, 2005).

Ogutua, Sylvester Ochieng, Dennis O. Ochieng, and Matin Qaim, "Supermarket Contracts and Smallholder Farmers: Implications for Income and Multidimensional Poverty", *Food Policy*, vol. 96 (August 2020), pp. 1–11.

Pinstrup-Andersen, P.P., and D.D. Watson, *Food Policy for Developing Countries* (Ithaca, NY: Cornell University Press, 2011).

Reardon, Thomas, and C. Peter Timmer, "Transformation of Markets for Agricultural Output in Developing Countries Since 1950: How Has Thinking Changed?", in R.E. Evenson, P. Pingali, and T.P. Schultz (eds.), *Handbook of Agricultural Economics, Volume 3: Agricultural Development: Farmers, Farm Production, and Food Markets* (Amsterdam: Elsevier, 2006), Chapter 13.

PART 5

Agricultural development in an interdependent world

Wheat being loaded on a ship for export

16 Agriculture and international trade

THIS CHAPTER

1 Explains why countries trade
2 Describes the recent experience of developing countries with trade and why trade patterns change as economic development occurs
3 Discusses problems that impede developing countries from realizing their trade potential with respect to agriculture

WHY COUNTRIES TRADE

The role of international trade in economic development was one of the first questions ever addressed by economists and has been hotly debated throughout history (see Box 16.1). Most economists agree that relatively open trade is helpful for successful economic development, and that trade restrictions generally make economic growth and poverty reduction slower and less sustainable. They also agree that trade generates both gainers and losers and that some of those gains and losses may be permanent for the individuals involved, especially when open trade is accompanied by rapid technological change. The gainers and losers may reside in more-developed or in developing countries. In this chapter, we ask why open trade facilitates economic growth, and why governments choose to restrict trade despite its potentially large net economic benefits.

Need for imports and exports

Trade facilitates development because it helps a country obtain greater benefits from its productive resources by exporting what it can produce

BOX 16.1 HISTORICAL ROOTS OF INTERNATIONAL TRADE DEBATE

Trade among countries has existed for thousands of years, most of that time in a very loosely structured system. By the sixteenth and seventeenth centuries, money, goods, and credit markets had developed to facilitate trade and colonial expansion. An economic doctrine known as *mercantilism* encouraged exports but discouraged imports (see Chapter 6). The preferred form of payment was gold rather than goods or currency. A wide range of restrictive trade policies was implemented, including tariffs, licenses, export subsidies, and general state control of international commerce. As the industrial revolution spread through Europe in the late 1700s, mercantilist ideas were increasingly questioned. Raw materials for expanding factory output and foods for factory workers were imported and markets for the output were sought abroad. Technological advances in transportation and communications further stimulated trade.

A strong movement toward economic liberalization began in the early 1800s. Perhaps the most important factor in the movement was the unilateral removal of trade restrictions in the United Kingdom. The world's leading economic power at the time, the United Kingdom repealed its Corn Laws in 1846, ending the world's first major price-support program for agricultural commodities. The Corn Laws were opposed by industrial and urban interests, and their repeal signaled an important shift in power away from the landed nobility. Britain then sought worldwide trade liberalization, with some success. World trade was relatively free until World War I, although several countries, including the United States and Germany, followed selective protectionist policies. World War I changed the trading environment. Industries, including agriculture, which expanded during the war, suffered slack demand and falling prices afterward. Governments attempted to protect these industries by introducing protectionist policies during the 1920s and 1930s. Since the 1940s, the world has struggled to remove these policies and has had some success. However, reducing protection for agricultural products has been especially difficult, and the last decade has seen an increase in trade restrictions in several nations.

relatively easily and importing items that are relatively more difficult to produce. Exports earn income and support jobs while imports supply goods to firms and consumers at lower cost than they could otherwise be supplied. Most countries import and export the same goods year after year, but especially in agriculture there can be wide fluctuations in quantities traded due to temporary shortages or surpluses. Absorbing change through fluctuations in trade volume can help keep domestic prices more stable than they would be with no change in quantities traded. Furthermore, most countries run persistent trade surpluses or deficits year after year, with offsetting flows of capital into or out of the country. Net inflows of foreign investment are matched by trade deficits, and net outflows are linked to trade surpluses. When investment flows change, there may be a need to alter trade patterns accordingly.

Comparative advantage

Surprisingly, the rationale for trade does not depend on absolute cost differences between countries. Absolute cost differences determine a country's wealth, not its pattern of trade. Trade is driven by *relative* cost differences among goods within each country, as countries export goods whose cost is relatively low in terms of other goods. This *principle of comparative advantage*, first articulated by David Ricardo in 1817, states that it is best for each country to export those goods for which it has the greatest relative cost advantage and to import goods which are relatively more costly to produce. The principle implies that one country could produce all goods at lower cost than other countries, yet it would still raise its standard of living through trade, exporting what it produces relatively best (see Box 16.2). What counts is the *opportunity cost* in terms of *other goods*.

Despite the logic of comparative advantage and the historical evidence of gains from trade, governments routinely intervene to limit imports and exports. Economists usually explain these interventions in terms of differences in lobbying power among those who gain and those who lose from these interventions. Other observers, however, have argued that trade restrictions are actually in the country's national interest. Proponents of restrictions often claim that trade opens the economy to increased exploitation by other countries, by multinational or state-supported corporations – such as those in China – and by the wealthy elites within their own countries. Another argument against open trade has been that the terms of trade, or the prices received for exports compared to the prices paid for imports, may decline over time (see Chapter 6 for a discussion of this "structuralist" perspective). Prices for developed-country products

BOX 16.2 ILLUSTRATION OF THE PRINCIPLE OF COMPARATIVE ADVANTAGE

To illustrate the principle of comparative advantage, consider two countries, each of which can choose how much to produce of two kinds of outputs: manufacturing (MFG) and agriculture (AGR). The production possibilities frontier (PPF) for each country is shown here, indicating the maximum (or total) amount of MFG and AGR that each country can produce given their resources and technology. For simplicity, both PPFs are shown as straight lines. In our example, country A can produce 15 units of MFG and no AGR, or 10 units of AGR and no MFG, and any combination in between such as 7.5 MFG and 5 AGR. Country B can produce up to 40 units of MFG and no AGR, or 20 units of AGR and no MFG, or any combination in between.

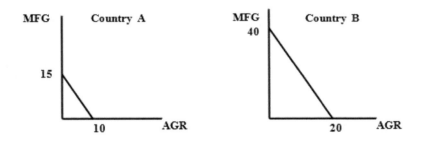

Each country can potentially gain from trade by exporting what it can produce at a lower relative cost as compared to the other country. In this example, the relative cost of production is shown by the slopes of the PPF lines. In country A, each unit of AGR costs 1.5 unit of MFG to produce, whereas in country B that same unit would cost 2 units of MFG. As a result, a trader could buy a unit of AGR in country A for a bit more than 1.5 units of MFG, and sell it to someone in country B for a bit less than 2 units of MFG, producing a total gain from trade of almost .5 units of MFG per unit of AGR that is exported from A to B.

How the gains from trade are divided between the countries depends on the relative bargaining power and the demands for MFG and AGR in each country, but the overall size of the gains and the direction of trade depend only on differences in relative costs. It does not matter whether A is always less productive than B, or AGR is always less productive than MFG. Country A can still exploit its comparative advantage, in this case by specializing in and exporting AGR to obtain more of both goods than it could produce in self-sufficiency. Likewise, Country B can exploit its comparative advantage (relative cost advantage) in MFG by specializing in and exporting MFG to Country A.

are also said to be high because of monopolistic behavior by sellers of developed-country products that are imported by developing countries and protectionist measures by governments in the more-developed countries. Some have also argued that dependence on international markets for food endangers national security since international markets are volatile and unpredictable. Others have argued that restrictions are needed because some countries do not play fair due to hidden subsidies to factories or farmers. Finally, advocates for trade restrictions have argued that "infant industries" may need to be protected from international competition in order to survive. They argue that solutions to these perceived problems are import-substitution policies that try to move a country toward self-sufficiency. Examples of these policies are direct import restrictions, setting of foreign exchange rates above the market equilibrium (which discourages exports for reasons discussed later in this chapter), state subsidies to specific industries, and export taxes that discourage exports and stimulate production for the local market instead.

Although most economists favor freer trade, there are debates within the economics discipline regarding (1) the degree to which any gains from trade will, in fact, be retained in a developing country and be relatively broadly distributed, and (2) the magnitude of the efficiency losses resulting from attempts to become relatively self-sufficient through import-substitution policies. Few economists dispute the *potential* for gains from trade, most desire that any gains be broadly distributed, and most agree that increased trade can result in both gainers and losers even if total gains are larger than total losses.

In recent years, most developing countries have chosen to be relatively open to international trade, with some variation in the degree of openness. Most empirical evidence supports the view that trade restrictions typically limit economic development. In fact, when the world or a group of countries wants to punish a nation, the first step taken is often to refuse to trade with it.

Gainers, losers, and the politics of trade policy

Despite the potential for significant economic gains from trade and accompanying specialization, international trade policies are a frequent topic of bitter dispute. Policymakers, farm groups, consumer advocates, labor leaders, and environmental groups constantly debate the benefits and costs of trade restrictions that affect exports, imports, the balance of payments, prices, jobs, and the environment. A major reason for such contentiousness is that many of the people who lose from freer trade are concentrated in specific locations and industries. Much of the tendency for governments to restrict trade stems from the fact that trade restrictions can generate highly concentrated and easily visible benefits for some industries, while spreading the costs of the restrictions broadly and less visibly among the population over time. Advocates for protection can readily identify the winners and tell their story, whereas the losses can be seen only through abstract reasoning and statistics.

The groups that are best able to act collectively and lobby policymakers tend to see trade policies enacted in their favor, even though doing so may impose greater costs on other, less influential groups. Agricultural lobbies are particularly strong in Europe and Japan and have obtained relatively large income transfers from other sectors. Within the United States, some commodity groups, such as those for sugar and cotton, have been particularly successful in securing government benefits over time. Representatives of various sectors may lobby together for favorable policies, forming coalitions either within or across larger political parties and interest groups.

An important fact about trade policy is that, while the debate often focuses on foreign countries, the actual effect of a policy change occurs mainly within the restricting country. Any trade restriction or its removal may have some impact on world prices and hence economic conditions in foreign countries, but most of its effect is on domestic prices and income transfers among the country's own citizens.

One study estimated that if borders were closed to trade for all products for 40 countries, including Japan, Korea, the United States, Canada, Mexico, China, Brazil, India, Indonesia, Taiwan, and most of Europe, real incomes would decline 28 percent for the richest 10 percent of the people in those countries and 63 percent for the poorest 10 percent.[1]

DEVELOPING COUNTRY EXPERIENCE WITH TRADE

During the 1950s and 1960s, import-substitution policies predominated in many developing countries. These inward-oriented policies helped produce a decline in the ratio of exports to GDP in many developing countries until the early 1970s. Since then, the ratio of exports to GDP has generally increased, paralleling an overall expansion in world trade. However, many developing countries still pursue import-substitution policies. Countries that followed these policies for several years, for example Argentina, India, and Egypt, tended to grow more slowly than those that followed more open-trading regimes, for example Malaysia, South Korea, and Botswana. While it is difficult to generalize based on a few cases, studies that have examined the statistical significance of trade restrictions have generally found a negative impact on economic growth.

It is often difficult to classify a country's trade policy as relatively open or relatively restricted because policies change over time. Many African governments, for example, imposed increasingly restrictive agricultural trade policies on themselves in the 1970s and then moved to more open trade in the 1990s.[2] The Mexican economy was quite closed until 1985 but has been relatively open since then. Even South Korea, which is often cited as an example of a successful export-oriented economy, has imposed substantial restrictions on trade from time-to-time. Trade intervention is usually a matter of degree.

Changing structure of trade

Total trade has grown for developing countries over the past 40 years. But the share of agricultural exports in developing country trade has declined steadily from about 60 percent of total exports in 1955 to less than 10 percent in recent years. This lower share partly reflects the import-substitution policies mentioned earlier, but it mainly reflects the impact of income growth, with faster increases in both demand and supply of manufactures than of agricultural products at the global level, as well as increased domestic demand for food within developing countries. Nevertheless, several developing countries still depend on a few agricultural exports for a major share of their foreign exchange earnings.

The dramatic shift in export composition toward manufactures is best illustrated by Southeast Asian countries such as Indonesia, Malaysia, the Philippines, Singapore, and South Korea, with the data shown in Table 16.1. As these countries invested in human and physical capital, their comparative advantage in exports shifted from land-intensive and low-skill, labor-intensive activities such as agriculture, to more skill-intensive and capital-intensive products such as manufactures. Agricultural exports were a very important source of foreign exchange earnings in the past, but other sectors grew faster over time.

Table 16.1 Structure of Exports for Selected Southeast Asian Countries, 1970–2018

Country	*Percentage share of total merchandise exports*									
	Agricultural commodities					*Manufactured products*				
	1970	*1980*	*1990*	*2010*	*2018*	*1970*	*1980*	*1990*	*2010*	*2018*
Indonesia	35	14	5	7	5	1	2	35	37	44
Malaysia	50	31	14	3	1	7	19	54	67	70
Philippines	26	6	2	1	1	8	21	38	57	84
Singapore	28	10	3	0	1	28	47	72	73	75
South Korea	7	1	1	1	1	77	90	94	89	88

Source: World Bank, World Development Indicators 2018 (online at www.worldbank.org/data)

As countries develop, their agricultural sectors do not disappear but instead tend to become more specialized. Tropical countries have a natural comparative advantage in relatively heat-tolerant tree crops, such as coffee, cocoa, tea, rubber, and bananas, or other crops that grow year-round, such as sugar. Technological change can affect where crops grow best, as shown for example by the increased exports of citrus and soybeans from developing countries.

Increased demand by more-developed countries for many of the agricultural exports of developing countries are limited due to relatively small income elasticities of demand for those commodities and, in some cases, to the development of synthetic substitutes (e.g., for rubber, jute, sisal, cotton). On the other hand, domestic demand for food within the developing countries often increases rapidly with development. Not only are populations growing, but a high proportion of any income increases are spent on food. The quantity consumed increases, and the mix of foods shifts toward more expensive products (often meats and vegetables, wheat, and certain other grains rather than roots). As a result, the more rapidly growing, middle-income countries have become less self-sufficient in food production over the past two decades, even as their agricultural production and incomes have risen. Their increased imports have come partly from other developing countries and partly from high-income food exporters such as the United States.

Some countries have reacted to increased domestic demand for food by setting artificially low prices for food commodities and overvaluing their exchange rates to tax exports and lower the prices of imports. These policies tend to be counterproductive, as they discourage production. The effects of exchange rate manipulation are discussed in more detail in Chapter 18.

Trade, employment, and capital interactions

Employment growth is crucial for economic development. While few people are totally idle, under-employment is pervasive in most developing countries. By under-employment, we mean people working only part-time or in very low-productivity jobs. Several possible linkages exist between trade and employment. One such linkage is the effect of trade on overall growth through more efficient resource allocation, assuming faster growth entails more employment. A second linkage is that export industries in countries in early stages of development tend to be labor-intensive, consistent with the Factor Endowment Theory of Trade (Box 16.3). Thus, increased exports might lead to greater employment.

BOX 16.3 FACTOR ENDOWMENT THEORY OF TRADE

The Factor Endowment Theory of Trade (often called the Heckscher–Ohlin–Samuelson Theory because it is derived from their work) argues that because countries have different factor endowments, they adopt different production techniques, and the result is profitable trade. A country with relatively abundant labor (compared to land and capital) will have a low wage rate relative to land prices, rents, and interest on capital-borrowing. Such a country will find it optimal to adopt labor-intensive rather than capital-intensive technologies. The opposite would be true for capital-abundant countries. Without trade, the price ratio of labor-intensive goods to capital-intensive goods will be lower in the labor-abundant country than in the capital-abundant country. Opening the country up to trade would mean that the labor-abundant country would export labor-intensive goods in exchange for capital-intensive goods. Trade will have the effect of increasing the demand for the abundant factor, thus bidding up its price, and increasing the supply of the scarce factor (in the form of imported goods), thereby reducing its price. Trade is expected to reduce factor price differences between countries.

Source: David Colman and Trevor Young, *Principles of Agricultural Economics: Markets and Prices in Less Developed Countries* (Cambridge: Cambridge University Press, 1989), pp. 232–234

A third possible linkage is that trade policies might influence the degree of labor intensity in all industries. For example, trade policies might encourage capital-intensive industries through subsidized capital-goods imports.

Empirical evidence suggests that increased exports from developing countries, including agricultural exports, have positive employment implications. Those countries that have followed import-substitution policies have suffered greater employment problems than more open economies. Research in several countries by the International Food Policy Research Institute (IFPRI) indicates that an export-oriented agriculture increases the demand for hired labor, raises family incomes, and benefits both landowners and landless laborers.[3] Small-scale farmers who produce sugarcane, non-traditional vegetables, and other cash crops for export usually maintain some production of subsistence crops as insurance against market and production risk, but these farmers also benefit from the additional income from the cash crops.

The role of trade in agricultural development

Agriculture has many roles to play in economic development, and trade can affect the relative importance of these different roles. In fact, an outward-looking trade orientation helps solidify the role of agriculture in development, especially if the outward orientation is accompanied by an agriculture- and employment-based growth strategy. Removal of impediments to trade will facilitate exports, and thus will enhance the foreign exchange contribution of agriculture. An open-trading regime helps provide accurate signals of relative resource scarcity to producers and to investors; the abundance of labor usually found in most developing countries signals the need for employment-intensive investment. With no bias in favor of capital-intensive industries, demands for capital-intensive manufacturing processes can be met through imports, increasing the importance of agriculture's labor contribution.

The food and fiber contribution of agriculture under an outward-looking strategy is usually of most concern to policymakers. Fear of excessive reliance on imports to meet domestic food needs can lead to protectionist policies. But protection raises the cost of food, and combining freer trade with more investment in domestic agricultural production usually results in faster and more stable economic growth. Of course, if growth in demand exceeds domestic food production, then imports would be needed to fill the gap, but these imports should be viewed as evidence of success in generating employment and income growth. Income growth will enhance food security and open trade will reduce reliance on often unstable domestic food production. Some policymakers have expressed concern that events such as global pandemics create problems with over-reliance on international food markets, but agricultural trade disruptions during the COVID-19 crisis have been relatively small.

TRADE IMPEDIMENTS

The wide variety of agricultural trade strategies in developing countries reflects differences in resource endowments, history, food security, sources of government revenues, balance of payments, and other factors. This variety also indicates differences in perceptions about the ability of markets to generate prices consistent with desired income distributions. No country operates with completely free trade. Many developing countries employ trade policies that discriminate against the agricultural sector, as discussed in Chapter 15. Domestic trade policies, however, are just one of the impediments to agricultural trade. In this section, we discuss the major constraints to trade, and in Chapter 17, we suggest potential solutions to trade problems. Impediments to agricultural trade for developing countries can be grouped into three major categories: (1) external demand constraints, including restrictive trade policies in other countries, (2) restrictive trade policies at home, and (3) market instability.

External demand constraints

Developing countries that export primary products are concerned that they face relatively inelastic demands for these products in more-developed countries. With inelastic demands, additional exports may result in a fall in world prices for the commodities. While individual countries face relatively elastic export demands, when several countries that export the same products, such as cocoa, coffee, tea, and bananas, all try to increase exports simultaneously, prices might fall by a higher percentage than export quantities increase. Thus, their collective export revenues could decline, even as export quantities grow. An example is the coffee crisis that occurred in the late 1990s when Vietnam, Indonesia, and other relative newcomers to coffee production expanded their exports. World prices of coffee fell to around $.50/lb. compared to average prices of $1.20/lb. during the 1980s. Prices during the early 2000s were so low that an estimated 540,000 workers in Central America lost their jobs as coffee farms discontinued harvesting.[4] After 2004, coffee prices partially recovered as supplies tightened, but temporary job losses caused permanent harm to many households. Sustained declines in export prices can cause worsening terms of trade in the long run as well. Historical evidence suggests that the terms of trade for developing countries may indeed have declined over time, as their output growth has outpaced increases in demand.[5]

Trade restrictions in more-developed countries

The demand for certain agricultural exports from developing countries is affected by trade restrictions in more-developed countries. More-developed countries are more protectionist of their agriculture than of their industrial sectors. More-developed countries often support farm prices above market equilibrium levels in hope of supporting farm incomes (see Chapter 15). Thus, they restrict imports to avoid supporting prices for the whole world. These restrictions particularly affect exports from temperate and sub-tropical areas of developing countries that compete with their agricultural products: commodities such as beef, certain fruits and vegetables, and sugar.

Raw tropical products such as cocoa and coffee face few restrictions because they do not compete with more-developed country production. However, semi-processed products, such as cocoa paste, and certain fibers, such as cotton, do face restrictions. Developing countries would like to export more processed commodities because they have a higher unit value and provide more employment.

Quotas and tariffs are two of the more common import restrictions placed on agricultural commodities by more-developed countries. An example of how an import tariff works to increase price in the country imposing it and to reduce imports from the exporting countries is illustrated in Figure 16.1. The tariff increases the price that domestic

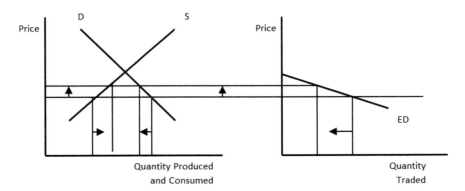

Figure 16.1 Effects of an import tariff
Note: the right-hand graph shows the excess demand schedule related to the country and commodity in question. It is constructed by subtracting the quantity supplied in the country from the quantity demanded below the equilibrium point.

consumers must pay for imports, which also raises the price they are willing to pay to local producers. In Figure 16.1, the country imposing the tariff is small in the world market, so the tariff does not alter the world price. However, if is country is large in the world market, such as the United States with sugar, a tariff (or a quota, which would act just like the tariff in its effects on the market) would depress the world price as well.

A few years ago, one study estimated that if the more-developed countries removed all barriers to market access for agricultural products from other countries, the world would gain about $44 billion, about a quarter of which would accrue to developing countries.[6] If all agricultural tariffs and subsidies were removed by more-developed countries, the largest individual country winners would be Brazil, Argentina, and India.

Subsidized agricultural prices in the more-developed countries encourage increased production in those countries, while high prices discourage consumption. If production exceeds consumption, stocks accumulate unless they are exported at subsidized prices. The additional volume of exports can depress world prices, making production elsewhere even less attractive. Dairy products and wheat are examples of subsidized exports of high-income countries. Urban consumers in developing countries can benefit from these policies, at least in the short run, due to lower prices, but farmers in those countries are faced with production disincentives and lower incomes. These price distortions, though benefiting farmers in more-developed countries, are globally inefficient. They create conditions for lower growth worldwide. One of the purposes of trade negotiations and agreements (discussed in Chapter 17) is to reduce these trade restrictions.

Restrictive trade policies at home

Many developing countries proclaim food self-sufficiency as an objective, but employ direct and indirect policies that, on net, tax farmers, subsidize consumers, and increase dependence on food imports. Examples of direct policies that influence agricultural trade are export taxes and subsidies, import tariffs, export and import quotas, import or export licenses, and government-controlled marketing margins. Overvalued and, in some cases, multiple exchange rates and high rates of protection for other sectors are the principal indirect means of discriminating against agriculture.

Agricultural export taxes are one of the oldest and most common trade interventions in developing countries. Export taxes tend to raise the prices of the products to foreign buyers and reduce the prices received by domestic producers. Producers of cocoa in Ghana, cotton in Mali, coffee in Togo, tobacco in Tanzania, and tea in India – to name just a few examples – typically receive less than the border prices for their products. Some of this difference is due to marketing system inadequacies (see Chapter 15), but a significant portion is caused by export taxes.

Some taxation of export crops involves direct taxation of products as they move through ports. Alternatively, public marketing agencies may be established that control marketing margins or set farm prices lower than market equilibrium. These agencies, often called marketing boards or parastatal marketing agencies, were discussed in Chapter 15. They are granted monopoly power for buying and selling the commodity, and they may set quotas for exports or imports. While they may be set up with the stated purpose of protecting domestic producers, they tend to evolve into institutions that extract resources from domestic producers and consumers alike. Several developing countries have reduced their use of parastatals over the past three decades.

Export taxes remain common in the developing countries because they are a relatively easy tax to institute and collect compared to alternatives such as income or land taxes. Export taxes generate government revenues and, in some cases, reduce exports and encourage the shifting of production from exports to domestic food crops.

Occasionally, developing countries impose export taxes in attempts to exploit monopoly power that they believe they hold in world markets. If a country is a large enough exporter in the world market to affect the world price, it can use a tax to raise the world price. Although the volume of trade would be lower following the imposition of the tax, the hope is that additional income is earned at the expense of purchasing countries because the price is higher. Ghana has used this rationale for its export tax on cocoa, Brazil for a tax on coffee, and Bangladesh for a tax on jute. Although some world price increase is possible, the ability of individual developing countries to exploit monopoly power for particular commodities is limited. Higher prices create incentives for increased production in other countries as well as for the development of substitute products.

Developing countries sometimes use export quotas to partially or totally restrict exports. These restrictions force the sale of the products in domestic markets, thereby reducing prices to consumers. The result, however, is to discourage domestic production and to generate profits for those holding the quota rights. Temporary export quotas are common during food price spikes or periods of high global food prices. India and Thailand applied them to rice during the food price spike in 2008, lowering prices at home but driving them higher globally.

Import tariffs and quotas are also used on agricultural products in developing countries and are commonly employed on industrial products as well. When an import tariff or quota is imposed on industrial goods, the prices of the goods are raised relative to those of agricultural goods, creating an indirect tax on agriculture. Another significant source of indirect taxation is exchange rate misalignments that result from both macroeconomic policies and direct industrial protection policies. When fiscal and monetary policies (see Chapter 18) lead to a higher rate of inflation at home than abroad, the value of the local currency falls. If governments fail to adjust the official exchange rate downward, the currency becomes *overvalued*. An overvalued currency makes exports from a country more expensive and imports into it cheaper. Thus, fewer goods are exported and more imported. The additional supply of agricultural products on the domestic market reduces farm and consumer prices. Exchange rate overvaluation is common in developing countries and historically has been severe at times in African countries such as Nigeria, Ghana, and Tanzania.

Countries sometimes establish a *multiple exchange rate system* in which different commodities are traded at different rates. For example, the government allows one rate of exchange for a commodity it wants to keep inexpensive in the country and another for a commodity it wants to make expensive. Multiple exchange rate systems often discriminate against the agricultural sector, although their use is less common than in the past.

Accurately measuring the effect of government policies on the prices received by farmers is difficult, in part because governments typically implement many different policies at once. The results of research to compare actual farm level prices with what farmers would have received under free-trade policies, across countries all around the world, are summarized in Table 16.2. The results in the table are averages for 75 countries, which together account for over 90 percent of the world's population, total income, and agricultural income. Policy effects were estimated for the major products in each country in each year, totaling more than 70 different products with an average of almost a dozen per country. Not all countries had data for the entire 1955–2007 period, but the average number of years covered is 41 per country.

The data in Table 16.2 illustrate how governments in Africa, Asia, and Latin America imposed heavy taxes on their farmers during the 1960s

Table 16.2 Percent Rate of Government Taxation (negative values) of or Support (positive values) to Agriculture in Selected Countries/ Regions, 1955–2015

	1960– 1964	1965– 1969	1970– 1974	1975– 1979	1980– 1984	1985– 1989	1990– 1994	1995– 1999	2000– 2004	2005– 2009	2010– 2014	2015
sub-Saharan Africa	-5	-11	-12	9	16	29	-9	-7	-6	-18	-3	2
Asia developing	-9	-4	-6	59	53	94	13	19	27	20	24	38
Latin America	-1	-4	-16	0	2	2	2	3	5	16	4	6
Eur. transition and Mediterranean	-26	-28	-15	13	23	39	6	25	28	13	9	7
Other high income	42	48	34	11	12	18	87	61	53	39	29	36
All countries	13	13	3	19	22	37	26	23	24	11	12	23

Source: World Bank, *Nominal Rate of Protection* Online Database; Kym Anderson and Signe Nelson, *Updated National and Global Estimates of Distortions to Agricultural Incentives, 1955 to 2011, Regional Aggregates* 2013; both available at www.worldbank.org/agdistortions

Note: Data shown are weighted averages of commodities in selected countries, based on gross value of agricultural production at undistorted prices.

and 1970s. In the 1980s, a wave of reform known as structural adjustment led many of these governments to reduce average tax burdens by lifting both exchange-rate distortions and direct trade restrictions. Some of these policy changes were imposed by foreign lenders so that borrowing countries could expand exports and repay their debts, but many were adopted voluntarily by developing-country governments seeking faster economic growth. Changing domestic socioeconomic conditions also led to policy change, particularly when higher incomes and other trends raised the relative political power of a country's farmers as opposed to its food consumers and taxpayers.

This rising political influence is reflected in Table 16.2 in the switch from taxing farmers to subsidizing them in Asia and Latin America, and in the particularly rapid rise in subsidy rates in the highest-income countries of Asia. This transition toward farm subsidies is a bit of a paradox in that farmers have greater political influence and more support from government after they are fewer in number and have already escaped extreme poverty. The situation may seem unusual, but as discussed earlier, lobbying is facilitated by smaller numbers, and richer countries can afford support easier than poor countries. Factors such as benefits and costs per person help explain why regions differ in the average tax or subsidy rates shown in the table.[7]

Policy changes that influence prices can lead to large responses in farm income and agricultural production. Heavy taxation of agriculture and trade restrictions constrain agricultural growth. By reducing farm incomes, they hasten the exodus of people from rural areas, creating social costs in urban areas, as sewer, water, health systems, and other infrastructure are stretched to their limits. Lower incomes in agriculture also reduce farmers' incentives to invest in land improvements such as irrigation and farm buildings, to adopt new technologies, and to support rural schools with local resources.

Arguments against a relatively free trade regime often are based on anticipated effects of trade on income distribution. The basic concern is that the benefits of trade may accrue to the wealthiest segments of society. While there is reason for concern that a disproportionate number of economic gains from trade might go to the wealthiest, historical evidence suggests that a high proportion of the benefits from trade *restrictions* also accrues to them. Trade restrictions provide a fertile environment for powerful domestic interest groups to pressure for advantages. The benefits of quota rights, export and import licenses, and subsidized inputs provide economic incentives for people to lobby for these privileges. Visible corruption often emerges as well. It is naive to assume that governments are simply selfless protectors of social welfare. They are politicians and civil servants who respond to pressures from private individuals and interest groups.

While many government employees act with the overall public interest in mind, they may also be just as concerned with their own self-interest as people are in the private sector. Self-interest can encompass monetary gain, reelection, promotion, or other rewards. And, even when there are no conflicts of public and private interests, administrative complexities associated with trade restrictions can lead to waste, costly time delays in marketing, and other types of inefficiency.

Market instability

Government officials in developing countries often argue that trade restrictions are needed to counter food insecurity and income risks associated with international trade. In fact, on occasion, rapid increases in staple prices have led to severe political crises. For example, in 2007 and 2008, the Egyptian government faced widespread protests in response to sharp rises in the price of bread. Price instability in international commodity markets is indeed large, but prices would also fluctuate domestically in the absence of trade.

Why are agricultural prices so variable? The central reason is that demand for most primary commodities is relatively inelastic. As weather changes and other factors cause supply to shift back and forth against an inelastic demand curve, prices vary substantially for small changes in quantity supplied (Figure 16.2). A shift back in food supply against an inelastic demand at a time of low food stocks was responsible for a rapid rise in world food prices during 2007–08, which in turn led many food surplus countries to restrict exports and food deficit countries to seek self-sufficiency. When trade restrictions are imposed in such a situation, however, prices in local markets become even more volatile than world prices because domestic demand tends to be even more inelastic than world demand.

One way for governments to reduce their country's vulnerability to fluctuations in commodity prices is to diversify by investing in a wider range of agricultural products and in other sectors. When these new enterprises are profitable, the result is sustained growth and greater stability. Unfortunately, some attempts at diversification impose taxes on successful industries while promoting less successful ones. Such promotion can reduce growth and worsen instability. Both diversification and stabilization are often most successful when they are driven by new technologies and accompanied by marketing improvements. These changes can make

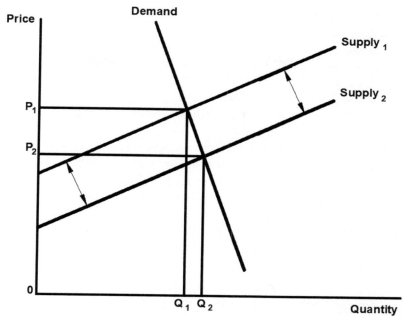

Figure 16.2 Small changes in the supply of agricultural products can result in large changes in price

production of major field crops more stable and facilitate introduction of products for which markets are growing, such as such as non-traditional fruits and vegetables. Diversification may be associated with higher levels of exports, but less overall exposure to single market risks.

SUMMARY

Proponents of trade restrictions argue that as countries become more integrated into the world economy, they open themselves up for exploitation by more-developed countries. Proponents of freer trade argue that it facilitates development and permits more efficient use of resources. It gives countries access to goods and services that otherwise would be unavailable or more expensive. Even well-motivated efforts to restrict trade, however, often serve merely to benefit the wealthy. Most developing countries do trade and also follow some restrictive trade policies. Many developing country exports come from agriculture. The preponderance of evidence supports the view that a relatively open trading environment is more conducive to economic development than a highly restrictive one.

Developing countries have a comparative advantage in several agricultural products, particularly tropical ones. They often become less self-sufficient in food in the middle stages of development. Trade tends to have favorable employment implications.

External demand constraints, market instability, and internal direct and indirect trade restrictions all impede exports from and imports into developing countries. Lack of access to developed country markets is probably the most severe external problem. Governments impose internal trade restrictions to raise revenue, to distribute income to particular groups in response to pressures from interest groups, to exploit monopoly power for certain export crops, and for reasons of food security. Indirect restrictions such as overvalued exchange rates are often greater sources of discrimination against agriculture than are direct restrictions such as export taxes and quotas.

IMPORTANT TERMS AND CONCEPTS

Comparative advantage

Export taxes

Foreign exchange rates

Free trade

Import substitution

International trade

Mercantilism

Overvalued exchange rate

Protectionism

Quotas

Tariffs

Terms of trade

LOOKING AHEAD

A variety of steps can be taken to enhance international trade. The next chapter considers those steps, including the role of regional groupings of countries, multilateral trade negotiations, and other changes in domestic and international policies.

QUESTIONS FOR DISCUSSION

1 Why do countries trade?

2 Why do some argue that the terms of trade turn against developing countries over time?

3 What is comparative advantage?

4 Has agriculture as a percent of total earnings increased or declined for developing countries over the past 40 to 50 years?

5 Why might a country's comparative advantage for particular products change over time?

6 Identify the possible linkages between trade and employment.

7 What are the major external trade impediments facing developing countries?

8 Why is world price instability a problem for developing countries?

9 What are the major direct and indirect agricultural trade restrictions employed by developing countries?

10 Why do developing countries impose trade restrictions?

11 Why does an overvalued exchange rate hurt agricultural exports from a country?

12 Which groups are most likely to benefit from restrictions on food exports from a country? Why?

NOTES

1 Pablo D. Fajgelbaum and Amit K. Khandelwal, "Measuring the Unequal Gains from Trade", *The Quarterly Journal of Economics*, vol. 31(3) (2016), pp. 1113–1180.

2 For details, see Kym Anderson and William A. Masters (eds.), *Distortions to Agricultural Incentives in Africa* (Washington, DC: The World Bank, 2008).

3 Several studies conducted by Joachim Von Braun and others at the International Food Policy Research Institute involved farm and household surveys in Guatemala, the Gambia, Rwanda, and elsewhere.

4 See Panos Varangis, Paul Siegel, Daniele Giovannucci, and Bryan Lewin, *Dealing with the Coffee Crisis in Central America: Impacts and Strategies* (Washington, DC: The World Bank Development Research Group Policy Research Working Paper 299, March 2003).

5 *Gross* terms of trade do not consider differences in costs of production between the products. It is difficult to draw a firm conclusion about the *net* terms of trade because improved technologies have reduced the cost of producing the exports as well. It is possible for the *gross* terms of trade to decline but the *net* terms of trade and comparative advantage for agricultural products to improve.

6 Thomas Hertel and Roman Keeney, "What Is at Stake: The Relative Importance of Import Barriers, Export Subsidies, and Domestic Support", in Kym Anderson and Will Martin (eds.), *Agricultural Trade Reform and the Doha Development Agenda* (Washington, DC: The World Bank, 2005), pp. 49–52.

7 Several papers have analyzed these data, including William A. Masters and Andres F. Garcia, "Agricultural Price Distortion and Stabilization: Stylized Facts and Hypothesis Tests", in Kym Anderson (ed.), *Political Economy of Distortions to Agricultural Incentives* (Washington, DC: The World Bank, 2009).

RECOMMENDED READINGS

Anderson, Kym, *Distortions to Agricultural Incentives: A Global Perspective, 1955 to 2007* (New York and Washington, DC: Palgrave Macmillan and The World Bank, 2009).

Bouet, Antoine, *The Expected Benefits of Trade Liberalization for World Income and Development: Opening the "Black Box" of Global Trade Modeling, Food Policy Review 8* (Washington, DC: International Food Policy Research Institute, 2008).

Trostle, Ronald, and Ralph Seeley, *Developing Countries Dominate World Demand for Agricultural Products* (Washington, DC: Amber Waves, U.S. Department of Agriculture, Economic Research Service, August 2013).

17 Trade policies, negotiations, and agreements

THIS CHAPTER

1 Explores solutions to internal constraints to international trade
2 Discusses international trade agreements and negotiations, regional cooperation, and other solutions to trade problems
3 Considers means of reducing price, production, and income instability problems associated with trade

REDUCING INTERNAL BARRIERS TO INTERNATIONAL TRADE

Barriers to expanded international trade in agricultural products are both self-imposed by developing countries and externally imposed on them by protectionist policies in more-developed countries. We begin by considering what developing countries can do internally to solve trade problems. Trade restrictions are imposed within developing countries in attempts to distribute benefits to particular groups, to generate government revenues, and to offset economic instability and food insecurity. Removing these restrictions may require institutional change to facilitate reform, alternative revenue sources to replace trade taxes that help pay for public services, and financing to pay the adjustment costs associated with short-term and potentially long-term losses for some groups of people so that long-term gains from adjustment can arise for the majority.

Institutional change to facilitate reform

A principal motive for trade restrictions is to redistribute income within the restricting country, transferring real income to one sector at the expense of others. Reforming such policies requires a shift in political influence, which usually comes from changes in social institutions. Civic organizations, the media, legal procedures, and administrative practices all help determine whether a particular sector – such as sugar refiners or steel producers – have the political influence needed to obtain favorable trade restrictions. Often, reforms arise not because favored groups lose some of their power but because other groups acquire more influence of their own and use that to obtain countervailing policies that level the playing field. Helping more groups acquire influence often involves lowering transactions costs and facilitating access to information among those who are relatively powerless. Doing so can help those individuals engage in collective action (such as informal lobbying and protesting), and thereby pressure the government for more favorable policies.

A concerted and sustained effort is needed to reform policies that benefit powerful groups. Transparency and accountability in government, facilitated by a free media and an independent judiciary, are essential to constrain unscrupulous behavior. Policy prescriptions mentioned in earlier chapters with respect to land tenure, environmental policy, price policy, and research policy are also relevant for trade policy because the same types of forces affect ability to modify trade policy.

One external means of encouraging internal policy reforms is for an organization such as the World Trade Organization (WTO) to help countries enter mutual commitments to favorable policies, and for lenders such as the International Monetary Fund (IMF) to require trade reforms as conditions for loans. This type of activity is viewed by many as meddling in the internal affairs of developing countries. And, to a certain extent, it is. It also places a high burden on international institutions to get their interventions right, lest they cause more harm than good. Sometimes, however, international actors can help a government undertake reforms that are known to be desirable but may not be politically feasible for them to accomplish without an external partner. Another means of encouraging internal policy reforms is through joining regional trade agreements.

Alternative revenue sources

Export taxes and import tariffs are among the easiest mechanisms for raising government revenues, but they are highly distortionary. They can be replaced with less-distorting revenue sources, such as income taxes, property taxes, and value-added taxes, but this kind of fiscal reform requires adequate record-keeping and accounting information about the domestic transactions to be taxed. Fortunately, some developing countries have built mechanisms to successfully implement value-added taxes, and the administrative burdens to reform tax regimes are not insurmountable. Converting quantitative restrictions (quotas) to export taxes or import tariffs as an intermediate step to their removal, while not removing the distortion, would at least provide more revenues to the government rather than to a few private individuals.

Foreign debt reduction would reduce the pressure on governments to generate revenues. The nature of debt problems in developing countries and potential solutions are discussed in Chapter 18. Several developing countries have realigned their exchange rates to encourage exports and facilitate debt reduction. But this solution is insufficient for several heavily indebted countries in sub-Saharan Africa without additional assistance from more-developed countries.

Bridge financing for adjustment costs

Developing countries often find it difficult to undertake necessary long-term policy reform because the short-term consequences can be severe. Devaluation of an overvalued exchange rate raises the cost of imports and reduces the cost of exports. While these cost changes improve the foreign-exchange balance and may improve economic efficiency, they also mean that fewer goods are in the domestic market, resulting in price increases in the short run. Food prices may rise, real incomes fall, and a disproportionate burden from devaluation may be placed on the poorest members of society. International organizations can play a role in providing financial assistance to help offset short-term *cost-of-adjustment* problems associated with policy adjustments.

REDUCING EXTERNAL CONSTRAINTS TO INTERNATIONAL TRADE

The primary methods that have been suggested as potential solutions to external trade constraints are trade negotiations and special preferences, regional cooperation, and product diversification. Countervailing trade restrictions to offset the external constraints also have been suggested, but they can generate their own set of problems.

Trade negotiations and special preferences

Bilateral and multilateral negotiations have provided opportunities for liberalizing external restrictions on developing country trade. Bilateral negotiations occur when one country negotiates preferential trade arrangements with a second country for either specific goods or whole categories of goods and services. For example, nation A might grant nation B preferential access to its sugar market – that is, reduce or remove restrictions to sugar imports from nation B – in exchange for special access to nation B's wheat market. Or, nation A, a more-developed country, might simply grant a special preference to nation B, a less-developed country. Numerous variations of bilateral trade negotiations and special preferences are found, but these types of negotiations and preferences have declined in recent years.

Since World War II, the primary focus for trade negotiations has been multilateral rather than bilateral, and in recent years multilateral negotiations have been more regional, involving small subsets of countries, than global. Global negotiations occurred under the auspices of the General Agreement on Tariffs and Trade (GATT) until 1994, and since then fall under the World Trade Organization (WTO). The GATT, signed in 1947, replaced a series of bilateral agreements that segmented world trade before the war. More than 100 countries were signatories to the GATT, and currently 164 countries are members of the WTO, its successor organization. The GATT and WTO have attempted to foster adherence to the principle that countries should not discriminate in the application of tariffs.[1] Nondiscrimination implies that bilateral preferential agreements are not allowed. The rules allow for exceptions for developing countries. Several developed countries maintain preferential trading arrangements with particular groups of developing countries for certain categories of products. For example, the United States instituted a Caribbean Basin Initiative that eliminated tariffs and quantitative restrictions for many agricultural products from Caribbean countries. Several countries in West Africa have had special preferences with France. Some developing countries have called for more generalized preferences to be granted to countries with incomes below a particular level.

The GATT contained provisions related to consultation and negotiation to avoid disputes, rules concerning non-tariff as well as tariff barriers, and agreements to periodic multilateral negotiations to lower trade barriers. Over time, success in reducing tariff barriers increased the importance of non-tariff barriers. Non-tariff influences on trade include, but are not limited to, health and safety regulations (see Box 17.1), domestic content restrictions, complex customs formalities and reporting requirements, and rules on intellectual properties.

BOX 17.1 ENVIRONMENTAL, HEALTH, AND SAFETY REGULATIONS

Environmental or health and safety regulations can have a significant effect on trade. The United States and other countries prohibit the importation of products with certain pesticide residues. Fresh or frozen beef is prohibited from countries that have a history of foot-and-mouth disease. Clearly, governments are wise to regulate trade in products potentially injurious to public health. More-developed countries usually have tighter environmental and food-safety regulations than less-developed countries. These regulations raise the cost of production so that without corresponding restrictions on trade, not only might there be environmental or health threats, but developed-country producers might also be placed at a competitive disadvantage. However, environmental or health and safety restrictions appear sometimes to be used arbitrarily to protect the economic health of an industry when the true human health hazard is seriously in doubt. As a result, recent multilateral trade negotiations have included tighter rules on when such restrictions can be applied.

Eight rounds of multilateral trade negotiations took place under the GATT. Most of the early rounds involved negotiations on tariffs and on rules for trading blocs such as the European Community (EC). The middle rounds increasingly focused on non-tariff issues. Agricultural trade restrictions received relatively little attention until the Uruguay Round from 1986 to 1994.[2] They were at the heart of the Doha Round negotiations under the WTO, also called the Development Round.

The Uruguay Round of the GATT produced the first serious attempt to address agricultural trade restrictions, including some of particular concern to developing countries. The reason for finally considering agricultural restrictions had little to do with agricultural development problems per se. By the mid-1980s, budget costs, shrinking foreign demand, and world surpluses that threatened a global trade war forced agricultural issues to the top of the GATT agenda. The Uruguay Round negotiations highlighted the divisions among more-developed countries and between more-developed and less-developed countries with respect to trade policy. It also illustrated the diversity of interests among less-developed countries. Net exporting developing countries were concerned about market access and effects of developed-country export subsidies. Net importing developing countries, while concerned about market access, were also concerned about possible rising prices in world markets, particularly for food grains.

The Uruguay Round ended with only a modest reduction in trade barriers but reoriented the trade debate in several respects. Prior to the Uruguay Round, trade in many agricultural products was unaffected by the tariff cuts that were made for industrial products in previous rounds. In the Uruguay Round, there was agreement to convert all non-tariff agricultural trade barriers to tariffs. These tariffs were subject to rules, called bindings, that limit countries' ability to increase them. The round also contributed to a shift in domestic support for agriculture away from those policies with the largest potential to affect production and, therefore, to affect trade flows. Countries accepted commitments to reduce expenditures on export subsidies and not to apply new subsidies to unsubsidized commodities. Because the base periods chosen for comparing levels of tariff protection had relatively high protection, the way non-tariff barriers were converted to tariff-equivalent rates, and the small percentage reductions agreed to, the overall reduction in trade barriers was quite small.[3] However, the base was established to build on in future negotiations, or so it was hoped at the time.

The Uruguay Round resulted in separate agreements on (1) sanitary and phyto-sanitary (SPS) measures to protect humans, animals, and plants from foreign pests, diseases, and contaminants and (2) intellectual property rights to protect patents, copyrights, and other such rights from infringement abroad. Both of these measures have been difficult for developing countries to accept. The SPS rules can be credited with increasing transparency of countries' SPS regulations and providing a means for settling disputes. Still, the rules can be manipulated to create barriers to trade that may not be related to SPS concerns. The rules state that science should be the deciding factor as to whether an imported product poses a threat, but science can still be debated. Intellectual property rights are monopoly rights that are granted to create incentives for private individuals and firms to innovate. However, they also can lead to companies charging high prices to poor countries for drugs and production inputs.

World Trade Organization
The WTO was created during the Uruguay Round and came into force in April 1994 to replace the GATT and strengthen the enforcement of international trade rules and the settling of trade disputes. For example,

a single country could no longer block formation of a dispute resolution panel or veto an adverse ruling by blocking the adoption of a panel report. However, it can still be difficult to get countries whose practices have been successfully ruled against to change their behavior, because the only sanction that the WTO can impose when a member government is found to have violated its commitments is to give to other governments the permission to impose limited, specific retaliatory sanctions.

More developing countries have joined the WTO than were members of the GATT. Because developing countries can vote as a bloc, they can force issues more strongly than before. Negotiations under the WTO can succeed only with concessions to developing country concerns. In a 2001 meeting in Doha, Qatar, developed countries agreed to place export subsidies higher on the agenda. They also agreed to some relief on intellectual properties, such as for drugs to fight AIDS. The Doha Round has been called the Development Round to indicate international commitment to addressing concerns of developing countries. In a 2003 ministerial-level WTO meeting in Mexico, a group of 21 developing countries (which altogether represented about two-thirds of the world's farmers) called for tighter domestic support restrictions for developed countries and more flexibility for special and differential treatment for developing countries. Their strong position was one reason that meeting broke down, but it marked a milestone in that for the first time, several developing countries negotiated as a bloc and were able to affect the outcome.

Most would argue that the WTO is potentially more of a friend than foe for developing countries. It has been estimated that global free trade would confer income gains of more than $100 billion annually to developing countries and reduce extreme poverty.[4] About half of those gains would arise from removing restrictions (e.g., tariffs and quotas) on exports from developing-country products to developed-country markets, especially in agricultural goods, textiles, and apparel. The gains from trade liberalization would be about twice the amount that developing countries currently receive from foreign development assistance. However, in the Doha Round negotiations, neither developed nor developing countries sought the degree of trade liberalization that would have come close to generating this level of benefits. In July 2008, Doha Round negotiations broke down over agricultural trade issues, especially a dispute over a mechanism that would allow poor countries to institute tariff protection for specific products if prices drop too low or there is a surge in imports. Negotiations eventually restarted, and a partial agreement was concluded in December 2013. Progress was made on issues such as simplifying customs procedures. However, the agreement to relax major agricultural trade constraints was minimal, and the conclusion of the Doha Round may have marked the end of significant progress in global multilateral trade liberalization for the foreseeable future.

One stumbling block related to agriculture was the request by India that poor countries, including India, be allowed to subsidize their agricultural sectors for an indefinite period of time. The United States objected but compromised on the issue. The compromise shields countries like India from WTO dispute challenges over their agricultural supports if they are transparent about them and do not sell the affected commodities in global markets. The agricultural portion of the deal also provides somewhat greater access to markets in Japan and the EU, which have quotas backed by high tariffs on certain goods.

The WTO now faces significant obstacles in its role as an international forum for trade negotiations. Some less-developed countries fear that developed countries will use labor standards as a protectionist tool. Others are concerned about the limited progress on strengthening anti-dumping rules. Europeans want stronger environmental rules than either the United States or developing countries would like, the latter preferring environmental issues to come under separate, non-trade agreements. The rise of populism in several countries, including the United States, has worked against freeing up trade in general.

China and the WTO

The large effect on world trade of China's economic growth and admittance to the WTO 2001 has been another obstacle to continued progress in liberalizing trade under the WTO. Growth in China's economy and trade has been positive for world welfare overall, but the gains have been widely dispersed, while the losers have been concentrated in trade-affected industries and the labor markets where they are located.[5] These industries and labor markets are found more in manufacturing than in agriculture, but given the size of the Chinese economy, the effects have been substantial. Trade adjustment programs for workers are minimal in more-developed countries and almost non-existent in developing nations. The result has been growing opposition to trade liberalization under the auspices of trade agreements such as the WTO. Some countries, including the United States, have raised tariffs against China, resulting in retaliation with reciprocal tariff increases and reduced economic growth in these countries. Larger and more creative trade adjustment programs to compensate losers from trade would be more likely to generate broad-based welfare gains than would higher tariffs.

Regional trade agreements

Perhaps in part due to difficulties in reaching agreement under the WTO, international trading relations have increasingly been influenced by growth in smaller regional organizations and trading groupings. The Economic Union in Europe and the North American Free Trade Area (NAFTA) are examples, but so too are free trade areas (FTAs) that have been established in the Asian–Pacific countries, the Andean countries and the southern cone countries in Latin America, in Southern Africa, and elsewhere. *Free trade areas* are trading blocs whose member nations agree to lower or eliminate tariffs and perhaps other trade barriers among themselves, but each country maintains its own independent trade policy toward nonmember nations. Free movement of production factors, such as labor, are usually not included.[6] More than 300 regional agreements have now been signed, many of them overlapping.

Reduced trade restrictions among a group of those countries could allow for increased specialization, economies of scale (particularly for manufacturers), and competition that reduces costs of production and improves economic efficiency. They could also affect labor standards, environmental protection, and intellectual property rights (see Box 17.2). Occasionally a group of countries can gain some market power through closer economic integration.

Regional economic groupings can be helpful to developing countries, but their usefulness can be limited by the similarity of products produced among the various countries in a region. For this reason, developing countries increasingly link to more-developed countries in these groupings. NAFTA is a good example, with Mexico linked to the United States and Canada. Trade liberalization under the NAFTA was accompanied by substantially larger volumes of trade of agricultural commodities among the three countries. NAFTA eliminated many tariffs and quantitative restrictions among the participants beginning in 1994, with progressive elimination of tariffs and other trade barriers over the 15-year period that followed. Both exports and imports grew in all three countries more than would have otherwise. The result was gains from trade as well as resource adjustments within individual commodity sectors.

Despite these gains, NAFTA and its successor, the U.S.–Mexico–Canada Agreement (USMCA), and other regional agreements remain controversial because some industries lose within each partner country and some trade is diverted from countries outside the agreement. Developing and more-developed countries fear for loss of jobs, and expanded regional trade creates many adjustment costs. Some also fear that the signing of regional trade agreements lessens incentives for countries to enter into meaningful multilateral negotiations at the global level.

BOX 17.2 THE TRANSPACIFIC PARTNERSHIP

The Transpacific Partnership (TPP) was a proposed free trade agreement, designed to be one of the most comprehensive FTAs in the world. It included enforceable labor standards, environmental protection, safeguarding of intellectual property rights, and restrictions on undervaluing exchange rates, in addition to almost complete elimination of tariffs among member nations. Its dispute settlement mechanism would allow TPP countries to adjudicate conflicts outside of the WTO. The TPP signatory nations included the United States, Japan, Canada, Australia, New Zealand, Mexico, Chile, Singapore, Vietnam, Malaysia, Peru, and Brunei, which together account for 40 percent of global trade. Agricultural interests in the United States, particularly the beef industry, favored joining the TPP because it would lower Japan's high tariffs on beef, from 38.5 percent to 9 percent. However, the proposed TPP had critics across the political spectrum, and the agreement was not ratified by the U.S. Congress after trade negotiators signed it in early in 2016. The United States officially withdrew from the agreement in early 2017. Many provisions of the TPP were U.S.-centric, and the agreement would have brought sizable U.S. economic benefits.

Following U.S. withdrawal from the TPP, the remaining 11 nations renegotiated the agreement and formed the Comprehensive and Progressive Transpacific Partnership (CPTPP), with many provisions removed that were favorable to the United States. The absence of the United States from the CPTPP has disadvantaged U.S. agriculture. For example, Japanese beef imports from Australia, Canada, New Zealand, and Mexico were up about half in 2019 compared to 2018, while exports of U.S. beef to Japan were down.

Due to losses incurred by withdrawing from the TPP, the United States negotiated a bilateral trade agreement with Japan in 2019, which included several agricultural commodities. Under the USJTA, which took effect in 2020, Japan agrees to reduce tariffs on over $7 billion of U.S. agricultural exports to Japan for commodities such as beef, pork, wheat, cheese, and wine.

REDUCING INSTABILITY

Many trade policy issues are related to price variability rather than average price levels for traded goods and foreign exchange earnings. Some of the main strategies used to address price risk include: diversification, commodity agreements, compensatory financing, enhanced use of market information, and temporary export restrictions.

Product diversification

Countries that receive a high proportion of their export earnings from one or two commodities could moderate the effects of external trade restrictions by diversifying their exports. The terms of trade can turn against any single product as substitutes are developed (e.g., for jute and sisal) or new technologies shift supply out against a relatively inelastic and slowly shifting world demand (e.g., peanuts). Even if progress is made through negotiations in opening up market access for commodities such as sugar or cotton or reducing explicit or implicit export subsidies for commodities such as peanuts, total removal of developed-country policy distortions is unlikely. Diversifying production of export and food crops can help not only to reduce the terms-of-trade problems arising from external constraints, but may also reduce risks associated with price, production, and foreign exchange variability.

The difficulty for developing countries is in deciding how much to diversify away from a commodity for which it has a strong comparative advantage. Diversification out of agriculture is a natural consequence of economic development that may eventually increase exchange-earnings stability, but too much diversification within agriculture can be a costly means of achieving stability.

Commodity agreements and buffer stocks

One approach to reducing price variability for individual commodities has been to develop international commodity agreements. Several of these agreements have been concluded in the past for commodities such as wheat, sugar, coffee, and cocoa. However, few of them have been effective for very long.

Some previous international commodity agreements, such as those for coffee and sugar, have attempted to stabilize prices but also to keep prices high, by restricting production through trade quotas. However, when production varies, these quotas can actually serve to destabilize world

An international agreement was in effect for coffee many years ago

prices. A third type of commodity agreement involves *buffer stocks*. With a buffer stock scheme, when supplies are high, the commodity is bought up and stored. These international stocks are intended to provide protection against a time when supply of the commodity drops for some reason. If there is a shortage, stocks would be released on the market to keep prices down. The agreement might specify a minimum and a maximum price, a buffer stock of say 15 percent of world production, a tax on imports or exports to build up the stocks, and perhaps some quotas for producing countries. Buffer stocks for commodities such as rice, whose global trade volumes represent only a small share of global consumption, might have helped during the global food price spike in 2007–08. The few exporters of rice invoked short-term restrictions on export due to concerns about meeting domestic demands, and global prices increased dramatically.

With most commodity agreements, exporters and importers have difficulty agreeing on an appropriate target price range. The agreements also have proven expensive to administer, especially buffer stock programs with their high costs of storage. Hence, they are seldom employed.

Compensatory financing schemes

Schemes aimed at stabilizing expenditures or earnings have been used as an alternative to direct intervention in commodity markets. The simplest approach has been compensatory financing schemes in which a reference amount is set for each country for its total export earnings or earnings from particular commodities. Upper and lower acceptable bounds are set around this amount. When earnings go below the lower bound, the CFS fills in the shortfall by providing cash or credit to the particular country. When earnings exceed the upper bound, participating developing countries may pay back what was previously taken out.

Although CFS programs rarely break even, they have been used at times by donor agencies to help specific developing countries. For example, a Compensatory Financing Facility (CFF) was established by the IMF to provide financial assistance to member countries experiencing temporary export shortfalls. To use the CFF, the IMF must be convinced that the country will seek means to correct its balance of payments problem in the case that export earnings shortfalls are caused by structural problems.

A second compensatory finance scheme was the STABEX, run by the European Union (EU) as part of the Lomé Convention.[7] The STABEX scheme was restricted to African, Caribbean, and Pacific countries and was aimed at stabilizing export earnings for 48 agricultural products. Usually, only exports to the EU were covered. A reference amount was set for each commodity based on the average value of exports for the products in the preceding four years. To qualify for compensation, export earnings had to fall at least 6.5 percent below the reference amount. All loans were interest free and the least-developed countries repaid nothing. The major commodities supported were cotton, sisal, coffee, cocoa, and peanuts. Major beneficiaries were Senegal, Sudan, Cote d'Ivoire, Mauritania, and Tanzania.

Enhanced use of market information, insurance, and derivatives

The difficulty of implementing any of the stabilization approaches previously discussed has led to the development of new, more market-based interventions. At the simplest level, governments seek to increase the flow of market information to facilitate commodity trading and storage. Governments can also help traders use well-regulated futures and options markets. These contracts are called derivatives, because they represent the right to buy or sell something else: they are derived from the commodity but are not the product itself. Derivative markets exist in London, New York, Sydney, and elsewhere; the largest futures market "exchange" is in Chicago. With futures markets, commodities can be bought and sold for delivery at a future date. Farmers or exporters can fix a price for goods to be sold later, thus reducing the risk. This activity is called *hedging*. Alternatively, sellers can insure against extremely low prices and buyers against extremely high prices by trading in options on futures contracts. Farmers or exporters can insure against low prices by purchasing an option to sell if prices fall to a specified level. If prices fall below that level, they can exercise their option to sell at that price. If prices rise above it, they lose what was paid for the option, but they can sell the products for the higher price.

Temporary export restrictions

One approach to stabilizing prices, which may be contrary to a country's signed trade agreements, is to impose temporary export restrictions during periods of abnormally high prices for food commodities such as rice and wheat. The purpose is to soften the blow of high prices on consumers. Once the food price spike has receded, the restrictions are removed. India and Thailand imposed such restrictions on rice in 2008 and removed them the following year. The United States imposed a similar restriction on soybeans during a price spike in 1973. As the United States learned the hard way, such restrictions can allow a country's competitors, such as Brazil in the case of U.S. soybeans, to grab part of the market for the commodity because importers begin to feel the previous supplier is unreliable.

SUMMARY

External demand constraints, market instability, and internal direct and indirect trade restrictions all impede exports from and imports into developing countries. Lack of access to developed country markets is probably the most severe external problem. Governments impose internal trade restrictions to raise revenue, to distribute income to particular groups in response to pressures from interest groups, to exploit monopoly power for certain export crops, and for reasons of food security. Indirect restrictions, such as overvalued exchange rates, may be more significant sources of discrimination against agriculture than are direct restrictions, such as export taxes and quotas.

Trade negotiations were undertaken under the GATT beginning in 1947 but before the 1990s did not address in any substantial way the restrictions on agricultural products that are important to developing countries. The WTO was formed during the Uruguay Round of negotiations to replace the GATT and currently has roughly 164 member-nations. Developing countries have more power in the WTO then they had under the GATT, but the WTO is currently struggling to maintain momentum in liberalizing multilateral trade policies. Regional economic groupings of countries have also become more prevalent and have increased regional trade, although their effects on total trade are less certain. International commodity agreements, compensatory financing, product diversification, enhanced use of market information, and temporary export restrictions have been used by developing countries to address economic instability.

IMPORTANT TERMS AND CONCEPTS

Compensatory finance

Doha Round

Free trade area

GATT

International commodity
  agreement

International trade

Multilateral trade negotiations

NAFTA/UCMCA

Protectionism

Quotas

Regional trade agreement

Tariffs

Terms of trade

Trade preferences

Uruguay Round

World Trade Organization

LOOKING AHEAD

The macroeconomic environment strongly influences agricultural production incentives, agricultural trade, and employment. Domestic macroeconomic policies affect key prices in the economy, including exchange rates, interest rates, wages, food prices, and land prices. Government revenues, taxation, borrowing, and inflation all influence agriculture. In the next chapter, we will consider the effects of both domestic macroeconomic policies and the world macroeconomic relationships. Attention is also devoted to world capital markets and the debt crises.

QUESTIONS FOR DISCUSSION

1 Why do developing countries impose trade restrictions?
2 What is the GATT and why did developing countries feel that it focused too little on their problems?
3 What is the WTO and why was it created?
4 What is the difference between multilateral and bilateral trade agreements?

5 What is the purpose of a compensatory finance scheme and how might one work?
6 Why might product diversification be helpful to developing countries?
7 What is a free trade area? Give an example.
8 How do buffer stocks relate in international commodity agreements?
9 How might enhanced information help reduce internal trade restrictions in developing countries?

NOTES

1 Nondiscrimination has been called the most-favored national principle: that a country should apply to other countries the same tariff levels that it applies to its most-favored nations.
2 Tariff rounds are frequently named after individuals or after locations where the initial discussions in the in the round take place. The Uruguay Round began with a meeting in Punta del Este, Uruguay, in 1986.
3 Developed countries committed to reducing tariffs by 36 percent from the levels in the late 1980s and developing countries by 15 percent. The Uruguay Round allowed countries to institute "tariff-rate quotas". A tariff-rate quota applies a lower tariff to imports below a certain quantitative limit (quota), and permits a higher tariff on imported goods after the quota has been reached. The purpose was to ensure that historical trade levels could be maintained, while creating some new trade opportunities. However, the effect has been to slow the rate of trade liberalization.
4 William Cline, *Trade Policy and Global Poverty* (Washington, DC: Institute for International Economics, 2004).
5 David H. Autor, "Trade and Labor Markets: Lessons from China's Rise", *IZA World of Labor* (2018), p. 431, doi:10.15185/izawol.431.
6 Free movement of factors is allowed in a tighter form of economic integration, such as a Common Market or an Economic Federation or Economic Union. One type of regional economic integration that is tighter than a free trade area but looser than a Common Market is a "Customs Union", in which member countries agree to a common trade policy against all outside countries.
7 The EU's economic arrangement with African, Caribbean, and Pacific countries, which replaced former colonial preference schemes, was originally spelled out in the Lomé Convention of 1975 and revised several times before being itself replaced by the Cotonou Agreement of 2000. Other arrangements include free access for many African, Caribbean, and Pacific products to EU markets and the European Development Fund, which administers foreign aid to these countries.

RECOMMENDED READINGS

Anderson, Kym, and Will Martin (eds.), *Agricultural Trade Reform and the Doha Development Agenda* (Washington, DC: The World Bank, 2005).

Cline, William, *Trade Policy and Global Poverty* (Washington, DC: Institute for International Economics, 2004).

International Agricultural Trade Research Consortium, www.iatrcweb. org/.

World Trade Organization, www.wto.org.

18 Macroeconomic policies and agricultural development

THIS CHAPTER

1 Discusses how government policies associated with taxation, spending, borrowing, interest rates, wage rates, the money supply, and exchange rates influence the performance of the agricultural sector
2 Examines why governments in less-developed countries tend to pursue specific types of macroeconomic policies
3 Describes the significance of the inter-relationships among macroeconomic policies across countries; international capital, labor, and product markets; and domestic agricultural markets

MACROECONOMIC POLICIES AND AGRICULTURE

Macroeconomic policies have a strong influence on output prices, factor prices, marketing margins, and, hence, on incentives for agricultural producers, consumers, and marketing agents. Foreign exchange rates, for example, affect export and import prices and quantities and, thus, output and input prices. Interest rates determine the cost of investments in machinery and equipment and, when combined with wage rates, the capital intensity of production. Interest rates also influence the cost of storage.

The macroeconomic environment conditions the rate and structure of agricultural and urban-industrial growth. Job creation and income growth and distribution are as much a function of macroeconomic policies as they are of policies and projects targeted at specific sectors. The short-run effects of macro-policies on employment and income distribution often differ substantially from their long-term effects. Real incomes of urban consumers can be sharply reduced in the wake of macroeconomic policy adjustments aimed at lowering public debt or controlling inflation. Policymakers may seek to offset short-run income and nutritional consequences of policy changes needed for long-term growth. During economic downturns, such as the steep reductions in employment and income associated with a virus pandemic, short-term income transfers to the poorest in the population can help reduce widespread hunger and avoid economic collapse.

Understanding the effects of macroeconomic variables on food and agriculture is important for designing economically and politically viable short- and long-run policies. When macro-policies create distortions such as overvalued exchange rates, heavily subsidized interest rates, or inflationary fiscal and monetary policies, agriculture is usually discriminated against and long-term prospects for development are compromised. Pressures build for major macro-policy reforms that, even if unintentionally, usually help the rural sector by increasing farm incomes and rural employment. Price increases and lower subsidies, however, necessitate painful adjustments by urban consumers. The pervasive nature of these macro-policy effects makes it imperative for those interested in agricultural development to understand how the macro-economy works.

Describing a macro-economy

The "macro-economy" is the aggregate of all economic activity in the country. It is the sum of the value of all individual goods and services, at the prevailing "macro prices" for foreign currency, capital, and labor that cut across all sectors. The value of the activity at current exchange rates, interest rates, and wage rates can be added up in terms of demand, supply, or income (see Figure 18.1). A country's gross domestic product (GDP), a measure of its domestically produced national income, will, in theory, be identical regardless of whether it is calculated by summing demands, supplies, or incomes. In practice, differences in measurement errors lead to different measures of income, depending on the adding up technique used. Macroeconomic policies in developed countries often focus on managing the demand side of the economy. Governments implement policies to stimulate private consumption or investment, use public expenditures to create demand, and closely manage trade. Policies in developing countries frequently are more concerned with managing

Demand Description	Supply Description	Income Description
Consumption	Agricultural production	Wages
+	+	+
Private investment	Industrial production	Interest
+	+	+
Government expenditures	Production of services	Rents
+	+	+
Excess of exports over imports	Government production	Profits
↓	↓	↓
Gross domestic product (GDP)	Gross domestic product	Gross domestic product
+		
Net income transfers abroad		
↓		
Gross national product (GNP)		

Figure 18.1 Three descriptions of a macro-economy

aggregate supply. Governments in developing countries tend to use the types of policies described in Chapter 15 to manage agricultural supply; similar policies affect the other productive sectors. Numerous developing countries have attempted to stimulate supply by involving the government directly in the production of goods and services.

Demand equals supply when the components in Figure 18.1 are expressed in real terms (inflation is netted out). The basic factors of production (land, labor, and capital), together with management, earn incomes when they produce goods and services. These incomes are spent on the components of aggregate demand; hence, total income equals GDP. Developing countries are often very concerned about the distribution of total income among wages, interest, rents, and profits, and undertake policies to manage this distribution.

The prices of goods and services are generally expressed in the country's currency units. The monetary value of a good or service can change due to inflation even when its real value has not changed. Policies that create inflation can change real values as well, though often indirectly. The causes of inflation are discussed later, but many of inflation's effects are, in a sense, unintended results of fiscal and monetary policies. We turn our attention to these policies first, highlighting their effects on agriculture. Then we consider the effects of macro-price policies, particularly those policies related to exchange rates, interest rates, and wage rates. Finally, we consider the effects of macro-policies on rural–urban terms of trade and land prices. The major macroeconomic and agricultural policy connections are summarized in Figure 18.2; these connections are described in the next sections.

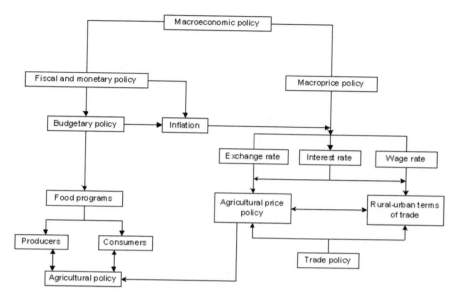

Figure 18.2 Major connections between macroeconomic policy and food policy
Source: Based on Fig. 5–1 in C. Peter Timmer, Walter P. Falcon, and Scott R. Pearson, *Food Policy Analysis* (Baltimore: Johns Hopkins University Press, 1983), p. 223

Fiscal and monetary policy

Fiscal policy is the use of taxes and spending by government to influence employment, income growth and distribution, and other objectives. *Monetary policy* is the use of the money supply and the interest rate to influence these things. The two kinds of policy are closely related. In particular, since the government can print money, expanding the money supply or borrowing from foreigners can be tempting alternatives to raising taxes. Governments differ substantially in their ability and willingness to run budget deficits, and in the way these deficits are financed.

Governments in developing countries often go into debt because of their many pressing needs and limited tax revenues. Tax collection, particularly income tax collection, is difficult and costly, and taxes are easy to evade in countries with poor information systems. Consequently, developing countries raise large proportions of their tax revenues from export taxes, import tariffs, and sales and value-added taxes, as these taxes tend to be easier to collect than others.

Because agriculture is usually the largest sector in the economy in developing countries, it generally provides more revenue to the government than it receives in return in the form of government programs. However, there are usually substantial budget allocations to the agricultural sector.

Programs for producers include items such as irrigation systems, roads, agricultural research and extension, market information, and certain output or input subsidies. Programs for consumers include items such as targeted and non-targeted food price subsidies. Many of the investments in agricultural research and extension, irrigation, roads, etc., also benefit consumers by lowering the price of food.

Foreign aid can ease some of these revenue needs, as discussed Chapter 19. A few countries have petroleum and other mineral resources that they can export so that foreign consumers help provide revenues for government spending. However, given the limitations to raising taxes, obtaining foreign aid, and exporting petroleum or minerals, most developing countries incur budget deficits. They meet these deficits by borrowing, often from abroad, or by increasing the money supply (whether by printing more money or other expansive policies).

Currently, several developing countries are heavily burdened by debts incurred through previous borrowing abroad. This debt problem and its causes, effects, and potential solutions are discussed later in the chapter. The debt incurred by borrowing can constrain the ability to take on additional debt. Consequently, domestic money supply and budget finance policies become that much more important. The size of the money supply must match the needs for operating capital in the productive sectors of the economy. However, when a country prints money to finance a large budget deficit, inflation is the usual result (see Box 18.1).

Inflation can be linked to increases in particular prices, for example, if a country devalues its exchange rate so the prices of all traded goods rise, or it keeps a fixed exchange rate and sees foreign prices rise. But in such cases, the rising prices of those items translate into economy-wide inflation only if the money supply rises accordingly. Otherwise, the prices of other things would fall, and only relative prices would change.

Whatever its source, inflation does not usually imply a change in all prices by the same amount, and so it creates some winners and some losers. Indeed, it often hurts agriculture because the prices of inputs usually rise by more than the prices of farm outputs. When inflation occurs, the foreign exchange rate should change to reflect the reduced value of the currency. Many developing countries do not allow this adjustment to take place completely. The resulting overvalued exchange rate increases the price of agricultural exports (thus reducing export demand) and makes food imports cheaper. The resulting increased supply of agricultural products on the domestic market reduces farm product prices. The foreign exchange rate policy is just one of the macro-price policies that have significant impacts on agriculture.

BOX 18.1 EFFECT ON INFLATION OF A GOVERNMENT BUDGET DEFICIT FINANCED BY EXPANDING THE MONEY SUPPLY

Inflation is a sustained rise in the general price level for a country's goods and services. It is usually measured by a price index. The following example, which draws on Figure 18.1, illustrates why expansion of the money supply to finance government budget deficits can create inflation. The aggregate supply of goods and services produced must equal the aggregate demand from total expenditures or, $Y = P \times Q = C + I + G + X - M$, where:

Y = monetary value of national output or income
P = price index for all goods and services produced
Q = quantity index for all goods and services produced
C = national consumption expenditures in private sector
I = national investment expenditures in private sector
G = government expenditures on consumption and investment
X = total value of exports
M = total value of imports

If government demand for goods and services (G) increases because the government prints money to pay for a budget deficit, the quantity produced of goods and services (Q) must increase, imports (M) must increase, or prices (P) will rise. Most developing countries do not have enough idle resources to meet this demand with enough Q. Changes in imports require foreign exchange. Thus, the usual result is an increase in prices.

Source: C. Peter Timmer, Walter P. Falcon, and Scott R. Pearson, *Food Policy Analysis* (Baltimore: Johns Hopkins University Press, 1983), pp. 227–228

Macro prices and agriculture

Governments use macroeconomic policies to influence inflation, provide incentives, and distribute income. Three prices – foreign exchange rates, interest rates, and wage rates – have major effects on the macro-economy and can be manipulated by the government. These *macro-prices* are all, in fact, determined by supply and demand conditions in their respective markets, so that if the government decides to set them by fiat, conditions of excess supply or demand can result. Two of these prices, interest rates and wage rates, signal the scarcity of basic factors of production, capital and labor. Governments often are tempted to set wage rates artificially high to directly raise incomes of workers. They are tempted to set interest rates low to encourage borrowing and investment. Wages set above the free market, equilibrium value determined by supply and demand conditions, will lead to excess supply of labor and, hence, unemployment. Interest rates set below equilibrium values will create excess demand for credit which will then have to be rationed. Government policy can be used to affect those macro prices indirectly by intervening to change the underlying supply and/or demand conditions. Public works projects, for example, stimulate demand for labor and could be used to raise wages.

The foreign exchange rate is relatively easy to control, and governments often do control it. Two other prices with major effects on the macro-economy, food prices and land prices, are influenced indirectly through exchange rate manipulations. These prices can also be affected directly by imposing tariffs or by government interventions in their respective markets.

Exchange rates

An exchange rate is the number of units of one currency that it takes to buy a unit of another currency, or the price of one currency in terms of another. For many relatively developed countries, the foreign exchange rate is determined in international money markets by the supply of and demand for a country's currency. For example, there is a demand for U.S. dollars in Japan in order to pay for agricultural products imported from the United States. Similarly, there is a supply of dollars in Japan coming from the purchase of Japanese cars by U.S. consumers. The balance of payments of any country summarizes all economic transactions between it and the rest of the world. The current account, largely reflecting trade balances in goods and services, is balanced by the capital account, which reflects changes in ownership of assets between countries. A country with a trade deficit (i.e., it currently imports more than it exports), by the nature of the accounting relationship, must run a capital account surplus (i.e., it is selling more of its assets) to foreign investors. Thus, the supply of, and demand for, dollars are affected by international trade and capital flows for investment or other purposes.

These same supply and demand factors exist in developing countries, but the exchange rates in some of these countries are set by governments rather than determined in currency markets. A developing country may fix or "peg" the value of its currency to that of a major trading partner such as the United States. For example, Honduras for many years fixed its currency, the Lempira, to the dollar at a rate of 2 Lempira equals 1 dollar. The Lempira then followed the fate of the dollar in foreign exchange markets. It declined in value when the dollar declined against third countries, and rose when the dollar rose.

A government can set a new official exchange rate to raise or lower the value of its currency. For example, Honduras eventually devalued its currency relative to the dollar and set it at a ratio of 4 to 1. In 2020, it is 25 to 1. This devaluation made imports into Honduras more expensive and its exports cheaper. In recent years, countries as diverse as Thailand, Indonesia, South Korea, Russia, Brazil, Argentina, and Turkey have used pegged exchange rates, at least for a period of time. In some cases, such as Ecuador, El Salvador, Panama, and Zimbabwe, the country has even done away with its currency and just used the dollar in its place. In other cases, countries have used what is called a crawling or soft peg, where the currency is allowed to shift gradually over time or move within a pre-specified range with respect to another currency.

Some countries overvalue their exchange rates for long periods of time. Overvalued exchange rates usually result from differences in inflation rates between a country and its major trading partners. Domestic inflation in the presence of fixed exchange rates means that imports seem cheaper relative to domestically produced goods. At the same time, exports from the country become more expensive abroad. But the market for foreign exchange in the country will not balance unless capital flows in; thus, the value of the currency is driven up. Any policy that creates inflationary pressures, such as government budget deficits or expansion of the money supply, will, when combined with fixed exchange rates, lead to overvaluation. Countries maintain overvalued exchange rates by controlling the movement of foreign exchange and foreign investment (see Box 18.2).

Countries overvalue exchange rates in part to keep domestic prices down. More imports and fewer exports mean more goods in the domestic market. The greater the domestic supply of goods relative to demand, the lower the price. The result of an overvaluation is that the prices of traded goods produced in the country, such as many agricultural goods, are depressed relative to those of non-traded goods and services. Thus, rural incomes tend to be lowered compared to urban incomes.

Devaluation may correct the problem, at least temporarily, but unless fiscal and monetary policies are changed to reduce either government expenditures or aggregate demand, inflation can quickly result in a reoccurrence of the overvalued exchange rate. Devaluation can also cause hardship on those who produce non-tradable goods and services and

BOX 18.2 HOW A GOVERNMENT MAINTAINS AN OVERVALUED EXCHANGE RATE

Since supply and demand factors determine exchange rates, if a government wishes to fix the official rate at a level other than its equilibrium, then it must intervene in the foreign exchange market. It can support an overvalued rate by selling foreign exchange reserves (dollars or some other currency) and purchasing its own currency, thus supporting its value. Overvaluation thus diminishes foreign reserves and cannot be sustained for long periods of time. In the absence of significant reserves, a government can restrict access to foreign currency at the official rate, and thus effectively ration the commodity (foreign exchange) for which excess demand exists. This rationing is usually implemented by imposing direct currency controls, by controlled allocations of foreign exchange to preferred importers, and by tariffs and other barriers to imports.

consume tradable goods; for example, civil servants and certain groups of factory workers. Food prices generally rise in response to currency devaluation, helping farmers and hurting urban consumers. Policies are often needed to protect the welfare of the very poor when a devaluation occurs, especially if the currency has been allowed to become substantially overvalued and a large adjustment is needed.

Over time, countries that are open to international capital flows have found that either a fixed exchange rate or a flexible exchange rate that is allowed to float against other currencies is more sustainable than an exchange rate that is managed by the government so it adjusts gradually. Countries with a history of monetary instability or that are closely tied in trade and capital flows to another country tend to be those with fixed rate systems.

In addition, many countries, for example Colombia, invoice a large share of their exports in dollars rather than their local currency, muting the effect of a devaluation of their currency on demand for their products. They do this type of invoicing to avoid erratic pricing of their products in global markets, as the dollar is the most widely used currency for international transactions. It means that devaluations of the country's currency against the dollar, rather than against the currencies of other countries with which they trade, have the largest effect on demand for their products.

Interest rates

The price of capital investment is represented by the interest rate. The interest rate reflects, in part, the productivity of capital or the opportunity cost of using capital for one purpose rather than another. Interest rates also reflect risk and the value of current as opposed to future consumption. Interest rates are determined by the interaction of the supply of investment funds, basically household savings, and the demand for these funds.

Governments can influence interest rates by setting them for public credit sources and by imposing regulations such as reserve requirements on private financial sources. In addition, the method by which the government finances a fiscal deficit affects interest rates. If a deficit is financed by domestic borrowing, then interest rates may rise in response to the increased demand for funds. The alternative means of financing deficits is to print money, a policy which is usually inflationary. Thus, higher interest rates in the presence of budget deficits can help keep inflation down. Macroeconomic policy with respect to interest rates often represents an attempt to balance the value of capital in increasing production with the valuation of future, relative to current, consumption.

Governments may set a maximum interest rate that can be charged by lenders. If the rate is set too low, excess demand for credit is created because demand for credit will exceed its supply. Under these circumstances, credit has to be rationed to borrowers who are fortunate to have access to the funds, and private lenders will have incentives not to lend or to circumvent the regulations. Formal lending institutions may be forced out of business. Moneylenders and other informal credit sources not under the control of the government find it easier to charge higher rates.

When interest rates are controlled, they may even be set below the inflation rate. When this happens, the real interest rate is, in fact, negative.[1] Negative real interest rates create credit crises since they spur demand for borrowing far above the supply of savings. Even less-extreme interventions can have negative effects, however, as they encourage use of government credit for those who can obtain it and drive out private credit institutions.

Wage rates

The primary source of income for most people in the world is returns to their labor. Hence, creating jobs at decent wages is essential to reductions in poverty and hunger. Governments recognize the importance of labor remuneration and often set minimum wages in an attempt to raise people out of poverty. Unfortunately, in low-income countries where most people are self-employed, minimum-wage legislation is a relatively impotent tool for raising returns to labor and can have unintended effects that hurt labor.

Labor markets are complex because they are segmented by skill levels, occupations, and locations. In rural areas, labor arrangements may include payment in kind (e.g., food or other goods), may involve conditional access to a piece of land, or may depend on other special relationships between employers and workers that are determined by local customs or institutions. Wages for unskilled workers in these areas may be close to the average product of labor rather than the marginal product (Chapter 6). This level in turn is close to a basic subsistence level. Minimum-wage legislation is virtually unenforceable in rural areas in developing countries.

In urban areas, minimum wage legislation has been successful in large industries and government organizations. People who are able to obtain jobs at or above the minimum wage clearly benefit. Unfortunately, by raising the price of labor, minimum wage legislation can reduce the demand for labor by these industries and organizations. Thus, unemployment (or excess supply of labor) may result in the short run. In the long run, the industries may adapt more capital-intensive technologies, further displacing labor, or close their doors and move to a country with lower and more flexible wages. The possibility of higher wages in the formal sector may attract more migrants to the urban area, even if jobs are scarce. This influx of migrants will also swell the informal sector. Consequently, minimum-wage legislation in the formal sector may, over time, depress wages in the informal sector. In summary, wages are an important macro-price, especially to the poor, but governments have limited ability to raise people out of poverty by legislating wage levels.

Prices of agricultural products and land

Agricultural prices are influenced by government interventions in output and input markets, as discussed in Chapters 15 and 16. Price supports, input subsidies, export taxes, and so on directly influence the terms of trade between the agricultural and nonagricultural sectors. Fiscal and monetary policies and macro-prices, however, usually have even larger effects on the terms of trade between the sectors than do the more direct price policies. For example, the agricultural sector produces a high proportion of tradable commodities. Thus, an overvalued exchange rate that encourages imports and discourages exports typically has a strong negative effect on the agricultural sector.

When macro-policies and prices discriminate against the agricultural sector so that agricultural prices are depressed, downward pressures are placed on land prices as well. Incentives are reduced for improving the land base or for developing technologies to utilize land more efficiently.

In summary, macro-prices reflect basic economic conditions in an economy. Unless agricultural productivity is increased, simply distorting these prices through government policies is likely to hinder the development process and create distributional effects that hurt the rural poor.

WHY GOVERNMENTS PURSUE PARTICULAR MACROECONOMIC POLICIES

Why do governments in developing countries often follow macroeconomic policies that discriminate against rural producers in favor of urban consumers? Why do they sometimes change course and introduce policy adjustments that partially reverse this discrimination? Political leadership and individual personalities play an important role; at the simplest level, governments follow policies that respond to the balance of political power within their countries. They distribute income in particular ways to help certain sectors, correct past problems such as external debts, reduce inflation, and react to changing world conditions that are beyond their control. Because food is a wage good (i.e., food is a high proportion of consumer budgets in developing countries), the interests of urban consumers coincide with owners of industrial firms. Consumers view lower-priced food as higher real wages, while industrialists see it as serving to decrease upward pressure on nominal wages. Thus, an overvalued exchange rate, for example, is a tempting quick fix for stimulating some forms of industrial growth, distributing income toward politically influential urban consumers and industrialists, and reducing inflationary pressures. If industries are exporters, however, the overvalued exchange rate will make their products less competitive in international markets.

The growth stimulus of macroeconomic intervention is often short-lived. Discrimination against agriculture reduces agricultural growth and investment and foreign exchange earnings from agricultural exports. A severely overvalued exchange rate can turn a food exporter into a food importer. Rural opposition to the macro-policies increases over time, inflation worsens due to higher food prices, and unemployment grows. Then, because pressures from urban groups continue, governments may subsidize agricultural inputs, raise output prices through subsidized market margins for food staples, and undertake other measures to reduce prices to consumers. In other words, they pursue partially offsetting policies. Governments institute such complex policies due to political expediency. Urban consumers and industrialists are potent pressure groups that demand low food prices and relatively more public goods for urban compared to rural areas.

Transactions costs and collective action

Both macroeconomic interventions and sector policies provide benefits to politically favored groups. Individuals may belong to several groups and may be simultaneously helped and harmed by different policies. The net benefit obtained from policy, often called political rents, is rarely clear. Macro-policy interventions are particularly difficult to observe. Thus, governments may provide direct subsidies to agricultural producers that are more than offset by overvalued exchange rates and still appear to be helping farmers. Food prices are kept low in urban areas, at least in the short run, and urban industrialists and civil servants, with better information than most farmers, press for the continuation of exchange rate distortions and other forms of protection that benefit the urban sector.

Rural and urban households can form coalitions and lobby collectively for their interests. The policy preferences of politicians and other government officials are affected by the relative strength of these rural and urban lobby groups. The urban lobby is often quite strong because it may represent a coalition of households, students, civil servants, military factions, labor unions, and industrialists.

It is not the sheer size of the urban lobby that gives it power to influence policy. The rural lobby is even larger in many developing countries. However, the urban lobby is much more concentrated geographically, and this concentration facilitates its ability to organize. Students are concentrated near universities, civil servants in government offices, and labor unions and industrialists in a relatively small, concentrated formal sector. The military is highly organized. If people decide to protest rising food prices, the costs of organizing and coming together for this purpose are relatively small in urban areas.

Because the urban lobby is made up of relatively small but homogeneous groups, members of these groups see the benefits of organizing collectively to press for their interests. Rural interest groups, particularly small-scale farmers, are so geographically dispersed that individual members often see few benefits to themselves. Communication is difficult so that even if collective benefits are perceived, the costs of organization and action are prohibitively high. Ironically, as development proceeds and the agricultural sector declines in relative and absolute size, its ability to organize and lobby often increases. Also, the cost to the government of subsidizing a small agricultural sector is lower than a larger sector. Therefore, once a country is relatively well-developed, it usually reduces its discrimination against agriculture. Over the past 20 years, we have witnessed this reduction in several developing countries, particularly those in Asia.

Sometimes government policies are motivated by corruption among politicians and other officials. Policy distortion creates gains for certain groups, and some of these gains are appropriated by individuals in public service as payment for instituting the policies.

Historical factors, structural adjustment, and external forces

A government is constrained by the accumulated effects of past policy choices interacting with worldwide economic conditions. One of the most dramatic examples of history colliding with external forces involves government debt. It is natural for developing countries to go into debt to some degree, but at the start of the 1980s, there was a simultaneous increase in international real interest rates and decline in world commodity prices that sharply increased the difficulty of repayment. Many countries, particularly in Latin America and in Africa, had no choice but to devalue their currencies and cut consumption expenditures in an effort to generate more foreign exchange. Similarly, painful "structural adjustment" programs were urged on other countries in the 1990s, when their sources of capital suddenly disappeared. The term "structural adjustment" is often associated with policies aimed at repaying government debt, usually foreign debt. This adjustment typically involves a devaluation of the foreign exchange rate to increase exports and reduce imports, a reduction in government spending and increase in tax collection, sale of government assets and the removal of restrictions on economic activity. The devaluation, privatization, and various types of liberalization may be needed because external debts cannot be reduced without earning or saving foreign exchange. Reduced government spending and increased efficiency in tax collection can bring spending more in line with revenues. The removal of policy distortions is needed to stimulate economic growth, although growth effects may take several years.

Some policy changes are made necessary by changing world economic conditions. A recession in the industrialized countries, for example, can reduce the demand for products from developing countries. High interest rates elsewhere in the world can exacerbate debt problems for developing countries. A shock to the oil market can strain exchange reserves for countries without petroleum. A recent example is the extreme shock

The poorest of the poor may need to be protected by targeted food subsidies during "structural adjustment"

that reverberated around the world during the global pandemic caused by coronavirus disease 2019 (COVID-19). The virus originated in China but quickly spread around the world, forcing economy-wide lockdowns. Policy changes are necessitated just to react to these external forces. In the next section, we examine how world macroeconomic linkages occur and how they affect developing countries.

WORLD MACROECONOMIC RELATIONSHIPS

Since the end of World War II, when there was virtually no international capital market, the international monetary system has grown to the point that transfers of capital between countries dwarf the value of international trade in goods. Capital flows ensure a close link between interest rates and exchange rates across countries and heavily influence countries' trade and their fiscal and monetary policy options.

A major change in the structure of the international economy was the shift, beginning in 1973, from a system of fixed exchange rates to one of bloc-floating exchange rates. With the fixed system, currencies around the world were fixed for long periods of time against the dollar.[2]

With the bloc-floating system, the values of major currencies are allowed to change rapidly against each other in response to market conditions. Some developing-country currencies, however, remain fixed to the major floating currencies such as the U.S. dollar.

Implications of well-integrated capital markets and bloc-floating exchange rates

A well-integrated international capital market and bloc-floating exchange rates mean that interest rates, capital movements, exchange rates, and trade are interconnected. They mean that fiscal and monetary policies in each country are tied into a single global macro-economy, with a common core rate of inflation and interest rates. For example, when the United States issues bonds to pay for a government budget deficit, the capital to buy those bonds usually comes from a wide range of foreign and domestic sources. The foreign purchase of U.S. bonds increases the demand for dollars, driving up the value of the dollar. It also reduces the capital available for other purposes, raising worldwide interest rates. The higher interest rate makes it harder for developing countries to pay off their remaining foreign debt, forcing them to reduce consumption more than they otherwise would.[3]

A higher value of the dollar makes U.S. exports more expensive abroad and encourages imports into the United States. Developing countries with currencies that are tied to the dollar will also find it harder to export and easier to import. Then, tradable goods sectors, such as agriculture, in those countries suffer from downward pressure on prices.

Governments often try to partially isolate their domestic agricultural sectors from changes in international markets, but any such isolation would mean loss of gains from trade and from access to foreign capital to facilitate development. Consequently, developing countries usually choose to absorb a certain amount of instability in interest rates, exchange rates, etc., caused by world macroeconomic forces in order to benefit from international goods and capital markets. These countries, however, may need to: (1) protect the poorest of the poor through targeted food subsidies or other means of ensuring basic food security, and (2) take full advantage of international schemes aimed at stabilizing foreign exchange, such as the compensatory finance arrangements discussed in Chapter 17. The International Monetary Fund (IMF) plays a role in helping to stabilize developing-country economies during financial crises. In a sense, the IMF is the closest thing the world has to an international central bank. However, the relatively small resource base of that institution and the lack of explicit mandate keeps its role circumscribed.

Changes in international comparative and competitive advantage

Comparative advantage increasingly is less influenced by physical resource endowments and more by human capital endowments. Government spending on education and agricultural research and the rapid international diffusion of certain technologies, particularly biotechnology, has the potential to influence human capital accumulation in many developing countries by improving education, nutrition, and incomes. These changes may eventually lead to restructured trade patterns.

Government macroeconomic and sector policies, however, can suppress underlying comparative advantage and distort a national economy away from what the physical and human resource base would seem to dictate. As exchange rates swing, so too does competitive advantage, in directions discussed previously. For example, a long decline in the value of the U.S. dollar can mislead U.S. producers and producers in other countries about their long-term ability to compete. A sustained rise in the value of the dollar can send opposite but still misleading signals. These movements can be induced by U.S. and foreign government macroeconomic policies that do not reflect any changes in fundamental comparative advantage.

The external debt problem: causes, effects, and potential solutions

It is natural for the governments of developing countries to borrow to finance productive investment. As long as a country has investment opportunities in the public or private sector that yield returns comfortably above the cost of funds in the world market, then such investments should be made even if external borrowing is required. The country will grow more rapidly and can export to repay the loans in the future. A country may also borrow at times to finance consumption, a policy that would be appropriate, for example, if a natural disaster or a short-run economic shock such as a pandemic makes it reasonable to sustain consumption even though current income is lower.

Borrowing is imprudent, however, when the debt is increased to cover longer-run consumption, questionable investments, large government deficits, or capital flight out of the country.[4] Imprudent, large-scale borrowing by the government occurred in many developing countries during the 1970s, particularly in Latin America and sub-Saharan Africa. The result was a *debt problem* that began in the early 1980s and has only slowly receded, until the recent COVID-19 pandemic increased it again. When a country has a debt problem, it lacks foreign exchange to make payment of interest and principal on its loans.

Causes of the debt problem

When a country makes more payments to the rest of the world than it receives in payments, it has a *current account deficit* (see Box 18.3). It has to sell off assets or borrow to finance the deficit. Several developing countries began running abnormally large current account deficits in 1973 when the price of oil skyrocketed. During the 1970s, commercial banks received a flood of dollars from the oil-producing countries. The banks loaned these dollars to developing countries to finance their current account deficits. Several Latin American and Asian countries appeared to be good risks because they had been growing rapidly. In Africa, growth had, for the most part, not occurred, but countries there borrowed from official sources such as the World Bank for development purposes.

By 1980, many developing countries were heavily in debt, which became hard to repay when worldwide interest rates rose sharply due to tight monetary policy in the United States and Britain. Debt repayment became even harder when a world recession struck in the early 1980s, depressing demands for exports from developing countries. The first reaction of countries seriously in debt was to refinance the loans and spread them out over a longer period of time. Several countries, however, found it difficult to service their debts (make scheduled interest and principal payments) or to acquire new funds. For Latin America, debt servicing exceeded 50 percent of the value of the region's exports during the early 1980s, and much of the debt was owed on loans at variable interest rates that were rising.

The first of the large debtors to announce it could no longer service its debts was Mexico in 1982. Other countries followed and the world community had a major financial problem on its hands. By 1986, more

---

BOX 18.3 CURRENT ACCOUNT DEFICIT

The current account deficit represents the excess of spending on imports and interest payments on the external debt over export revenues. In other words, it equals the trade deficit plus interest payments. The current account deficit in a particular year also represents the increase in the net debt for a country. Unless the trade surplus is large enough, the mere existence of an external debt means that interest on that debt will cause the debt to keep growing.

than 40 countries in Latin America, Africa, and elsewhere had encountered severe financial difficulties. Except for the Philippines, countries in Asia largely escaped severe debt problems.

Comparisons of the external debt situation between 1970 and 2017 for low income, middle-income, and several individual countries are presented in Table 18.1. For developing countries, external debts as a percent of GNP were two to three times as great in 1990 as they were in 1970. By 1990, developing countries owed more than a $1.3 trillion. Debt service was running more than $100 billion per year. Twelve of the 17 countries identified by the World Bank as heavily indebted were in Latin America and the Caribbean. Africa's debt of more than $110 billion was three times the value of all its annual exports. Cote d'Ivoire provides an example of the severity of the debt problem: with a population of 12 million in 1990, it owed $15 billion or $1250 per citizen in a country with an annual per capita income of about $800. Forty percent of the country's export receipts were needed just to service the debt.

After 2000, there was gradual debt reduction in most developing countries until 2010, especially middle-income countries. Since then, debt levels have crept up again for many countries. Some attempts have been made to forgive debts for the most highly indebted, least-developed counties, and economic growth in several Latin American countries and the Philippines reduced debt problems there until recently. A number of Latin American and East Asian countries have experienced other

Table 18.1 Indicators of Debt Service for Developing Countries

Country or country group	External debt service as a percentage of gross national income					
	1970	1980	1990	2000	2010	2017
Low income	17	44	88	83	26	30
Middle income	10	20	33	34	22	25
Colombia	33	21	46	35	23	41
Brazil	14	32	27	39	16	27
Morocco	25	46	85	55	30	46
Philippines	33	54	70	62	27	19
Cote d'Ivoire	26	77	187	124	49	34
Nigeria	7	15	120	80	4	11
Niger	5	35	73	97	27	42
Cameroon	14	46	61	111	12	30

Source: World Bank, World Development Indicators Online Database

short-term financial crises over the past three decades, but the roots of those problems are distinct from debt crises.

Effects of the debt problem

When a country attempts to reduce its external debt, domestic consumption must be cut to free up resources to produce goods that can be exported to earn foreign currency for debt service. Reductions in import demand are needed to save foreign exchange. Not all of the reduced spending affects traded goods. Some of it falls on non-traded goods and services when labor and capital shift to production of traded goods for export.

Within the country, prices of traded goods must rise relative to wages and other prices to encourage production of traded goods and to discourage domestic consumption. Exchange rate devaluation is one means of bringing about these adjustments in relative prices. Devaluation, however, takes time to have the desired effect. Thus, policymakers typically find ways to reduce imports in the short term by means such as tariffs or import quotas. Because some of the imports are raw materials or producer inputs, economic growth often is slowed as well.

Spending cuts and devaluations are painful because they inherently involve reductions in real income for the country. The cuts usually include reductions in basic services for the poor. Devaluations effectively cut real wages. As a currency is devalued, the country has to give up more in terms of domestic resources to earn each unit of foreign currency. The country is essentially selling its labor and other resources more cheaply on world markets.

Some developing countries had overvalued exchange rates prior to their debt problems; thus, adjustments were needed irrespective of the debts. The devaluations raised the domestic prices of many agricultural products, helping the farm sector. However, the resulting higher food prices hurt the poor disproportionately.

When countries can no longer borrow enough to meet shortfalls, they often loosen the money supply by printing money or other means. Printing money usually increases inflation. Devaluation and import restrictions contribute to these inflationary tendencies. They also hurt markets for U.S. farm products.

When the debt crisis first hit, a major concern was the impending peril to the world financial system. The fear was that countries such as Mexico, Brazil, and Argentina would default on their loans, causing large commercial banks to go bankrupt. The threat to the banking community eventually receded as threatened banks reduced their outstanding loans to developing countries and increased their revenues set aside to cover disruptions in debt service. The threat to the poor in developing countries, however, receded slowly.

Solutions to debt problems

External debt problems of developing countries impose costs on debtors and creditors. One potential solution is for developing countries to default on the loans. Total default would have the advantage of relieving pressures to cut government spending and to export more to service the debt. The disadvantages are that the creditors might seize debtors' overseas assets, and creditors might seize payments to firms that attempt to export to the debtor and payments made by firms that attempt to import from it. Thus, the country might lose some potential gains from trade. In addition, the country might find future borrowing more difficult. As a result, relatively few countries have totally defaulted on their loans.

When considering solutions to debt problems, it is important to separate the two different groups of countries whose governments have large debt problems. One group consists of low-income, mostly African countries that owe money largely to governments or to multilateral lending agencies. The second group is composed of countries, primarily in Latin America, that owe money mainly to commercial banks.

Because the lowest-income debtors owe mostly to governments, the creditor countries can mandate debt relief or restructuring without interfering in private international capital markets. Creditors can respond to the debt crisis in ways consistent with their humanitarian beliefs or foreign policy objectives. Low-income debtor countries can turn to the Paris Club for help with debt relief, such as extending the repayment period or granting a moratorium on payments during short-term crises (see Box 18.4). Partial debt forgiveness for some of the poorest countries has occurred. The Enhanced Heavily Indebted Poor Country (HIPC) debt relief initiative, established by the World Bank and IMF in 1996, reduced debt for 28 HIPCs, and the Multilateral Debt Relief Initiative agreed to by G8 countries in 2005 provided additional debt relief to HIPCs. Recent increases in debt for African countries is largely due to loans from China. The COVID-19 pandemic that began in 2020 is making these loans difficult to repay.

The solutions to debt problems for the countries with commercial debts are different from those for the HIPCs because solutions operate within the context of international capital markets. Any solution will affect the distribution of the debt burden among debtors, private creditors, and the public in creditor countries.

BOX 18.4 THE PARIS CLUB

The Paris Club is a forum for negotiations on countries' debts to government creditors. The Club, formed in 1956 in response to Argentine debt difficulties, has no set membership. The participants in any Paris Club negotiation are the debtor government and its creditors, who traditionally meet under the chairmanship of a senior French treasury official. All creditors are treated equally in Paris Club rescheduling negotiations. Debtor countries approaching the Paris Club are usually required to conclude an agreement with the IMF for an IMF loan and an IMF-approved program for restructuring economic policies. An example of IMF conditions would be reductions in government spending and fewer restrictions on exports.

Source: P. Krugman and M. Obstfeld, *International Economics* (Cambridge, MA: MIT Press, 1988), p. 596

Potential solutions to the commercial debt problem include: debt rescheduling, restructuring of economic policies within debtor nations, debt-for-equity swaps, cash buybacks of debt, debt-for-conservation swaps, to name a few, as well as "growing out of debt". Debt rescheduling involves extending the repayment period for loans, altering interest rates, and forgiving part of the principal. Efforts to restructure economic policies involve reducing exchange rates to discourage imports and to encourage exports, cutting government spending, and otherwise liberalizing the economy through reduced government intervention in markets and marketing.

Most countries' debt sells at a discount on a secondary market in which the debt can be shifted from bank to bank or to other institutions. The debt sells at a discount because creditors believe they will not be repaid in full. For example, each dollar of Peru's debt sold for about 5 cents on the secondary market in 1991. Debtor countries can sometimes buy back part of their debt with cash or by swapping government-owned assets (such as stock in publicly owned companies). Unfortunately, the secondary value goes up as countries attempt to buy back their own debt. In a few cases, for example in Costa Rica, outside groups bought up and eliminated part of the debt in exchange for government assurances of protecting rainforests or other natural resources. This type of activity is called a debt-for-conservation (nature) swap.

Rescheduling debts over a longer period of time at fixed but below market interest rates would eventually solve debt problems because countries could grow out of their debt. However, no single bank has an incentive to act alone. Debt reduction, like domestic bankruptcy, needs an institutional setting to bring it about. Even when it is in the collective interests of the banks to reduce the debt, each bank has an incentive to insist on full payment of its own loans. If one bank does grant a concession to lower the interest rate or principal, it becomes more likely that other banks will collect their loans. Hence, each bank waits around for other banks to voluntarily reduce the interest rate or principal owed so they can get a "free ride".

Developed countries have been reluctant to play too large a role in debt relief for fear of large budget expenditures. While there have been humanitarian grounds for debt relief through Paris Club negotiations for the poorest countries, the arguments carry less weight for debt relief in Latin America if that relief comes at the expense of foreign assistance to even poorer countries in Africa and Asia. The solution for Latin American countries has been primarily to reduce the debt burden as a proportion of national incomes through gradual economic growth. However, the economies of many Latin American countries struggled throughout the 2010s and are now suffering severely under the COVID-19 pandemic, which makes growing out of debt extremely difficult.

In late 2020, many of the largest countries of the world signed on to a "common framework" for relieving debts of the poorest 73 countries. The framework is limited, requires debtors to submit to IMF-style policy prescriptions, and for all public creditors to do their share. Additional cooperation on debt relief is needed.

Financial crises in Latin America and Asia

In the 1990s, a series of shorter-run financial crises occurred in Latin America (1994–95), East Asia (1997), Russia (1998), and Brazil (1998–99). The impacts of the crises spread to other countries and regions. There were some similarities among the crises. In most cases, there were increased private capital flows into the countries shortly before the crises, including both bank lending and private investments. The IMF gradually had relaxed its rules on capital flows and encouraged capital movements. Real exchange rates generally had appreciated as well, especially in Mexico and Thailand. When investors became nervous, they pulled their money out and the governments were forced to let their currencies depreciate. Problems worsened when neighboring countries were forced to depreciate their currencies and investors withdrew their money. As capital dried up in the affected countries, investment stalled, and the countries went into deep recessions. In some cases, the countries had problems with deficit spending or inflation before these crises, but in many cases not.

The crises demonstrated that completely deregulated capital flows carry both benefits and costs. Advantages to the borrowers include resources to finance investments with high social returns and to compensate for balance of payments problems and recessions. The disadvantages are that foreign investors might withdraw their money quickly, thereby destabilizing the economy. Also, the money may go toward projects that are too risky if the investors think that the government or the IMF will bail them out. In addition, capital flows can affect the exchange rate. If capital suddenly starts to flow out, the government must choose between higher interest rates or depreciation of the exchange rate.[5]

Governments can reduce the chances of financial crises by stronger regulation of domestic banking and financial institutions, and improving information flows with respect to economic and financial conditions. The IMF can assist by helping devise solutions in times of crisis while providing some financial assistance when private funds are not available. The IMF must distinguish between countries that are being fiscally irresponsible from those that are financially sound but are suffering sudden capital outflows due to temporary regional or global events.

Governments cannot simultaneously fix the value of the exchange rate and use macroeconomic policy tools to offset economic problems if capital is allowed to flow in or out of the country freely. Therefore, some countries choose to have a flexible exchange rate with relatively free capital flows allowing more flexibility in their macroeconomic policies. Others choose to fix their exchange rates and institute some controls on capital flows to minimize the danger of financial crises. This combination also allows more macroeconomic policy flexibility. A third group of countries decide to fix their exchange rates and allow free capital flows but give up the ability to influence their macro-economies. The latter countries are usually small ones with major trading partners to which they tie their currency. They also want to encourage strong foreign capital investment, and therefore do not want to institute capital controls.

SUMMARY

Macroeconomic policies have a strong influence on prices and marketing margins, and hence on incentives for economic agents. A macro-economy can be described in terms of aggregate demand, supply, or income.

Policies in developing countries are frequently aimed at the supply side of the economy. Both fiscal and monetary policies influence inflation. Developing countries often go into debt because of many pressing needs and limited tax revenues.

Governments use foreign exchange rates, interest rates, and wage rates to influence trade, investment, and incomes. Some developing countries overvalue their exchange rates, a policy which discourages exports and encourages imports. They often subsidize interest rates. Agricultural and land prices are influenced by macroeconomic policies.

Governments pursue particular macroeconomic policies to stimulate economic growth, distribute income, correct debt problems, lower inflation, and so on. Policies are influenced to a large extent by urban lobbies. Forces external to the country also come into play. Well-integrated capital markets and bloc-floating exchange rates tie economic policies of developing to developed countries.

While it is natural for governments in developing countries to borrow to finance investment, massive borrowing during the 1970s, followed by high interest rates and tight money in the early 1980s, led to a severe debt problem that has taken decades to solve. Many of the loans in Latin America were from commercial banks, and many of the loans in sub-Saharan Africa were from official sources. Countries were forced to adjust their economies by exporting more, importing less, and reducing government spending in order to pay off debts. The debt problem has only slowly been solved. Much of the burden of adjustment has fallen on the developing countries themselves. Structural adjustment programs often hurt the poor in the short run, highlighting the need for safety-net programs and debt forgiveness.

In recent years, several developing countries have experienced short-run financial crises in which private capital has flowed out rapidly, causing severe economic downturns. Capital controls are a possible remedy for capital outflows, but may come at the cost of reduced foreign investment. Some countries with flexible exchange rates choose to allow free capital flows, but then attempt to manage their macro-policies to offset the dangers of the sudden capital flows.

IMPORTANT TERMS AND CONCEPTS

Balance of payments	Fiscal policy
Bloc-floating exchange rate	Free rider
Capital flight	International capital market
Current account deficit	Macro-prices

Debt crisis
Debt-for-conservation swaps
Debt-for-equity swaps
Debt relief
Debt rescheduling
External debt
Financial crisis

Monetary policy
Money supply
Over-valued exchange rate
Paris Club
Secondary market
Structural adjustment program
Urban lobby

LOOKING AHEAD

International relations between more-developed and less-developed countries are influenced in major ways by foreign assistance programs. In the following chapter, we discuss the various types of foreign assistance, motivations for the aid, and effects on the less- and more-developed countries.

QUESTIONS FOR DISCUSSION

1 What are the three ways a macro-economy can be described so as to arrive at gross domestic product (GDP)?
2 What do we mean by a country's "fiscal policy"?
3 What are the two primary monetary policies that can be used to finance a government deficit, and what are their effects?
4 What are the major macro-prices that governments often try to set?
5 Why do countries overvalue their currencies, and what is the effect of overvaluation?
6 What are the advantages of high versus low interest rates?
7 How are wage rates determined, and what are the advantages and disadvantages of minimum wage laws?
8 How are land prices affected by macroeconomic policies?
9 Why do governments pursue particular macroeconomic policies?
10 How does a bloc-floating exchange rate system differ from a fixed exchange-rate system?
11 How are interest rates, capital movements, exchange rates, and trade interconnected?
12 How might a macroeconomic policy suppress the comparative advantage of a country in producing a particular good?
13 Why is it natural for developing countries to borrow from developed countries?
14 Describe the major causes of the debt crisis.

15 Why have many heavily indebted countries devalued their currencies?
16 Why has voluntary rescheduling of debt servicing by commercial banks not resolved the debt crisis?
17 Why are the urban poor often hurt more by structural adjustment than are semi-subsistence farmers?
18 What are the pros and cons of a developing country defaulting entirely on its debts?
19 What were the causes of financial crises in Asia and Latin America in the 1990s?
20 Who are the HIPCs?

NOTES

1 The *real* interest rate is equal to the nominal interest rate minus the rate of inflation.
2 The fixed exchange-rate system had been established at the Bretton-Woods Conference in 1944. Trade expanded rapidly under this system, but the system eventually became unworkable when certain currencies, particularly the U.S. dollar, became seriously overvalued and others, particularly the German deutschemark and Japanese yen, became severely undervalued.
3 Capital flows can also keep interest rates low in some cases. For example, in 2005, China eagerly purchased U.S. bonds even though interest rates were low, which meant that the United States did not have to raise interest rates to sell bonds to finance its budget deficit. These low rates kept the demand for home mortgages and other loans strong, stimulated the U.S. economy as people were willing to borrow and spend, and contributed to a bubble in the housing market. That bubble subsequently burst and the housing market collapsed with major recessionary implications.
4 Capital flight occurs when capital leaves a country due to perceived risk at home. Capital flight, however, is difficult to distinguish from normal capital flows. It often occurs when the government borrows foreign exchange and makes it available to residents at a subsidized price. People acquire this foreign exchange, if they can, and move it to banks or other investments abroad.
5 Joseph Joyce, "The IMF and Global Financial Crises", *Challenge*, vol. 43 (July–August 2000), p. 98.

RECOMMENDED READINGS

The Economist, "The Mundell-Fleming Trilemma: Two out of Three Ain't Bad", August 26, 2016, p. 51.
United Nations Conference on Trade and Development, *Sovereign Debt Crisis: From Relief to Resolution* (Washington, DC: UNCTAD Policy Brief No. 3, April 2012).

19 Capital flows, foreign assistance, and food aid

THIS CHAPTER

1 Examines the nature of public and private capital flows to developing countries, including the rationale for and major types of foreign assistance to agriculture
2 Discusses the types, objectives, and effects of food aid programs in less-developed countries
3 Identifies means for improving the effectiveness of foreign assistance.

DEVELOPMENT ASSISTANCE PROGRAMS RELATED TO AGRICULTURE

Flows of capital into developing countries can help overcome a shortage of capital relative to labor. Private capital flows, however, may be insufficient to meet development needs for several reasons. Restrictions on investments and other forms of capital flows in developing countries create risks for private investors, as do political and legal uncertainty and long gestation periods for projects. Many key forms of infrastructure, such as roads, have attributes of public goods, and it is difficult to charge for use of public goods. All these factors reduce the willingness of the private sector to undertake investments and, hence, can slow the flow of capital into developing countries. The absence of sufficient incentives to invest can also stem from incomplete development of international capital institutions. Foreign development assistance (aid) is one possible solution to help reduce the resulting capital imbalance, including assistance to the agricultural sector.

Foreign aid in support of agriculture in developing countries has taken many forms, and the nature and magnitude of its effects have generated considerable debate. Multiple objectives drive all foreign aid programs, with the result that the distribution of aid among different countries often bears little relation to need as manifested by hunger, poverty, or presence of market failure. Hence, we begin this chapter by examining the reasons for foreign assistance.

Rationale for foreign capital flows and assistance

From a donor's perspective, the rationale for foreign aid in general, as well as for aid to agriculture, rests on humanitarian (moral or ethical), political (strategic), and economic (commercial) grounds. Several variants of the humanitarian argument have been made based on compensation for past injustices, uneven distribution of global natural resources, and a moral obligation to help the least-advantaged members of society. The premise is that the emergence of international economic and political interdependencies has extended the moral basis for distributive justice from the national to the international sphere. Foreign assistance to agriculture can benefit one of the largest and poorest sectors in most developing countries.

The political self-interest rationale is based on the idea that aid will strengthen the political commitment of the recipient to the donor(s). Aid is often given during or immediately after wars and conflicts when there is an opportunity for political realignment or as part of a negotiated agreement to provide aid in exchange for certain political or military actions.

The argument that aid serves a country's economic self-interest is based on the idea that aid increases exports from and employment in the donor country. For example, producers of food grains in the United States benefit from food aid to the extent that it increases total quantities demanded. Food aid may open markets to a country's exports by initiating commercial contacts. In general, foreign aid to agriculture can improve nutrition and stimulate economic growth, thereby, in low-income countries, stimulating demand for agricultural imports and, by extension, donor exports. Much foreign assistance is tied to the purchase of goods, such as food or equipment, from the donor. These purchases directly benefit producers in the donor countries.

This complex set of reasons for foreign assistance means that foreign aid does not always go to where need is greatest. The fact that aid is

Table 19.1 Top Ten Recipients of U.S. Official Development Assistance

Rank	1960–1969	1970–1979	1980–1989	1990–1999	2000–2009	2010–2017
1	India	Israel	Israel	Egypt	Iraq	Afghanistan
2	Viet Nam	Viet Nam	Egypt	Israel	Afghanistan	Pakistan
3	Pakistan	India	El Salvador	Haiti	Egypt	Kenya
4	Korea	Egypt	Bangladesh	El Salvador	Colombia	Ethiopia
5	Brazil	Indonesia	Philippines	Philippines	Sudan	Iraq
6	Turkey	Pakistan	Pakistan	Somalia	Ethiopia	Jordan
7	Egypt	Korea	Sudan	Bolivia	Jordan	Tanzania
8	Chile	Bangladesh	Costa Rica	Nicaragua	Pakistan	Haiti
9	Indonesia	Cambodia	Honduras	Bangladesh	DRC	DRC
10	Taiwan	Jordan	Turkey	Peru	Kenya	Nigeria

Source: OECD, QWIDS Online Database

given in part for donor self-interest purposes would seem to impose on donors some obligation to ensure that the distribution and types of foreign assistance provided do not harm the recipients.

Most of the top ten recipients of U.S. foreign assistance by country over time, since 1960, are shown in Table 19.1. Most of the top ten recipients were in Asia, including a number of countries that later enjoyed rapid economic growth and earned high incomes as allies and commercial partners with the United States. Aid flows declined for many years, and the top ten list evolved in response to conflicts and peace accords. Israel and Egypt were the top recipients in the 1980s and 1990s. In recent years, total U.S. aid flows have almost doubled their level in the 1960s (in constant dollars), and Iraq and Afghanistan have risen to the top of the top ten list, while countries in sub-Saharan Africa have entered the top ten list, including D. R. Congo, Sudan, Ethiopia, Tanzania, and Nigeria.

Foreign aid in the context of other capital flows

Foreign aid is not the largest type of capital flow to developing countries. Larger flows occur in the private sector through private investment from abroad and through individual remittances from migrants abroad to their families back in developing countries. Private investment can be large, but flows are limited to particular sectors and countries and have fluctuated widely over the years. Remittances tend to be more stable than private investment, have grown rapidly, and are about three times as large as foreign aid. In 2019, the total amount of remittances received by low- and middle-income developing countries is estimated to have exceeded $554 billion, or more than 2 percent of their total income.[1] According the World Bank, the top recipients of officially recorded remittances in 2019 were India ($83 billion), China ($68 billion), Mexico ($38 billion), the Philippines ($35 billion), and Egypt ($27 billion). Other large recipients were Nigeria, Pakistan, Bangladesh, Vietnam, and Ukraine. As a percentage of GDP, the top recipients of remittances in 2012 were Haiti (37%), South Sudan (34%), Kyrgyz Republic (29%), Tajikistan (28%), Nepal (27%), Honduras (22%), and Lesotho (21%). Many of these remittances were sent back by young, well-educated migrants who transferred money for consumption by family members, although increasingly these funds have been used for investment purposes as well (see Box 19.1).

BOX 19.1 REMITTANCES AS A DEVELOPMENT TOOL

Remittance transfers are generally small amounts sent to family members through wire transfers, banks, or hand-carried to individuals in developing countries. Improving how remittances are transferred could have a big impact on development. Efficiency can be improved by lowering the costs and risks of transferring money through more cooperation and better regulation of international financial institutions. Steps are also needed to improve the enabling environment within recipient countries through reforms of banking systems, more transparent rules of access, encouraging acceptance of small-scale deposits, and so on. Incentives can be given for participation in the formal financial sector to help mobilize savings of remittance recipients and other potential small-scale customers. Steps to encourage use of remittance funds for private productive investments will channel these funds into capital accumulation and away from short-term consumption. Well-defined legal and regulatory frameworks will help build confidence of remitters to make productive investments and lower risks of losing their investments. Many of these steps would have the side benefit of mobilizing all forms of small-scale savings and investments, and this micro-finance can facilitate broad-based growth.

See Samuel Munzele Maimbo and Dilip Ratha, *Remittances: Development Impact and Future Prospects* (Washington, DC: World Bank, 2005).

Foreign aid is different from private investment or remittances in that, by definition, it uses government or philanthropic funds to serve a public purpose. Total foreign assistance encompasses official development assistance plus military assistance and export credits. Often, private funds from voluntary agencies are included. Foreign development assistance, as the term is used in this chapter, excludes the military-related component and export credits, while the term *official development assistance* (ODA) excludes private fund transfers as well. To qualify as any type of foreign assistance, the resources transferred must be sent from donor(s) to a recipient without a commensurate return flow of resources. Foreign assistance may be used to create good will, build political support, and so on, but direct payments to the donor country are not made in return.

At one extreme, foreign development assistance can occur as loans at near-market interest rates. At the other, this assistance can be an outright grant. In the middle, the assistance can be a loan at a concessional (below-market) interest rate or with a maturity period longer than that commercially available. Foreign development assistance also can come in the form of food aid or as technical assistance to provide needed expertise. To be classified as ODA by the Development Assistance Committee of the Organization for Economic Cooperation and Development (OECD), the assistance must have at least a 25 percent grant element.[2] The grant element is defined as the excess of the loan or grant's value over the (present) value of repayments calculated with a 10 percent interest rate.

Trends in ODA amounts are shown in Table 19.2. In the early 1960s, U.S. foreign aid was about 60 percent of global foreign aid. U.S. assistance then declined while others expanded their aid programs, such that by the 1990s the U.S. was giving only about one-sixth of the global aid total. In the early 2000s, ODA from the United States and other donors grew again, but has remained fairly stable in real terms for the last decade. Aid for agriculture declined until 2008 and then increased before stabilizing.

Development assistance programs

Modern foreign aid programs began after World War II with recovery assistance provided by the United States to war-torn Western Europe and East Asia. A wider U.S. development assistance program grew out of President Harry S. Truman's inaugural address of January 20, 1949. Truman called for a "bold new program for making the benefits of scientific advances and industrial progress available for the improvement and growth of underdeveloped areas".[3] The program provided technical

Table 19.2 United States and World Official Development Assistance (ODA), 1960–2019 (Millions, 2019 U.S. dollars)

Year	Total world ODA	U.S. ODA	US as % of total
1960	31,607	18,656	59.0
1965	40,855	25,329	62.0
1970	34.731	16,144	47.0
1975	49,164	15,364	31.2
1980	67,801	18,399	27.1
1985	59,210	19,293	32.6
1990	95,191	19959	21.0
1995	91,895	11,495	12.5
2000	77,511	14,284	18.4
2005	138,360	35,657	25.8
2010	149,981	34,618	23.1
2015	141,605	33,351	23.6
2016	153,740	36,516	23.8
2017	153,845	36,123	23.5
2018	152,502	34,337	22.5
2019	147,371	33,889	23.0

Source: OECD, QWIDS Online Database, 2020 (deflated by U.S. GDP price deflator to convert data to constant 2019 US$)

assistance to Taiwan, South Korea, and other countries in Southeast Asia, the Middle East, and the less-developed countries of Europe. The program was followed by other programs which were consolidated in 1961 to form the U.S. Agency for International Development (USAID). USAID remains the principal development assistance agency of the United States Government.

Other donor countries have development assistance efforts and similar agencies leading their foreign aid programs, such as the Japan International Cooperation Agency (JICA), the U.K. Department for International Development (DFID), and the Canadian International Development Agency (CIDA). During the 1950s, assistance was extended by the United Kingdom, France, the Netherlands, and Belgium to their former colonies. The list of donors grew during the 1960s and includes most members of OECD, many members of the Organization of Petroleum Exporting Countries (OPEC),[4] and other "emerging" donors such as China, Brazil, and Russia. Even though the U.S. gives more ODA than any other country, in recent years it has ranked near the bottom among OECD countries in terms of the ratio of ODA to GNI, a rough measure of the ability to "afford" aid. In 2019, it gave 0.16 percent, while the weighted average across all OECD countries was 0.30 percent.[5]

The actual content of foreign assistance programs varies widely over time and across donors. In 2019, the biggest area of emphasis for U.S. assistance was health and long-term economic development, short-term humanitarian emergency assistance, and improving governance institutions in developing countries. Governance received little aid in the 1970s, but such programs began to grow rapidly in the 1980s. The health area includes, among other programs, population, reproductive health, and HIV/AIDS prevention. Food aid was the largest area of focus in the 1970s and the 1980s, but has since fallen significantly. The agriculture, forestry, and fishery sector was the second largest sector in the 1970s and 1980s, but is now far down the list and included under the economic development and environment areas. Foreign assistance to agriculture includes such diverse components as aid used for agricultural research and extension, irrigation projects, rural roads, agricultural education and training, flood control projects, health and nutrition improvement programs, community development projects, and agricultural value chains and policy assistance. Comparing the aid allocations of the United States with those of other donors reveals that other donors place greater emphasis on aid to education and debt reduction.

Not all development assistance is administered through government agencies. Governments sometimes contract for aid delivery through non-profit, non-governmental organizations (NGOs), which are often also supported by private charitable donations and commercial activities.[6] Several of the largest nonprofit NGOs have religious affiliations, such as Catholic Relief Services or Lutheran World Relief; the biggest of these is a non-denominational Christian organization, World Vision International, whose operations in 2019 involved over $2.9 billion in revenue plus in-kind donations.[7] Most NGOs specialize in specific areas. For example, the International Committee of the Red Cross and Doctors without Borders specialize in the health sector, while Heifer International specializes in animal agriculture. Some NGOs have major advocacy programs, such as Oxfam and Bread for the World.

NGOs differ widely in their sources of revenue. For example, the Bangladesh Rural Advancement Committee (BRAC) is a large NGO providing micro-finance and other commercial services. In 2018, BRAC reported total expenditures of $728 million.[8] Development assistance can be channeled through for-profit firms as well as NGOs. The use of private contractors to deliver foreign aid services is particularly important for the United States, where firms routinely bid for contracts from USAID and other government agencies on a commercial basis.

Although most foreign aid funding comes from governments, private philanthropy also plays an important role in international development. The Rockefeller Foundation and other donor organizations made key contributions throughout the twentieth century. In the 1990s, large-scale philanthropy by individuals such as George Soros and Ted Turner became important, followed by major grants from Bill and Melinda Gates and from Warren Buffett, whose combined grant making contributed over $1.3 billion for global health and over $1.8 billion for global development in 2012. These and countless other acts of individual generosity, alongside the even larger taxpayer-funded programs, create many opportunities to meet new challenges. Managing aid in a cost-effective manner, however, is still a significant challenge.

Multilateral assistance programs

Much aid is bilateral, or country-to-country, but a second approach to giving and managing aid is for multiple donors to combine their resources through multilateral organizations in which donated funds are pooled and managed for a common purpose. Combining funds helps donors to leverage their contributions, obtain access to specialized professional staff and impartial management, and address problems best addressed through multi-nation efforts.

The leading multilateral organization for international development is the World Bank, which was created in 1944. Unlike other development agencies, the Bank disburses few donor funds as grants – and unlike other banks, it does not take deposits. Instead, the World Bank uses donor contributions to guarantee the repayment of funds borrowed from investors, and it then lends at low interest rates to developing countries. The World Bank has more than 180 country members and consists of three major arms that together represent the largest source of long-term multilateral economic development assistance. The first arm, the International Bank for Reconstruction and Development (IBRD), established in 1945, makes long-term loans at interest rates related to its own cost of borrowing, mostly for large-scale projects. The second arm, the International Development Association (IDA), established in 1960, uses profits on the IBRD loans and other funds to subsidize loans to the poorest 82 countries. Loans from IDA have 25–40-year repayment periods at little or no interest. IDA also provides grants and debt relief to countries with severe debt problems. The third arm, the International Finance Corporation (IFC), is a profit-making enterprise and is funded by capital from its member countries. It makes loans to the private sector, mixed (public/private) enterprises, and government-owned agencies that channel financial assistance to the private sector. Two other arms of the World Bank are the Multilateral Investment Guarantee Association (MIGA) and the International Centre for the Settlement of Investment Disputes.

In addition to the World Bank, there is a set of regional development banks for Latin America, the Caribbean, Asia, Africa, and Eastern Europe. These banks operate in a similar way to the World Bank, but on a smaller scale. The World Bank is also complemented by the International Monetary Fund (IMF), a sister organization whose purpose is to make short-term, emergency loans for macroeconomic stabilization, as opposed to the long-term development objectives of the multilateral banks. The World Bank and IMF are the major multilateral sources of development funding, but large numbers of technical staff provide assistance through the other UN agencies described in Box 19.2.

BOX 19.2 MAJOR UNITED NATIONS AGENCIES FOR FINANCIAL AND TECHNICAL ASSISTANCE TO DEVELOPING COUNTRIES

The *United Nations Development Programme* (UNDP) is the central funding and coordinating mechanism within the United Nations for technical assistance to developing countries.

The *United Nations Fund for Population Activities* (UNFPA) helps countries gather demographic information, undertake family planning projects, and formulate population policies and programs.

The *United Nations Children's Fund* (UNICEF) provides technical and financial assistance to developing countries for programs that benefit children and for emergency relief for mothers and children.

The purpose of the *Food and Agriculture Organization* (FAO) is to raise nutrition levels and standards of living by improving the production and distribution of food and other commodities derived from farms, fisheries, and forests. It also helps countries with food emergencies.

The *World Food Programme*'s (WFP) purpose is to stimulate economic and social development through the use of food aid and to provide emergency food relief.

The *World Health Organization* (WHO) conducts immunization campaigns, promotes and administers research, and provides technical assistance to improve health systems in developing countries.

The *United Nations Education, Scientific, and Cultural Organization* (UNESCO) promotes international intellectual cooperation in education, science, culture, and communications.

The UNDP, UNFPA, WFP, and UNICEF are funded through voluntary contributions, public and private, while FAO, WHO, and UNESCO are funded primarily through assessments on member nations with some additional voluntary contributions and other sources of funds.

Source: Details on UN agencies are provided at www.un.org

Effects of foreign assistance

The economic effects of development assistance on recipients are the regular subject of debate in the popular press and among policymakers. The effects of aid can be assessed at the project, the sector, or the national level. At the project level, rates of return have been calculated for individual investments such as roads, schools, or agricultural research. These calculations typically yield high returns: for example, the World Bank's independent evaluation group estimated the real rate of return for each of 396 projects that ended between 1995 and 2000, and found an average return of 22 percent per year.[9] This payoff is much higher than the interest paid to borrow these funds, which suggests that increased lending for similar investments would raise total economic growth rates.

Given the high rates of return to many aid projects, questions are raised about why private lending has not been more forthcoming, or why concessional loans are needed. An important part of the answer is that returns to aid are spread among the recipient population in ways that a private company could not capture to repay its investors. For example, aid that helps a small child avoid malnutrition or attend school can generate benefits far in excess of its cost, but those benefits cannot be seized by a lender. Indeed, aid is most effective when it focuses on precisely these kinds of public services that will not be provided by private firms. The developing country's own governments cannot provide enough of these public goods because they lack the tax base or administrative capacity to finance them, either from current revenues or to repay its own loans. As a result, public-sector development assistance from richer to poorer countries has an important role to play in making the world economy more efficient as well as more equitable.

At the sector or national levels, development assistance can augment domestic savings, help provide foreign exchange, and minimize adverse impacts of needed policy reforms. These effects can stimulate growth. Many studies have attempted to assess the impact of development assistance at the national level as it affects savings, investment, or growth. Generally, the results have been positive but, in many cases, inconclusive. The fundamental problem is that aid typically flows to countries in trouble and so is usually associated with bad economic outcomes, even though without aid the outcome might have been worse. Poor countries face many different kinds of problems, from natural disasters and disease to wars and corruption. A widely cited view suggests that aid has positive effects on growth only in countries with good fiscal, monetary and trade policies, but other studies suggest that aid has helped even in countries with weak governments.

The small size of aid relative to other capital sources, as described previously, undoubtedly has contributed to many of the inconclusive findings about the effects of aid on growth. It is also difficult to measure the effects of aid without breaking it down into its different types and the different reasons for which it is given. For example, aid for infrastructure may have different impacts on growth than aid for policy reform or for emergency food relief. Emergency food relief programs may be very effective at reducing hunger and human suffering associated with short-term problems, but their effects on aggregate growth can be hard to measure.

Despite a relatively weak link between aid and aggregate economic growth, for reasons outlined earlier, aid has helped reduce poverty and improved the quality of life of the poor. Targeted aid has helped eradicate smallpox, put polio on the brink of eradication, reduced death from diarrheal diseases, and reduced the incidence and severity of many illnesses. These results will, over time, contribute to economic growth and development, but their effects are indirect and hard to measure. Investments in education together with research and dissemination of new technologies may be among the most effective kinds of aid for reducing poverty, especially in Africa, where the level of such investment has been low and where rural poverty is particularly severe.[10]

Effects on donors

Many donor countries believe that development assistance is effective in stimulating growth in developing countries but ask whether the effects on their own countries are negative. In other words, they question whether their economic self-interest is served by aid. For example, farm groups and the farm press in the United States frequently express concern that foreign aid may be generating foreign competition. Several studies have assessed whether foreign aid to agriculture does indeed hurt U.S. farmers. These studies have found that for particular commodities in particular countries at particular stages of development, foreign competition is increased as a result of aid. However, they also have found that agriculture as a whole in donor countries is helped by foreign aid to agriculture in developing countries.[11]

One reason farmers in donor countries benefit from aid to agriculture in developing countries is that agricultural growth in developing nations increases incomes, and these incomes, in turn, stimulate food demand. Middle-income countries, particularly, still have relatively high population growth rates and high income elasticities of demand for food. Demands shift toward higher-quality grains and livestock products as incomes rise. Consequently, when agricultural production rises in these countries, if domestic economic policies permit that production growth to stimulate other sectors of the economy, the result is an expansion in food demand that must be met partially through food imports. Of course, when countries eventually reach higher incomes, their growth in food demand slows. If and when most of the currently developing countries reach that status, trade will be governed by comparative advantage and trade-distorting policies. Development assistance to agriculture will no longer be an issue.

In summary, while empirical evidence is not always conclusive about the effects of development assistance in general or to agriculture in particular, it appears that positive but modest gains are likely for both recipients and donors. It is unlikely that large gains will be realized except in a few small countries because aid usually represents a small portion of ODA.

FOOD AID

Food aid has been an important and controversial dimension of foreign assistance since the mid-1950s. Its importance relative to other kinds of aid has fallen over time, but it is still a significant component of U.S. foreign assistance. The United States has been the largest source of food aid since the enactment of the Agricultural Trade Development and Assistance Act of 1954, commonly referred to as Public Law (P.L.) 480, now called the Food for Peace program. Food aid once represented about one-half of U.S. grain exports, but in recent years it has declined to a small fraction of those exports. In 2018, the United States donated $4 billion in food aid as compared to selling $143 billion in agricultural exports.

The role and effects of food aid have been controversial because of its many purposes. Food aid fulfills a humanitarian and development mission, has helped, at least in the past, to dispose of commodity surpluses, and also serves foreign policy objectives. While this multiplicity of objectives has added instability over time to food aid allocations, it also has strengthened the political support for maintaining food-aid programs within the donor countries.

Critics of food aid have argued, among other things, that unrestricted cash donations would be preferable to food in the speed and cost with which it could be transferred. The recipient nation could then purchase food from the neatest and cheapest source. Since 2016, the use of cash in place of in-kind food donations to meet emergency food needs has expanded.

History of food aid

The history of food aid to developing countries is marked by shifting emphases on its multiple objectives. From 1959 to 1965, the United States and Canada were particularly concerned about disposal of farm surpluses, developing markets for farm products, and providing emergency food relief. Most of the aid provided during this period was in grain, but several other products were given, including tobacco (Box 19.3).

Food aid has helped alleviate hunger in Ethiopia

BOX 19.3 THE UNITED STATES P.L. 480 FOOD AID PROGRAM

Since 1954, most U.S. food aid activities have been coordinated under Public Law 480, the Food for Peace program. Numerous amendments and extensions have been added to the original act, but its major provisions fall under three titles:

Title I allows recipient governments to buy grain on credit with interest rates of 3 percent or less over 20 to 40 years, repayable in local currency. However, Title I is no longer funded. When it was funded, governments could sell the grain they received internally and use the profits for development. The low interest rates and long repayment period meant that almost 70 percent of the food aid loan was a grant. Title I was formerly the most important component of P.L. 480, but by the early 2000s, it had shrunk substantially, and by 2014, it was no longer funded at all.

Title II involves gifts of food for emergency relief and for economic development, and in 1991 it surpassed Title I as P.L. 480's largest component. It now accounts for the bulk of the program. Food is given to and distributed by private agencies such as CARE, who use the food for infant feeding programs and for mother and child health programs in addition to emergency distribution. Shipping and labor are paid for by the U.S. government. Food given under Title II also is used in food-for-work programs.

Title III involves using food aid in government-to-government programs to support economic development, but has not received funding since 2001.

Other titles in the U.S. food aid program exist, but food aid is now dwarfed by agricultural export credit programs that support commercial grain exports.

In 1961, an amendment was added to P.L. 480 to permit food to be used for economic development instead of being restricted to emergency relief. Improved export markets, led by demand growth in developing countries, reinforced the objective that food aid helps develop markets.

The era from 1966 to 1972 was a period of heavy use of food aid for emergency relief, particularly in drought-stricken areas of South Asia. Self-help of recipients also was promoted during this time. The United States, European Community, and Canada increased shipments of food aid for emergency relief in this period, which might be called the idealistic era of food aid.

Unfortunately, any idealism with respect to food aid programs was pretty much destroyed by the cutbacks in food aid that followed food price increases from 1972 to 1975. The United States had depleted its grain surplus by exporting commercially to the Soviet Union and other countries. From 1972 to 1973, U.S. commercial grain exports doubled and the volume of food aid fell in 1974 to its lowest level since the enactment of P.L. 480.

In 1975, the U.S. Congress instituted more humanitarian and development criteria for receiving food aid by passing the International Development and Food Assistance Act. This legislation called for increased food aid to the poorest countries. The remainder of the 1970s also saw increasing food aid quantities from EC countries. The use of food aid for political purposes also increased after 1975. For example, U.S. food aid to Bangladesh declined from 1.15 million tons in 1975 to 0.34 million tons in 1985, while food aid to Egypt increased from 0.58 to 2.00 million tons. This increase to Egypt was directly linked to the Camp David Peace Accord between Egypt and Israel, which was signed in 1979. Food aid quantities increased in the mid-1980s in response to severe drought problems in Ethiopia, the Sudan, and other sub-Saharan African countries. In the 1960s, most food aid went to Asia and Latin America. By the mid-1980s sub-Saharan Africa was absorbing as much food aid as the much more populous Asia.

Since the year 2000, the use of food aid for emergency assistance, as opposed to support for economic development, has expanded significantly. Much of the food aid flows to relieve suffering in conflict countries. In-kind food shipments remain important, but since 2016, the use of food vouchers and cash transfers for food have grown.

Types of food aid programs today

Emergency food aid grabs the headlines as it relieves suffering associated with droughts, flooding, and/or conflict in countries such as Ethiopia, South Sudan, Bangladesh, Afghanistan, Syria, Yemen, and Somalia. Emergency food aid is essential for reducing acute hunger problems. It is estimated that food aid under P.L. 480 has reached between 3 and 4 billion people in 150 countries since 1954. It helped feed tens of millions of people in 55 countries in 2019.

The possibilities of using food aid to foster long-term development are more closely linked to program or project food aid than to emergency food aid. These uses are more controversial than emergency food assistance, in part due to cost and in part due to fears that the food may discourage local food production.

Program food aid is, in many respects, similar to more general financial assistance, as it provides currency to buy imports, in this case food that can be sold or otherwise distributed in the domestic market. This aid fosters the development of marketing linkages with the donors, helps the recipients save foreign exchange, and the funds generated by food sales can be used for development. Some donors participate in determining how the funds generated by commodity sales are used. Donors may insist that funds be used for investments in the agricultural sector or to support specific policy changes affecting agriculture.

Project food aid is aimed at meeting specific development objectives. Projects tend to be multiyear, to be targeted at nutritionally vulnerable individuals or groups, and may involve food in exchange for work on the project. Donor and recipient countries agree on who will be targeted by the project, the amount of food each individual receives, the delivery system for the food, and the design, implementation, and monitoring of project activities. Most projects are in the rural sector and can vary in size from a few hundred thousand dollars to $100 million or more. Food aid projects may involve forestry development, soil conservation and watershed management, resettlement projects, training, development of irrigation works, and construction and maintenance of rural roads.

Effects of food aid

The positive and negative effects of food aid on recipient countries have been studied and debated for years. On the positive side, food provides real resources that can be used to expand investment and employment. Food aid can have a disproportionate but positive effect on disadvantaged groups, notably by supporting specific nutrition or food-for-work projects or by providing food to the poor for free or at subsidized prices. Food can be used to help recipient governments support storage and stabilization schemes to provide a small buffer against poor production years.

Food aid also can have adverse effects on the recipients. These potential adverse effects can occur in a number of ways: (1) disincentive effects on local agricultural production through reduced prices because of greater supply, (2) dependency effects because the government may substitute food aid for agricultural development programs, and (3) uncertainty of food aid quantities from year to year.

The disincentive issue has been examined empirically, and some studies have found a production disincentive, but most have not. The disincentive effect is minimized if food aid is given or sold to people who otherwise could not afford the food. Transferring food is like transferring income. The quantity of the aid compared to the country's overall food production is important. It appears that there has been a disincentive effect in Egypt due to the large quantities of aid shipped, but it is difficult to sort out the impact of food aid from other policy-induced distortions. Even when food aid reduces prices, it is likely to benefit the poor, who generally purchase more food grains than they sell.

The idea that food aid creates dependency has been examined less frequently than the disincentive issue. Food aid is no different from other aid in that, by providing resources, it may lead to less effort to raise revenues domestically or to promote agricultural development. Most donor countries find public opinion is generally supportive of food aid, especially when it is used in visible programs to prevent starvation.

Food aid is used in Kenya to help pay labor for road construction

SUMMARY

Foreign development assistance in support of agriculture in developing countries has been substantial, taken many forms, and generated considerable debate. The rationale for foreign aid rests on various political and economic interests as well as humanitarian grounds, so aid does not always go to where need is greatest. Aid may be channeled through government agencies, NGOs, or private contractors, and comes mainly from donor-country governments but also from charitable donations and philanthropies. Some aid is a simple grant, but much of it comes as loans at below-market interest rates. Foreign aid to agriculture includes aid for agricultural research and extension, irrigation projects, rural roads, agricultural policy assistance, and many other items.

The United States is the largest donor country, but the share of total ODA coming from the United States has declined over time. The U.S. has been active in giving food aid, which provides emergency relief in times of severe shortage, and supports specific development projects and programs. Food aid also provides a means for donor countries to pursue foreign policy objectives.

IMPORTANT TERMS AND CONCEPTS

Bilateral aid
Concessional interest rates
Economic self-interest
Food aid
Foreign development assistance
International Bank for
   Reconstruction
   and Development
International Finance Corporation

International Development
   Association
Multilateral aid
Non-governmental organization
Official development assistance
Public Law 480
The World Bank
U.S. Agency for International
   Development

LOOKING AHEAD

This chapter concludes the section of the book concerned with macroeconomic and international issues affecting development. The book concludes with a discussion of how the various components required for agricultural development can be combined in an overall strategy. An assessment of future development prospects is provided, and suggestions are made for how you as individuals can contribute to solving the world food–poverty–population problem.

QUESTIONS FOR DISCUSSION

1 What is the rationale for foreign development assistance?
2 What are the major types of foreign development assistance?
3 What are some of the major effects of foreign development assistance on recipients and donors?
4 Distinguish between bilateral and multilateral aid.
5 Give several examples of foreign aid to agriculture.
6 How do NGOs differ from official sources of foreign development assistance?
7 What are the three major arms of the World Bank and how do they differ?
8 Which country is currently the largest bilateral donor of foreign aid?
9 Why might foreign development assistance help U.S. farmers?
10 What are the objectives of food aid?
11 What is the case for and against food aid?
12 How have food aid programs changed over time?
13 What is the difference between program and project food aid?
14 Why might food aid have disincentive effects, and what might be done to minimize these effects?

NOTES

1 Data in this section are World Bank staff estimates, updated periodically and available online through www.worldbank.org/remittances.
2 The OECD is an organization of 30 industrialized nations designed to promote economic growth and stability among these relatively high-income countries and in the world as a whole.
3 Harry S. Truman, *Inaugural Address of the President* (Washington, DC: Department of State Bulletin 33, January 1949), p. 125.
4 OPEC is a group of countries devoted to seeking agreement among themselves regarding selling prices and other issues related to oil exports. OPEC members include Algeria, Ecuador, Gabon, Indonesia, Iran, Iraq, Kuwait, Libya, Nigeria, Qatar, Saudi Arabia, the United Arab Emirates, and Venezuela.
5 See https://data.oecd.org/oda/net-oda.htm#indicator-chart.
6 A detailed analysis of NGOs in U.S. foreign aid is provided by Rachel McCleary and Robert J Barro, "Private Voluntary Organizations Engaged in International

Assistance, 1939–2004", *Nonprofit and Voluntary Sector Quarterly*, vol. 37(3) (September 2008), pp. 512–536.

7 World Vision International, *Accountability Report 2019*, www.wvi.org.

8 BRAC, *Audited Financial Statements, Year Ended December 2018*, www.brac.net.

9 World Bank, *Annual Review of Development Effectiveness*, 2000, supplement Table 13a, www.worldbank.org.

10 See Colin Thirtle, Lin Lin, and Jenifer Piesse, "The Impact of Research-Led Agricultural Productivity Growth on Poverty Reduction in Africa, Asia and Latin America", *World Development*, vol. 12(31) (December 2003), pp. 1959–1975.

11 See, for example, David Kraybill, Stephanie Mercer, and Joseph Glauber, *How the United States Benefits from Agricultural and Food Security Investments in Developing Countries* (Washington, DC: BIFAD, 2019), pp. 1–43.

RECOMMENDED READINGS

Barrett, Christopher B., and Daniel G. Maxwell, *Food Aid After Fifty Years: Recasting Its Role* (New York: Routledge, 2005).

Collier, Paul, *The Bottom Billion* (New York: Oxford University Press, 2008).

Easterly, William, *The Elusive Quest for Growth* (Cambridge, MA: MIT Press, 2002).

Kraybill, David, Stephanie Mercer, and Joseph Glauber, *How the United States Benefits from Agricultural and Food Security Investments in Developing Countries* (Washington, DC: BIFAD, 2019).

Lancaster, Carol, *Foreign Aid: Diplomacy, Development, Domestic Politics* (Chicago: University of Chicago Press, 2007).

Norton, George W., *Hunger and Hope: Escaping Poverty and Achieving Food Security in Developing Countries* (Long Grove, IL: Waveland Press, 2014), Chapter 15: "Doing Well by Giving Goods".

Riddell, Roger, *Does Foreign Aid Really Work?* (Oxford: Oxford University Press, 2007).

20 Lessons and perspectives

THIS CHAPTER

1 Summarizes how the various components required for agricultural development can be combined to increase agricultural productivity and stimulate economic growth and development
2 Discusses how principles discussed in this book can be used to assess future prospects for agricultural development in developing countries
3 Suggests ways that individuals can contribute to reducing the food–poverty–population problem

AN INTEGRATED APPROACH TO AGRICULTURAL DEVELOPMENT

Substantial progress has been made in reducing poverty and hunger in the world, but major challenges remain to continue that progress, especially for a sizeable set of countries in sub-Saharan Africa. Climate change, conflicts, pandemics, resistance to trade and migration, growing water scarcity, soil degradation, and rising inequality are just some of the headwinds that can stall or reverse the downwards trends in poverty and hunger experienced over the last 30 years. It is easy to get discouraged about prospects for eliminating human suffering in the world. Progress in sub-Saharan Africa and in parts of Asia and Latin America remains painfully slow. However, several countries, especially in Asia, have experienced rapid economic growth in recent years, with major reductions in poverty and hunger and improvements in health.

Many governments have actively sought scientific and policy solutions to the fundamental problems that cause human suffering, even as other governments seem oblivious or unconcerned. Over the past several years, numerous prescriptions have been implemented or suggested to accelerate agricultural development, although none has been universally successful. Import substitution, domestic and trade policy liberalization, land reform, foreign aid, education, privatization, integrated rural development projects, agricultural research, and other solutions have been offered. Some suggestions have contributed to development; others have not or have done little.

While economic development has been slow and uneven, the progress realized by some countries lends optimism for others. Globally, the percentage of people living in poverty fell from 35 percent in 1990 to about 10 percent in 2020, and the number of people in extreme poverty fell from 1.9 billion to 650 million. The absolute number of undernourished people fell from about 1 billion to 800 million despite rapid growth in population. While poverty and malnutrition rose during the COVID-19 pandemic, they may trend down again if countries cooperate and escape the trap of becoming too insular. Cooperation has helped the world survive difficult periods in the past and should do so in the future.

Several lessons have been learned about what is required to stimulate agricultural and overall economic development. One lesson is that there are no panaceas; development requires a mix of institutional and technical changes that work best in combination. Technical change is important but creates winners and losers. Institutional changes are required for not only efficiency improvements but also social protection. Institutions that are appropriate for one country will not necessarily work in another, but policies or institutions that provide incentives for investment, good behavior, and social protection are fundamental. A second lesson is that development takes time, and many of the research, infrastructure, and other investments necessary for long-run sustainable development have impacts long after they are implemented. This time lag requires patience and political stability. A third lesson is that developing countries are primarily responsible for their own development, although interdependence in trade and capital flows means that developed-country policies can assist or retard that development. A few years ago, the United Nations and its member states established a series of millennium development goals for 2015 that would significantly reduce poverty, hunger, and disease while promoting education, gender equality, and environmental sustainability.[1] Significant progress was been made toward achieving the goals, but few countries attained them in their entirety. In 2015,

UN countries adopted a new set of 17 Sustainable Development Goals (SDGs) for the world to achieve by 2030. The first three SDGs, no poverty, zero hunger, and good health and well-being, appear unattainable in light of the recent COVID-19 pandemic, but significant progress is possible if not likely once the pandemic passes.

In *Economics of Agricultural Development*, you have examined the many dimensions of world food–poverty problem (see top of Figure 20.1). You have considered the interconnections among these problems and their linkages to nutrition, health, population, and the

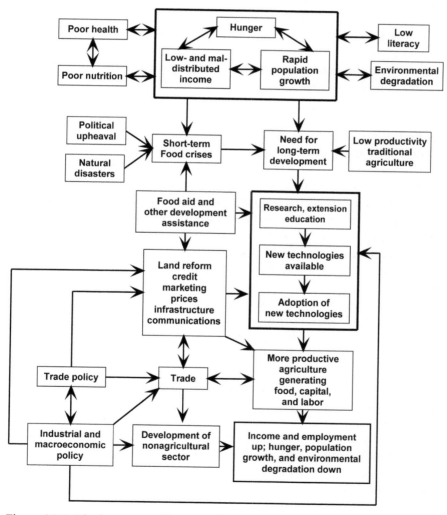

Figure 20.1 The hunger problem and the solution process

environment. There is enough total food in the world at the moment, but hunger is caused by food price volatility and conflict and by distributional problems that cause poverty. There are short-term food crises and long-term or chronic malnutrition. You have considered economic development theories, the role of agriculture in those theories, and the nature of existing agricultural systems. You have learned that most developing-country farmers are relatively efficient at what they do, but have low productivity because of their limited access to resources, their existing technological and institutional environments, and the pervasive climatic, market, and other risks they face. Having learned something about the dimensions of the problem, the role of agriculture in economic development theories, and the nature of agriculture in developing countries, you then examined several components of the development process. Let's review the inter-relationships among those components and assess where the need is greatest for additional insights with respect to the development process.

Technical and institutional change in agriculture

In the 1950s, many development experts felt that the keys to agricultural development were capital investment and the transfer of technologies from more-developed countries. By the 1960s and 1970s, it was clear that technology transfers and capital investment had a role, but that other factors were equally or more important. Differences in resource bases across countries meant that indigenous research and extension were crucial. Education was required if countries were to produce, adapt, transfer, and receive new technologies. By the 1990s, countries that were successful in agricultural development had put in place a research and technology transfer system that included: (1) agricultural research stations and educational institutions, (2) a mechanism for linking those stations to on-farm research and testing, and (3) ties between the national research system and the international agricultural research and training network.

As important as local capacity for agricultural research and extension is, the last several years have also demonstrated the need for a series of policy or institutional reforms related to the agricultural sector. These reforms have proved important because of not only their influence on production incentives and the distribution of economic gains, but also their influence on the types of technologies produced and adopted. Land reform, improved credit policies, expanded and more efficient agricultural marketing systems, nondiscriminatory pricing policies, rules on intellectual property protection, efficient means of managing risks, and incentive systems to reduce environmental externalities are examples of the institutional changes that may be required.

New technologies are not gifts of nature, and institutional changes do not magically appear. New technologies require research investments, and the levels and types of technologies produced and subsequently adopted are influenced by changes in relative prices of inputs and outputs. Institutional changes also are induced by changes in relative prices and by technical change.

The logic of the induced technical and institutional change theories and their apparent empirical verification in several countries, particularly in East Asia, give cause for optimism. However, the failure of many countries to follow a path of sustained development has forced economists to broaden the induced innovation theory. This broadening has come by incorporating transactions costs and collective action into the theory, and closer attention to human behavior.

The fact that information is not perfect and is costly to acquire, and that people are willing to exploit a situation at the expense of others, has received particular attention. If one group has greater access to information than another, that group can – and is likely to – act collectively to press for policies or new technologies that benefit it at the expense of others. If a small but wealthy elite with large landholdings finds it cheaper to acquire information and act collectively, it may press for technical and institutional changes for personal benefit at the expense of the masses. The elite may press for changes that not only distribute income in its favor but also reduce agricultural growth because the resulting technologies and policies may not be appropriate for the resource base in the country.

Factors that can help reduce transactions costs are those factors that reduce information costs. Improved roads and communications infrastructure are examples, and new communications technologies can have dramatic impacts even in remote areas. More widespread access to market information is allowing producers to make decisions that increase economic efficiency. Widespread access to education is also critical, as education allows people to better use information. Changes in land policies can help in some countries, as can institutional change to enhance contracting, improve the legal infrastructure, and provide certain types of regulations.[2] In some cases, freer markets to provide efficient price signals to individual farmers are needed. As development occurs, agricultural marketing chains become longer and more complex, necessitating government rules and regulations to guide a largely private marketing sector.

Markets are generally held to be the best means of transmitting signals to actors. In developing countries, however, market imperfections due

Young boys in Guatemala

to transactions costs, unequal asset distributions, and other factors are the norm. These factors reduce efficiency but also increase variability in prices and exacerbate risks for producers and consumers. Public sector involvement is legitimate and necessary to reduce these imperfections and allow markets to function. Government involvement can be justified to provide "public goods", to create equal access to opportunities, and to achieve equity outcomes consistent with society's wishes.

Macroeconomic and international institutional changes

In the 1950s and 1960s (and to some extent before and after), some economists in developing countries recommended policies that discouraged agricultural exports and encouraged production of goods that would substitute for imports. The argument for these policies was based on potential or perceived exploitation of developing countries by more-developed countries, and recently by the concerns over market disruptions during pandemics. However, countries that have integrated more closely into international markets have tended to develop more rapidly than those that have closed or isolated their economies. The more rapid development is due in part to the lower level of rent-seeking behavior and corruption as well as the increased efficiency gains from trade and specialization.

Some countries that discriminated against agricultural trade encouraged capital-intensive imports, causing capital-intensive industries to develop in labor-abundant countries. These industries placed a drag on economic development because human resources, freed up by increases in agricultural productivity, were under-employed.

For more than four decades, several developing countries have suffered from heavy external indebtedness. Some debt reduction for the lowest-income, heavily indebted countries has occurred, but gradual economic growth that reduces debt as a proportion of the national income is the primary means of resolving the debt problem for most countries. Economic stimulus programs in response to COVID-19 have sharply increased debt levels in many countries.

Continued efforts by developing countries to reduce overvalued exchange rates and to phase out policies such as export taxes can help to stimulate agricultural growth. Phasing out implicit or explicit taxes, however, will necessitate new mechanisms for generating government revenues, such as land or income taxes. These mechanisms become more feasible as land titling and information flows improve. New institutions will be needed along with increased government responsibilities. Reduced trade restrictions by developed countries as a result of negotiations under the auspices of the WTO and regional trade agreements have helped some developing countries, but additional trade liberalization and reduced restrictions on international migration are needed. The latter provides scarce labor in countries with low population growth rates and valuable remittances back to developing countries.

Capital flows and foreign assistance

Capital flows have provided a two-edged sword for many countries, particularly in Asia and Latin America. Capital inflows have helped stimulate investments and growth, but have led to financial crises when outflows occur rapidly over a short period of time. For example, the crisis that spread through East Asia in 1997 had devastating, if short-term, impacts on human welfare. The worldwide economic crisis that began with the freezing of lending by US and European banks in 2008 contributed to a recession whose economic growth and employment impacts were felt for a decade. Each developing country must decide upon the appropriate mix of regulations for capital flows, exchange rate policies, and freedom to adjust its macro-economic policies. Flawed decisions can lead to economic instability and stagnation.

Economic development assistance can help relieve short-term food crises and can contribute to longer-term development. Emergency food aid is essential for averting famine following natural disasters and major political upheavals. Longer-term financial aid could help to further reduce the debt problem in several countries and provide real resources for development.

Aid effectiveness could be improved by longer-term commitments and increased donor coordination. Less tying of aid to factors such as procurement from donor sources, but increased tying of aid to institutional changes that eliminate distortions or reduce transactions costs would help.

Coordinated international action has been successful in dealing with specific development problems. International support for agricultural research led to productivity increases that enhanced food security, reduced famines in highly populated areas, and helped alleviate rural poverty. Success also brought complacency and agricultural R&D slowed from the 1970s to the 1990s. Worldwide immunization efforts, coordinated by the World Health Organization, have significantly reduced deaths due to common childhood diseases. Concerted efforts to provide food to famine victims have reduced famine mortalities. Similar international coordination could be helpful for reducing debts, assisting policy reforms, and for other specific actions.

In summary, it is clear that many pieces are needed for a country to solve its development puzzle. Enhanced information flows are vitally important for agricultural development.

ASSESSING FUTURE PROSPECTS

Several countries in Asia have grown at relatively rapid rates for more than three decades (despite some short-term financial instability). Rapid growth has occurred as well in select countries in Latin America and in part of Africa. But masses of impoverished people still live in South Asia and in much of sub-Saharan Africa. Hunger problems persist despite increased per capita food production in the world over the past 50 years. Poverty rates have fallen, but environmental problems worsened in several countries. What does the future hold for reducing hunger, poverty, population growth, and environmental problems? Let's consider some of the underlying forces at work.

Supply and demand for food

The real price of food in the world trended slightly downward for more than 50 years as supply growth outstripped demand growth. For the past two decades, food prices have been volatile and trended slightly upward. Agricultural productivity growth has slowed, while the demand for more and higher quality foods continue to grow. The major long-run food supply shifters are new technologies and the competition with energy for use of agricultural resources. The major demand shifters are population and income growth. As we look to the future, population will continue to grow, but the *rate* of population growth will continue to fall. Incomes have increased rapidly in several Asian countries, including China and India with their massive population bases. Continued income growth is likely, although perhaps at a slower rate than recent years. Asia has two-thirds of the world's population and, as a region, has the best chance of continued supply increases due to research-induced technical change. Food production per capita will likely continue to increase in the region, but income-based growth in demand is likely to keep food prices high (Box 20.1). There will be increased diversification away from rice as diets change with higher incomes. Demands for animal proteins and fruits and vegetables are likely to increase, with implications for production and marketing systems.

BOX 20.1 THE PROSPECTS FOR CEREAL TECHNOLOGIES

The spectacular burst in yield potential from new varieties of rice and wheat that began the green revolution has not been repeated. Rice yields on experimental farms have not grown dramatically since the introduction of IR-8 in 1966. However, the difference between yields on the best farms and the yields on experiment stations has shrunk dramatically since 1970, particularly in Asia. This reduced difference is due to widespread irrigation, high application of fertilizer, and good management. Future gains in rice production must come increasingly from rain-fed upland and deep-water areas, unless new biotechnologies yield breakthroughs.

The prospects for wheat and maize are more optimistic than for rice, even in the short run. The Centro de Mejoramiento de Maiz y Trigo (CIMMYT) reports a continued increase in the yield potential of wheat, of about 1 percent annually. Substantial progress has been made toward breeding in disease resistance, especially against wheat leaf-rust. Yield growth for wheat in less favorable conditions has been less spectacular. High-yielding varieties for low-rainfall marginal areas are limited, and there are virtually no new varieties for the lowland humid tropics. Major breakthroughs in these areas may pave the way for a technology-driven boom in wheat yields. Maize shows the most promise. There is a large gap between experiment station and farmer's yields, and weed control seems to be a critical problem. Human-based solutions to weed problems provide opportunities for increased employment while increasing maize yields.

In terms of genetic engineering and other biotechnologies in general, the outlook is promising but uncertain. Many improvements, such as increased insect/disease and drought resistance, are on the horizon, but public fears about biotechnologies in developed countries have slowed the development and spread of these technologies in developing countries as well. Accelerated use of marker-assisted breeding for major crops promises to speed up genetic improvement and the release of improved varieties.

In Latin America, increased food production per capita is likely, but not at a rapid rate. Debt problems continue to linger in many countries, limiting public investments in agriculture. Population growth rates have already slowed there, except in a couple of countries, facilitating a per capita increase in food demand. Continued urbanization and income growth will imply higher and more varied food demands and changes in food marketing and trade. Overall, demand growth may outstrip supply growth for the region.

Agriculture has improved in some countries in sub-Saharan Africa, but others in the region will continue to experience disease and stagnant per capita growth in food production. Increased investments in education and agricultural research systems have been realized, but population growth rates remain high. If income increases can be realized, population growth may decelerate, but environmental problems appear to have degraded the resource base in parts of the Sahel to the point of reducing productivity. Climate change will exacerbate the problem. AIDS, malaria, and COVID-19 remain serious health problems, and religious extremism is fomenting conflict. Seventy percent of food demand growth over the remainder of this century will occur in Africa, so meeting the world food problem means addressing African food systems.

Institutional changes

Hunger is more of a governance, institutional, or social protection problem than a food supply issue. Improved information technologies and infrastructure development have improved information flows in some developing countries, which should facilitate political and institutional changes that offer favorable opportunities for development. Reductions in transactions costs may induce the development of technologies that are better suited to the relative resource scarcities of the countries than was the case previously. Increases in market-oriented policies may continue to create efficiency gains, as they have in Asia. Many governments in Latin America and Africa have laid groundwork for these types of efficiency gains if they can avoid conflict.

Technological innovation and efficiency gains are not enough to solve poverty and hunger problems, because innovations and efficiency changes generate winners and losers. Safety nets need expanding, including cash transfers and food assistance. Crop insurance and other institutional means of managing risks will be needed. Finding ways to mitigate and adapt to climate change will be essential.

Obesity is also a growing food-related problem in developing countries. As the value of time rises with economic development, people spend more on processed food, contributing to obesity. Starchy staples are cheaper than vegetables and animal proteins, creating an additional contributing factor to obesity in low-income households. Increased availability of highly nutritious foods, education, and policies that encourage reduced consumption of starchy sweet foods may help. Currently, more than a third of the world cannot afford a healthy diet.

Technological changes

Growing land and water scarcity along with soil and disease problems will increasingly constrain agricultural growth. Technological innovation, combined with policy and social changes, can relieve these constraints. Genetic improvements, increased biological control, and improved management designed not only for productivity growth but for stress tolerance, biofortification, and reduced post-harvest losses are essential. Agricultural research is a costly but high-payoff investment.

Globalization versus isolation

The willingness of more-developed countries to provide foreign assistance and international institutional changes to help poor countries is important but constantly in flux. The relatively wealthy countries of the world must resist isolationist temptations when economies struggle or pandemics arise. Terrorist activities and pandemic threats may stimulate countries eventually to seek longer-term solutions to problems abroad. A long-term goal of promoting democracy and freedom and minimizing damage from global pandemics can only be attained through steps to reduce poverty and build economic opportunity. Solutions to many security, income, hunger, health, and environmental problems require international cooperation. Isolation, as opposed to more open trade and immigration policies' combined social safety nets, can come at a high cost for more-developed and developing countries.

HOW YOU CAN HELP

You, as individuals, can do a great deal to help reduce hunger, poverty, ill health, environmental degradation, and other development problems. Some of you can get involved directly through working for grass-roots organizations in developing countries. The Peace Corps is an example in the United States, but there are many others. For those from developed countries, spending time living and working in a developing country can greatly improve your understanding of development problems. We are each captive of the pictures in our mind, and living in a developing country provides a more accurate picture of the world.

    Getting directly involved in influencing the fortunes of others can bring you a feeling of significance or satisfaction. The frustrations of

People in developing countries can benefit from grass-roots help

working with desperately poor people are many. If you are not an optimist, you may not want to try. However, if you are adventurous, flexible, and somewhat persistent, you may want to consider working at a grassroots level in a developing country.

Some of you can obtain a graduate education to become animal scientists, plant breeders, plant pathologists, entomologists, agricultural economists, soil scientists, microbiologists, or some other type of agricultural scientist needed to help solve world food, income, and environmental problems. Employment opportunities exist for rewarding careers at universities and in international agricultural research centers, national research centers, and private firms. Until the world's population stabilizes, the battle to keep world food production increasing at roughly 2 to 3 percent per year will continue.

Most of you will take very different career paths, but the opportunity always exists to contribute to solving poverty problems through financial contributions to private voluntary organizations. All of you can strive to keep informed about what is happening in the world outside your state and country. You can try to keep politicians informed and let them know that you support foreign assistance contributions to countries where needs are greatest.

SUMMARY

In this chapter, but also in the whole book, we have stressed the interrelatedness of hunger, health, population, environmental, and poverty problems. There are no panaceas, but rather a set of interconnected pieces to a development puzzle. We have learned over the years what many of these pieces are, especially a variety of improved institutions that affect agriculture. In this chapter, we stressed the importance of enhanced-information flows if broad-based development is to occur. Open economies, safety nets, and development policies that do not discriminate against agriculture are essential.

IMPORTANT TERMS AND CONCEPTS

Agricultural scientist
Enhanced information flows
Feeling of significance
Interdependence

No panacea
Social safety nets
Supply and demand shifters

QUESTIONS FOR DISCUSSION

1 Why might there be room for guarded optimism with respect to future agricultural and economic development?
2 Describe the interconnectedness among the pieces that can contribute to solving the development puzzle.
3 How has the theory of induced technical and institutional innovation been broadened and why?
4 What factors can help reduce transactions costs?
5 Why have relatively open economies grown more rapidly than relatively closed economies?
6 What factors will determine the long-run future price of food in the world?
7 Why do enhanced information flows offer favorable prospects for development?
8 What might you as an individual do to help solve hunger, poverty, and other development problems?

NOTES

1 See Jeffrey Sachs, *Investing in Development: A Practical Plan to Achieve the Millennium Development Goals* (London: Earthscan Publishing, The Millennium Project, 2005).
2 For example, regulations may be needed to reduce environmental externalities, to provide food safety standards, and for other purposes.

RECOMMENDED READING

Norton, G., *Hunger and Hope: Escaping Poverty and Achieving Food Security in Developing Countries* (Long Grove, IL: Waveland Press, 2014), Chapter 16.

Thurow, R., *The Last Hunger Season: A Year in an African Farm Community on the Brink of Change* (New York: Public Affairs, 2013).

Glossary of selected terms

agricultural extension: The process of transferring information about improved technologies, practices, or policies to producers, consumers, or policymakers.

agricultural productivity: Level of agricultural output per unit of input.

balance of payments: Difference between receipts from all other countries and payments to them, including all public and private transactions.

bilateral: Two-party or two-country, such as aid from one country to another.

biotechnology: A set of tools, including traditional breeding techniques, that alter living organisms, or parts of organisms, to make or modify products; improve plants or animals; or develop micro-organisms for specific uses. Modern biotechnology includes use of recombinant DNA, monoclonal antibodies, and novel bio-processing techniques, among others.

birth rates and death rates: The number of births or deaths per 1,000 population in a year.

buffer stocks: Supplies of a product that are stored and used to moderate price fluctuations. These stocks are sold during periods of rising prices, and purchased when prices fall.

capital accumulation: Investment.

common property: Property for which the rights of use are shared and ownership is not private but shared by all.

comparative advantage: Ability of a country to produce a good or service at a lower opportunity cost than another country can. The theory of comparative advantage implies that a country should devote its resources not to all lines of production, but to those it produces most efficiently.

concessional: Subsidized, usually used with respect of interest on loans.

conditional cash transfer program: Program designed to reduce poverty making a welfare payment conditional upon the receiver meeting certain criteria such as enrolling children in school and getting regular health check-ups.

debt rescheduling: Extending the repayment period for loans, altering interest rates, forgiving part of the principal, or some combination of the three.

demographic dividend: Economic growth in a country that results from increased spending on investment rather than on dependents. It occurs for a period of 20–30 years after a significant drop in birth rates.

demographic transition: The historical shift of birth and death rates from high to low levels in a population. Death rates usually decline before birth rates, resulting in rapid population growth during the transition period.

discount rate: The value used to determine the present value of future cash flows arising from a project or an investment.

economic development: Improvement in the standard of living of an entire population. Development requires rising per capita incomes, eradication of absolute poverty, reduction in inequality over the long term, and increased opportunity of individual choice.

economic or structural transformation of an economy: The increase in the size of the nonagricultural sector relative to agriculture that occurs in all economies as economic growth occurs.

elasticity: A measure of the percentage response of one variable (for example, quantity demanded) to a 1 percent change in another variable (for example, price).

experiment station: A center or station at which scientists conduct research.

external debt: Debts owed by the government in one country to creditors in another country.

externality: An economic impact of an activity by an individual or business on other people for which no compensation is paid. Externalities may be positive or negative and are often unintentional.

foreign assistance or foreign aid: Includes financial, technical, food, and military assistance given by one or several countries to another country. This assistance may be given as a grant or subsidized loan.

foreign exchange rate: The number of units of one currency that it takes to buy a unit of another currency.

free rider: An individual or business that receives the benefits of the actions of another individual or business without having to pay for those benefits.

free trade area: A block of countries that agree to lower or eliminate tariffs and other trade barriers among themselves, but each country maintains its own independent trade policy toward nonmember nations.

General Agreement on Tariffs and Trade (GATT): Multilateral agreement, originally negotiated in 1947, for the reduction of tariffs and other trade barriers. The agreement provides a forum for intergovernmental tariff negotiations.

globalization: The increasing integration of economies around the world, particularly through trade and financial flows. Also refers to the movement of people and knowledge across international borders.

green revolution: The dramatic increases in wheat and rice harvests that were achieved in the late 1960s, primarily in Asia and Latin America, following the release of fertilizer- and water-responsive, high-yielding, semi-dwarf varieties of those crops.

high-yielding variety: Varieties of plants that have been improved through agricultural research so that they yield more per amount of input than the traditional varieties.

human capital: The level of education, skills, knowledge, health, and nutrition of an individual or a population.

import substitution: Actions by a government to restrict imports of a commodity to protect (from international competition) and encourage domestic production of the good.

induced innovation theory: A theory that hypothesizes that technical change is induced by changes in relative resource endowments and by growth in product demand; institutional change is induced by changes in relative resource endowments and by technical change.

institutions: Organizations or rules of society. Government policies, regulations, and legal systems are examples.

integrated pest management: The coordinated use of biological, cultural, and chemical pest control practices to reduce insects, diseases, and weeds. The purpose is to control pests in both an economically and ecologically sound manner.

intellectual property rights: Laws regulating the copying of inventions, identifying symbols, and creative expressions. These laws encompass four separate and distinct types of intangible property – patents, trademarks, copyrights, and trade secrets.

international agricultural research centers (IARCs): The set of agricultural research centers supported by a group of public and private funding sources. These centers provide improved technologies and institutional arrangements to help developing countries increase their food production. Funding is coordinated by the Consultative Group on International Agricultural Research (CGIAR).

international capital market: The transfers of capital (money) among countries in response to short- and long-term investment opportunities.

international commodity agreement: A formal agreement among the major producing and consuming countries of a commodity that specifies a mechanism for stabilizing price. An agreement may specify import and export quotas for each country.

International Monetary Fund (IMF): An international financial institution designed to: (1) promote international monetary coordination; (2) foster international trade; (3) facilitate stabilization of exchange rates; (4) develop mechanisms for multilateral transactions between members; and (5) provide resources for enhanced international financial stability.

land reform: An attempt to change the land tenure system through public policies.

land tenure: The rights and patterns of control over land.

law of diminishing returns: In the production of any commodity, as more units of one factor of production are added to a fixed quantity of another factor (or factors), the additions to total output with each subsequent unit of the variable factor will eventually begin to diminish.

less-developed country (developing country) (LDC): Generally refers to countries in which per capita incomes are below $6,000, although a few countries with higher incomes consider themselves to be less developed or developing.

market failure: When markets fail to efficiently organize production or allocate goods in a way that maximizes social welfare.

micro-finance: Small-scale provision of credit, savings, and insurance services, usually to the very poor.

moneylender: An informal lender whose business it is to lend money to borrowers, usually at high interest, with little or no collateral or paperwork.

money supply: Currency plus money that can be easily withdrawn from checking or savings accounts.

monopoly power: When a single seller or united group of sellers has the power to alter the market price as opposed to having to just accept the market price.

monopsony: A market with a single buyer.

multilateral: Refers to many countries as opposed to two countries (bilateral). Examples are multilateral aid, multilateral trade, and multilateral agreements.

multiple exchange rates: When a country sets different rates between its currency and foreign currencies depending on the class of imports. May be used to control foreign exchange by limiting certain types of imports.

official development assistance (ODA): Foreign assistance that excludes military-related assistance, export credits, and private fund transfers while having at least a 25 percent grant element. The grant element is defined as the excess of the loan or grant's value over the (present) value of repayments calculated with a 10 percent interest rate.

opportunity cost of capital: The rate of return on the best alternative use for the funds. It is the cost of alternative investments forgone when a particular investment is made.

overvalued exchange rate: When the official value of a currency is too high given the exchange rate that would otherwise prevail in international money-markets given the supply and demand for the country's currency.

parastatal: An institution, such as a marketing board, that is used by a government to control the production, distribution, international trade, and domestic price of a product. This product might be an agricultural good or an input such as fertilizer.

production function: Describes, for a given technology, the different output levels that can be obtained from various combinations of inputs or factors of production.

production possibilities frontier: The trade-off between the maximum amount of two goods that can be produced in a country given existing production technologies and the available productive resources.

protectionism: A reaction by an industry or a country to foreign competition. That reaction is usually manifested through tariffs, quotas, or other means of reducing imports to shield domestic producers.

public goods: Goods or services that are non-rival (consumption or use by one person does not preclude consumption by another) and non-exclusive (a person cannot be excluded from consumption or use, except at prohibitively high costs).

scale-neutral technology: A technology that can be employed equally well by any size firm.

social cost: The total value of resources used in production of a good, including the value of externalities, which are not borne by the producer of the good or reflected in the market price.

structural adjustment program: Government program aimed at adjusting the economy to reduce imbalances between aggregate supply and demand. Structural adjustment programs typically involve: devaluation of the foreign exchange rate to increase exports and reduce imports, reduced government spending, and removal of many government policies that distort prices, including barriers to trade.

subsidized (concessional) credit: Loans made with interest rates below the rates prevailing in the market.

sustainable development: Development that meets the needs of the present without compromising the ability of future generations to meet their own needs.

tariff: A tax or duty placed on goods imported into a country.

technology: The method for producing something. New technologies are often embedded in inputs, for example seeds or machines. Technological progress occurs when more output is obtained from the same quantity of inputs. Technology transfer occurs when methods (perhaps embedded in materials) from one location are applied in a second location.

terms of trade: The relationship between the prices of two goods that are exchanged; for example, the price of an export good relative to the price of an import good. When the price of an export good increases relative to the price of an import good, the terms of trade have increased for the export and are said to be favorable.

trade preferences: Refers to favorable tariff treatment accorded by one country or group of countries to exports of certain other countries.

transactions costs: The costs of adjustment, of information, and of negotiating, monitoring, and enforcing contracts.

World Bank: The major multilateral-funded organization that makes loans to developing countries. It contains the International Finance Corporation, the International Bank for Reconstruction and Development, and the International Development Association.

World Trade Organization (WTO): The international institution created in 1994 to replace the GATT and strengthen enforcement of international trade rules and the settling of trade disputes.

Works cited

Acemoglu, Daron, and James A. Robinson, *Why Nations Fail: The Origins of Power, Prosperity, and Poverty* (New York: Random House, 2012).

Akroush, S., K. Shideed, and A. Bruggeman, "Economic Analysis and Environmental Impacts of Water Harvesting Techniques in the Low Rainfall Areas of Jordan", *International Journal of Agricultural Resources, Governance and Ecology*, vol. 10(1) (2014), pp. 34–49.

Alesina, Alberto, Paola Giuliano, and Nathan Nunn, "On the Origins of Gender Roles: Women and the Plough", *Quarterly Journal of Economics*, vol. 128(2) (2013), pp. 469–530.

Alkira, Sabina, Ruth Meinzen-Dick, Amber Peterman, Agnes R. Quisumbing, Greg Seymour, and Ana Vaz, "The Women's Empowerment in Agriculture Index", *World Development*, vol. 52 (2013), pp. 71–91.

Alston, Julian M., Connie Chan-Kang, Michele C. Marra, Philip G. Pardey, and T.J. Wyatt, *A Meta-Analysis of Rates of Return to Agricultural R&D* (Washington, DC: International Food Policy Research Institute, IFPRI Research Report 113, 2000).

Alston, Julian M., George W. Norton, and Philip G. Pardey, *Science Under Scarcity: Principles* and *Practice for Agricultural Research Evaluation and Priority Setting* (Ithaca, NY: Cornell University Press, 1995).

Amaya, Nadezda, and Jeffrey Alwang, "Women Rule: Potato Markets and Access to Information in the Bolivian Highlands", *Agricultural Economics*, vol. 43(4) (2012), pp. 403–413.

Anderson, Kym, *Distortions to Agricultural Incentives: A Global Perspective, 1955 to 2007* (New York and Washington, DC: Palgrave Macmillan and The World Bank, 2009).

———, ed. *Political Economy of Distortions to Agricultural Incentives* (Washington, DC: The World Bank, 2009).

Anderson, Kym, and Will Martin (eds.), *Agricultural Trade Reform and the Doha Development Agenda* (Washington, DC: The World Bank, 2005).

Anderson, Kym, and William A. Masters (eds.), *Distortions to Agricultural Incentives in Africa* (Washington, DC: The World Bank, 2008).

Anderson, Kym, and Signe Nelson, *Updated National and Global Estimates of Distortions to Agricultural Incentives, 1955 to 2011, Regional Aggregates 2013*, www.worldbank.org/agdistortions, accessed November 1, 2020.

Autor, David H., "Trade and Labor Markets: Lessons from China's Rise", *IZA World of Labor* (2018), p. 431, doi:10.15185/izawol.431

Baldwin, Richard, *The Great Convergence: Information Technology and the New Globalization* (Cambridge, MA: Harvard University Press, 2016).

Banerjee, Abhijit, and Ether Duflo, *Poor Economics: A Radical Re-Thinking of the Way to Fight Global Poverty* (New York: Public Affairs, 2011).

——, *Good Economics for Hard Times* (New York: Public Affairs, 2019).

Banerjee, Abhijit, Dean Karlan, and Jonathan Zinman, "Six Randomized Evaluations of Microcredit: Introduction and Further Steps", *American Economic Journal: Applied Economics*, vol. 7 (2015), pp. 1–21.

Barrett, Christopher B., and Daniel G. Maxwell, *Food Aid After Fifty Years: Recasting Its Role* (New York: Routledge, 2005).

Baumol, William J., "Williamson's the Economic Institutions of Capitalism", *Rand Journal of Econometrics*, vol. 17 (1986).

Beintema, Nienke, Gert-Jan Stads, Keith Fuglie, and Pail Heisey, *ASTI Global Assessment of Agricultural R&D Spending, Developing Countries Accelerate Investment* (Washington, DC: IFPRI, 2012).

Bell, Clive, "Reforming Property Rights in Land and Tenancy", *World Bank Research Observer*, vol. 5 (July 1990), pp. 143–166.

Benjamin, Dwayne, "Can Unobserved Land Quality Explain the Inverse Productivity Relationship?", *Journal of Development Economics*, vol. 46 (1995), pp. 51–84.

Bennett, M.K. "International Disposition in Consumption Levels", *American Economic Review*, vol. 41 (September 1951), pp. 632–649.

Bevis, Lea, and Christopher Barrett, "Close to the Edge: High Productivity at Plot Peripheries and the Inverse Size-Productivity Relationship", *Journal of Development Economics*, vol. 143 (2020).

Bill and Melinda Gates Foundation, *Annual Report 2018*, www.gatesfoundation.org.

Binswanger, Hans P., "Agricultural Mechanization: A Comparative Historical Perspective", *World Bank Research Observer*, vol. 1 (January 1986), pp. 27–56.

Binswanger-Mkhize, Hans P., Camille Bourguignon, and Rogier van den Brink (eds.), *Agricultural Land Redistribution: Toward Greater Consensus* (Washington, DC: The World Bank, 2009).

Binswanger, Hans P., and Mark R. Rosenzweig (eds.), *Contractual Arrangements, Employment and Wages in Rural Labor Markets in Asia* (New Haven, CT: Yale University Press, 1984).

Boo, Katherine, *Behind the Beautiful Forevers* (New York: Random House, 2012).

Borrelli, Pasquale, David A. Robinson, Panos Panagos, Emanuele Lugato, Jae E. Yang, Christine Alewell, David Wuepper, Luca Montanarella, and Cristiano Ballabio, "Land Use and Climate Change Impacts on Global Soil Erosion by Water (2015-2070)", *Proceedings of the National Academy of Sciences*, vol. 117(36) (September 2020), pp. 21994–22001.

Boserup, Esther, *The Conditions of Agricultural Growth* (London: Allen and Unwin, 1965).

——, *Women's Role in Economic Development* (London: Allen and Unwin, 1970).

Boucher, D., P. Elias, K. Lininger, C. May-Tobin, S. Roquemore, and E. Saxon, *The Root of the Problem: What's Driving Tropical Deforestation Today?* (Cambridge, MA: Union of Concerned Scientists, 2011).

Bouet, A., *The Expected Benefits of Trade Liberalization for World Income and Development: Opening the "Black Box" of Global Trade Modeling* (Washington, DC: International Food Policy Research Institute, Food Policy Review 8, 2008).

BRAC, *Audited Financial Statements, Year Ended December 2018*, www.brac.net.

Bromley, Daniel W., and Devendra P. Chapagain, "The Village Against the Center: Resource Depletion in South Asia", *American Journal of Agricultural Economics*, vol. 68 (December 1984), pp. 868–873.

Brooks, Karen, J. Luis Guasch, Avishay Braverman, and Csaba Csaki, "Agriculture and the Transition to Market", *Journal of Economic Perspectives*, vol. 5(4) (Fall 1991), pp. 149–162.

Burnside, Craig, and David Dollar, "Aid, Policies and Growth", *American Economic Review*, vol. 90 (September 2000), pp. 775–786.

Caldwell, J.C., and T. Schindlmayr, "Historical Population Estimates: Unraveling the Consensus", *Population and Development Review*, vol. 28(2) (2002), pp. 183–204.

Caplan, Bryan, and Zach Weinersmith, *Open Borders: The Science and Ethics of Migration* (New York: First Second Press, 2019).

Carter, Michael, Alain de Janvry, Elisabeth Sadoulet, and Alexandros Sarris, "Index Insurance for Developing Country Agriculture: A Reassessment", *Annual Review of Resource Economics*, vol. 9 (2017), pp. 421–438.

CGIAR Science Council, *Science for Agricultural Development: Changing Contexts and New Opportunities* (Rome: Science Council Secretariat, 2005).

Christensen, Cheryl, et al., *Food Problems and Prospects in sub-Saharan Africa: The Decade of the 1980's* (Washington, DC: U.S. Department of Agriculture, Economic Research Service, Foreign Agricultural Research Report No. 186, August 1981).

Cline, William R., *Trade Policy and Global Poverty* (Washington, DC: Institute for International Economics, 2004).

Cline, William R., and Trevor Young, *Principles of Agricultural Economics: Markets and Prices in Less Developed Countries* (Cambridge: Cambridge University Press, 1989).

Collier, Paul, *The Bottom Billion* (New York: Oxford University Press, 2008).

Cotula, Lorenzo, Sonja Vermeulen, Rebeca Leonard, and James Keeley, *Land Grab or Development Opportunity? Agricultural Investment and International Land Deals in Africa* (London and Rome: IIED/FAO/IFAD, 2009).

Coudouel, Aline, and Stefano Paternostro (eds.), *Analyzing the Distributional Impact of Reforms* (Washington, DC: The World Bank, 2005).

Dalgaard, Carl-Johan, Henrik Hansen, and Finn Tarp, "On the Empirics of Foreign Aid and Growth", *The Economic Journal*, vol. 114(496) (June 2004), pp. F191–F216.

Deaton, Angus, *The Analysis of Household Surveys* (Baltimore: Johns Hopkins University Press, 1997).

De Brauw, Alan, Valerie Mueller, and Hak Lim Lee, "The Role of Rural-Urban Migration in the Structural Transformation of sub-Saharan Africa", *World Development*, vol. 62 (November 2014), pp. 33–42.

Deininger, Klaus, "Land Policy Reforms", *World Bank's Poverty and Social Impact Analysis*, http://go.worldbank.org/L8N5DAY120, accessed December 16, 2013.

Deininger, Klaus, and Songquing Jin, "Tenure Security and Land-Related Investment: Evidence from Ethiopia", *European Economic Review*, vol. 50 (July 2006), pp. 1245–1277.

———, "Land Sales and Rental Markets in Transition: Evidence from Rural Vietnam", *Oxford Bulletin of Economics and Statistics*, vol. 70 (February 2008), pp. 67–101.

———, "Securing Property Rights in Transition: Lessons from Implementation of China's Rural Land Contracting Law", *Journal of Economic Behavior and Organization*, vol. 70 (2009), pp. 22–38.

de Janvry, Alain, "The Role of Land Reform in Economic Development: Policies and Politics", *American Journal of Agricultural Economics*, vol. 63 (May 1981), pp. 384–392.

de Janvry, Alain, and Elizabeth Sadoulet, *Development Economics: Theory and Practice* (New York: Routledge, 2016).

Dercon, Stephan, and Pramila Krishnan, "In Sickness and in Health: Risk Sharing Within Households in Rural Ethiopia", *Journal of Political Economy*, vol. 108(4) (August 2000), pp. 688–727.

de Waal, A., and A. Whiteside, "New Variant Famine: AIDS and Food Crisis in Southern Africa", *The Lancet*, vol. 362 (October 11, 2003).

Diaz-Bonilla, Eugenio, and Sherman Robinson, "The WTO Can Help World's Poor Farmers", *International Herald Tribune*, March 28, 2001.

Dixon, John, Aidan Gulliver, and David Gibbon, *Farming Systems and Poverty: Improving Farmers' Livelihoods in a Changing World* (Rome and Washington, DC: FAO and the World Bank, 2001).

Doss, Cheryl, "Men's Crops? Women's Crops? The Gender Patterns of Cropping in Ghana", *World Development*, vol. 30(11) (2001).

———, "The Effects of Intrahousehold Property Ownership on Expenditure Patterns in Ghana", *Journal of African Economies*, vol. 15(1) (2005), pp. 149–180.

Doss, Cheryl, Ruth Meizen-Dick, Agnes Quisumbing, and Sophie Theis, "Women in Agriculture: Four Myths", *Global Food Security*, vol. 16 (2018), pp. 69–74.

Duckham, Alec N., and G.B. Masefield, *Farming Systems of the World* (London: Chatto and Windus, 1970).

Easterly, William, *The Elusive Quest for Growth: Economists Adventures and Misadventures in the Tropics* (Cambridge, MA: MIT Press, 2001).

The Economist, "The Mundell-Fleming Trilemma: Two Out of Three Ain't Bad", August 26, 2016, p. 51.

Ellis, F., *Rural Livelihoods and Diversity in Developing Countries* (Oxford: Oxford University Press, 2000).

Emerick, Kyle, Alain de Janvry, Elisabeth Sadoulet, and Manzoor H. Dar, "Technological Innovations, Downside Risk, and the Modernization of Agriculture", *American Economic Review*, vol. 106 (2016), pp. 1537–1561.

Evenson, R.E., P. Pingali, and T.P. Schultz (eds.), *Handbook of Agricultural Economics, Volume 3: Agricultural Development: Farmers, Farm Production, and Food Markets* (Amsterdam: Elsevier, 2006).

Fajgelbaum, Pablo D., and Amit K. Khandelwal, "Measuring the Unequal Gains from Trade", *The Quarterly Journal of Economics*, vol. 31(3) (2016), pp. 1113–1180.

Fan, Shenggen, and Connie Chan-Kang, *Road Development, Economic Growth and Poverty Reduction in China* (Washington, DC: International Food Policy Research Institute, Research Report No. 138, 2005).

FAO, "The State of Food Security and Nutrition in the World, 2020", http://www.fao.org/3/ca9692en/online/ca9692en.html#:~:text=The%20State%20of%20Food%20Security%20and%20Nutrition%20in,Programme%20%28WFP%29%20and%20the%20World%20Health%20Organization%20%28WHO%29.

FAOSTAT Data, 2019, 2020, http://www.fao.org/faostat/en/#home.

Fletschner, Diana, "Women's Access to Credit: Does It Matter for Household Efficiency?" *American Journal of Agricultural Economics*, vol. 90 (2008), pp. 669–683.

Food and Agriculture Organization of the United Nations, *Global Forest Resources Assessment 2010 – Main Report* (Rome: FAO, Forestry Paper No. 163, 2010), www.fao.org/docrep/013/i1757e/i1757e00.htm.

———, *The State of Food and Agriculture: Women in Agriculture: Closing the Gender Gap for Development* (Rome: Food and Agriculture Organization of the United Nations, 2011).

———, *Country Gender Assessment of Agriculture and the Rural Sector in Nepal* (Kathmandu: FAO, 2019), p. ix, http://www.fao.org/3/CA3128EN/ca3128en.pdf.

———, *State of Food Security and Nutrition in the World 2020* (Rome: FAO, 2020).

Foster, A., and M. Rosenzweig, "A Test for Moral Hazard in the Labor Market: Contractual Arrangements, Effort, and Health", *Review of Economics and Statistics*, vol. 76 (1994), pp. 213–227.

Foster, J., J. Greer, and E. Thorbecke, "A Class of Decomposable Poverty Measures", *Econometrica*, vol. 52 (1984), pp. 761–766.

Foster, Phillips, and Howard D. Leathers, *The World Food Problem* (Boulder, CO: Lynne Reinner Publishers, 2017).

Fuglie, Keith O., and Nicholas E. Rada, *Resources, Policies, and Agricultural Productivity in sub-Saharan Africa* (Washington, DC: U.S. Department of Agriculture, Economic Research Service, Report 145, February 2013).

Gittinger, J. Price, Joanne Leslie, and Caroline Hoisington (eds.), *Food Policy: Integrating Supply, Distribution, and Consumption* (Baltimore: Johns Hopkins University Press, 1987).

Global Nutrition Report, 2018, https://globalnutritionreport.org/reports/global-nutrition-report-2018/.

Grosh, Margaret, Carlo del Ninno, Emil Tesliuc, and Azedine Ouerghi, *For Protection and Promotion: The Design and Implementation of Effective Safety Nets* (Washington, DC: The World Bank, 2008).

Haggblade, Steven, Peter Hazell, and Thomas Reardon, *Strategies for Stimulating Poverty-Alleviating Growth in the Rural Nonfarm Economy in Developing Countries* (Rome: International Food Policy Research Institute, EPTD Discussion Paper No. 93, 2002).

Hansen, M.C., P.V. Potapov, R. Moore, M. Hancher, S.A. Turubanova, A. Tyukavina, D. Thau, S.V. Stehman, S.J. Goetz, T.R. Loveland, A. Kommareddy, A. Egorov, L. Chini, C.O. Justice, and J.R.G. Townshend, "High-Resolution Global Maps of 21st-Century Forest Cover Change", *Science*, vol. 342 (November 15, 2013), pp. 850–853, http://earthenginepartners.appspot.com/science-2013-global-forest.

Hareau, Guy, George W. Norton, Bradford Mills, and Everett Peterson. "Potential Benefits of Transgenic Rice in Asia: A General Equilibrium Analysis", *Quarterly Journal of International Agriculture*, vol. 44 (2005), pp. 229–246.

Harrison, Ann, *Globalization and Poverty* (Chicago: University of Chicago Press, 2007).

Hayami, Yujiro, and Vernon W. Ruttan, *Agricultural Development: An International Perspective* (Baltimore: Johns Hopkins University Press, 1985).

Holloway, Kris, *Monique and the Mango Rains* (Long Grove, IL: Waveland Press, 2007).

Hossain, Mahabub, *Credit for Alleviation of Rural Poverty: The Grameen Bank of Bangladesh* (Washington, DC: International Food Policy Research Institute Research Report No. 65, February 1988).

International Agricultural Trade Research Consortium, http://www.iatrcweb.org/.

International Food Policy Research Institute, *PROGRESA – Breaking the Cycle of Poverty* (Washington, DC: IFPRI, 2002).

———, *2020 Global Food Policy Report: Building Inclusive Food Systems* (Washington, DC: IFPRI, 2020).

International Fund for Agricultural Development, *Rural Poverty Report 2011* (Rome: Quintily Press, November 2010).

International Labor Organization, *Facts on Microfinance for Decent Work* (Geneva: ILO, 2010).

International Organization for Migration, *World Migration Report* (Geneva: IOM, 2020).

IPCC, *Climate Change and Land: Summary for Policymakers, Special Report* (Geneva: IPCC, 2020), p. 41.

ISAAA, *Global Status of Commercialized Biotech/GM Crops* (Ithaca, NY: ISAAA Brief No. 54, 2018).

Jensen, Robert T., and Emily Oster. "The Power of TV: Cable Television and Women's Status in India", *Quarterly Journal of Economics*, vol. 124(3) (2009), pp. 1057–1083.

Joyce, Joseph, "The IMF and Global Financial Crises", *Challenge*, vol. 43 (July–August 2000), pp. 88–107.

Junhua, Ehou, "Economic Reform: Price Readjustment (1978–87)", *Chinese Economic Studies*, vol. 24(3) (Spring 1991), pp. 6–26.

Karlan, Dean, and Jacob Apple, *More Than Good Intentions* (London: Dutton, 2011).

Koppel, Bruce M. (ed.), *Induced Innovation Theory and International Agricultural Development: A Reassessment* (Baltimore and London: Johns Hopkins University Press, 1995).

Kraybill, David, Stephanie Mercer, and Joseph Glauber, *How the United States Benefits from Agricultural and Food Security Investments in Developing Countries* (Washington, DC, BIFAD, 2019), pp. 1–43.

Kremer, Michael, and Alaka Holla, "Improving Education in the Developing World: What Have We Learned from Randomized Evaluations?", *Annual Review of Economics*, vol. 1 (2009), pp. 513–542.

Krugman, P., and M. Obstfeld, *International Economics* (Cambridge, MA: MIT Press, 1988).

Lancaster, Carol, *Foreign Aid: Diplomacy, Development, Domestic Politics* (Chicago: University of Chicago Press, 2007).

Lancet Global Health, vol. 3(9), https://www.thelancet.com/journals/langlo/home.

Landsburg, Steven, *The Armchair Economist: Economics and Everyday Life* (New York: Free Press, 1995).

Lin, Justin Y., "The Household Responsibility System Reform and the Adoption of Hybrid Rice in China", *Journal of Development Economics*, vol. 36(2) (1991), pp. 353–373.

———, "Agricultural Development in China", in Carl K. Eicher and John M. Staatz (eds.), *International Agricultural Development* (Baltimore: Johns Hopkins, 1998), Chapter 31.

Loomis, Robert S., "Agricultural Systems", *Scientific American* (September 1976), pp. 98–105.

Lybbert, Travis J., and Michael R. Carter, "Bundling Drought Tolerance and Index Insurance to Reduce Rural Household Vulnerability", in Arsenio M. Balisacan, Ujjayant Chakrovarty, and Majah-Leah V. Ravago (eds.), *Sustainable Economic Development: Resources, Environment and Institutions* (Oxford: Academic Press, 2015), pp. 401–414.

Maimbo, Samuel Munzele, and Dilip Ratha, *Remittances: Development Impact and Future Prospects* (Washington, DC: World Bank, 2005).

Markandaya, Kamala, *Nectar in a Sieve* (New York: New American Library, 1954).

Masters, William A., *Government and Agriculture in Zimbabwe* (Westport, CT: Praeger, 1994).

———, "Paying for Prosperity: How and Why to Invest in Agricultural Research and Development in Africa", *Journal of International Affairs*, vol. 58(2) (2005), pp. 35–64.

McCleary, Rachel, and Robert J. Barro, "Private Voluntary Organizations Engaged in International Assistance, 1939–2004", *Nonprofit and Voluntary Sector Quarterly*, vol. 37(3) (September 2008), pp. 512–536.

McLeman, Robert, "International Migration and Climate Adaptation in an Era of Hardening Borders", *Nature Climate Change*, vol. 9 (2019), pp. 911–918.

Meinzen-Dick, Ruth, Agnes R. Quisumbing, Julia Behrman, Patricia Biermayr-Jenzano, Vicki Wilde, Marco Noordeloos, Catherine Ragasa, and Nienke Beintema, *Engendering Agricultural Research*. IFPRI Research Monograph (Washington, DC: International Food Policy Research Institute, 2011).

Mellor, John W., *Agricultural Development and Economic Transformation* (Cham, Switzerland: Palgrave Macmillan, 2017).

Minot, Nicholas, and Todd Benson, *Fertilizer Subsidies in Africa: Are Vouchers the Answer?* (Washington, DC: IFPRI Issue Brief 60, 2009).

North, Douglas, "Institutions, Transactions Costs, and Economic Growth", *Economic Inquiry*, vol. 25 (1987), pp. 415–418.

Norton, George W., *Hunger and Hope: Escaping Poverty and Achieving Food Security in Developing Countries* (Long Grove, IL: Waveland Press, 2014).

Norton, George W., E.A. Heinrichs, Gregory C. Luther, and Michael E. Irwin (eds.), *Globalizing Integrated Pest Management: A Participatory Research Process* (Ames, Iowa: Blackwell Publishing, 2004).

OECD, QWIDS Online Database, https://stats.oecd.org/qwids/.

Ogutua, Sylvester O., Dennis O. Ochieng, and Matin Qaim, "Supermarket Contracts and Smallholder Farmers: Implications for Income and Multidimensional Poverty", *Food Policy*, vol. 96 (August 2020), pp. 1–11.

Olson, Mancur, Jr., "Big Bills Left on the Sidewalk: Why Some Nations Are Rich and Others Are Poor", *Journal of Economic Perspectives*, vol. 10 (Spring 1996), pp. 3–24.

Ostrom, Elinor, *Governing the Commons: The Evolution of Institutions for Collective Action* (Cambridge: Cambridge University Press, 1990).

———, "The Challenge of Common-Pool Resources", *Environment: Science and Policy for Sustainable Development*, vol. 50(4) (2011), pp. 8–21.

———, "Reflections on 'Some Unsettled Problems of Irrigation'", *American Economic Review*, vol. 101(1) (2011), pp. 49–63.

Oweis, T., "Rainwater Harvesting for Restoring Degraded Dry Agro-Pastoral Ecosystems; a Conceptual Review of Opportunities and Constraints in a Changing Climate", *Environmental Reviews* (2016), doi:10.1139/er-2016-0069.

Pardey, Philip G., Nienke Beitema, Steven Dehmer, and Stanley Wood, *Agricultural Research: A Growing Divide* (Washington, DC: IFPRI, 2006).

Pinstrup-Andersen, Per, *Food Subsidies in Developing Countries* (Baltimore: Johns Hopkins University Press, 1988).

Pinstrup-Andersen, Per, and R. Pandya-Lorch (eds.), *The Unfinished Agenda: Perspectives on Overcoming Hunger, Poverty, and Environmental Degradation* (Washington, DC: International Food Policy Research Institute, 2001).

Pinstrup-Andersen, Per, and D.D. Watson, *Food Policy for Developing Countries* (Ithaca, NY: Cornell University Press, 2011).

Population Reference Bureau, Inc., *2019 World Population Datasheet*, https://www. prb.org/2019-world-population-data-sheet/.

Qaim, Matim, "Role of New Plant Breeding Technologies for Food Security and Sustainable Agricultural Development", *Applied Economic Perspectives and Policy*, vol. 42(2) (2020), pp. 129–150.

Quisumbing, Agnes, Lynn R. Brown, Hillary Sims Feldstein, Lawrence Haddad, and Christina Peña, *Women the Key to Food Security* (Washington, DC: International Food Policy Research Institute, August 1995).

Quisumbing, Agnes, R. Meinzen-Dick, T. Raney, A. Croppenstedt, J.A. Behrman, and A. Peterman (eds.), *Gender in Agriculture and Food Security: Closing the Knowledge Gap* (New York: Springer, 2012).

Quisumbing, Agnes, and Lauren Pandolfelli, "Promising Approaches to Address the Needs of Poor Female Farmers: Resources, Constraints, and Interventions", *World Development*, vol. 38(4) (2010), pp. 581–592.

Riddell, Roger, *Does Foreign Aid Really Work?* (Oxford: Oxford University Press, 2007).

Robinson, Marguerite S., *The Micro-Finance Revolution: Sustainable Finance for the Poor* (Washington, DC: The World Bank, 2001).

Roodman, David, *Due Diligence: An Impertinent Inquiry into Microfinance* (Washington, DC: Center for Global Development, 2011).

Runge, C. Ford, Benjamin Senauer, Philip G. Pardey, and Mark W. Rosegrant, *Ending Hunger in Our Lifetime: Food Security and Globalization* (Baltimore: Johns Hopkins University Press, 2003).

Sachs, Jeffrey D., *The End of Poverty: Economic Possibilities for Our Time* (New York: Penguin, 2005).

———, *Investing in Development: A Practical Plan to Achieve the Millennium Development Goals* (London: Earthscan Publishing, The Millennium Project, 2005).

Sahn, David E. (ed.), *Causes and Implications of Seasonal Variability in Household Food Security* (Baltimore: Johns Hopkins University Press, 1987).

Sarma, J.S., *Cereal Feed Use in the Third World: Past Trends and Protections to 2000* (Washington, DC: International Food Policy Research Institute, Research Report No. 57, December 1986).

Schady, Norbert, and José Rosero, "Are Cash Transfers Made to Women Spent Like Other Sources of Income?", *Economics Letters*, vol. 101 (2008), pp. 246–248.

Schramm, Gunter, and Jeremy J. Warford (eds.), *Environmental Management and Economic Development* (Baltimore: Johns Hopkins University Press, 1989).

Schultz, Theodore W., *Transforming Traditional Agriculture* (Chicago: University of Chicago Press, 1964).

Scobie, Grant M., and Rafael Posada, "The Impact of Technical Change on Income Distribution: The Case of Rice in Colombia", *American Journal of Agricultural Economics*, vol. 60(1) (February 1978), pp. 85–92.

Scoones, Ian, Nelson Marongwe, Blasjo Mavedzenge, Jacob Mahenehene, Felix Murimbarimba, and Chrispen Sukume, *Zimbabwe's Land Reform: Myths and Realities* (Suffolk: Boydell and Brewer, 2010).

Sethi, Vishal, "Life in a Slum: Ugly Face of India", *The Times of India*, August 17, 2016.

Sharma, Shalendra, "The Truth About Foreign Aid", *Challenge* (July–August 2005), pp. 11–25.

Shouying, Liu, Xiong Xuefeng, and Long Tingyu, "Rural Land Rights in China: Evolution and Case Studies", *China Economist*, vol. 15 (March–April 2020), pp. 109–120.

Siegel, Paul B., and Jeffrey Alwang, *An Asset Based Approach to Social Risk Management* (Washington, DC: Human Development Network, Social Protection Unit, The World Bank, SP Discussion Series 9926, October 1999).

Skjonsberg, Else, *Change in an African Village: Kefa Speaks* (West Hartford, CT: Kumarian Press, 1989).

Stiglitz, Joseph, "Overseas Aid Is Money Well Spent", *Financial Times*, April 14, 2000.

Taylor, J. Edward, *Essentials of Development Economics* (Berkeley, CA: Rebel Text, 2013), p. 230.

Thirlwall, A.P., *Growth and Development* (New York: Palgrave Macmillan, 2011).

Thirtle, Colin, Lin Lin, and Jenifer Piesse, "The Impact of Research-Led Agricultural Productivity Growth on Poverty Reduction in Africa, Asia and Latin America", *World Development*, vol. 12(31) (December 2003), pp. 1959–1975.

Thurow, Roger, *The Last Hunger Season: A Year in an African Farm Community on the Brink of Change* (New York: Public Affairs, 2013).

Timmer, C. Peter, *Getting Prices Right: The Scope and Limits of Agricultural Price Policy* (Ithaca, NY: Cornell University Press, 1986).

Timmer, C. Peter, Walter P. Falcon, and Scott R. Peterson, *Food Policy Analysis* (Baltimore: Johns Hopkins University Press, 1983).

Todaro, Michael P., *Economic Development* (New York: Prentice Hall, 2011).

Trostle, R., and R. Seeley, *Developing Countries Dominate World Demand for Agricultural Products* (Washington, DC: Amber Waves, U.S. Department of Agriculture, Economic Research Service, August 2013).

Truman, Harry S., *Inaugural Address of the President* (Washington, DC: Department of State Bulletin 33, January 1949).

UNICEF, WHO, and World Bank, *Joint Child Malnutrition Estimates, Regional and Global Joint Estimates*, 2019, https://www.who.int/nutgrowthdb/estimates/en/.

United Nations Conference on Trade and Development Program, *Human Development Report 2007* (New York: Palgrave Macmillan Press, 2007).

———, *Human Development Report 2011* (New York: Palgrave Macmillan, 2011).

———, *Sovereign Debt Crisis: From Relief to Resolution* (Washington, DC: UNCTAD Policy Brief No. 3, April 2012).

———, *Human Development Report 2013* (New York: Palgrave Macmillan, 2013).

———, *2019 Human Development Report* (New York: UNDP, 2019), p. 252.

———, *Sustainable Development Goals*, 2020, https://www.undp.org/content/undp/en/home/sustainable-development-goals.html.

United Nations Conference on Trade and Development Program, Department of Economic and Social Affairs, *International Migration*, 2019, https://www.un.org/en/development/desa/population/migration/publications/migrationreport/docs/InternationalMigration2019_Report.pdf.

———, *Population Division, World Population Prospects: The 2019 Revision, Highlights* (ST/ESA/SER.A/423), 2019, https://population.un.org/wpp/Publications/Files/WPP2019_Highlights.pdf.

United Nations Conference on Trade and Development Program, Food and Agricultural Organization, *Global Forest Resources Assessment 2010 – Main Report* (Rome: FAO, Forestry Paper No. 163, 2010).

———, *Population Division, World Population Prospects: 2019 Revision Database*, https://population.un.org/wpp/.

United Nations Conference on Trade and Development Program, Secretariat, Population Division of the Department of Economic and Social Affairs, *World Population Prospects: The 2019 Revision* (New York: United Nations, 2019).

U.S. Census Bureau, 2010, https://www.census.gov/prod/cen2010/cph-2-1.pdf.

U.S. Department of Agriculture, *Census of Agriculture*, various years, https://www.nass.usda.gov/AgCensus/.

Varangis, Panos, Paul Siegel, Daniele Giovannucci, and Bryan Lewin, *Dealing with the Coffee Crisis in Central America: Impacts and Strategies* (Washington, DC: The World Bank Development Research Group Policy Research Working Paper 299, March 2003).

Vollrath, Dietrich, "Land Distribution and International Agricultural Productivity", *American Journal of Agricultural Economics*, vol. 89 (February 2007), pp. 202–216.

Vollrath, Dietrich, and Ruth Meinzen-Dick, *Land Grabbing by Foreign Investors in Developing Countries: Risks and Opportunities* (Washington, DC: IFPRI Policy Brief 13, 2009).

Voosen, Paul, "Earth's Climate Destiny Finally Seen More Clearly", *Science*, vol. 369 (July 24, 2020), pp. 354–355.

Walraven, Gijs, *Health and Poverty: Global Health Problems and Solutions* (London: Earthscan, 2011).

World Bank, *Annual Review of Development Effectiveness*, 2000, supplement Table 13a, www.worldbank.org.

———, *Engendering Development* (New York: Oxford University Press, 2001).

———, *Agricultural Risk Management in the Face of Climate Change* (Washington, DC: World Bank, 2015), https://openknowledge.worldbank.org/handle/10986/22897, License: CC BY 3.0 IGO.

———, *Future of Food: Shaping a Climate-Smart Global Food System* (Washington, DC: World Bank, 2015), p. 32.

———, *World Development Indicators 2018*, 2019, https://datacatalog.worldbank.org/dataset/world-development-indicators.

———, *World Development Report 2008, Agriculture for Development* (New York: Oxford University Press, 2008).

———, *World Development Report 2009: Reshaping Economic Geography* (Washington, DC: The World Bank, 2009).

———, World Development Indicators Online Database, https://datatopics.worldbank.org/world-development-indicators/.

World Bank, and the International Fund for Agricultural Development, *Gender in Agriculture Sourcebook* (Washington DC: The World Bank, 2009).

World Commission on Environment and Development, *Our Common Future* (New York: Oxford University Press, 1987).

World Health Organization, *Investing in the Future: A United Call to Action on Vitamin and Mineral Deficiencies, Global Report*, 2009, https://www.who.int/vmnis/publications/investing_in_the_future.pdf?ua=1.

———, 2020, https://www.who.int/gho/malaria/en/.

———, https://www.wto.org/english/tratop_e/agric_e/agric_e.htm.

World Vision International, *Accountability Report 2019*, www.wvi.org.

Zeddies, J., R.P. Schaab, P. Neuenschwander, and H.R. Herren, "Economics of Biological Control of Cassava Mealybug in Africa", *Agricultural Economics*, vol. 24(2) (2001), pp. 209–219.

Zeller, Manfred, and Richard L. Meyer, *The Critical Triangle of Microfinance: From Vision to Reality* (Baltimore: Johns Hopkins University Press, 2003).

Index

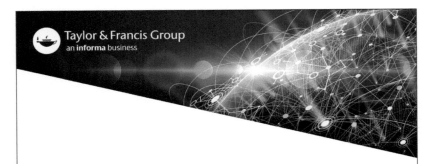